DEBATING
CULTURAL
HYBRIDITY

POSTCOLONIAL ENCOUNTERS

A Zed Books series in association with the International Centre for Contemporary Cultural Research (ICCCR)

Series editors: Richard Werbner and Pnina Werbner

This series debates the making of contemporary culture and politics in a postcolonial world. Volumes explore the impact of colonial legacies, precolonial traditions and current global and imperial forces on the everyday lives of citizens. Reaching beyond postcolonial countries to the formation of external ethnic and migrant diasporas, the series critically theorises

- the active engagement of people themselves in the creation of their own political and cultural agendas;
- the emerging predicaments of local, national and transnational identities and subjectivities;
- the indigenous roots of nationalism, communalism, state violence and political terror;
- the cultural and religious counter-movements for or against emancipation and modernity;
- the social struggles over the imperatives of human and citizenship rights within the moral and political economy.

Arising from the analysis of decolonisation and recolonisation, the series opens out a significant space in a growing interdisciplinary literature. The convergence of interest is very broad, from anthropology, cultural studies, social history, comparative literature, development, sociology, law and political theory. No single theoretical orientation provides the dominant thrust. Instead the series responds to the challenge of a commitment to empirical, in-depth research as the motivation for critical theory.

Other titles in the series:

Richard Werbner and Terence Ranger, eds, *Postcolonial Identities in Africa* (1997).

Tariq Modood and Pnina Werbner, eds, *The Politics of Multiculturalism: Racism, Identity and Community in the New Europe* (1997).

DEBATING CULTURAL HYBRIDITY

Multi-Cultural Identities and
the Politics of Anti-Racism

EDITED BY **PNINA WERBNER**
AND **TARIQ MODOOD**

ZED BOOKS
London & New Jersey

Debating Cultural Hybridity was first published in 1997 by
Zed Books Ltd, 7 Cynthia Street, London N1 9JF, UK, and
165 First Avenue, Atlantic Highlands, New Jersey 07716, USA

Second impression, 2000
Typeset in Monotype Bembo by Lucy Morton, London SE12
Printed and bound in Malaysia

A catalogue record for this book is available from the British Library

Library of Congress Cataloging-in-Publication Data

Debating cultural hybridity : multi-cultural identities and the
   politics of anti-racism / edited by Pnina Werbner and Tariq Modood.
        p.   cm.
     Based on a European workshop convened in Dec. 1994, at Holly Royde
   Conference Center, Univ. of Manchester.
     Includes bibliographical references and index.
     ISBN 1-85649-423-3 (hb). — ISBN 1-85649-424-1 (pb)
     1. Multiculturalism—Europe—Congresses. 2. Racism—Political
   aspects—Europe—Congresses. 3. Ethnicity—Political aspects—
   Europe—Congresses. 4. Communication and culture—Europe—
   Congresses. 5. Europe—Race relations—Congresses.   I. Werbner,
   Pnina.   II. Modood, Tariq.
   HM276.D37   1997
   305.8'0094—dc20

                                              96-28109
                                              CIP

ISBN 1 85649 423 3 (Hb)
ISBN 1 85649 424 1 (Pb)

CONTENTS

PREFACE

This book results from a European Workshop convened in December 1994 at Holly Royde Conference Centre, University of Manchester. The title of the workshop was 'Culture, Communication and Discourse: Negotiating Difference in Multi-Ethnic Alliances'. It was convened jointly by the editors, Pnina Werbner, Research Administrator of the International Centre for Contemporary Cultural Research (ICCCR), Universities of Keele and Manchester, and Tariq Modood, Senior Research Fellow at the Policy Studies Institute (PSI), London. The workshop was generously funded by the Economic and Social Research Council, UK, and by the European Union through its COST A2 Migration Programme on 'Multiculturalism, Democracy and European Integration'. Altogether, forty scholars from Europe and the United Kingdom were supported by the two funding bodies. The editors would like to thank the ESRC and the Economic Union, as well as the ICCCR and PSI, for their generous support.

Thanks are due to several people who made the project possible. Laura Turney helped prepare the manuscript for publication, and gave unstintingly of her time and good will. Gabriele Schroter, Kingsley Purdam and Katherine Tyler, postgraduate students at Keele and Manchester, all worked tirelessly to make the workshop a success. Michel Arens, Secretary of COST A2, sorted out all the administrative complexities with great skill. John Hutnyk and Bobby Sayyid, postdoctoral fellows at the ICCCR, gave support, encouragement and labour. Finally, Richard Werbner, Director of the ICCCR, helped make it all possible.

This is one of two volumes to come out of the conference. The second volume, *The Politics of Multiculturalism: Racism, Identity and Community in the New Europe*, co-edited by Tariq Modood and Pnina Werbner, complements and augments the debates about culture and hybridity put forth here, through a range of ethnographic case studies from different European countries.

The issue of Europe's cultural integration and our ability to redress the predicaments experienced by racialised ethnic minorities living in our midst, or cope with the influx of migrants and refugees entering the Union, make the issue of 'culture' as pressing as ever. We hope that the present volume sheds some light on the complexity – and yet also inherent flexibility – of 'culture' and identity, their potential openness as well as their closures. It is this openness, the essentially hybrid nature of all culture, that makes the vision of European integration a possible future reality.

Pnina Werbner and Tariq Modood

INTRODUCTION:
THE DIALECTICS OF
CULTURAL HYBRIDITY

Pnina Werbner

THE POWER OF CULTURAL HYBRIDITY

The current fascination with cultural hybridity masks an elusive paradox. Hybridity is celebrated as powerfully interruptive and yet theorized as commonplace and pervasive. Born out of the paradigmatic shift in theory from the modernist to the postmodernist, the paradox is energised by anti-essentialist, anti-integrationist zeal.

The power of cultural hybridity – one side of the paradox – makes sense for modernist theories that ground sociality in ordered and systematic categories; theories that analyse society as if it were bounded and 'structured' by ethical, normative dos and don'ts and by self-evident cultural truths and official discourses. In such theories, it makes sense to talk of the transgressive power of symbolic hybrids to subvert categorical oppositions and hence to create the conditions for cultural reflexivity and change; it makes sense that hybrids are perceived to be endowed with unique powers, good or evil, and that hybrid moments, spaces or objects are hedged in with elaborate rituals, and carefully guarded and separated from mundane reality. Hybridity is here a theoretical meta-construction of social order.

But what if cultural mixings and crossovers become routine in the context of globalising trends? Does that obviate the hybrid's transgressive power? And if not, how is postmodernist theory to make sense, at once, of both sides, both routine hybridity and transgressive power? Even more, what do we mean by cultural hybridity when identity is built in the face of postmodern uncertainties that render even the notion of strangerhood meaningless? When culture itself, all cultural categories, are – as Hans-Rudolf Wicker and Alberto Melucci argue – reflexively in doubt, unstable and lacking cognitive faith or conviction? How do the subjects of (post)modern nation-states respond to such ambivalences and the sheer efflorescence of cultural products, ethnicities and identities? This is a central question in postmodernist theory, and one that the contributors to this volume directly address.

The paradox leads us to ask about the *limits* of cultural hybridity, demarcated not only by hegemonic social formations but by ordinary people. What are the forces, Jonathan Friedman asks, that generate *anti-hybrid*, essentialising discourses stressing cultural boundedness, ethnicity, racism or xenophobia? And how are we to theorise the ambivalences and multiplicities contained in these forces? Why do strangers continue to pose a threat, despite the fact that the very meaning of strangerhood, might seem to be elusive and meaningless in what Zygmunt Bauman defines as an age of 'heterophilia'?

Modernist hybridity theory made its heuristic gains on very different frontiers. Starting from an assumption about cosmic and social ordering, Claude Lévi-Strauss analysed tricksters as ambiguous and equivocal mediators of contradiction (1963); Victor Turner explored the anti-structural properties of liminality and hybrid sacra (1967); while Mary Douglas recognised the dangerous or beneficial powers of exchange inherent in anomalous conflations of otherwise distinct categories (1966; 1975).[1] Starting from a perspectival position *within* society, these outstanding contributions to modernist anthropology stressed the capacity of hybrid symbolic monstrosities to challenge the taken-for-granteds of a local cultural order, and thus to recover a critical cultural self-reflexivity. Their theoretical stance allowed them to explain why dangerous mixings were culturally marked and hedged with taboos.

Along with that, modernist hybridity theory looked to sites of resistance and exclusion, as in Foucault's analysis of heterotopic spaces (Foucault 1986). Similarly, Barthes (1972), Bourdieu (1984) and Bakhtin (1984) analysed popular mass culture and carnival as subversive and re-vitalising inversions of official discourses, high-cultural aesthetic forms or the exclusive lifestyles of dominant elites. Such popular mixings and inversions, like the subversive bricolages of youth cultures analysed by Hebdige (1979), are 'hybrid' in the sense that they juxtapose and fuse objects, languages and signifying practices from different and normally separated domains and, by glorifying natural carnality or 'matter out of place', challenge an official, puritanical public order. Indeed, the ordering tendencies of modernity are, Bauman argues, the key to understanding intolerance towards 'strangers' in the modern nation-state, leading either to their expulsion/elimination or to their assimilation (Bauman 1989; see also this volume, Chapter 3). This also explains why the defence of hierarchy and elite privilege in colonial settler societies was buttressed, Papastergiadis shows, by a pervasive fear of 'racial' hybridity.

From a postmodern perspective, it might seem self-evident that essentialising ideological movements need to be countered by building cross-cultural and multi-ethnic alliances. But cross-cultural or gendered politics, the politics of anti-racism or of transversal alliances, turn out to be fraught with the very same sorts of difficulties that generate the contemporary dual forces of hybridity and essentialism in the first place. Rather than being open and subject to fusion, identities seem to resist hybridisation. The result, Nira Yuval-Davis argues, is that the creation of new oppositional alliances aiming to transcend differences must contend with the resistance of activists to a fusing of their identities and subject positions. What makes for that resistance, and why is it so difficult, Alastair Bonnett and Michel Wieviorka ask, to be an anti-racist? Why is cultural racism a pervasive force, as Tariq Modood claims, and to what extent do ethnic demotic discourses that fuse identities coexist with essentialist discourses that deny such fusings – a question explored by Gerd Baumann. We need to interrogate, Werbner argues, the schismogenetic forces that undermine coexistence, however uncertain and fragmentary, and precipitate polarising essentialisms.

This subject – the attack on or the possibility of transcending and negotiating cultural difference – was the theme of the conference for the present volume. The title of the conference, 'Culture, Communication and Discourse: Negotiating Difference in Multi-Ethnic Alliances', was open enough to allow participants to raise concerns that seemed most pressing at the present theoretical moment. These turned out to be the place and meaning of cultural hybridity in the context of growing global uncertainty, xenophobia and racism. It is significant that all the contributors are European sociologists and social anthropologists. In Europe, hybridisation and xenophobia seem at first glance to be conflicting political forces. Yet counterposed to the destructive power of xenophobia or fetishised 'culture' are also the cultural claims made by minorities and small European nations to be recognised as different, and to retain their right to practise distinctive cultures and religions.

How are we to make sense of such claims when the very concept of culture disintegrates at first touch into multiple positionings, according to gender, age, class, ethnicity, and so forth? As Culture evaporates into a war of positions, we are left wondering what it might possibly mean to 'have' a cultural 'identity'. In the present deconstructive moment, any unitary conception of a 'bounded' culture is pejoratively labelled natural-istic and essentialist. But the alternatives seem equally unconvincing: if 'culture' is merely a false intellectual construction, a manipulative invo-cation by unscrupulous elites or a *bricolage* of artificially designed capitalist consumer objects – a feature of late capitalism stressed by John Hutnyk – where does the destructive or revitalising power of cultural identities and hybridities come from?

The attempt to grapple with these questions and the ambivalences they imply is what makes the present debate so compelling and, indeed, so novel and fresh. We have moved beyond the old discussions that start from certain identities, communities and ordered cultural categories into unchartered theoretical waters. Inadequate, too, are the old modernist insights into the nature of liminality, the place and time of betwixt-and-between, of carnivals, rituals of rebellion and rites of cosmic renewal, or of boundary-crossing pangolins, ritual clowns, witches and abominable swine. We need to incorporate these insights into a broader theoretical framework which aims to resolve the puzzle of how cultural hybridity manages to be both transgressive and normal, and why it is experienced as dangerous, difficult or revitalising despite its quotidian normalcy.

Before attempting to trace what the contours of an emergent theory of hybridity that is postmodern, post-colonial and late-capitalist might be, I want to draw upon a crucial distinction made by Bakhtin. This distinction helps to sweep away much unnecessary confusion plaguing postmodernist discussions of hybridity. It also creates a bridge to earlier modernist approaches, I believe, and thus enables us to draw on the insights developed by these approaches in our attempt to explain why, on a culturally hybrid globe, cultural hybridity is still experienced as an empowering, dangerous or transformative force. Conversely, we can be-gin to consider why borders, boundaries and 'pure' identities remain so important, the subject of defensive and essentialising actions and reflec-tions, and why such essentialisms are so awfully difficult to transcend.

INTENTIONAL HYBRIDITIES

In his work on the dialogic imagination, Bakhtin makes a key distinc-tion between two forms of linguistic hybridisation: unconscious, 'organic' hybridity and conscious, intentional hybridity. For Bakhtin, hybridisation is the mixture of two languages, an encounter between two different linguistic consciousnesses (1981: 358). Organic, unconscious hybridity is a feature of the historical evolution of all languages. Applying it to culture and society more generally, we may say that despite the illusion of boundedness, cultures evolve historically through unreflective borrowings, mimetic appropriations, exchanges and inventions. There is no culture in and of itself. As Aijaz Ahmad puts it, the 'cross-fertilisation of cultures has been endemic to all movements of people ... and all such movements in history have involved the travel, contact, transmutation, hybridisation of ideas, values and behavioural norms' (Ahmad 1995: 18). At the same time – and this amplifies Bakhtin's point – organic hybridisation does not disrupt the sense of order and continuity: new images, words, objects, are integrated into language or culture unconsciously. Yet despite the fact, he says, that 'organic hybrids remain mute and opaque, such unconscious hybrids ... are pregnant with potential for new world views' *like a form of new consciousness* (ibid.: 360).

Hence organic hybridity creates the historical foundations on which aesthetic hybrids build to shock, change, challenge, revitalise or disrupt through deliberate, intended fusions of unlike social languages and images. Intentional hybrids create an ironic double consciousness, a 'collision between differing points of views on the world' (ibid.; see also Young 1995: 21–5). Such artistic interventions – unlike organic hybrids – are internally dialogical, fusing the unfusable.

Bakhtin's distinction is useful for theorising the simultaneous co-existence of both cultural change and resistance to change in ethnic or migrant groups and in nation-states. What is felt to be most threatening is the deliberate, provocative aesthetic challenge to an implicit social order and identity, which may also be experienced, from a different social position, as revitalising and 'fun'. Such aesthetic interventions are thus critically different from the routine cultural borrowings and appropriations by national and ethnic or migrant groups which unconsciously create the grounds for future social change. This is a feature of discourse highlighted by Gerd Baumann: while demotic discourses deny boundaries, the dominant discourses of the very same actors demand that they be respected.

The danger that the aesthetic poses for any closed social universe with a single monological, authoritative, unitary language is that of a heteroglossia 'that rages beyond the boundaries' (Bakhtin 1981: 368). Lotman's 'semiosphere' is an attempt to theorise this heteroglossia in centre–periphery terms (Papastergiadis). Intentional heteroglossias relativise singular ideologies, cultures and languages. Organic hybridisation casts doubts on the viability of simplistic scholarly models of cultural holism.

Several of the contributors to this volume (Wicker, van der Veer, Baumann) reflect on the limitation of earlier anthropological models of bounded cultures and societies. Radical critics of anthropology even suggest, according to Wicker, that culture as a complex whole perpetuates earlier notions of race. These are outlined here by Papastergiadis in his discussion of the painful reflections of Octavio Paz and Gilberto Freyre on Mexican and Brazilian notions of hybrid contamination. Critics of holistic cultural models cite New Right claims about the intrinsic incommensurability of cultures as proof that multiculturalist notions that start from ideas about the homogeneity (and hence boundedness) of culture are dangerously essentialist. As several contributors stress, such assumptions reify 'culture' in substantivist terms, as object, in a logic that seems, on the surface at least, inimical to individual and universal rights.

There is, however, a tremendous irony in the historical revisionism that equates anthropological theories of cultural holism with racism: both Durkheim's society and Boas's culture were, after all, powerful analytical tools used to disprove evolutionary, racist theories. Notwithstanding the often bitter anthropological disagreements between structuralists and relativists, their common purpose was (and is) to demonstrate that the apparently bizarre, primitive or barbaric beliefs and customs of the 'natives' were rational, moral and meaningful, if they were seen in context. Second, they aimed to prove that cultures had value in their own terms, were vital for human diversity, and hence also had a rightful claim not to be destroyed in the name of Europe's civilising mission.

The irony of anthropology's postmodernist critique of cultural or social holism is compounded by its enunciation at the present poststructuralist moment, marked, above all, by its sceptical denial of even the possibility of universal rationality, truth and morality (Friedman, Bauman). We may say that rather than being racist, Lévi-Strauss's or Durkheim's ideas about the socially embedded nature of truth, as developed by modernist anthropologists, anticipated poststructuralist claims that knowledge and truth are the authoritative effects of language games, discourses and interpretive communities. James Clifford puts the latter position sharply when he argues that universal humanist claims are 'meaningless, since they bypass the local cultural codes that make personal experience articulate' (Clifford 1988: 263).

Be this as it may, what has evidently rendered holistic models of culture and society unviable is the reality of postwar population movements, transnational capitalism, global telecommunications and the explosion of consumption. What now seems pressing is to theorise the problems of cultural translation and reflexivity, inter-ethnic communication and cross-cultural mobilisation, hybridity and creolisation. To use Bakhtin's metaphor: in a globalising world, monological national languages cannot escape the sense of being surrounded by an 'ocean of heteroglossia'. This, Bakhtin suggests, undermines the authority of reified custom and tradition, of mythological and magical thought (Bakhtin 1981: 368).

We need, however, to guard against a stereotyped view of 'tradition' that anthropologists have worked hard to dispel: the mistaken assumption that mythology and ritual cannot be subversive of the normative. In reality, pre-industrial societies too have their aesthetic, 'magical', interruptive moments; moments in which internal conflicts and perspectival oppositions are exposed through ritual humour, monstrous objects and liminal actions. Pulsating through the apparently monological cultures of these societies, such liminal moments challenge the pretence of consensus and singularity. Hence, rather than being merely a recursive reinscription of authority, myth, magic and ritual – like the modern novel – use aesthetic hybrid forms that juxtapose unlike images to play out implicit social conflicts, challenge authority and subvert everyday morality.[2]

One might even suggest – extending Peter van der Veer's argument – that the transgressive and reflexive nature of the modern novel is equivalent to such rituals, an institutionalised form of opposition enshrined by 'enlightened' modern bourgeois society. As such, the novel creates dialogical hybridity and reflexiveness without necessarily posing a threat to a liberal social order. One has only to think of the elaborate ceremonials of publicity accompanying the launch of a new novel, its aesthetic design and set-aside spaces (it must not, of course, either be destroyed or be taken too seriously) to unmask its hidden ontology: a ritualised object hedged with taboos, a modern-day equivalent of liminal sacra, boundary-crossing pangolins or humanised cassowaries.

The illusion that globalisation is refracted through creolised cultures is challenged by a recognition of the artifice of postmodern life and the ability of the media not only to reflect human action but, Melucci argues, to produce reality. The well-meaning cultural 'smorgasbord' of World Music Festivals, John Hutnyk finds, packages and fetishises uniqueness and authenticity in a commodified form that ironically renders Third World musical works, however hybrid, equal in their difference, rather than uniquely transgressive. The question Hutnyk considers is whether any real politics of resistance can be fought through such artifices.

This is a serious question: what kind of influence do aesthetic works by diasporic black and Third World intellectuals have upon the realities of ethnicity, racism or nationalism? The urgency of this question stems from what we see as an unwarranted tendency to use these artistic 'texts' – films, novels, poetry, popular music – as documentary springboards for global theorising about society and culture. Against this tendency we want to argue, as sociologists and anthropologists, for a need to locate these 'ritual' objects vis-à-vis their various constituencies. More importantly, we question how quotidian cultural meanings, fusions and excluding essentialisms are actively and dialectically negotiated, in practice, and formulated strategically, through joint political action; and what kind of limits are set by ordinary people on the practice and discourse of cultural hybridity.

Wicker's essay, which opens the volume, draws on Bourdieu's theory of habitus as cultural disposition and practice to suggest that we need to ask not why creolisation occurs, but why actors in a negotiated field of meanings constantly attempt to deny and defy these processes of hybridisation. The move Wicker defines is from cultural complexity to complex wholeness; but in reality, postmodern negotiated orders may be elusive and rare political achievements. If complex (pre-industrial) cultures were marked, as we have seen, by endemic (if somewhat predictable) conflicts, cultural complexity is quite obviously full of fissiparous dissonance. Here the constant tendencies are towards fragmentation, requiring a new form of self-consciously hybrid politics.

CYBORG POLITICS

Cyborg politics is a term drawn from Haraway's mythological text to define a politics that seeks to build non-hegemonic resistance movements out of respect for the intersecting particularities of multiple identity positions. Haraway's cyborg is constituted by a struggle against 'unity-through-domination or unity-through-incorporation [that] ... undermines all claims to an organic or natural standpoint' (1991: 157). As Modood shows, some oppressed groups in Britain have felt excluded from the terms of anti-racism and from coercive definitions of equality and unity. Not all minority groups are equally oppressed in the same way. The cyborg's artificial 'birth' is a result of a growing reflexive realisation of an absence of any privileged subjects who might 'claim innocence from the practise of domination' (ibid.). The underlying fear fuelling the cyborg is of the self-destructiveness of 'totalising' (even if seemingly progressive) oppositional ideologies.

Cyborg politics – or 'transversal' politics, as Nira Yuval-Davis calls them – are about opening up and sustaining dialogues across differences of ideology, culture, identity and social positioning. The recognition of the right to be different animates and sustains such exchanges, despite conflictual perceptions and partial agreements. What *is* accepted, in other words, is the enormous potentiality of *imperfect* communication. Transversal politics thus organise and give shape to heteroglossia, without denying or eliminating it.

Transversal politics start from a denial of essentialist, fixed constructions of cultures, nations and their boundaries, and the reduction of ethnicity to 'culture'. Such politics also reject any universal essentialising,

Externous Post-Modernis

such as that of women's oppression, because this leads to a construction of Women as a basically homogeneous group sharing the same interests, their individual identities merged into the identity of the collectivity. But equally rejected are essentialist assumptions of 'difference' – being black (or white) women, middle- or working-class, and so forth. Yet postmodernist constructions of hybridised female identities, Yuval-Davis proposes, are almost as problematic, since not only do they obscure real inequalities of power between women, they also resort to 'strategic' essentialising as a way out of their own constructivist aporias, and these instrumental inventions come ultimately to be reified as realities via social movements and state policy practices.

A true transversal politics depends on participants' retaining a strong sense of their own 'rootedness' and individual commitments, along with respect for the commitments and interests of others. This is also, it appears, the nub of Modood's contribution, which advocates an anti-racist politics that prefers 'cultural' over 'colour'-based (i.e. racialised) identities as the basis for alliance. But whose 'culture'? In the post-material world, Melucci suggests in his analysis of ecological movements, individuals' rootedness is itself in doubt. They must learn to live with a multiple sense of self. In order to mobilise against coercive planetary codes and operational languages that organise global social life, subjects have to lay claim to personal or group autonomy. Obviously, however, to achieve this, individuals and collective actors must first construct the identity, meaning and underlying moral values constituting who they themselves are. They must recover their own 'mosaic' identities, as Michael Fischer has suggested (Fischer 1986).

This is not an easy quest, Melucci argues, since we live in an age of heightened reflexivity, enmeshed in multiple bonds of belonging in a proliferating number of different symbolic worlds. Moving between these universes of experience, we are compelled to make constant choices and constantly learn quite new social languages. Paradoxically, heightened autonomy, the imperative to choose, can lead to uncertainty, fear of change and a sense of loss. This is also the point emphasised by Bauman.

The conceptualisation of such a fractured self must avoid the danger of dissolving self and identity into an essential nucleus, a metaphysical continuity. The key to this, as Bauman also proposes, is the notion of responsibility, responsibility to and for others and the world, by 'positioning myself in my relations with others and by taking my place in the world' (Melucci). This is precisely what young Asian radicals achieve through music (Hutnyk) or Pakistani immigrants through gestures of giving that define community and identity (Werbner).

But the negotiation of this responsibility, given that relations are based entirely on choice, is, Melucci argues, fragile and precarious, threatening to disintegrate into a 'catastrophic individualism'. The only solution is to accept the imperfection of social exchange and communication, respect the autonomy of co-actors, and create solidarity through an awareness of its fragility, by meta-communicating about goals and choices. The challenge is to formulate an agreed cultural ethos and language with which to 'create the world'.

The proliferation of lifeworlds and choices evoked in Melucci's analysis is inversely produced in the 'explosion and dispersal' of accusations of racism described by Michel Wieviorka. This expansion in the very understanding of what racism means has led inevitably to a fragmentation of prior anti-racist solidarities. It is particularly acute in France, where 'racism' is a term attached to all forms of discrimination, so that even the police are said to suffer from it! But, as Wieviorka rightly points out, the old vocabulary of racism has become unacceptable everywhere. Similarly, Whiteness, Alastair Bonnett shows, cannot escape the essentialism imposed on it by the new logic of racism.

If everyone and no one is a racist, and anti-racists are accused of fomenting racism by stigmatising 'ordinary' (only slightly ethnocentric) folk, or 'racialising' culture in their calls for multiculturalism, what possible shape can an anti-racist movement assume? Wieviorka suggests, first, the need for precise definitions which avoid banalising the term and, particularly, a need to specify what we mean by 'cultural' racism. We should be careful, he warns, not to confuse intercultural tensions with the naturalising tendency of cultural racism to perceive culture as being organically, innately different. Racism either subordinates by positing universal human differences, or differentiates by perceiving the commingling of two cultures as a 'natural' threat. Usually, it does both. The hybridity of racism, we might say, consists in its capacity to merge incoherent and heterogeneous effects and elementary forms into a singular hatred of the Other.

Anti-racist movements cannot afford to reflect back this hybrid incoherence, Wieviorka argues. Yet this is precisely what they tend to do – universalists who affirm equality, citizenship and individual rights clash with multiculturalists who make claims for collective cultural rights, each accusing the other of being racists. With such friends, as the saying goes, who needs enemies? It is here that a cyborg politics is essential to navigate the impossible path between the Scylla of universalism and the Charybdis of differentialism. Wieviorka leaves us to imagine the shape such a dialogue might take.

The obstacles faced by transversal politics are highlighted by the plethora of reificatory labels undermining British and American anti-racist projects.

In a far-reaching critique, Bonnett proposes that, although the contingent nature of 'race' or 'Black' identifications is now accepted, anti-racists still subvert their own anti-essentialist project by defining Whites as essentially oppressive, homogeneous, immutable and intrinsically racist. Rather than acknowledging that all ethnic labels, including White, are historically sited, we continue to grasp 'whiteness' outside history and geography, removed from any social context. The problem is that White public expressions of guilt ('confessional' strategies) only serve, ironically, to site whiteness as the 'altruistic' moral centre of anti-racist discourse.

The essentialising of Whites as racists fractures potential anti-racist alliances by excluding the dominant majority from the anti-racist project, and denying the very possibility that identities may be hybrid, uniquely personal or fused (Hutnyk, Baumann, Werbner). Rather than strategic essentialism, Bonnett proposes, what is needed is strategic *deconstruction*: a continuous process of self-monitoring reflexiveness that explores the personal experiences of people of all 'races', while exposing the constructedness of all political categories including Whiteness, Blackness, and race itself. We are back with cyborg politics.

Our examples suggest that, as Yuval-Davis puts it, the 'boundaries of ... dialogue are determined by the message rather than the messenger'. It remains unclear, however, whether such highly reflexive cyborg politics can ever lead to more liberating forms of sociality between activists, a fusing of unfusable subject positions, the fabulation by collective actors of new aesthetic myths and shared social memories of triumphs and tribulations. Will these replace the utopian and yet, at the same time, imperfect and fragmentary communicative 'noise' of the cyborg with more earthy human realities of joint physical action, of performative gestures that extend *metonymic* connections between activists rather than stressing their symbolic separations?

In ethnic mobilisations, unlike cyborg politics, the 'message' is often merely an excuse for sociality and cultural creativity (Werbner). Rather than being a rare achievement, the sheer sociality of activism usually takes precedence over any instrumental goals, however noble. There is thus a real and *politicised* difference, we argue, between ethnics and cosmopolitans.

THE POLITICS OF HYBRIDITY: COSMOPOLITANS AND TRANSNATIONALS

I draw this distinction from Ulf Hannerz's work on globalising cultural complexity (1992). Cosmopolitans – to expand on his definition – are multilingual gourmet tasters who travel among global cultures, savouring cultural differences as they flit with consummate ease between social worlds. Such gorgeous butterflies in the greenhouse of global culture are a quite different social species from the transnational bees and ants who build new hives and nests in foreign lands. Transnationals are people who move, often in great swarms, in order to create collective 'homes' around them wherever they happen to land. There is no question of simply replicating culture here. This is where the zoological metaphor breaks down. Like cosmopolitans, transnationals are also cultural hybrids, but their hybridity is unconscious, organic and collectively negotiated in practice. Like cosmpolitans, they think globally, but their loyalties are anchored in translocal social networks and cultural diasporas rather than the global ecumene. Most translocals have to contend with incredible social and economic hardships, and they draw on culturally constituted resources of sociality and mutual aid for survival. They actively construct 'community' to shield them from racist rejections, but also to compete for honour, to have fun, to worship, and to celebrate – together – collective rites of passage or ceremonies of nostalgic remembrance for a lost home (Werbner). They draw boundaries which become buttresses against what they perceive to be dangerous incursions and deliberate, *external*, transgressive hybridity (Modood, van der Veer, Baumann).

What is evident, then, is that hybridity, much like contemporary religious syncretism, is a collective condition perceived by actors them-selves to be potentially threatening to their sense of moral integrity, and hence subject to argument, reflection and contestation: a highly politicised form (see the contributions on syncretism in Stewart and Shaw 1994). No longer unconscious in the postmodern world, cultural hybridity has become instead a reflexive moral battleground between cultural purists and cultural innovators, a cultural 'thing' in itself, defined in a field of contestation.

Jonathan Friedman argues for the need to locate Third World diasporic intellectuals as a special class of cosmopolitans who have a positioned interest in perpetuating notions of hybridity without modernism. The old intellectual elites, he recalls, countered cultural diversity by promoting universalist ideas of social justice, equality and individual rights that trans-cended cultural difference. But multiculturalism signals the decline of modernism – a view Friedman shares with Bauman. The hollow claims of the new intellectuals to be voices from the margins are exposed, however, by global trends towards ethnicisation: the real voices from the margins want no truck with hybridity. The reality is one of fragmenta-tion and ghettoisation, of ethnic primordialism in the face of a weakened nation-state.

In interrogating the contributions of Paul Gilroy and Homi Bhabha, Friedman opens a debate that animates much of the present volume.

Without doubt, the three great contemporary prophets of hybridity –
Hall, Gilroy and Bhabha – have precipitated a scientific revolution in the
study of cultural politics that has compelled us to revise the very problems
we address. Stuart Hall's road-to-Damascus conversion from black radical
to hybrid radical, in a talk presented at the British Film Institute in 1988
(Hall 1992), pronounced the 'end of the innocent black subject', confessed
that 'ethnicity' might be a legitimate force of resistance (rather than a
disguised form of white racism), and rendered racism itself ambivalent:
fractured by positioned genders, ethnicities and specular 'desires'.

Hall's consistently original contributions to the debate on hybridity
are grounded, above all, in the Gramscian idea that hegemony or
counter-hegemony must necessarily be constituted through alliances across
differences. Drawing on Derrida's work on *différance* as both the same
and different, anticipatory as well as present, and on Lacanian psychoanalytic notions of gender and its ambivalences (Hall 1990), Hall remains
committed, pragmatically, to the urgent need to create alliances against
conservative, 'Thatcherite' forces, and an acceptance of the limitations to
any joint project imposed by the interests of other actors 'positioned'
differently in this project. For Hall, identity is a vision for the future, a
mobilising call. His work, discussed here by Papastergiadis, reveals that
cyborg politics have their theoretical ground in Gramsci's notions of
alliance and hegemony.

Gilroy's project is to take on both essentialism, in the form of Afro-
centric claims to authenticity, and anti-essentialism, which sees blackness
as an unwarranted holistic construction. The continuity of the black
subject, he suggests, can be found in its simultaneous belonging and
engagement with the darker side of modernity. The Black Atlantic for
Gilroy is a continuously changing, hybridising counter-culture, a genuine
community of sentiment responsive to slavery and racism, neither a mere
construction nor a pre-modern unchanging whole. He demonstrates the
contingent unity of this black diaspora through a detailed analysis of
aesthetic works by black intellectuals and musicians, and the way these
works travel or have travelled within and across black diasporic communities, as well as beyond them.

The problem with Gilroy's work, Friedman finds, is its fundamentally
ambivalent posture with regard to the ethnicisation process itself, expressed in the desire for something truly cosmopolitan. Hybridisation is
a politically correct solution to an anti-ethnic or nationalist agenda; yet
it is completely remote from the real global, *anti-ecumenical* processes that
the weakening of the nation-state as a modernist project has precipitated.

So while Gilroy recognises that identities have depth and are not
totally instrumental and manipulable, he still seems to imply, like Iain

Chambers, that self-consciously ethnic identities are 'bad', and that nationalism remains the source of all evil. Against that, Friedman, citing Lévi-Strauss, argues that ethnocentrism and racism are not the same, and should not be conflated – a view echoed by Werbner, Wieviorka, van der Veer and Yuval-Davis.

How to cope with ethnocentrism is, of course, at the heart of the postmodern aporia: if there are no universal values or rationality, as postmodernists claim, it makes no sense to speak of morality and truth outside cultural communities of language. But if 'culture' itself is seen to be a universally evil force, where does the truth lie? The nihilism evident in this set of equations has been attacked variously by Habermas, MacIntyre and Norris (see his discussion, 1993). Even Foucault, Norris shows, began to dissociate himself from his earlier monological vision of discourse. He argued for the possibility of emancipation through an aesthetic project of the self but, more importantly, he emphasised the subject's ability to distance itself from, and engage critically with, a dominant discourse (Norris 1993: 91). We find the equivalent in Spivak's project of 'speaking against the grain' from within hegemonic 'colonial' discourse.

This implies that hybridity is not the only mode of resistance to homogenising ideologies: whether nationalism or ethnicity are 'good' or 'evil' depends on the ability (and right) of members of ethnic or national collectivities to engage in reflexive self-critical distancing from their own cultural discourses, and hence also to recognise the potential validity of other discourses/communities of language. Such a critical self-distanciation from within discourse differs, it should be stressed, from Homi Bhabha's interruptive hybridity from the margins, although it opens up a space for it; nor (to return to Friedman) does it imply, as Geertz seems to, that to solve global intolerance, everyone in the world must become an anthropologist.

For Homi Bhabha, nationalism is never homogeneous and unitary; it is the liminal space created by the permanent *performative* transgression of national grand narratives, eternal and 'pedagogic', by the 'shreds and patches' of the quotidian 'daily plesbicite' of many national voices (1994: 142, 158), by cultural discourses from the margins. Drawing on Derrida, Bhabha locates agency in the act of interruptive enunciation. As Gilroy too argues, this creates a 'double consciousness', a split subject, a fractured reality. To an anthropologist this echoes with familiar tropes: liminal masks, possessed 'lions', ritual clowns or anomalous creatures from beyond the boundaries all create such double consciousnesses – except that the discursive setting is the nation, and the marginal, hybrid, anomalous, betwixt-and-between, highly potent creatures are postcolonial migrants, or, more specifically, their creative works of high culture.

It is this *intellectualising* of everyday realities and material interests that Friedman criticises, but also the assumption that there ever were 'pure' cultures. All cultures are always hybrid, as both Bakhtin or Lévi–Strauss argue from different vantage points. To speak of cultural 'mixing' makes sense only from *inside* a social world. Hybridity is meaningless as a description of 'culture', because this 'museumises' culture as a 'thing'. The hybridity discourse celebrated by the new diasporic intellectuals is, Friedman feels, merely a form of moral self-congratulation – a view echoed in Hutnyk's account. Culture as an analytic concept is always hybrid (Friedman, Wicker), since it can be understood properly only as the historically negotiated creation of more or less coherent symbolic and social worlds.

Peter van der Veer reflects on the preoccupation of Cultural Studies with nomadism, travel and margins. His scepticism about the empowering transformative potentiality that Bhabha attributes to literary works arises from what he shows to be the liberal, romantic, *Enlightenment* topos these works evoke. Appropriating the toolkit of his intellectual opponents, he embarks on a finely textured and nuanced analysis of two novels, V.S. Naipaul's *The Enigma of Arrival* and Salman Rushdie's *The Satanic Verses*. Naipaul's book, he suggests, is a 'mortuary ritual' around the theme of migrancy, uprootedness and death, all allegories of modernity. Both Indian migrant and English farmer are exposed in the novel as rootless and plagued by a sense of loss, ironically mirroring each other's nostalgia for Empire.

But the main criticism directed by van der Veer against post-colonial critics like Bhabha is a substantive one. For Bhabha, the blasphemy of *The Satanic Verses* epitomises the power of hybridity to challenge the purity of 'tradition' through a 'poetics of reinscription'. Van der Veer's view – underwritten by Werbner's analysis of the schismogenetic nature of essentialism and the Rushdie affair – is that such blasphemy merely polarises and sharpens moral oppositions: this particular form of newness that comes into the world is, he finds, alienating and sterile. The irony, he notes, is that it is religious migrants who are in the vanguard of a new European multiculturalism, yet they are dismissed and condemned as purists by elitist, bourgeois, 'enlightened' intellectuals. From a quite different, feminist perspective, Yuval-Davis also points out that, *contra* Bhabha, not all minority voices from the margins are progressive. Indeed, one might add, indigenous, 'white', racist and xenophobic discourses of the underprivileged at the margins have historically been just as pernicious as those of national elites, despite a Marxist tendency to privilege the latter.[3]

THE POWER TO NAME:
HYBRIDITY VERSUS ESSENTIALISM

Ambivalence is a key term that is often substituted for hybridity in (post-)colonial/diasporic discourse. It seems to mark not merely Bhahba's liminal 'fluctuation between a thing and its opposite' (Young 1995: 61) but the distorted specularities of colonial racism highlighted by Fanon and Ashis Nandy (Werbner, Papastergiadis). Ambivalence is the 'colonial mirror of production' where, according to Michael Taussig, racism rehearses mimetically its 'love–hate relation with [its own] repressed sensuosity', embodied in the physicality of the racialised other (1993: 66, 67). The psychoanalytic gaze thus highlights biological and sexual as well as metaphorical repulsion and desire: according to Young, 'colonial novels in English betray themselves as driven by desire for the cultural other' (1995: 3). It is this potent mixing of magnetising otherness, sexuality and culture that makes racism itself, according to Rattansi (1992; 1995), essentially ambivalent (or 'hybrid'). The further logical step is to argue that there are no clear differences between racism and ethnicity, between essentialising discourses of otherness and multicultural identities. All is hybrid. We are back, it seems, in the Alice-in-Wonderland world described by Wieviorka.

Against this conflation of racism with ethnicity, we interrogate here the difference between a shifting, hybridising politics of cultural multiplicity (Werbner, Baumann, Hutnyk) and racism as a violating, exclusionary process of essentialism that ultimately seeks to negate ambivalence (Werbner, Bonnett). Since our shared assumption is that culture is always sited and negotiated, we also argue for the possibility of new, positive ethnic anti-racist identity fusions, transcending fragmentation and beyond cyborg politics (Baumann, Hutnyk, Bonnett, Werbner).

While racists are not particularly consistent in their likes and dislikes, as Modood shows, they do consistently tend to differentiate between their racialised objects of desire/disgust: they are 'cultural' racists rather than 'just' racists. In a postmodern age of uncertainty, Bauman proposes, difference has itself, paradoxically, come to be reified by both the Left and the Right.

Resonating with Wieviorka's, Melucci's and Friedman's analyses of the postmodern condition, Bauman suggests that in the postmodern world, identities are *palimpsest*, rootless and in constant flux. Yet notwithstanding the uncertainties, alienations and fears of postmodernity, it has opened up a real opportunity for individual self-fulfilment and emancipation. Against the old modernist, obsessively organising state, unable to live with strangers, the present efflorescence of cultural and subcultural differences has made difference the very organising principle of post-modern existence. To talk of strangers no longer makes sense. Ours is a *heterophilic* age.

But, paradoxically, cultural difference has also become the basis for an exaggeration of difference and, with it, the incommensurability of cultures. Racist differentialism and liberal or social communitarianism – ideologies of the Right and the Left – abandon universalist notions of responsibility, of the individual as a life project, in order to revalorise closed cultures, roots and traditions. Against uncertainty, their desire is to 're-embed' what modernity disembedded. In this hybrid discourse of 'community' and 'rights', multiculturalists deny the universalist, self-emancipatory challenge of modernism, founded upon assumptions of the inalienable right of individuals to choose, irrespective of tribe or nation. They thus fail to recognise that the new, postmodern freedom depends on recognising the rights of all – of strangers *qua* individuals – while at the same time denying the right of anyone to define who strangers are.

Yet, as we saw, it cannot be assumed *a priori* that all appeals to community and nation are intrinsically racist. New Right discourses may be better conceived of as disguised appeals by unscrupulous politicians to a more pervasive, 'vulgar' street racism, as Miles has argued (1993: 71–8). The hybrid discourse of the New Right – cultural rights plus social exclusion – generates an apparent ambivalence, but this should not delude us into thinking that racism is ambivalent in the same way multiculturalism and ethnicity are. Cultural racism is, in Bauman's words, 'an essentialism not yet unmasked'. But what, precisely, is this racism? How are we to recognise it as different and apart from ethnicity, patriotism, multiculturalism or ethnocentrism?

To disentangle this question in all its multiple strands, we need to start from the fact that discourse is performative, not a text to be analysed in abstraction. Racism and ethnicity are, we argue, distinct social processes of public communication, enunciation, elicitation, action and reaction. This accords with Bhabha's privileging of the performative and the interruptive, and it is a key to unlocking the divide between the ambivalences of racism and the multiplicities of multicultural identities.

Perhaps one might begin by considering the nature of ethnicity, a subject to which anthropologists have given a good deal of thought. In an original contribution to this field, Gerd Baumann distinguishes between two forms of discursive praxis – 'dominant' and 'demotic' – routinely deployed by the residents of a single multi-ethnic urban neighbourhood in London. The dominant discourse reifies community and culture as essences, he proposes, by demarcating currently accepted divisions between South Asian British settlers, based upon religious affiliation and nationality. The demotic discourse transgresses these divisions in sited interaction. In particular, young South Asians create a shared popular culture across these major divisions, fusing their identities as South Asians through popular cultural aesthetic forms. They intentionally subvert the normative boundaries of 'community' set by their parents. Nevertheless, the same people who use demotic discourses revert to the dominant discourse on public occasions, while any public challenge to this reifying discourse (as was attempted by a local women's group) is likely to bring upon the offenders the full wrath of community elders.

The point is, Baumann argues, that neither discourse is 'false'; they constitute a dual discursive competence that renders 'culture' and 'community' active terms of debate and negotiation in everyday life or *vis-à-vis* the local state. For ethnic activists, reified cultural emblems are mobilising banners, not terms of analytic debate. They draw on common-sense ideas to objectify culture, community, ethnos and even 'race' as self-evident homologues, while at the same time being aware of remaking, reshaping and re-forming these very terms in other contexts.

In these circumstances, negotiating alliances is not via a cyborg politics of respect but by a remaking of culture itself, much of it through fun and music, in dialectical tension with a more monological discourse. This liminal discursive space – in many senses reminiscent of Bhabha's third space – while it is replete with essentialist ideas about culture and community, is not – as Werbner proposes – ambivalent in the same sense as racism is.

The urgent need, Werbner argues, is to distinguish the pernicious essentialising of racism, a reification of categories that does not admit its own contingent ambivalence, from the normal objectifications of ethnicity that foreground cultural identities situationally through dynamic processes of '(pre)figuring' and 'grounding'. Here Werbner draws on anthropological insights, reiterated recently by Strathern (1991), about scale as well as positioning, to illuminate the way people 'play' with their identities while still valorising them. Like Gilroy, she finds that diasporic identities 'on the margins' are grounded in sentiment and constituted as moral virtue. The emancipatory motifs they encapsulate are not merely discursive; they are materially embodied by subjects in response to the experience of racist violation, but also through gestures of 'reaching out' to morally valued others, enacted performatively in invisible diasporic spaces, far from the public eye. The reason ethnic identities remain contingent has to do with their responsiveness to context, and hence lack of fixity: as Baumann and Yuval-Davis also note, ethnicity is as much the product of *internal* arguments of identity and contestation as of external objectifications.

Unlike ethnicity, pernicious essentialism precipitates a schismogenetic process. The pathological ambivalences of racism or xenophobia are the very motor that drives polarising processes forward through a series of agonistic moral panics, towards violent exclusions, assimilations and denials. The emergence of Islamphobia in Europe exemplifies this process, Werbner demonstrates. From this perspective racial violence is intentionally exemplary and theatrical, and all racist essentialisms are implicitly or explicitly violating of self and subjectivity. The imbrication of racism in destructive sentiment is what makes its ambivalences pathological and non-contingent – a feature highlighted by Fanon (1963). This leads Werbner to criticise post-colonial/modern theories, such as those of Rattansi or Bhabha, which tend to conflate the distorted specularities of colonial/racial 'desire' with the hybridities and multiplicities of ethnicity or multiculturalism. The obvious danger we need to guard against, Werbner contends, is of essentialising all essentialisms as the same, a confusion that ends up criminalising ethnicity and exonerating racism. We need instead to follow Fanon or Nandy (1983) in recognising the polarising and distorting features of racist encounters.

Against a fragmented cyborg politics, the materiality of racial suffering can potentially lead to the invention of allegories that 'travel', and hence to the 'imagining' of moral and aesthetic communities of suffering *across* social and cultural divisions. As we have seen, there are strong centrifugal forces that act to fracture such communities of sentiment, but the embodied nature of the shared experiences of oppression does appear to create at least the grounds for such fusions. The emergence of anti-racist unities against the grain is the central message of Hutnyk's contribution.

MIMESIS, CROSSOVER AND CREATIVITY

Speaking in an age of reflexive global heterophilia, Hutnyk probes the implications of Adorno's insight into the commodification of difference: in capitalist production, mimesis, crossover and unique authenticity – apparently quite discrete aesthetic impulses – are merged in an underlying uniformity. The World Music Festival, a 'progressive' event promoting world peace and understanding, is an ironic text of the cacophony of global emancipatory struggles, a scene where 'authenticity operates through incomprehension'. The multiplicity of 'traditions', genres and modern crossovers must, Hutnyk speculates, make marketing a nightmare, leading to essentialist definitions of culture, blind to their own incoherence. In the process of co-optation all semblance of unique voice or value seems to get lost. Ironically, hybridity-talk is itself in danger of becoming just such another marketable commodity.

Here Hutnyk echoes van der Veer's scepticism about the power of literary works to disrupt. At the same time, the accessibility of the new technology leads to opposed processes: of global homogenisation on the one hand, and autonomous creativity on the other. The question is: can there be political resistance through music in and against the market? To answer this, we need to start from the fact that Adorno and Hork-heimer, Hutnyk insists, have been misunderstood. While the two scholars recognised the fascist potential of mass culture, they also saw its revital-ising power as a counter to high culture. What they really objected to was the dilution of popular culture by bourgeois tastes.

Despite its embeddedness in capitalism, Womad can also be seen to open up a genuine liberatory space that escapes commodity fetishism and the indiscriminate promotion of rampant creativity and 'mix'. This is exemplified in the political work of some Asian bands that fuses their identity as Asian, Muslim and black in an explicit critique of racial oppression. What these young Asians signal is that Hall's 'innocent black subject' is still vitally present: it has not been erased in the face of ethnic difference. So, too, Gilroy's reluctance to work with the notion of 'black' that includes Asian politics in Britain is misconceived. Too much hybridity, as Spivak says, leaves all the old problems of class exploitation and racial oppression unresolved. Far from being a radical project, hybridity turns out, Hutnyk contends, to be a political cul-de-sac which trivialises black political activity.

But what would a radical hybridity look like? As an example, he brings us the lyrics of a Bengali band that are informed by the experience of multiple oppressions – of racism, colonialism and capitalism. It is only such aesthetic fusions of collective subjectivity, he feels, that can resist the homogenising influences of the market.

CONCLUSION: THE PROCESS OF HYBRIDITY

In the postmodern imaginary, hybridity invades whole areas of socio-logical discourse, subverting and conflating long-established classes and categories. Thus Actor Network Theory defines hybridity as the product of mixed networks of people-objects (Latour 1993; Callon and Law 1995). Objects are prosthetic extensions of persons; persons materially consti-tuted by objects. Hi-tech threatens to conflate the 'division between the human and the nonhuman' (Strathern 1996: 519); commerce, to patent Culture plus Nature (ibid.: 524). The conceptual efflorescence of terms for heterogeneity, for 'mixed narratives', is often as infinite and shapeless as the networks supposedly embodying it (ibid.: 522–3).

Perhaps it is true, as Papastergiadis suggests, that one of the achievements of poststructuralist theory has been to liberate the subject from notions of fixity and purity of origin. In the process, hybridity as a loaded discourse of dangerous racial contaminations has been transformed into one of cultural creativity: 'insults' have been turned into 'strengths'.

But, as we have argued here, there are problems with this celebration of hybridity by post-colonial intellectuals, as well as with the conception of 'the migrant' as the exemplary embodiment of this double consciousness (Ahmad 1995: 13). In a scathing critique, Ahmad argues that hybridity fails to move beyond the ephemeral and the contingent; thus it masks long-term social and political continuities and transformations. In the real world, however, political agency is 'constituted, not in flux and displacement but in given historical locations' (ibid.: 16), by having a coherent 'sense of place, of belonging, of some stable commitment to one's class or gender or nation' (ibid.: 14). Echoing the contributions in this volume, Ahmad finds that the conditions of ethical responsibility, moral action and committed positioning are the subjective foundations of any (oppositional) politics that wants to effect real change.

What is needed, in other words, is a *processual* theory of hybridity, one that goes beyond the recognition that monological discourses are in permanent tension with a 'sea of heteroglossia'. Such a theory must differentiate, in the first instance, between a politics that proceeds from the legitimacy of difference, in and despite the need for unity, and a politics that rests on a coercive unity, ideologically grounded in a single monolithic truth. Second, it must explain how and why cultural hybrids are still able to disturb and 'shock' – and thus to heighten reflexivity and 'double consciousness' – in a postmodern world that celebrates difference through a consumer market that offers a seemingly endless choice of 'unique' identities, subcultures and styles.

These questions are tied theoretically. One of the advances made by anthropologists in the study of liminal moments has been to move beyond a simple stress on anti-structure as effervescence, *communitas* and egalitarian amity to an appreciation that liminality is itself structured processually. In this process, categories are exaggerated and caricatured in order to be worked upon and reconfigured so as to reconstitute the condition of participants.[4] Ritual hybrids not only raise consciousness; they are performatively powerful, polluting, fertilising or purifying. By analogy, we need to think in our discussions of multiculturalism and anti-racism of the way discourses interact to create bridges or precipitate polarising processes. It is in this spirit that Yuval-Davis and others argue here that one tendency of multiculturalism is to exaggerate cultural 'difference', and thus valorise 'fundamentalist' cultural self-definitions among minorities; while by contrast, as Hutnyk and Baumann suggest, a radical hybridity may emerge out of the homogenising culture industry in response to violence and suffering. Hence, too, cyborg politics may be the only viable form of alliance in the context of reflexive, 'high' modernity.

The challenge, then, is to develop processual models of hybridity to replace the current stress on contingent hybridity, a self-congratulatory discourse which leads nowhere. In order to do so we must start from the understanding that in Europe today, neither nations nor the nation's ethnic 'margins' are homogeneous; both are battlegrounds of contested moralities. The centre, far from being monological, has its own official forms of institutionalised dissent and indigenous rituals of rebellion – novels and other works of high or popular culture (thus 'the canon' in English literature consists primarily of works that have transgressed and challenged the inequities and hypocrisies of class, hierarchy and moral puritanism, while popular music, in its evocations of love, sensuality and play, subverts the mundane stress on disciplined bodies and compliant regimentation). We need to consider precisely what it is that cultural hybridity and essentialism from the margins do in this context. Even if we think that they expose the transparency of ethnocentric hegemonic cultural assumptions, we have to recognise the differential interests social groups have in sustaining boundaries. It is this interest in the boundary that makes the experience of hybridity disturbing and shocking for some, while for others it is revelatory. But thinking about process, we need also to ask: what are the consequences of this encounter for the margins? Again, a focus on hybridisation as process reveals the fissions in the margin: strategies of co-optation, resistance or genuine fusions divide the margins to create the crosscutting ties between centre and margin and the periodic moral panics that demonise margin and centre dialectically.

This complexity of process renders multiculturalism an important rhetoric and an impossible practice. As a rhetoric, it challenges any conception of the nation as a cultural whole, mutating nationalism into a hybridised cultural subjective consciousness that can act as a bulwark against racism. The mediating objects enabling this rhetoric – aesthetic creations of diasporic artists, writers, film makers or chefs – are in this sense important and merit attention. So, too, are the sometimes strident voices of religious leaders. Multiculturalism as a set of assumptions posits that marginal culture(s) in a postmodern world have to be accorded respect; that we underestimate the sentimental and moral roots of cultural identity – defined at a particular scale and historical moment – at our peril (Taylor 1994). This is an issue we explore more fully in the second volume arising out of the conference, *The Politics of Multiculturalism: Racism, Identity and Community in the New Europe* (Modood and Werbner 1997).

But against the rhetoric of multiculturalism, the impossibility of multiculturalism as fixed policy practice stems, as most of us have sought to show here, from the intrinsically sited, negotiated, hybrid and yet morally committed nature of 'culture' and ethnicity. In reality there are no fixed cultures in modern nation-states; only political imaginaries of pure or impure cultural horizons.

NOTES

This chapter has benefited greatly from the perceptive comments of Richard Werbner, as well as from long conversations about cyborgs with my postgraduate student, Katherine Tylor.

1. Lévi Strauss analyses the role of tricksters and clowns as mediators of opposite terms in mythic thought who thus help to achieve the 'purpose of myth [which] is to provide a logical model capable of overcoming contradiction' (1963: 229). He notes that as mediators, tricksters 'must retain something of that duality – namely an ambiguous and equivocal character' (ibid.: 226). Victor Turner sees the exaggerated features of hybrid masks and figurines of initiation rituals as a 'primordial mode of abstraction ... [that] is made into an object of reflection' (1967: 103). Hence 'liminality ... breaks, as it were, the cake of custom and enfranchises speculation ... a certain freedom to juggle with the factors of existence' (ibid.: 106). Similarly, Mary Douglas proposes that the cult of the Pangolin, an anomalous creature that conflates categories normally kept apart, 'invite[s its] initiates to turn round and confront the categories on which their whole surrounding culture has been built up and to recognise them for the fictive, man-made, arbitrary creations that they are' (Douglas 1966: 169–70). Further, she concludes elsewhere that 'a people who have nothing to lose by exchange and everything to gain will be predisposed towards the hybrid being.... A people whose experience of foreigners is disastrous will cherish perfect categories, reject exchange and refuse doctrines of mediation' (Douglas 1975: 307).

2. The idea that ritual is a site for the enactment of social oppositions and conflicts was early developed by Gluckman (1963) in his notion of rituals of rebellion, and by Turner (1967). Both Douglas and Turner see the liminal as a space of anti-structure from which hierarchy may be challenged through humour (Douglas 1968) or egalitarian 'communitas' (e.g. Turner 1974: 166–230). A broad range of anthropological studies build on these foundational insights to demonstrate the oppositional nature of ritual hybrids. As an example, one may take studies of spirit possession, shamanism and exorcism that analyse how mundane reality is overturned through oppositional hybrid figures and symbolic actions (Lambek 1981; Kapferer 1982; Boddy 1989; R. Werbner 1989; Tsing 1993); while culture itself may be composed of conflicting discourses (Abu-Lughod 1986; Hutchinson 1996). Geertz's analysis of the Balinese cockfight (1973: 412–53) highlights its reflexive and oppositional dimensions as an inversion of mundane values. Other studies address more explicitly the resistance to (post-)colonialism through hybrid images – for example, Taussig's Marxist gloss on the hybrid fetish-god of the Bolivian tin mines (1980); Comaroff (1985) on Zionist churches as 'subversive

bricoleurs'; P. Werbner (1990) on British–Pakistani migrant wedding ritual clowns; Cohen (1993) on the Notting Hill carnival; and Stoller (1995) on Hauka spirit possession. The idea that ritual in pre-industrial societies is merely formal and inscriptive, reflecting authority structures and eternal verities (Bloch 1986: 1–11), is thus rejected by most anthropologists.

3. See, for example, Wallerstein's contributions in Balibar and Wallerstein (1991); and Miles (1993).

4. The processual nature of the liminal phase is stressed by Kapferer (1982); R. Werbner (1989); P. Werbner (1990); Handelman (1990). The contested nature of the very definition of liminality is stressed in studies of pilgrimage (see, for example, the contributions to Eade and Sallnow 1991).

REFERENCES

Abu-Lughod, Lila (1986) *Veiled Sentiments: Honour and Poetry in Bedouin Society.* Berkeley, CA: University of California Press.

Ahmad, Aijaz (1995) 'The Politics of Literary Postcoloniality'. *Race and Class* 36, 3: 1–20.

Bakhtin, Mikhail (1981) *The Dialogic Imagination*, trans. Caryl Emerson and Michael Hosquist. Austin, TX: University of Texas Press.

Bakhtin, Mikhail (1984) *Rabelais and His World*, trans. Helen Iswolsky. Bloomington, IN: Indiana University Press.

Balibar, Étienne and Immanuel Wallerstein (1991) *Race, Nation and Class: Ambiguous Identities.* London: Verso.

Barthes, Roland (1972) *Mythologies.* London: Paladin.

Bauman, Zygmunt (1989) *Modernity and the Holocaust.* Cambridge: Polity Press.

Bhabha, Homi (1994) *The Location of Culture.* London: Routledge.

Bloch, Maurice (1986) *From Blessing to Violence.* Cambridge: Cambridge University Press.

Boddy, Janice (1989) *Wombs and Alien Spirits.* Madison, WI: University of Wisconsin Press.

Bourdieu, Pierre (1984) *Distinction.* London: Routledge & Kegan Paul.

Callon, Michael and John Law (1995) 'Agency and the Hybrid *Collectif*'. *The South Atlantic Quarterly* 94, 2: 481–508.

Clifford, James (1988) *The Predicament of Culture: Twentieth-Century Ethnography, Literature, and Art.* Cambridge, MA: Harvard University Press.

Cohen, Abner (1993) *Masquerade Politics: Explorations in the Structure of Urban Cultural Movements.* Berkeley, CA: University of California Press.

Comaroff, Jean (1985) *Body of Power, Spirit of Resistance.* Chicago: University of Chicago Press.

Douglas, Mary (1966) *Purity and Danger.* London: Routledge & Kegan Paul.

Douglas, Mary (1968) 'The Social Control of Cognition: Some Factors in Joke Perception'. *Man* (n.s.) 3: 361–76.

Douglas, Mary (1975) *Implicit Meanings.* London: Routledge & Kegan Paul.

Eade, John and Michael Sallnow (1991) *Contesting the Sacred: The Anthropology of Christian Pilgrimage.* London: Routledge.

Fanon, Frantz (1963) *The Wretched of the Earth*, trans. C. Farrington. London: Penguin.

Fischer, Michael M. J. (1986) 'Ethnicity and the Post-Modern Arts of Memory', in James Clifford and George E. Marcus (eds) *Writing Culture: The Poetics and Politics of Ethnography*. Berkeley, CA: University of California Press: 194–233.

Foucault, Michel (1986) 'Of Other Spaces'. *Diacritics* 16, 1: 22–7.

Geertz, Clifford (1973) *The Interpretation of Cultures*. London: Hutchinson.

Gilroy, Paul (1993) *The Black Atlantic: Modernity and Double Consciousness*. London: Verso.

Gluckman, Max (1963) *Order and Rebellion in Tribal Africa*. London: Cohen & West.

Hall, Stuart (1990) 'Cultural Identity and Diaspora', in Jonathan Rutherford (ed.) *Identity: Community, Culture, Difference*. London: Lawrence & Wishart.

Hall, Stuart (1992) 'New Ethnicities', in James Donald and Ali Rattansi (eds) *'Race', Culture and Difference*. London: Sage in association with the Open University.

Handelman, Don (1990) *Models and Mirrors: Towards an Anthropology of Public Events*. Cambridge: Cambridge University Press.

Hannerz, Ulf (1992) *Cultural Complexity: Studies in the Organization of Meaning*. New York: Columbia University Press.

Haraway, Donna (1991) *Simians, Cyborgs and Women: The Reinvention of Nature*. London: Free Association Books.

Hebdige, Dick (1979) *Subculture: the Meaning of Style*. London: Methuen.

Hutchinson, Sharon (1996) *Nuer Dilemmas: Coping with Money, War and the State*. Berkeley: University of California Press.

Kapferer, Bruce (1982) *A Celebration of Demons*. Oxford: Berg.

Lambek, Michael (1981) *Human Spirits: A Cultural Account of Trance in Mayotte*. Cambridge: Cambridge University Press.

Latour, Bruno (1993) *We Have Never Been Modern*, trans. C. Porter. London: Harvester Wheatsheaf.

Lévi-Strauss, Claude (1963) *Structural Anthropology*, trans. Claire Jacobson and Brooke Grundfest Schoepf. London: Penguin.

Miles, Robert (1993) *Racism after 'Race Relations'*. London: Routledge.

Modood, Tariq and Pnina Werbner (1997) *The Politics of Multiculturalism: Racism, Identity and Community in the New Europe*. London: Zed Books.

Nandy, Ashis (1983) *The Intimate Enemy: Loss and Recovery of Self Under Colonialism*. Delhi: Oxford University Press.

Norris, Christopher (1993) *The Truth about Postmodernism*. Oxford: Blackwell.

Rattansi, Ali (1992) 'Changing the Subject? Racism, Culture and Education', in James Donald and Ali Rattansi (eds) *'Race', Culture and Difference*. London: Sage in association with the Open University: 11–48.

Rattansi, Ali (1995) '"Western" Racisms, Ethnicities and Identities in a "Postmodern" Frame', in Ali Rattansi and Sallie Westwood (eds) *Racism, Modernity and Identity on the Western Front*. Cambridge: Polity Press: 15–86.

Stewart, Charles and Rosalind Shaw (eds) (1994) *Syncretism/Anti-Syncretism: The Politics of Religious Synthesis*. London: Routledge.

Stoller, Paul (1995) *Embodying Colonial Memories: Spirit Possession, Power and the Hauka in West Africa*. New York: Routledge.

Strathern, Marilyn (1991) *Partial Connections*. Savage, MD: Rowman & Littlefield.

Strathern, Marilyn (1996) 'Cutting the Network'. *JRAI* 2, 3: 517–35.

Taussig, Michael T. (1980) *The Devil and Commodity Fetishism in South America.* Chapel Hill, NC: University of North Carolina Press.

Taussig, Michael T. (1993) *Mimesis and Alterity: A Particular History of the Senses.* New York: Routledge.

Taylor, Charles (1994) *Multiculturalism: Examining the Politics of Recognition.* Princeton, NJ: Princeton University Press.

Tsing, Anna L. (1993) *In the Realm of the Diamond Queen.* Princeton, NJ: Princeton University Press.

Turner, Victor (1967) *The Forest of Symbols: Aspects of Ndembu Ritual.* Ithaca, NY: Cornell University Press.

Turner, Victor (1974) *Dramas, Fields and Metaphors: Symbolic Action in Human Society.* Ithaca, NY: Cornell University Press.

Werbner, Pnina (1990) *The Migration Process: Capital, Gifts and Offerings among British Pakistanis.* Oxford: Berg.

Werbner, Richard (1989) *Ritual Passage, Sacred Journey.* Washington, DC: Smithsonian Institution Press.

Young, Robert (1995) *Colonial Desire: Hybridity in Theory, Culture and Race.* London: Routledge.

PART ONE

HYBRIDITY, GLOBALISATION AND THE PRACTICE OF CULTURAL COMPLEXITY

2

FROM COMPLEX CULTURE

TO CULTURAL COMPLEXITY

Hans-Rudolf Wicker

INTRODUCTION

Certain ideas have a lasting impact on the intellectual landscape by solving complex problems with apparent ease and in altogether unexpected ways (Langer 1984). They operate as organisers on different levels of society, and focus scientific attention. As grand designs, they usually proceed through phases of formation, scientific dissemination, discursive adaptation and popularisation, until they finally reach the stage of consolidation. If, in the course of time, an idea of this order proves its usefulness, it will – its proper explanatory range now clearly established – become an integral part of the fundamental scientific vocabulary. By contrast, a concept that turns out to be of little explicative value or – worse still – that tends to dissolve order when it is implemented practically or politically, will most probably never survive the stage of clarification, and will have to be removed from the list of truth-generating concepts.

There are many notions of this kind; some have proved their usefulness and continue to be of value, while others, having revealed themselves as misleading, have been consigned to history, at least where science is concerned. As an example of the useful and now firmly established ideas of this type we might name the Darwinian law of natural selection, which, after countless digressions into the social sciences, finally found its proper place in biology. Communication is another useful idea. Established as a theory in the late 1940s, the idea of communication mushroomed during the 1960s and 1970s, and found its way into almost every branch of science. It was not unusual at the time for reality to be interpreted exclusively as a world of signals, describable entirely in terms of communication such as sender, receiver, code, sign, channel, information, redundancy, entropy, and so on (Köck 1987). Currently, the idea of communication could be said to be passing through its consolidation stage.

Race is a *grande idée* of a different kind which came into pre-eminence in the eighteenth and nineteenth centuries as the notion of order *par excellence*. On the European continent – and most notably in the German-speaking parts – the idea of race was so thoroughly discredited through political implementation that it has been – and may well remain – banished from the social sciences as an affirmative element of order for ever. This is not the case in the Anglo-Saxon world, however, where race (and racism), although reinterpreted and stripped of its main biologist components, continues to serve as an important analytical tool in the social sciences.

My contribution focuses on an idea which – not for the first time – is currently undergoing the process of consolidation. There is still no conclusive evidence to enable us to decide whether it will come to be regarded as false and be discarded, or whether it will be kept on as a useful tool for the interpretation and ordering of reality. Hotly debated in the social sciences, often indiscriminately used in the media, claimed by the political Left as a framework for emancipative efforts from the bottom up and by the political Right as an element of order and delimitation from the top down, the idea I am referring to is 'culture'.

The idea of culture appears in a wide variety of contexts and has experienced a veritable boom since the 1970s, spawning a whole string of new compound words formed with multi-, pluri-, inter-, and trans-culturalism, as well as many different ethno-fashions. Much the same thing is happening in science, where research activities dealing directly with concepts of culture are multiplying and becoming increasingly differentiated. In the words of Susanne Langer (1984), we could say that the concept of culture is passing through a period of widespread and indiscriminate use in different social spheres, a period remarkable for the fact that the idea is assumed to be useful in naming and solving social problems which, in fact, it cannot possibly help to solve. Starting from this somewhat paradoxical situation concerning the explanatory scope of the culture concept, I shall (1) begin by describing the classical concept of culture; then (2) turn to the most important points of criticism concerning concepts of culture; and finally (3) discuss those relevant contemporary aspects which force us to develop a new concept of culture.

CULTURE AS A COMPLEX WHOLE

Few concepts have been as pervasively effective in ethnology as the often-quoted passage from E.B. Tylor's *Primitive Culture* (1958: 1) which describes culture – and civilisation – as, in the widest sense, a complex whole which includes knowledge, religious beliefs, art, morals, laws, and customs – in other words, all the skills and characteristics human beings acquire as members of a society. Although he was still influenced by the evolutionism of his century, which saw culture as a civilising achievement and an ennoblement of the spirit, Tylor prepared the ground for a post-evolutionary and post-colonial view of culture.

With regard to this transition, it is important to remember that the claim to a civilising development and the resulting imperative to break down and do away with traditions – such as the shackles of feudalism – are immanent to the bourgeois–evolutionist conception of culture, while post-evolutionism no longer equates the idea of culture with the striving for progress but with unbroken and persisting traditions.

In America more than elsewhere, Tylor's definition provided social scientists in the first half of the twentieth century with a theoretical framework for the establishment of a post-colonial context of interpretation. Cultures now came to be described, by turns, as complex *wholes* or as *sums* of characters in the form of ideas, representations, beliefs, behaviours and activities, referring in each instance to a *totality* (Kroeber and Kluckhohn 1952: 81–8). Representing cultures as *wholes* permitted (1) the search for patterns that give expression to supra-individual entities; (2) the treatment of totalities in their distinctions – thus clearing the way for cultural delineations and cross-cultural comparisons; and finally, (3) the ethnographic treatment of parts of these cultural wholes.

Representing the first viewpoint are theories which attempt to narrow down the conceptual terms describing the sum of all these things – culture – and their workings. Émile Durkheim's *représentations collectives* belong in this category, as do the 'stereotyped manners of thinking and feeling' (Malinowski 1972: 23) that constitute the 'spirit of a culture', and also the idea of cultures as *super-organic* units (Kroeber 1952) that generate *patterns of culture* (Benedict 1966) which, in the words of Parsons and Shils (1990: 40), 'guide choices of concrete actors'. In this view, culture feeds people tradition (Benedict 1966: 167), and guides them in their everyday thinking and acting.

Point two refers to the temptation – inherent in this conception of culture – to grasp the uniqueness of entities only by emphasising their difference. Although cultural collectivities and cultural patterns are not unequivocally determinable, at least their existence is documented by the fact that they differ from each other: 'some of the phenomena of culture – as, for instance, distinctive customs' (Kroeber 1952: 118). Thus, in a first step, the distinction between belonging to a culture and being alien to it is turned into a fundamental principle of human existence (Benedict 1966: 5); in a second step, mutual marginalisation is converted – via the postulate of cultural equivalence – into a demand for reciprocal recognition that finds its ultimate expression in the concept of cultural relativism.

The last point follows from the two that precede it. Starting from Tylor's definition of culture, cultural anthropology has set itself the task of recording and analysing, in their respective uniqueness, all the separate parts whose sum makes up the complex whole – systems of beliefs, myths, social structures, economic formations, and so on. In this century alone, enormous amounts of data from unique cultures have been recorded and published in this way.

The idea of culture as the expression of a *complex whole* manifesting itself alternately in fixed social structures, in stereotypical patterns of thought, action and beliefs (culture as pattern, as matrix, as stencil, or as filter), in the way of life of a people, or even in the processes of adaptation to the environment, is not devoid of a scholastic undertone. Culture is conceived of in terms of objectifying philosophies with, presumably, no need for an active subject at all. In the classical concept, individuals appear mostly as carriers of culture. They exist for the sole purpose of lending expression to their culture, which, through them, is able to fulfil its true destiny.

CRITICISM OF THE COMPLEX WHOLE

The classical concept of culture has its origins in the study of small societies with relatively well-defined cultural borders and only a small degree of internal social differentiation, which, to the observing ethnologist, appear as the very image of cultural homogeneity, cultural coherence and cultural continuity. Even without considering the validity of such a culture concept for the interpretation of small societies, the problem remains whether this classical design can actually be transferred from small, closed societies to large and complex ones. Parsons and Shils, whom we have quoted above, were by no means the only ones to shift the quest for the complex whole to industrial societies. After World War II, the search for the *shared cultural tradition* (Parsons 1951: 12) and the complex whole in the heart of modern society became practically a must.

Although various sciences today are developing a more critical and discriminating approach to culture, the effects of 'the complex whole' continue to be felt. Totalities of this kind tend to surface whenever the inner structure of a culture concept is based on ideas of homogeneity, coherence and continuity, referring to comparable supra-subjective entities, which, in turn, raise once more the question of cultural relativity or, obversely, of cultural compatibility. The dispute over cultural relativism, anti- and anti-anti-relativism (Geertz 1984) – much like the controversy surrounding the notion of multiculturalism – is essentially a moral dispute over the call to tolerance and the limits of tolerance towards foreigners, a dispute which is understandable if one assumes that cultural wholes actually exist.

If Esser (1983: 31) is willing to recognise the independence of ethnic, cultural and religious groups within multicultural societies, he implicitly introduces the notion of autonomous cultural wholes and tolerance between these wholes. If the Canadian government sees the recognition of cultural diversity and identity as the basis of a multicultural state policy (Berry 1994), it presumes the existence of cultural wholeness. The moment one's own way of life and that of others are presented as goods deserving of protection, they become comparable entities and are set up in relation to homogeneous and coherent cultural orders in the classical sense. By supposing the incompatibility of cultures, as he does in his discussion of the emerging multicultural society – which he perceives as a danger to the social order – Hoffmann-Novotny (1992: 24–7) also falls back on the classical category of the complex whole which is prerequisite to the delimitation and comparability of cultures. The list of examples expressing similar notions of culture is virtually endless. They are particularly numerous in descriptions and analyses of subcultures and ethnic communities (for a critique, see Anthias and Yuval-Davis 1992: 157–98), but they also appear in studies which attempt to think of Western society as a culture and try to outline its basic premises as a coherent whole (Sahlins 1976).

The practice of blindly adopting classical concepts of culture in recent scientific discussions has repeatedly been criticised. Apart from a certain type of postmodern disapproval, which tends to view all scientific descriptions of the foreign as mere phenomenologies of difference (Clifford and Marcus 1986), there are two main lines of criticism. Critics of the first kind view the classical definition of culture as a continuation of older concepts of race, and propose to remove both race and culture from the list of useful analytical categories. They argue that just as physiological characteristics had been insufficient to group people into concrete, unchanging and non-overlapping 'races', cultural signs are too vague and ambivalent to define and separate cultural units (Kahn 1989: 18–19).

Culture, like race, is perceived as defying definition (Ingold 1994: 329), and this, the critics maintain, suggests that both categories are ideological systems of classification of a kind which can be understood only in their proper historical context, and which powerful political systems use to construe order. Relativist proposals such as 'to each people its cultural identity; to each culture its own moral values, its political traditions, its rules of behaviour' (Finkielkraut 1990: 95) are dismissed as descendants of a tradition that originates with Herder's notion of 'Volksgeist'; and the latter, by refusing the absolute and the universal, is seen as leading straight to the following doctrine:

> Prejudice is good in its proper time: because it brings happiness. It tightens the bonds of peoples grouped around their centre, it strengthens their stock, makes their nature bloom, makes them more ardent also and more blissful in their inclinations and purposes. (Herder 1984: 619)

As Finkielkraut puts it, culture changes into a product of political collectivities who use the processes of integration and marginalisation to promote and strengthen the collective 'We'. Such a reading – culture as classification of order – is justifiable to the extent that the New Right does, indeed, base its policy of integration and marginalisation on the 'principle of the radical incommensurability of the different cultural forms' (Taguieff 1992: 237). The link between racism and culture is thus clearly established. Culture in this form 'opens the floodgates of un- controlled irrationalism' (Dittrich and Radtke 1990: 24) – an irrational- ism implicit in the concept of multiculturalism as well (Radtke 1990) – and opposes the principles of a rational order of modernity with its universal norms and values based on the equality of all human beings. Thus, both neo-racists and critics of neo-racism implicitly and without reflection base their views on concepts of cultures as complex wholes: the former by objectifying cultural difference (Taguieff 1992: 238); and the latter by relying on views of progress and modernisation, and perceiving the existence of cultural difference, and of culture in general, as the sole result of state control and state policy – in other words, by putting the existence of objective global equality above the negation of the existence of objective cultural difference.

The second faction, whose theories also question the classic concept of culture to a certain extent, are the ethnicity researchers. While the classical definition of culture seemed to explain cultural borders quite naturally as stages of transition from one cultural system to another, eth- nicity research actually studies the ethnic borders themselves, and the mechanisms used to preserve them. Probably the most important inno- vation resulting from this approach concerned the fact that ethnic lines of separation were found to constitute and preserve themselves through processes of ascription – to self and other. The origins of these processes of ethnicity, however, could not, it was argued, be traced to the different cultural representations of the groups involved (Barth 1969). Although cultural phenomena can be diacritical elements of delimitation strategies, they do not reveal sufficient information to *explain* the existence of ethnic borders and conflicts.[1]

Much of the research concerning ethnic groups in industrial countries is based on the ethnic delimitation model. The strength of the new doctrine lies in its ability to explain why groups within nation-state systems who mark themselves off from each other by means of ethnic categories need not necessarily be very different in terms of culture. The ethnicity model thus takes into account the fact that the cultural convergence which inevitably takes place between interacting groups – the very social dynamics that sociology tried to subsume under the concept of assimilation early on – does not necessarily 'soften' ethnic borders. Ethnic marginalisation is conceivable even under conditions of full cultural assimilation (Glazer and Moynihan 1975). It thus resists the liberal proposal to define ethnic difference as a relic of pre-modern forms of social organisation, and therefore doomed to extinction. The ethnicity model also reveals that ethnic borders are actively worked on from both sides of the boundary. This aspect is significant because the integration of ethnic groups in a nation-state is characterised by an imbalance of power, and is thus asymmetrical. In this context, the explicit strengthening and mobilising of ethnic ties is a strategic device which may enable minorities to attain specific emancipative group objectives. Similarly, the state may choose to work with ethnic categories for specific purposes of social and political control (Cohen 1974; Glazer and Moynihan 1975: 10).

These two schools of cultural criticism have two things in common. One: they do not question the basic premiss of early American cultural anthropology, which states that human beings are generally to be regarded as cultural beings who are formed by processes of enculturation and who, at the same time, participate in this forming through interaction. Two: both camps agree in their criticism of cultural concepts which lead to clearly delimited, homogeneous and coherent cultural units, and therefore lend themselves to the establishment of cultural types that can be instrumentalised. This applies to cultural, ethnic and racialised boundaries (Anthias and Yuval-Davis 1992) as well as the social segments which, owing to their power to classify and to define, are in a position to draw, naturalise and instrumentalise boundaries of this kind.

PREREQUISITES FOR A MODIFIED
CONCEPT OF CULTURE

Before we can set out to find a new definition of the concept of culture, we need to free ourselves from the object of research on the basis of which the classical concept of culture was originally founded – that is, the small, strongly integrated, barely differentiated societies equipped with unique systems of social organisation, values and religious beliefs which, even as ethnography was beginning to observe them, were already being destroyed or forcefully integrated into nation-states and colonial systems. Characteristics such as invariance, exclusive territoriality, cultural incommensurability, cultural bias and cognitive limitation, whose inscription into the concept of culture by way of the study of archaic societies was incidental rather than conscious, have lost all meaning today. Vectors for a new concept of culture which adequately consider the most important characteristics of modern social development should look as follows.

For one thing, we need to accept the fact that cultures and ethnic groups as actual, autonomous totalities do not exist – or, at least, no longer exist. Notions such as Swiss, Turkish or Chinese culture are too diffuse, and do not refer to coherent and historically independent cultural patterns and grammars (Keesing 1974: 73; 1987: 161). Today, ethnic groups exist only within nation-states, and in interaction within and with these. They are either the product of nation-state strategies or so involved in these through mechanisms of state integration and assimilation that they can no longer be understood without concepts of identity – and border-generating processes of inter-ethnic dialectics. On the other hand, the significance of primordial invariants, the social facts that generate a sense of belonging, such as quasi-kinship, language, religion, customs and morals (Geertz 1963: 105–57) are no longer taken for granted anywhere, and are often perceived as threatened. In just the same way as culture and ethnic group are now freed from their existence as timeless essentials, a revised concept of culture can no longer be based on an assumption of an experience of restrictive and passive forces of eternal validity and uniform bias.

A second factor which increasingly undermines the classical concept of culture is the breaking up of the territorial borders of cultures and ethnic groups through a variety of forms of contemporary migration. Country-to-city migration and international migration generate interactions between people from fundamentally different backgrounds, and carry with them the seed of modification and change at the expense of time-honoured loyalties. When ethnic groups lose their territorial ties through migration – Appadurai (1991: 192) speaks of *de-territorialisation* as a new dynamic and constituent principle of culture – and require such makeshift concepts as 'transnational cultural communities' or 'transnational ethnic groups' for their collective description, then the search for their 'true' culture would seem to be rendered obsolete. Emigration and re-emigration, as well as the general global flow of information via mass media, migrant networks, and so on, lead to the emergence of cultural significations which resist all but the most syncretic designations. The space once perceived to be occupied by timeless, traditional essence and uniqueness is lost for ever.

Third, one of the achievements of modernism is to have disengaged communication and interaction from face-to-face relations between its actors, thus clearing the way for the development of global forms of communication and interaction. Driven by worldwide, norm-generating flows of capital, goods and data, globalisation efforts are omnipresent. They are producing transnational, transethnic and transcultural networks of communication and interaction in a powerfully staged attempt at creating a global ecumenical community (Hannerz 1992: 217–67; King 1991), typified by integration and a homogenisation of norms. And here again – only this time on a global scale – we find the characteristic particulars once used to define the classical culture concept. After its deconstruction through colonialism and modernism, and – at a later stage – through postmodernist approaches, the small culture, with its limited territory and its specific logic, is now being re-enacted on a higher plane. This process of transformation will not be clearly under-stood unless it is placed in the context of the universalist–rationalist ide-ologies of Enlightenment and the victory of the capitalist system. The emerging new perspective, characterised by the dialectic of universalism and particularism, suggests a separation of (global) culture and (local) identity, as expressed in the title of a monograph on the small Afro-Caribbean state of St Kitts–Nevis, *Global Culture, Island Identity* (Olwig 1993), or – equally telling – in the advertising slogan of a media giant: 'Think Global – Act Local'.

Fourth, one final important point which is closely related to the tendencies described above is the process of creolisation. Creole culture signifies, on the one hand, the distinctive mixture of linguistic and cultural elements in the Afro-Caribbean region, resulting from the area's unique historical development. On the other hand, creolisation refers to a cultural concept diametrically opposed to the Tylor model. From the viewpoint of creolisation, culture as an invariable and homogeneous whole makes no sense at all. On the contrary: a Creole-type model of culture will, by definition, accent internal variation, diachronicity and transitions – the kinds of events that Bickerton (1975) has tentatively described as intersystemic – and thus arrive at an entirely new mani-festation of cultural continuity.

Whereas the classical concept of culture was based on the inner logic and inherent laws of a culture – on a tangible structure, in other words – the Creole model postulates that intersystems have no uniform rules and invariant characteristics, and that their only system of classification consists of a set of rules of possible transformations (Drummond 1980: 352–553). The thesis that 'structure' is merely the result of a large number of variations and transitions has far-reaching consequences. It challenges Saussure's doctrine that *la langue* can be understood as a fixed and struc-tured whole by proposing that 'a language' can be described only in its variations (Bickerton 1975: 179). Applied to ethnology, this amounts to saying that culture – far from being a complex whole in the form of identifiable structures or significations – exists only in its variations and transitions. Culture in itself, then, is the result of past, present, and fu-ture processes of creolisation. Consequently, such an approach no longer focuses on a coherent cultural grammar – the pattern of Ruth Benedict, the 'elementary structure' of Émile Durkheim and Claude Lévi-Strauss, the basic personality structure of Abraham Kardiner – but on the rules of transformation responsible for cultural continua.

CULTURE AS THE ABILITY TO TAKE MEANINGFUL INTERSUBJECTIVE ACTION[2]

On the basis of what we said above, any definition of culture will have to consider the fact that today's world is one single horizontally and vertically integrated field of economic and social interaction, with an uneven distribution of power among its subfields. In this global space, unbroken traditions, developed regionally and in relative singularity, have ceased to be the norm. In the place of local authenticity we now encounter processes of creolisation. In so far as locally limited traditions still do exist, their particularistic world-views and structures are transient, residual or even purely reactive in character, and as such often merely the expression of secondary traditionalisation. Only a handful of strong subfields of power – which, privileged by their exceptional economic status, have access to the instruments necessary for the construction of coherent globality – can conceivably view themselves as possessing a truth untouched by the ravages of time.

Concepts of culture that face up to contemporary realities will no longer be preoccupied with the eternal and unchanging, and will make room for change as an implicit aspect of culture. By way of active and reactive processes of resistance and accommodation, the ability to act culturally guarantees the possibility of change, that is, of creolisation. Culture can no longer be represented by the metaphor of the timeless and suspended complex whole. A much more fitting allegorical expression for a new view of culture is the river, forever changing within given perimeters of space and time, and eluding the grasp of science because of its liquid nature as a process. In this way, the concept of a coherent culture yields to the concept of a flowing cultural complexity (Hannerz 1992; Barth 1993: 339). In its changing form, culture works intersystemically through its innate rules of transformation; cultural continua are invisible except as great numbers of variations. Two fundamental conclusions can be drawn so far.

First, the fairly trivial proposition advanced by the American school of cultural anthropology: that a human being develops into a social, cultural and therefore viable being only through the processes of primary and secondary socialisation – and the dialectic of socialisation and individuation – remains valid, albeit reinterpreted and limited in scope. The incorporation of values, norms and meanings continues to be part of becoming human even in a field of social and cultural complexity. However, the process of humanisation must be freed from the unilinear cultural determinism of the classical period of American anthropology, when the human mind was perceived as being literally swamped by tradition and culture (Sapir 1917: 441), and subjective character was relegated to a passive, incarcerated existence. According to recent findings in linguistic socialisation, enculturation implies *active, context-orientated appropriation* of knowledge and significations within the framework of *guided participation* (Rogoff 1990: 100), where subjective thinking and objective structure constitute and change each other in a unified process of interaction (Schieffelin and Ochs 1986: 183).

The question 'how could culture be formative and yet the individual be directive?' (Fox 1991b: 104) is sufficiently answered by pointing out that both culturalisation and individuation result from one and the same development. This theoretical position induces a shift in perspective away from the perception of culture as something in itself, towards those dynamic and complex fields of negotiation, invested with various degrees of defining power, which emerge from partly divergent and contradictory lines of exploration and discourse. Evidently, such a concept of culture must do without grammar or syntax, as these would merely serve to imply the existence of a coherent logic.

Culture does not equal language in its different manifestations (body language, symbolic language, fashion language, etc.), nor does it equal text, or a library of texts, which can be grasped by thick description (Geertz 1987). It is exclusively the ability to produce reciprocal symbolic relations and to form meaning through interaction. Enculturative inter-action therefore consists in the active appropriation of variants pertaining to language, classification, values and norms. Like the notion of 'partici-patory observation', the idea of 'active appropriation' contains two inter-weaving conceptions which cease to contradict each other only in actual practice: that of an imagined, external object which changes its nature in the course of appropriation.

To avoid promoting an overly positivistic view of science in talking about cultural ability, we should not dwell exclusively on the omnidirec-tional human negotiating potential. 'Limits to the negotiability of culture' (Douglas 1978: 6) are defined by the structural facts of a social field. They limit the choice of suitable and preferred alternatives of thinking, perception and action which interplay to create durable dispositions and field-specific strategies of habit or interaction. The incorporation of struc-ture and the exteriorisation of interiority contain the field-specific cultural bias (ibid.), that 'durable way of behaving, speaking, walking, and – in-cluded also – of feeling and thinking' which Bourdieu summed up in the term hexis (1976: 195).

A conception which replaces the principle of culture as a reality *sui generis* by a principle of semiotic practice (Vervaeck 1984) – culture as a set of specific dispositions, acquired by individuals in the process of living, which permit the intersubjective formation of signification and meaning-ful action – has far-reaching consequences for the current controversy surrounding the question of multiculturalism. By refusing monolinear and single-cause concepts of culture, we strip all notions based on such concepts of their relevance, including the very ideas of multiculturalism and pluriculturalism, as well as terms of integration such as cultural assimilation, melting-pot, and so forth (Nyberg Sørensen 1993: 31). Because meanings are negotiated directly in (political, social and eco-nomic) practice, integration in analytical terms can no longer be described as the change from one cultural system to another. Instead, integration becomes a social field of interaction in itself, wherein processes of creolisation occur with increasing frequency to produce culture in the form of new habits, and from which emerge the categories of a new public sphere.

What needs to be explained, then, is not why creolisation, as a result of the interactive search for meaning and generation of symbols, does occur but, on the contrary, the fact that the cultural ability for interac-tive signification is thwarted by the prescription of one-sided assimilation in specific social situations where the actors from certain fields of origin are virtually denied access to the power of defining. In trying to account for the successes, failures and difficulties of the integration of migrants in any given society, recourse cannot be taken to notions of culture, cultural bias, or even the incompatibility of cultural values and norms. Culture has no *facultas* of its own – no independent *proprietas*. Culture is a modal *accidens* equipped only with *dispositio* and *habitus*, and thus has no proper force of its own – it neither resists nor adapts and assimilates. There is no cultural being.

At best – following the praxiology of Bourdieu (1976 [1972]: 139–202) – culture is expressed in and through those durable dispositions which form the habits of people and which, as linkages of objective structures and subjective thinking, give expression to social fields. In this sense, it is not *the* Turkish culture that determines the integration process of Turks in Switzerland but, on the one hand, the migrants' social field of origin (rural, urban, social class, degree of literacy, etc.) which generates and naturalises durable dispositions in the form of action strategies and world-views, and, on the other, the social fields in the country of admission into which the migrants are to be integrated and whose residents, obviously, have equally naturalised habits. Dispositions permit the search for alternative action strategies, and enable individuals to participate in processes of integration and creolisation, respectively. However, since dispositions are inert – *hysteresis* is the term Bourdieu uses in this context – and the dynamics of adaptation are thus reduced, the change from one field to another – from lower to higher social stratum, from country to city, from one country to another – is characteristically slow. It is not cultural persistence, therefore, that is responsible for the typical formation of field-related or field-ethnic enclaves – particularly among first-generation immigrants – but the dialectic of existing barriers of integration and the staying power of habits.

This brings us to the second conclusion which can be drawn from the new understanding of culture discussed above. Briefly stated, it says that although the ability to act meaningfully and in a symbolic way allows for the construction of united and closed worlds of signification, the existence of social and political collectivities cannot be explained through culture, but only through social and political practice. Once culture is no longer viewed as a diction of complex wholes but as the expression of a semiotic praxiology, ethnology faces the methodological imperative to refrain from linking culture to terms of collectivity that suggest the existence of a culture-bound object. On the analytical level – and only there – collective action and culture are to be considered as separate fields. They cannot even be interpreted as being congruent where native ideology actually suggests such a proximity – as in 'that's the way our culture is' (Handler 1985). Ethnic groups and cultures, ethnic and cultural identities – terms and social practices, in other words, which project an image of unified collective actors – are the object of analysis, not the object of an implicitly given culture (Kirshenblatt-Gimblett 1992: 53). By the same token, this automatically voids all assumptions concerning possible 'objective cultural differences' that might exist between such collectivities of actors, as well as those suggesting that traditions – which generate meaning for and legitimate the existence of such collectivities – might be the expression of specific cultures. Culture only provides the means for social interaction and for the generation of intersubjective symbols, but it is not responsible for the results of these processes, such as the emerging social and political collectivities or more or less binding symbolic worlds.

It may well be that the very perspective which proposes a limited reading of the impact of culture can help to explain why, by way of intersubjective practice, collectivities keep forming which demand to be labelled, and attempt to come close to the image of imagined complex wholes. They are marked by rituals that project complex wholes by way of specific dramaturgies, and include different ethnic groups and political organisms – from primitive communities to nation-states – engaged contextually, sporadically or steadily in the work of producing collective identities. The image of complex wholeness projected by such social and political units, at least on a symbolic plane, often includes the very characteristics – homogeneity, coherence and consistency – which, as we have just argued at great length, cannot be considered attributes of 'culture'. What a formation of this kind may currently lack in terms of inner logic can be generated by way of the production of communality. The tuning-in of social and political bodies in the sense of a unity of feeling (Fernandez 1986) includes both the positioning within a common history and the rhythmisation of experience. While, in the final analysis, the existence of complex wholes cannot be denied, they must not be seen as cultures based on an unquestionable logic. Formations of this kind use only the intersubjective abilities – of culture – to build monolithic and truth-generating symbolic worlds. This is why they elude the concept of culture, and require for their understanding scientific concepts that give priority to the question of the social power to define.

CONCLUSION

We can now answer – at least tentatively – the question raised at the beginning of this chapter as to the meaning and range of culture as a scientific concept in the future. The division of the classical concept of culture into culture – meaningful action and the intersubjective generation of symbols – on the one hand, and complex wholeness – a constituted, delimitable collectivity – on the other, makes sense inasmuch as it clearly defines different levels of analysis. Criticism of the concept of culture used in classical ethnology is mainly directed at the mixing of culture and complex totality, not at the concept of enculturation. While the construction of complex wholeness is seen as a societal process moving between opposing poles of ideological argumentation – from essentially given (orthodox) to contextually construed (heterodox) – the question regarding the specific and field-related tools of human perception, thinking and action must be discussed at a different level. Reduced to its essentials, like so many other key concepts of science before it, a new and straightforward concept of culture will be based on this second level in order to be a scientifically valid tool for future analysis.

NOTES

1. Regrettably, ethnicity today is often used as a synonym for 'culture' in the classical sense. When Richard H. Thompson remarks 'or ethnicity ("tribal", linguistic, national, religious, or other cultural characteristics)...' (1989: 1), or Lawrence H. Fuchs states that 'Religion, language, and ancestral customs constituted the major expressions of ethnicity (1992: 46), they are both using ethnicity in the same essentialist manner as Geertz uses 'culture' (1963: 109) in his attempt to isolate the perceived primordial attachments of culture. It seems pointless to deconstruct the classical concept of culture, only to charge its successor with exactly the same meanings. In my text I adhere to the border-constituting sense of ethnicity as proposed by Barth (1969).

2. I would like to express my gratitude to Dr Alex Sutter, who – through his involvement with the phenomenon of culture from a philosopher's point of view – has been very helpful with his suggestions concerning the material in this chapter.

REFERENCES

Anthias, Floya and Nira Yuval-Davis (1992) *Racialised Boundaries. Race, Nation, Gender, Colour and Class and the Anti-racist Struggle*. London and New York: Routledge.

Appadurai, Arjun (1991) 'Global Ethnoscapes: Notes and Queries for a Trans-national Anthropology', in Richard G. Fox (ed.) *Recapturing Anthropology: Working in the Present*. Santa Fé: School of American Research Press: 191–210.

Barth, Fredrik (1969) *Ethnic Groups and Boundaries: The Social Organisation of Culture Difference*. Bergen–Oslo: University Forlaget.

Barth, Fredrik (1993) *Balinese Worlds*. Chicago: University of Chicago Press.

Benedict, Ruth (1966 [1935]) *Patterns of Culture*. London: Routledge.

Berry, John W. (1994) 'Coûts et avantages du multiculturalisme, un point de vue canadien', in Marie-Claire Calos-Tschopp (ed.) *Europe: Montres patte blanche!* Geneva: Centre Europe-Tiers Monde: 415–33.

Bickerton, Derek (1975) *Dynamics of a Creole System*. Cambridge: Cambridge University Press.

Bourdieu, Pierre (1976 [1972]) *Entwurf einer Theorie der Praxis*. Frankfurt am Main: Suhrkamp.

Clifford, James and George E. Marcus (eds) (1986) *Writing Culture: The Poetics and Politics of Ethnography*. Berkeley, CA: University of California Press.

Cohen, Abner (ed.) (1974) *Urban Ethnicity*. London: Tavistock.

Dittrich, Eckard J. and Frank-Olaf Radtke (eds) (1990) *Ethnisität*. Opladen: Westdeutscher Verlag.

Douglas, Mary (1978) *Cultural Bias*. London: Royal Anthropological Institute of Great Britain and Ireland. Occasional Paper 35.

Drummond, Lee (1980) 'The Cultural Continuum: A Theory of Intersystems'. *Man* 15: 352–74.

Esser, Hartmut (1983) *Die fremden Mitbürger*. Düsseldorf: Patmos.

Fernandez, James W. (1986) 'The Argument of Images and the Experience of Returning to the Whole', in Victor W. Turner and Edward M. Bruner (eds) *The Anthropology of Experience*. Urbana and Chicago: University of Illinois Press: 159–87.

Finkielkraut, Alain (1990 [1987]) *Die Niederlage des Denkens*. Hamburg: Rowohlt.

Fox, Richard G. (ed.) (1991a) *Recapturing Anthropology: Working in the Present*. Santa Fé: School of American Research Press.

Fox, Richard G. (1991b) 'For a Nearly New Cultural History', in Richard G. Fox (ed.) *Recapturing Anthropology: Working in the Present*. Santa Fé: School of American Research Press: 93–113.

Fuchs, Lawrence H. (1992) 'Thinking about Immigration and Ethnicity in the United States', in Donald L. Horowits and Gérard Noiriel (eds) *Immigrants in Two Democracies: French and American Experience*. New York: New York University Press: 39–65.

Geertz, Clifford (1963) 'The Integrative Revolution: Primordial Sentiments and Civil Politics in the New States', in Clifford Geertz (ed.) *Old Societies and New States: The Quest for Modernity in Asia and Africa*. New York: The Free Press: 105–57.

Geertz, Clifford (1984) 'Distinguished Lecture: Anti Anti-Relativism'. *American Anthropologist* 86: 263–78.

Geertz, Clifford (1987) *Dichte Beschreibung*. Frankfurt am Main: Suhrkamp.

Glazer, Nathan and Daniel P. Moynihan (eds) (1975) *Ethnicity: Theory and Experience*. Cambridge, MA and London: Harvard University Press.

Handler, Richard (1985) 'On Dialogue and Destructive Analysis: Problems in Narrating Nationalism and Ethnicity'. *Journal of Anthropological Research* 41, 2: 171–82

Hannerz, Ulf (1992) *Cultural Complexity: Studies in the Social Organization of Meaning*. New York: Columbia University Press.

Herder, Johann Gottfried (1984) 'Auch eine Philosophie der Geschichte sur Bildung der Menschheit', in Johann Gottfried Herder, *Werke*, Bd. 1. Munich: C. Hanser.

Hoffmann-Novotny, Hans-Joachim (1992) *Chancen und Risiken multikultureller Einwanderungsgesellschaften*. Bern: Schweizerischer Wissenschaftsrat.

Ingold, Tim (1994) 'Introduction to Culture', in Tim Ingold (ed.) *Companion Encyclopedia of Anthropology*. London and New York: Routledge: 329–49.

Kahn, Joel S. (1989) 'Culture. Demise or Resurrection', *Critique of Anthropology* 9, 2: 5–25.

Keesing, Roger M. (1974) 'Theories of Culture'. *Annual Review of Anthropology* 3: 73–97.

Keesing, Roger M. (1987) 'Anthropology as Interpretive Quest'. *Current Anthropology* 28: 161–76.

King, Anthony D. (ed.) (1991) *Culture, Globalisation and the World-System: Contemporary Conditions for the Representation of Identity*. London: Macmillan.

Kirshenblatt-Gimblett, Barbara (1992) 'Performing Diversity', in Daun Ake, Billy Ehn and Barbro Klein (eds) *To Make the World Safe for Diversity*. Helsingborg: Schmidts Bocktryckeri: 51–62.

Köck, Wolfram K. (1987) 'Kognition – Semantik – Kommunikation', in Siegfried J. Schmidt (ed.) *Der Diskurs des Radikalen Konstruktivismus*. Frankfurt am Main: Suhrkamp: 340–73.

Kroeber, Alfred R. (1952 [1917]) 'The Superorganic', in Alfred R. Kroeber (ed.) *The Nature of Culture*. Chicago: University of Chicago Press: 22–51.

Kroeber, Alfred R. and Clyde Kluckhohn (1952) *Culture: A Critical Review of Concepts and Definitions*. New York: Random House/Vintage.

Langer, Susanne K. (1984 [1942]) *Philosophie auf neuem Weg. Das Symbol im Denken, im Ritus und in der Kunst*. Frankfurt am Main: Fischer.

Malinowski, Bronislaw K. (1972 [1922]) *Argonauts of the Western Pacific*. Thetford: Lowe & Brydone.

Nyberg Sørensen, Ninna (1993) 'Creole Culture, Dominican Identity'. *Folk* 35: 17–35.

Olwig, Karen Fog (1993) *Global Culture, Island Identity: Continuity and Change in the Afro-Carribean Community of Nevis*. Chur: Harwood Academic Publishers.

Parsons, Talcott (1951) *The Social System*. New York and London: The Free Press/Collier-Macmillan.

Parsons, Talcott and Edward Shils (1990) 'Values and Social Systems', in Jeffrey C. Alexander and Steven Seidman (eds) *Culture and Society. Contemporary Debates*. Cambridge: Cambridge University Press.

Radtke, Frank-Olav (1990) 'Multikulturell – Das Gesellschaftsdesign der 90er Jahre'. *Informationsdienst sur Ausländerarbeit*, 4, 90, S: 27–34.

Rogoff, Barbara (1990) *Apprenticeship in Thinking: Cognitive Development in Social Context*. New York: Oxford University Press.

Sahlins, Marshall (1976) *Culture and Practical Reason*. Chicago: University of Chicago Press.

Sapir, Edward (1917) 'Do We Need a "Superorganic"?' *American Anthropologist* 19: 441–7.

Schieffelin, Bambi B. and Elinor Ochs (1986) 'Language Socialisation'. *Annual Review of Anthropology* 15: 163–91.

Taguieff, Pierre-André (1992) 'Die Metamorphosen des Rassismus und die Krise des Antirassismus', in Uli Bielefeld (ed.) *Das Eigene und das Fremde*. Hamburg: Junius: 221–68.

Thompson, Richard H. (1989) *Theories of Ethnicity. A Critical Appraisal*. New York: Greenwood Press.

Tylor, Edward B. (1958 [1871]) *Primitive Culture*. New York: Harper Torchbooks.

Vervaeck, Bart (1984) 'Towards a Semantic–Praxiological Approach to Culture Creation', in Rik Pinxten (ed.) *New Perspectives in Belgian Anthropology*. Göttingen: Herodot: 37–62.

3

THE MAKING AND UNMAKING

OF STRANGERS

Zygmunt Bauman

All societies produce strangers, but each kind of society produces its own kind of strangers, and produces them in its own inimitable way. If the strangers are the people who do not fit the cognitive, moral or aesthetic map of the world – one of these maps, two, or all three – if they, therefore, by their sheer presence, make obscure what ought to be transparent, confuse what ought to be a straightforward recipe for action, and/or prevent the satisfaction from being fully satisfying, pollute the joy with anxiety while making the forbidden fruit alluring; if, in other words, they befog and eclipse the boundary lines which ought to be clearly seen; if, having done all this, they gestate uncertainty, which in its turn breeds the discomfort of feeling lost – then each society produces such strangers; while drawing its borders and charting its cognitive, aesthetic and moral maps, it cannot but gestate people who conceal borderlines deemed crucial to its orderly and/or meaningful life, and are thus charged with causing the discomfort experienced as the most painful and least bearable.

The most oppressive of nightmares that haunted our century, notorious for its fears, gory deeds and dreary premonitions, was best captured in George Orwell's memorable image of the jackboot trampling the human face. No face was secure – everyone was liable to be charged with the crime of trespassing or transgressing. And since humanity bears ill all confinement, while the humans who transgress the boundaries turn into strangers, everyone had reason to fear the jackboot made to trample the strangers in the dust, squeeze the strange out of the human, and keep all those not-yet-trampled-but-about-to-be-trampled away from the mischief of boundary-ignoring.

Jackboots are part of a uniform. Elias Canetti wrote of 'murderous uniforms'. At some point of our century it became common knowledge that men in uniforms are to be feared most. Uniforms were the insignia of the servants of the State, that source of all power, and, above all, of coercive power. Wearing uniforms, men became that power in action; wearing jackboots, they trampled, and trampled at the behest and in the name of the State. That State which dressed men in uniforms so that they should be allowed and instructed to trample was the State which saw itself as the fount, the guardian and the sole guarantor of orderly life, a dam protecting order from chaos. It was the State that knew what that order should look like, and had enough strength and arrogance not only to proclaim all other states of affairs to be disorder and chaos, but also to force its subjects to live up to such a condition. This was, in other words, the modern State – one which legislated order into existence and defined order as the clarity of binding divisions, classifications, allocations and boundaries.

The typical modern strangers were the reverse of the State's ordering zeal. What the modern strangers did not fit was the vision of order. When you draw dividing lines and set apart what is so divided, everything that blurs the lines and spans the divisions undermines the work and mangles its products. The semantic under- and/or overdetermination of the strangers corrupted neat divisions and blurred the signposts. Their mere being around interfered with the work which the State swore to accomplish, and undid its efforts to accomplish it. The strangers exuded uncertainty, where certainty and clarity should have ruled. In the harmonious, rational order about to be built, there was no room – there could be no room – for 'neither–nors', for those who sat astride, for the cognitively ambivalent. This order-building was a war of attrition waged against the strangers and the strange.

In this war (to borrow Lévi-Strauss's concepts) two alternative but also complementary strategies were intermittently deployed. One was *anthropophagic*: annihilating the strangers by *devouring* them and then metabolically transforming them into a tissue indistinguishable from one's own. This was the strategy of *assimilation* – making the different similar; smothering cultural or linguistic distinctions; forbidding all traditions and loyalties except those meant to encourage conformity to the new and all-embracing order; promoting and enforcing one, and only one, measure of conformity. The other strategy was *anthropoemic*: *vomiting* the strangers, banishing them from the limits of the orderly world and barring all communication with those inside. This was the strategy of *exclusion* –

confining the strangers within the visible walls of the ghettos or behind the invisible yet no less tangible prohibitions of *commensality, connubium* and *commercium*; expelling the strangers beyond the frontiers of the managed and manageable territory; and, when neither of these two measures was feasible, destroying them physically.

The most common expression of the two strategies was the notorious clash between the liberal and the nationalist/racist versions of the modern project. People are different, implied the liberal project, but they are different because of the diversity of local, particularistic traditions in which they grew and matured. They are products of education, creatures of culture, and hence pliable and amenable to reshaping. With the progressive universalisation of the human condition – which means nothing else but the uprooting of all parochiality and the powers bent on preserving it, and consequently setting human development free of the stultifying impact of the accident of birth – that predetermined, stronger-than-human-choice diversity will fade away. Not so, objected the nationalist/racist project. Cultural remaking has limits which no human effort can transcend. Certain people will never be converted into something other than what they are. They are, so to speak, beyond re-pair. One cannot rid them of their faults; one can only rid them of themselves, complete with their oddities and evils.

Cultural and/or physical annihilation of strangers and the strange was, therefore, in modern society and under the aegis of the modern State, a *creative* destruction: demolishing, but building at the same time; mutilating, but also straightening up.... It was part and parcel of the on-going order-building effort, its indispensable condition and accompaniment. And vice versa – whenever building-order-by-design is on the agenda, certain inhabitants of the territory, to be made orderly in the new way, turn into strangers who need to be eliminated.

Under the pressure of the modern order-building urge, the strangers lived, so to speak, in a state of suspended extinction. They were, by definition, an anomaly to be rectified. Their presence was defined *a priori* as temporary, much as the current stage in the prehistory of the order yet to come. A permanent coexistence with the stranger and the strange, and the pragmatics of living with strangers, did not need to be faced point-blank as a serious prospect. And it would not need to be, as long as modern life remained a life-towards-a-project, as long as that project remained collectivised into a vision of a new and comprehensive order, and as long as the construction of such an order remained in the hands of a State ambitious and resourceful enough to pursue the task. None of these conditions seems to be holding today, though, at a time which Anthony Giddens (1991) calls 'late modernity', Ulrich Beck (1992) 'reflexive modernity', George Balandier (1994) 'surmodernity', and I, together with many others, have chosen to call postmodern; the time we live in now, in our part of the world.

DISEMBEDDING INTO SETTING AFLOAT

In its order-building pursuits, the modern State set about discrediting, disavowing and uprooting *les pouvoirs intermédiaires* of communities and traditions. If it were accomplished, this task would 'disembed' (Giddens 1991) or 'disencumber' (MacIntyre 1985) individuals, give them the benefit of an absolute beginning, set them free to choose the kind of life they wish to live, and to monitor and manage its living in the framework of legal rules spelled out by the sole legitimate legislating powers, those of the State. The modern project promised to free the individual from inherited identity. Yet it did not take a stand against identity as such, against having identity, against having a solid, resilient and immutable identity. It only transformed the identity from a matter of ascription into achievement, thus making it an individual task and the individual's responsibility.

Much like that global order which collectively underwrote individual life-efforts, the orderly (comprehensive, cohesive, consistent and continuous) identity of the individual was cast as a *project*, the *life-project* (as Jean-Paul Sartre, with an already retrospective wisdom, articulated it). Identity was to be erected systematically, floor by floor and brick by brick, following a blueprint completed before the work started. The construction called for a clear vision of the final shape, careful calculation of the steps leading towards it, long-term planning and seeing through the consequences of every move. Thus, there was a tight and irrevocable bond between social order as a project and individual life as a project; the latter was unthinkable without the former. Were it not for the collective efforts to secure a reliable – lasting, stable and predictable – setting for individual actions and choices, constructing a lasting and stable identity and living one's life towards such an identity would be all but impossible.

Settings appear reliable (1) if their life expectancy is by and large commensurate with the duration of the individual identity-building process; and (2) if their shape seems immune to the vagaries of fads and foibles promoted singly or severally (in sociological jargon: if the 'macro-level' is relatively independent of what goes on at the 'micro-level'), so that individual projects can be sensibly inscribed in a trustworthy, unyielding external frame. This was the case, by and large, throughout most of modern history, the notorious modern acceleration of change notwithstanding. 'Structures' (from physical neighbourhoods to currencies) appeared to be endowed with enough resilience and solidity to withstand all inroads of individual endeavours and survive all individual choice, so that the individual could measure himself up against the tough and finite set of opportunities, convinced that his choices can be, in principle, rationally calculated and objectively evaluated. Compared to the biologically limited span of individual life, the institutions embodying collective life (and the nation-state above all) appeared truly immortal. Professions, occupations and related skills did not age more quickly than their practioners. Neither did the principles of success: delaying gratifications paid off in the long run, and the savings book epitomised the rationality of long-term planning. In a modern society which engaged its members primarily in the role of producers/soldiers (Bauman 1995), adjustment and adaptation pointed one way only: it was the fickle individual choice which needed to take stock as well as notice of the 'functional prerequisites' of the whole, in more than one sense – to use Durkheim's apt phrase – 'greater than itself'.

If these are indeed the conditions of the reliability of settings, or of the appearance of the settings as reliable, the context of postmodern life does not pass the tests. Individual life-projects find no stable ground on which to cast anchor, and individual identity-building efforts cannot rectify the consequences of 'disembedding' and arrest the floating and drifting self. Some authors (notably Giddens) point to the widely fashionable efforts of 're-embedding'; however, being postulated rather than pre-given, and sustained solely by notoriously erratic supplies of emotional energy, the sites of the sought 're-embedment' are plagued with the same unsteadiness and eccentricity that prompt the disembedded selves to seek them in the first place. The image of the world generated by life concerns is now devoid of the genuine or assumed solidity and continuity which used to be the trademark of modern 'structures'. The dominant sentiment is the feeling of uncertainty – about the future shape of the world, about the right way of living in it, and about the criteria by which to judge the rights and wrongs of one's way of living. Uncertainty is not exactly a newcomer in the modern world, with its past. What is new, however, is that it is no longer seen as a mere temporary nuisance which, with due effort, may be either mitigated or completely overcome. The postmodern world is bracing itself for life under a condition of uncertainty which is permanent and irreducible.

DIMENSIONS OF THE PRESENT UNCERTAINTY

Many a feature of contemporary life contributes to the overwhelming feeling of uncertainty: to the view of the future as essentially un-decidable, un-controllable and hence frightening, and to the gnawing

doubt whether the present contextual constants of action will remain
constant long enough to enable reasonable calculation of its effects....
We live today – to borrow the felicitous expression coined by Marcus
Doel and David Clarke (forthcoming) – in an atmosphere of *ambient fear*.
Let us name just a few of the factors that are responsible for this.

1. The new world disorder. After half a century of clear-cut divisions,
obvious stakes and evident political purposes and strategies, came a world
devoid of visible structure and any – however sinister – logic. The power-
bloc politics which dominated the world frightened us with the awesome-
ness of its evident possibilities; whatever has replaced it frightens us with
its lack of consistency and direction – and so it is threatening in the
boundlessness of its possibilities. Hans-Magnus Enzensberger in Germany
fears the impending era of the civil war (he has counted about forty
such wars being waged today, from Bosnia through Afghanistan to
Bougainville). In France, Alain Minc writes of the coming New Dark
Ages. In Britain, Norman Stone asks if we are not back in the medieval
world of beggars, plagues, conflagrations and superstitions. Whether this
is or is not the tendency of our time remains, of course, an open question
which only the future will answer, but what really matters now is that
auguries like these can be publicly pronounced from the most prestigious
sites of contemporary intellectual life, listened to, pondered and debated.

The 'Second World' is no more; its former member countries woke
up – to use Claus Offe's felicitous phrase – to the 'tunnel at the end of
the light'. But with the demise of the Second World, the 'Third World',
too – once, in the Bandung era, constituting itself in opposition to power
blocs as the third force, and proving to be such a force through playing
up the fears and inanities of the two power-greedy world empires – has
quit the world political stage. Today, twenty or so wealthy but bothered
and unselfassured countries confront the rest of the world, which is no
longer inclined to respect their definitions of progress and happiness, yet
by the day grows ever more dependent on them for preserving whatever
happiness, or mere survival, it can scrape together by its own efforts.
Perhaps the concept of the 'secondary barbarisation' best sums up the
overall impact of the modern metropolis on the world periphery.

2. Universal deregulation, the unquestionable and unqualified priority
awarded to the irrationality and moral blindness of market competition,
the unbounded freedom granted to capital and finance at the expense of
all other freedoms, a tearing up of the socially woven and societally
maintained safety nets, and a disavowal of all but economic reason, gave
a new impetus to the relentless process of polarisation, one halted (only
temporarily, as we know now) by the legal frameworks of the welfare

state, trade-union bargaining rights, labour legislation, and – on a global scale, though in this case much less convincingly – by the initial effects of world agencies charged with the redistribution of capital. Inequality – intercontinental, interstate and inter-societal (regardless of the level of GNP boasted or bewailed by the country) – once more reaches proportions which the world, once confident of its ability to self-regulate and self-correct, seemed to have left behind once and for all. By cautious and, if anything, conservative calculations, rich Europe counts among its citizens about three million homeless, twenty million unable to find employment, and thirty million living below the poverty line. The switch from the project of community as the guardian of the universal right to a decent and dignified life to the promotion of the market as the sufficient guarantor of the universal chance of self-improvement adds further to the suffering of the new poor, glossing poverty with humiliation and with denial of consumer freedom, now identified with humanity.

The psychological effects, however, reach far beyond the swelling ranks of the dispossessed and the redundant. Only the few powerful enough to blackmail other powerful people into the obligation of a golden handshake can be sure that their home, however prosperous and imposing it may seem today, is not haunted by the spectre of tomorrow's downfall. No jobs are guaranteed, no positions are foolproof, no skills are of lasting utility. Experience and know-how turn into liabilities as soon as they become assets; seductive careers all too often prove to be suicide tracks. In their present form, human rights do not entail the acquisition of the right to a job, however well performed, or – more generally – the right to care and consideration for the sake of past merits. Livelihood, social position, acknowledgement of usefulness and the entitlement to self-dignity may all vanish together, overnight and without notice.

3. The other safety nets, self-woven and self-maintained, those second lines of trenches once offered by the neighbourhood or the family, where one could withdraw to heal the bruises acquired in the marketplace, if they have not fallen apart, have at least been considerably weakened. The changing pragmatics of interpersonal relations (the new style of 'life politics', as described with great conviction by Anthony Giddens), now permeated by the ruling spirit of consumerism, and thus casting the other as the potential source of pleasurable experience, is partly to blame: whatever else it is good at, it cannot generate lasting bonds, and most certainly not the bonds which are presumed to be lasting and treated as such. The bonds which it does generate in profusion have in-built until-further-notice and withdrawal-at-will clauses, and promise neither the granting nor the acquisition of rights and obligations. The slow yet relent-

less dissipation and induced forgetting of social skills bears another part of the blame. What used to be put together and kept together by personal skills and the use of indigenous resources tends now to be mediated by technologically produced tools purchasable on the market. In the absence of such tools, partnerships and groups disintegrate – if, that is, they emerge in the first place. Not only the satisfaction of individual needs but the presence and resilience of collectivities become to an ever greater extent market-dependent, and so duly reflect the capriciousness and erraticism of the marketplace.

4. As David Bennett observes, 'radical uncertainty about the material and social worlds we inhabit and our modes of political agency within them ... is what the image-industry offers us' (1994: 30). Indeed, the message conveyed today with great power of persuasion by the most ubiquitously effective cultural media (and, let us add, easily read by the recipients against the background of their own experience, aided and abetted by the logic of consumer freedom) is a message of the essential interdeterminacy and softness of the world: in this world, everything may happen and everything can be done, but nothing can be done once and for all – and whatever happens comes unannounced and goes without notice. In this world, bonds are dissembled into successive encounters, identities into successively worn masks, life history into a series of episodes whose sole lasting importance is their equally ephemeral memory. Nothing can be known for sure, and anything which is known can be known in a different way – one way of knowing being as good or as bad (and certainly as volatile and precarious) as any other. Gambling is now the rule where certainty was once sought, while taking risks replaces the stubborn pursuit of goals. Thus there is little in the world which one could consider solid and reliable, nothing reminiscent of a tough canvas on which one could weave one's own life itinerary.

Like everything else, the self-image splits into a collection of snapshots, each having to conjure up, carry and express its own meaning, more often than not without reference to other snapshots. Instead of constructing one's identity, gradually and patiently, as one builds a house, through the slow accretion of floors, rooms and connecting passages, a series of 'new beginnings', experimenting with instantly assembled yet easily dismantled shapes, is painted one over the other: a *palimpsest identity*. This is the kind of identity that fits the world in which the art of forgetting is an asset no less – if no more – important than the art of memorising; in which forgetting, rather than learning, is the condition of continuous fitness; in which ever new things and people enter and exit, without much rhyme or reason, the field of vision of the stationary camera of attention, and where memory itself is like videotape, always ready to be wiped clean in order to admit new images, and boasting a lifelong guarantee thanks only to that wondrous capacity of endless self-effacement.

These are some – certainly not all – of the dimensions of postmodern uncertainty. Living under conditions of overwhelming and self-perpetuating uncertainty is an experience altogether different from a life subordinated to the task of identity-building and lived in a world bent on the construction of order. The oppositions which, in that other experience, underlaid and endorsed the meaning of the world and of the life lived in it, lose in the new experience much of their meaning and most of their heuristic and pragmatic potency. Baudrillard has written profusely about this implosion of sense-giving oppositions. Yet alongside the collapse of the opposition between reality and its simulation, truth and its representation, comes the blurring and watering down of the difference between the normal and the abnormal, the expectable and the unexpected, the ordinary and the bizarre, domesticated and wild – the familiar and the strange, 'us' and the strangers. Strangers are no longer authoritatively preselected, defined and set apart, as they used to be in times of the state-managed, consistent and durable programmes of order-building. They are now as unsteady and protean as one's own identity; as poorly founded, as erratic and volatile. *L'ipséité*, that difference which sets the self apart from the non-self and 'us' from 'them', is no longer determined by the preordained shape of the world, nor by command from on high. It needs to be constructed, and reconstructed, and constructed once more, and reconstructed again, on both sides at the same time, neither side boasting more durability, or just 'givenness', than the other. Today's strangers are by-products, but also the means of production, in the incessant – because never conclusive – process of identity-building.

THE TWISTING ROAD TO SHARED HUMANITY

The essential difference between the socially produced modality of modern and postmodern strangers, for the reasons listed above, is that while modern strangers were earmarked for annihilation, and served as borderlines for the advancing boundary of the order-under-construction, the postmodern ones are – by joyful or grudging, but common, consent – here to stay. To paraphrase Voltaire's comment on God: if they did not exist, they would have to be invented.... And they are, indeed, invented, zealously and with gusto – patched together out of salient or minute and unobtrusive distinction marks. They are useful precisely in their capacity as strangers; their strangerhood is to be protected and lovingly preserved. They are indispensable signposts in a life-itinerary without plan and direction. They must be as many and as protean as the successive and parallel incarnations of identity in never-ending search for itself.

In an important respect, and for important reasons, ours is a *heterophilic* age. For sensation-gatherers or experience-collectors that we are, concerned (or, more exactly, forced to be concerned) with flexibility and openness rather than fixity and self-closure, difference comes at a premium. There is a resonance and a harmony between the way we experience our identity problems and the plurality and differentiation of the world in which these identity problems are dealt with, or which we conjure up in the process of that dealing. It is not just that we need strangers around because, owing to the way we are culturally shaped, we would miss precious life-enhancing values in a uniform, monotonous and homogeneous world; more than that – such a world without differences could not, by any stretch of the imagination, evolve out of the way in which our lives are shaped and carried on. The age of anthropophagic and anthropoemic strategies is over. The question is no longer how to get rid of the strangers and the strange, but how to live with them – daily and permanently. Whatever realistic strategy of coping with the unknown, the uncertain and the confusing can be thought of, it must start from recognising this fact.

And, indeed, all strategies still in competition today seem to accept this. One may say that a new consensus is emerging. If the Left and the Right, the progressivists and the reactionaries of the modern period, agreed that strangerhood is abnormal and regrettable, and that the superior – because it was homogeneous – order of the future would have no room for strangers, postmodern times are marked by an almost universal agreement that difference is good, precious, and in need of protection and cultivation. In the words of that towering figure of the postmodern intellectual Right, Alain de Benoist: 'We see reasons for hope only in the affirmation of collective singularities, the spiritual reappropriation of heritages, the clear awareness of roots and specific cultures' (1977: 19). The spiritual guide of the Italian new fascist movement, Julius Evola, is even more blunt: 'The racists recognise difference and want difference' (1985: 29). Pierre-André Taguieff (1988) sums up the postmodern rearticulation of the racist discourse in his coining of the term 'differentialist racism'.

Note that these self-admittedly right-wing, even fascist, professions of faith no longer propose, unlike their precursors, that differences between people are immune to cultural interference, and that it is beyond human power to make someone into someone else. Yes, they say, differences – our differences, the stranger's differences – are all human products, culturally produced. But, they add, different cultures produce their members in different shapes and colours – and *this is good*. Thou shalt not join together what culture, in its wisdom, set apart. Let us, rather, help culture – any culture – to go its own separate, and better, inimitable way. The world will be so much richer then.... The striking thing, of course, is that a reader, unaware that the author of the first quotation was Benoist, could be forgiven for mistaking it for a Left programmatic statement; and that Evola's sentence would lose none of its conviction were the word 'racist' replaced by 'progressive', 'liberal', or – for that matter – socialist.... Are we not all *bona fide* differentialists today? Multiculturalists? Pluralists?

So it happens that both Right and Left agree today that the preferable mode of living with strangers is to keep apart. Though perhaps for different reasons, both resent and publicly denigrate the universalist/ imperialist/assimilationist ambitions of the modern State, now debunked as innately proto-totalitarian. Disenchanted or repelled by the idea of legislated uniformity, the Left – which, being Left, cannot live without hope – turns its eyes towards 'community', now hailed and eulogised as the long-lost, now rediscovered true home of humanity. To be a born-again communitarian is widely considered today as the sign of a critical standpoint, leftism and progress. Come back community, from the exile to which the modern State confined you; all is forgiven and forgotten – the oppressiveness of parochiality, the genocidal propensity of collective narcissism, the tyranny of communal pressures and the pugnacity and despotism of communal discipline. It is, of course, a nuisance that one finds in this bed some unwelcome and thoroughly repulsive fellows. How to keep the bed to oneself, how to prove that the unwelcome fellows have no right to be in it – this seems to be the problem.

I propose that the racist fellows in the bed of communitarianism are perhaps a nuisance for its new occupants, but by no means a surprise. They were there first, and it is their birthright to be there. Both occupants, the old ones and the new, have been lured into that bed by the same promise and the same desire – of 're-embedding' what has been 'disembedded', of release from the formidable task of individual self-construction, and from even more awesome and burdensome individual responsibility for its results.

The old racism turned its back on the emancipatory chance entailed in the modern project. I propose that, true to its nature, it now turns its back on the emancipatory chance which the postmodern context of life holds. Only now, out of curious amnesia or myopia, it is not alone in doing so. It sings in chorus with the lyrical voices of a growing number of social scientists and moral philosophers who extol the warmth of communal homes and bewail the trials and tribulations of the un-encumbered, homeless self.

This is a type of critique of the emancipatory failure of modernity which holds no hope for emancipation: a misdirected and, I would say, retrograde critique of the modern project, as it proposes only to shift the site of disablement and subordination from the universalist State to the particularist tribe. It only replaces one 'essentialism', already discredited, by another, not yet fully unmasked in all its disempowering potential. True, communal self-determination may assist the initial stages of the long process of re-empowerment of human subjects – give the first push towards a fully fledged citizenship. But there is a dangerous and easily overlooked point where re-empowerment turns into a new disempowerment, and emancipation into a new oppression. Once on this road, it is difficult to sense where to stop; and, as a rule, it is too late to stop once that point has been recognised after the event.

But there is another, true emancipatory chance in postmodernity: the chance of laying down arms, suspending border skirmishes waged to keep the stranger away, taking apart the mini-Berlin Walls erected daily to keep distance and to separate. This chance does not lie in the celebration of born-again ethnicity and in genuine or invented tribal tradition, but in bringing to its conclusion the 'disembedding' work of modernity: through revealing conditions of individual freedom which transcend both national and ethnic/tribal limitations; through focusing on the right to choose as the sole human universality, on the ultimate, inalienable individual responsibility for that choice, and on the complex State- or tribe-managed mechanisms aimed at depriving the individual of that freedom of choice and that responsibility. The chance of human togetherness depends on the rights of the stranger, not on the question of who – the State or the tribe – is entitled to decide who the strangers are.

REFERENCES

Balandier, Georges (1994) *Le Dedale*. Paris.
Bauman, Zygmunt (1995) *Life in Fragments: Essays in Postmodern Morality*. Oxford: Blackwell.
Beck, Ulrich (1992) *Risk Society: Towards a New Modernity*, trans. Mark Ritter, London: Sage.
Bennett, David (1994) 'Hollywood's Indeterminacy Machine'. *Arena* 3/94.
de Benoist, Alain (1977) *Dix ans de combat culturel pour une Renaissance*. Paris: GRECE.
Doel, Marcus and David B. Clarke (forthcoming), 'Transpolitical Urbanism: Suburban Anomalies and Ambient Fear', in C. Hamilton and G. Crysler (eds) *Street Wars: Space, Power and the City*. Manchester: Manchester University Press.
Evola, Julius (1985) *Eléments pour éducation raciale*. Paris: Puiseaux.
Giddens, Anthony (1991) *Modernity and Self-Identity: Self and Society in the Late Modern Age*. Cambridge: Polity Press.
MacIntyre, Alasdair (1985) *After Virtue: A Study in Moral Theory*. London: Duckworth.
Taguieff, Pierre-André (1988) *La Force du préjugé: Essai sur le racisme et ses doubles*. Paris: La Découverte.

IDENTITY AND DIFFERENCE IN A GLOBALIZED WORLD

Alberto Melucci

SUBJECTS OF ACTION IN A PLANETARY SOCIETY

In this chapter I address the ways in which individual and collective identity is constructed in a complex, planetary society where both individuals and groups are given increasing chances and resources for an autonomous definition of themselves, and are simultaneously exposed to stronger pressures to conform to systemic regulations, to incorporate into their behavioural patterns the deep cognitive and motivational structures that anonymous apparatuses impose on them through the hidden encoding of the informational flow.

Highly differentiated systems allocate increasing amounts of resources to individuals, who use them to become autonomous subjects of action; but such systems also exact increasing integration. In order to maintain themselves, they must extend their control by regulating the deep-seated sources of action and by interfering with the construction of its meaning. Contemporary conflicts reveal the contradictions in this process, and bring to the fore actors and forms of action which cannot be fitted into the conventional categories of modern industrial conflict, competition among interest groups or political struggles. The production and reappropriation of meaning seem to lie at the core of contemporary conflicts; this entails a careful redefinition of what collective action is about, and what forms of action display the presence of social conflicts.

Today, information is a crucial resource, and contemporary systems depend upon it increasingly for their survival and development. In the course of the last thirty years, the capacity to gather, process and transmit information has grown to a level unprecedented in human history. This phenomenon increases the artificiality of social life as a collective construct. Everyday experiences unfold in an environment wholly produced by society; and nature itself, even where it is preserved in its 'natural' state, depends on cultural choices, political decisions and economic policies which ensure its protection. The media represent and reflect human action, but they gradually acquire an independent ability to produce reality because their messages are incorporated and reproduced in social praxis, in a spiral which seems destined to feed upon itself and grow in a never-ending process. Events are located in a planetary space, and seem to free themselves from the place in which they occur and from the population directly involved: their symbolic impact on the world system shifts space–time co-ordinates.

Information societies develop a cultural production which is no longer governed by the imperatives of survival or reproduction. In this respect they are truly 'post-material' societies, and they produce a 'cultural surplus' which increases the range of available options far beyond the current capacity for action of individuals and groups. But control over the production, accumulation and circulation of information is ensured by codes which organise information and render it comprehensible. Power transforms itself and comes to coincide with operational languages, with the formal rules that organise and construe the flow of messages. Under the operational logic which governs the great contemporary organisations, information is not a shared and universally available resource; it is an empty sign system whose keys are accessible only to a small number of people, a system which operates at the level of the planet. Access to knowledge beyond information, the ability to decipher signs in order to grasp their meaning – these are at stake in the confrontation among new forms of power and the emerging social actors who engage themselves in new conflicts.

In systems of high information density, individuals and groups must possess a certain degree of autonomy and formal capacities for learning and acting which enable them to function as reliable, self-regulating units capable of producing, receiving and exchanging information. Simultaneously, highly differentiated systems shift their control from the content of social action to its languages, from the external regulation of behaviour to interference in the cognitive and motivational preconditions for it. Conflicts tend to arise in those areas of the system most directly involved in the production of information and communicative resources, but at the same time subjected to intense pressures for integration. The crucial dimensions of daily life (time and space, interpersonal relations, birth and death), the satisfying of individual needs in the marketplace and within welfare systems, the shaping of personal and social identity in education, leisure, physical and psychological well-being – these are constructed today through the production and processing of information. Dimensions that were traditionally regarded as 'private' (the body, sexuality, affective relations) or 'subjective' (cognitive and emotional processes, motives, desires) or even 'biological' (the structure of the brain, the genetic code, reproductive capacity) now undergo social control and manipulation. Over these domains the technico-scientific apparatus, the agencies of information and communication, the decision-making centres which determine 'policies', wield their power. But these are precisely the areas where individuals and groups lay claim to their autonomy, where they conduct their search for identity by transforming them into a space where they reappropriate, self-realise, and themselves construct the meaning of what they are and what they do.

Conflicts are therefore carried forward by temporary actors who bring to light the crucial dilemmas of current society. The conflicts I describe here (which do not exhaust the range of social conflicts) concern the production and appropriation of resources which are crucial for a global society based on information. These same processes generate both new forms of power and new forms of opposition: conflict emerges only in so far as actors fight for control and the allocation of socially produced potential for action.

The forms of power now emerging in contemporary societies are grounded in an ability to 'inform' (which literally means to 'give form'). The collective action of contemporary movements occupies the same terrain and is in itself a message broadcast to society, conveying symbolic forms and relational patterns that cast light on 'the dark side of the moon' – a system of meanings that runs counter to the meaning that the apparatuses seek to impose on individual and collective events. Instrumental rationality appears to apply solely to procedures, and to impose the criterion of efficiency and effectiveness as the only measure of meaning. The collective action of contemporary movements reveals that the neutral rationality of means masks interests and forms of power; that it is impossible to confront the massive challenge of living together on a planet – now become a global society – without openly discussing the 'ends' and 'values' that make such cohabitation possible. Such movements highlight the insuperable dilemmas facing complex societies and, by doing so, force them openly to assume responsibility for their choices, their conflicts and their limitations.

BECOMING INDIVIDUALS

The scenario of complexity, of a system which by now irreversibly incorporates the entire planet and faces a future threatened by catastrophe, has deeply eroded the optimism of the myths of salvation. Nevertheless, we still hold on to the most exalting and dramatic legacy of modernity: our need and duty to exist as individuals. Modern individuals think of themselves as subjects of action capable of purposive and meaningful behaviour, but they also function as the co-ordinates in a network of communality and communication.

In information societies, individual consciousness becomes ever more reflexive. What matters now is not merely learning, but learning how to learn: how to control our cognitive and motivational processes and to adapt them to new problems. Technological power is accompanied by the exponential growth of symbolic possibilities, of self-reflexive activities, of the capacity to reflect and represent reality through a multitude of languages. This capacity seems to be gradually replacing reality itself, so that we inhabit a world constructed out of the images we ourselves have created, a world where we are no longer able to distinguish reality from the reality of the image.

Individuals find themselves enmeshed in multiple bonds of belonging created by the proliferation of social positions, associative networks and reference groups. We enter and leave this system much more often and much more rapidly than we used to in the past. We are migrant animals in the labyrinths of the world metropolises; in reality or in the imagination, we participate in an infinity of worlds. And each of these worlds has a culture, a language and a set of roles and rules that we must adapt to whenever we migrate from one to another. Thus we are subjected to mounting pressure to change, to transfer, to translate what we were just a moment ago into new codes and new forms of relation.

We transform ourselves into sensitive terminals, transmitting and receiving a quantity of information which far exceeds that of any previous culture. Our means of communication, our work environment, our interpersonal relationships, even our leisure, generate information addressed to individuals who must receive, analyse and store it in memory, and almost always respond with further information.

The rhythm of change accelerates at an extraordinary pace. The multiplication of our social memberships, the constant surge of possibilities and messages, floods the field of our experience. The traditional co-ordinates of personal identity (family, church, party, race, class) weaken. It becomes difficult to state with certainty who we are: the question 'Who am I?' constantly presses for an answer. Our presence urgently needs a firm foundation; we search for permanent anchors, and question our own life stories. Are we still who we were? Can we still stay the same as we respond to what will be asked of us even tomorrow? We scan our pasts and our futures through different lenses as we shift among the regions of experience. In the age of speed, we no longer have a home. We constantly have to build one, like the three little pigs in the fairy tale, or we have to carry it on our backs like snails.

Everyday time is multiple and discontinuous because it entails the passage from one universe of experience to another: from one membership network to another, from the language and codes of one social sphere to those of another semantically and affectively very different from it. Time loses its uniformity, and follows a variable rhythm imposed by the flow and quality of the information we receive and transmit. Our perception expands and shrinks, slows and accelerates; we can no longer rely on the certainty of the end-directedness of time, the notion modernity fed with its myths of progress and revolution. We, the bewildered witnesses to the demise of the great stories of salvation, are haunted by our destiny of choice. To cope with the possible which seduces and threatens us, we are compelled to take the risk of decision-making (of which catastrophe is the extreme image and metaphor).

Choosing seems now to be our inexorable fate. If the fields of our experience differentiate themselves, we cannot transfer the same patterns of action from one to another. Whenever we move from one setting or system of relations to another, we know that experience gained elsewhere cannot be transposed to it, and that we must learn to cope with the new system's languages and rules. Variability, as another feature of complex systems, has a frequency and an intensity unparalleled in any other society of the past. We thus find it increasingly difficult to transfer the same pattern of action from one time to another, and we are unable to rely on our previously acquired abilities to solve new problems. Lastly, complexity provides opportunities that far exceed the effective capacity for action of individuals or groups. We are constantly aware that our field of action is much wider than the actual capacities we possess.

In terms of everyday experience, the result of these processes is that uncertainty has become a stable component in our behaviour. We cannot move from one context to another and use what we have acquired elsewhere; we cannot pass from one time to another and transfer what we already are or know; we cannot act without choosing among the possible options, without therefore having some of them dissolve into the unreal and bringing others to reality. Many of our routine tasks become exercises in problem-solving which compel us to acquire information, read the instructions and, in the end, make a choice.

The imperative that immediately arises from uncertainty, therefore, is the necessity to choose. We thus find ourselves caught up by the paradox where choice becomes destiny because it is impossible not to choose among the options available. The extension of our life-chances – that is, of the range of individual autonomy expressed as choice-making that has always been associated with the idea of will and freedom – also entails the unavoidable obligation to choose. Even non-choice constitutes a choice because it means rejecting an opportunity, which is also a choice.

This situation aggravates the ambivalence intrinsic to every experience of change. Change is a goal that we find desirable and towards which our search for the new and the different is directed. But change also threatens our security, and our established and habitual rules. Thus, when we are facing change, we are always torn between desire and fear, between anticipation and uncertainty. This highly risky and unpredictable game has no guaranteed successful outcome; we may succeed, we may fail, but we are always exposed to the danger of losing ourselves.

The paradox of choice therefore creates a new kind of psychological pressure, and confronts us with new problems. Choosing among so many possibilities is a difficult undertaking, and what we discard is always more than what we choose. There is an inescapable sense of loss which generates the main forms of contemporary psychological suffering. Depression comes from the pure experience of loss without a distinct object, and so does a different but complementary reaction, the attempt to take up all the options: here the self fragments as it seeks to deny the partial nature of every choice by separating out its inner reality or multiplying his/her efforts into an endless spiral which eventually exhausts the person.

THE MULTIPLE SELF AND RESPONSIBILITY

Even when our anxiety falls short of the extreme stage of psychic malaise, our self undergoes a profound process of transformation which splits it into multiple units. Descriptions of the multiplicity of the self usually stress its variations over time and the discontinuities among the identifications forced upon us by rapid change. Equally important – perhaps even more so – is the multiplicity that derives from uncertainty and the paradox of choice. Our self simultaneously comprises a number of components, and the deepest-seated aspect of uncertainty is structured precisely by our difficulty in identifying with only one of them, and by the requirement that we should do so in order to act. Hence, not only is it difficult to identify ourselves over time and to state that we still are who we used to be; also – and perhaps even more so – it is hard to decide at any particular moment which self among many is ours.

It is not surprising, therefore, that identity should become a problem. First, the multiple experience of the self obliges us to abandon any static view of identity, and examine the dynamic processes of identification. The concept of identity is a substantialist notion which refers to a permanent essence as the foundation of identification. Instead of conceiving of a subject as endowed with an essential nucleus defined metaphysically, we must direct our attention to the processes by which individuals construct their identities. Identity as a multiple self becomes *indentitisation*.

Secondly, the multiplication of the self forces us to recognise the place of individual action in social life. In contemporary systems the construction of the meaning of action shifts to the individual, who thus becomes a social actor in the true sense of the word. In the societies of the past, the meaning of individual behaviour was always sought on some plane of reality lying above or below the individual – nature, the kinship system, the state, class, or Society itself with a capital 'S' as a metaphysical entity. Today, individuals have greater resources with which to develop their own individuality, and social action involves us as individuals because we are able to produce autonomously and to recognise the meaning of what we are doing. From the metaphysical notion of the individual subject, we therefore shift our attention to the processes that change individuals into individuals, the processes which enable each of us to become an autonomous subject of action. The individuality of a multiple self becomes *individuation*.

The new inequalities and imbalances within national societies and on the world scale refer to the unequal distribution of these resources among individuals and groups.

Thus characterised, the identity of a self becomes more of a field than an essence: not a metaphysical reality but a dynamic system defined by recognisable opportunities and constraints. Identity is both a system and a process, because the field is defined by a set of relations, and is simultaneously able to intervene to act upon itself and to restructure itself. Two crucial and perplexing problems arise here: the continuity of the self, and the boundaries of the self. Synchronically, the problem is one of deciding where the subject of action begins and where it ends; diachronically, we must establish how this subject persists through time. If we continue to think in terms of states and essences, the rushing flow of differentiation processes, the variability and the excess of opportunities that characterise a global society render these two problems insoluble.

One frequent way out of the impasse is to dissolve the self and eliminate the social actor. Thus identity becomes merely a presentation of self, a game of masks, a play acted out on the public stage which disguises a void. Or we must once again attach ourselves to a stable nucleus in a desperate attempt to reconstitute an essence – for example, by re-viving primary bonds of belonging, like kinship or local and geographical ties. This reawakening of primary identities, this need to anchor oneself to something essential which is permanent and has visible confines, lies at the basis of many contemporary collective phenomena. Ethnic or geo-graphical identification, the attachment to traditional culture, express the attempt to resist the dissolution of identity as an essence and the diffi-culty of accepting it in the form of a relation.

It is in order to counteract this dissolution that we must begin to conceive of identity as a field comprising both freedoms and constraints. Only then can the problem of its boundaries and its permanence be recast. The boundaries of identity can be conceived of as the recognition of constraints and the interplay between their aperture and closure. The problem of its continuity can be dealt with by changing its form so that it becomes no longer a passage among various metaphysical states but the process-bound organisation of various systems of relations.

This perspective leads directly to the topic of responsibility. If identity is a process of identitisation, and if the individual coincides with his or her action of self-identification, the problem becomes that of defining who chooses how the field is to be organised: synchronically (who am I at this moment?) and in time (who am I today compared with yesterday or tomorrow, compared with memory or projection?). The topic of responsibility becomes a crucial one, and the term 'responsibility' itself should be taken in its most literal and profound sense: as capacity to respond.

If identity is no longer an essential nucleus or a metaphysical con-tinuity, definition of its borders and maintenance of its continuity are entrusted to our capacity to respond – that is, to our ability to recognise and choose among the opportunities and constraints present in the field of relations that constitute us at any given moment. The very definition of the capacity to respond has a dual meaning: there is responding for (answering for) and responding to, recognising what we are and locating ourselves in our relations.

My responsibility towards that field of opportunities and constraints which constitutes 'I myself' is on the one hand a capacity to respond for, by assuming limitation, memory, biological structure and personal history; on the other, it is the capacity to respond to, by choosing among opportunities and grasping them, by positioning myself in my relations with others and by taking my place in the world.

Metamorphosis is the response to a world which compels us to multiply our faces, languages and relations. It is a warm response, not lacking in fear and anxiety but likewise never lacking in love. Without compassion for oneself and for others, without hope and humility, it is impossible to change form. One can only change masks, relying (but for how long?) on the vacuous game of self-representation.

Standing at the point where numerous circuits of information intersect, at the junction of complex relational networks, individuals are in danger of being overwhelmed by noise, of being lacerated by too many exchanges and too many desires. They can preserve their unity only by learning to open up and close down, to move into and withdraw from the flow of messages and possibilities.

It therefore becomes vital for each of us to find a rhythm which governs our entry to and exit from the relations that enable us to give and receive information, without losing the sense of communication and without neutralising the social bond which makes it meaningful.

SOCIAL MOVEMENTS AS MESSAGES IN A GLOBALIZED WORLD

But far from prefiguring a society that is characterised by Eros, creativity and expression, or by the cold harmony of a totalitarian community, the view I am proposing here is one in which the ambivalent, non-reducible quality of human action is accentuated, on both an individual and a collective scale. It sets us down squarely in the middle of the paradox of human sociability: the fact that the individual cannot be seen only in terms of relationships, the singular reduced to the plural, uniqueness to communication; at the same time, it reveals our radical need to coexist. It implies constant tensions, polarities and shadows, not light only.

When relations between humans are entrusted almost entirely to choice, the foundation of solidarity becomes fragile and the social contract leans towards the precarious. The social fabric threatens to unravel, and a catastrophic individualism could take its place.

But the very acceptance of the fact that not everything in our relations can be calculated, nor exchange necessarily be all-satisfying – the indomitable uniqueness which characterises the experience of every individual – this acceptance can become the foundation for a new autonomy, one that is able to strengthen solidarity with a lucid passion. This awareness of fragility can be the beginning of a change in the ethical choices which are the basis of coexistence.

We need new ethics which do not exempt us from the risk of choice, and will enable us to meta-communicate about the goals and criteria behind the choices themselves; a situational ethic, capable of lending dignity to the individual decision and repairing the links between genders, cultures, the individual and the species, living beings, the cosmos.

The discovery that our salvation is no longer guaranteed by historical destiny is the rocky coastline upon which the ship of Western rationalism has been wrecked, together with its claims to absolute truth and its will to supremacy. What floats to the surface is a hope for meaningful human existence, reasonable in coexistence and in the experience of our limits.

If values no longer bear the seal of the absolute, their only foundation lies in man's capacity for agreement. *Homo sapiens*, the erect species with the gift of thought, is faced with the task of recognising his position 'between heaven and earth', as the ancient wisdom of the East would put it: accepting his roots in the earth under his feet and reaffirming his heavenly aspirations, symbolised by his head's skyward orientation.

Between these two poles defining the boundaries of the human condition, detached from nature by their capacity for language but tied to it by their bodies, the men and women of the era of complexity will have to look to language and to the body for the basis of an ethics capable of dealing with the problems of a planet entirely shaped by the hand of man.

The body delineates the limits of nature within us and without: the great rhythms of birth and death, the permanent link to the cycles of day and night, the seasons, growth and aging. In a world built by technology, equilibrium and change depend on our choices; rhythm and respect for limits no longer exist, if they ever did, as the spontaneous result of a nature 'mother and teacher'. Instead, they are the product of individual and collective choices, of a conscious morality which assumes responsibility for nature while responding to it (responsibility implies, in fact, answering for and answering to).

It is precisely this twofold meaning of the word 'responsibility' which roots ethics in language. Culture is the space in which every moral choice is bound to take form. In the planetary society of information, to name things is to bring them into existence. What should be done with language? This is the new frontier of the ethics of complexity. How and to what end should we use the power of naming which enables us to create the world and force it to conform to the signs with which we give it (or neglect to give it) voice? It is language which meets the challenge of meaning or its reduction to signs. It is through language that, today, even nature can be named or erased.

Between the body and language – or rather, between the various languages with which we give a name to our world – we must be able to move with flexibility, open to change but respecting our limits. There is no longer a stable anchor to the criteria and values that guide our choices, other than that which we are able to create together, acknowledging their man-made character and temporal boundaries. For individuals, as for the species as a whole, this means accepting a finite existence and the possibility of change. Thus the theme of metamorphosis, of the ability to assume new forms, returns as a condition for coexistence.

Contemporary social movements, like those that have emerged over the last twenty-five years, are the first harbingers of this enormous cultural change which is already taking place. To reduce them only to their political outcomes is like believing that our shadow could exist without our person – like believing that contemporary movements could exist without personal involvement in the crucial issues of the time and without a search for new politics. The politics of the 'new' social movements are eminently personal politics, rooted in a profound need of the inhabitants of a global world to exist as autonomous individuals, capable of respect and communication.

Contemporary social movements remind us by their forms of action that we can work more on processes than on contents to face the challenges and dilemmas of a complex world. By including care for the question of meaning as an important part of present collective tasks, people who today are willing to contribute to a democratic society, more just and compassionate on the world scale, should be able to take responsibility both for the global planet and for the personal planet.

Precisely because of the role played by information, the transnational character of contemporary problems and conflicts, and the global interdependence of the planetary system in general become increasingly evident. The world system is formally constituted by a network of relationships among sovereign states. In reality, however, it has been dominated over the last fifty years by the logic of power blocs, and lacerated by the imbalances between North and South. The collapse of the Soviet empire has removed one of the central pillars of this equilibrium based on power, inequality and dependence. The changes, however, have not affected the prevailing logic of the world system, having only introduced an element of instability and uncertainty into its principally unaltered operation. Simultaneously, however, it has made the crisis of the international (in reality, interstate) system even more evident: the model of the nation-state, which enclosed multiple peoples and cultures within the boundaries of a centralised political order, is tottering, while a vast quantity of still-unresolved 'national' issues come to the fore, together with the importance of ethnic and cultural differences. The nation-states are losing their authority as, towards the top of the system, planetary interdependence and the emergence of transnational political and economic forces shift the locus of real decision-making elsewhere, while, towards the bottom, the proliferation of autonomous decision-making centres endows the 'societal' level of present-day societies with a power they never knew during the development of the modern state.

Behind the questions raised by ethnic, nationalistic and cultural conflicts, behind the legacy of unresolved tensions left as the aftermath of
the development and decline of the modern state, and even behind the
resistance by minority cultures to modernisation, which might appear
anachronistic, an entirely new perspective emerges today: the plea for
society to be given the power to decide its own existence and control its
own development, framed by new relations among the components constituting planetary reality (individuals, groups, cultures, 'nations'). A new
model of intra- and inter-society relations is one of the greatest contemporary aspirations. Humankind must make an enormous effort to give
political shape to its co-living; a political arrangement able to govern the
plurality, autonomy and richness of difference – but one, however, which
also expresses humanity's shared responsibility for the fate of the species
and the planet, and of each individual.

REFERENCES

Anderson, Benedict (1991) *Imagined Communities*. London: Verso.
Bauman, Zygmunt (1991) *Modernity and Ambivalence*. Cambridge: Polity Press.
Berman, Paul (ed.) (1992) *Debating P.C.: The Controversy Over Political Correctness
    on College Campuses*. New York: Dell.
Bruner, Jerome (1991) 'The Narrative Construction of Reality'. *Critical Inquiry* 18:
    1–21.
Crook, Stephen, Jan Pakulski and Malcolm Waters (1992) *Postmodernization: Change
    in Advanced Society*. London: Sage.
Featherstone, Mike (1992) *Consumer Culture and Postmodernism*. London: Sage.
Geertz, Clifford (1983) *Local Knowledge*. New York: Basic Books.
Gilroy, Paul (1993) *Small Acts*. London: Serpent's Tail.
Maffesoli, Michel (1995) *The Time of the Tribes*. London: Sage.
Maheu, Louis (ed.) (1995) *Social Movements and Social Classes: The Future of Collec-
    tive Action*. London: Sage.
Melucci, Alberto (1989) *Nomads of the Present. Social Movements and Individual Needs
    in Contemporary Society*. Philadelphia, PA: Temple University Press.
Melucci, Alberto (1994) 'A Strange Kind of Newness: What's "New" in New
    Social Movements?', in Enrique Larana, Hank Johnston and Joseph R. Gusfield
    (eds) *New Social Movements: From Ideology to Identity*. Philadelphia, PA: Temple
    University Press.
Melucci, Alberto (1996a) *The Playing Self: Person and Meaning in the Planetary Society*.
    Cambridge: Cambridge University Press.
Melucci, Alberto (1996b) *Challenging Codes: Collective Action in the Information Age*.
    Cambridge: Cambridge University Press.
Taylor, Charles (1989) *Sources of the Self: The Making of the Modern Identity*. Cam-
    bridge, MA: Harvard University Press.
Taylor, Charles (1992) *Multiculturalism and 'The Politics of Recognition'*. Princeton,
    NJ: Princeton University Press.
Touraine, Alain (1994) *Critique of Modernity*. Oxford: Blackwell.

5

GLOBAL CRISES, THE STRUGGLE FOR CULTURAL IDENTITY AND INTELLECTUAL PORKBARRELLING: COSMOPOLITANS VERSUS LOCALS, ETHNICS AND NATIONALS IN AN ERA OF DE-HEGEMONISATION

Jonathan Friedman

INTRODUCTION

Everyone knows that the world is changing in profound ways. We know this change via direct experience of increasing urban violence and the volatile emergence of underclasses, not only in the United States but now on a large scale in the former European welfare states. We read about ethnic violence, of demands for cultural rights, but also of global reach, internationalised markets, increasingly sensitive currency and stock markets, of fabulously wealthy stars and 'star-fuckers', of disappearing company and state funds, of globalised drug trafficking, terrorist bombings, and so on, all reported on the global news networks. We are told that the world is one place now, but not in Eastern Europe and the former Yugoslavia, the Middle East or Africa, or in our own inner cities. We are told that the world is one place, but for whom, one might ask! I have argued that these phenomena are *not* expressions of globalisation as such, of the emergence of a new global reality, a stage in social evolution ... from national to global ... 'once we were at home, but now we are everywhere'. Instead there are a number of parallel processes which, rather than being evolutionary, indicate a decline, expressed as a complex but unitary process of fragmentation. The logic of this process is expressed in the homology that links otherwise separate domains. These are as follows:

1. The fragmentation of the public sphere of knowledge production.
2. The ethnification of the nation-state via three separate processes of fragmentation:
   (a) indigenisation;
   (b) regionalisation;
   (c) ethnification of migrants and nationals.
3. A context of increasing economic polarisation and the emergence of marginalised populations in the centre of the system, the ghettoisation of the national sphere which accompanies its ethnification.

These processes are closely interrelated. The process of fragmentation is equivalent to a localisation of identification. The regional is a primary expression of the breakdown of the homogeneous nation-state as a geographic region. This is a process that is well under way in Europe, but one that has been discussed in other parts of the world that are undergoing similar breakdowns.

Indigenisation combines a strong sense of region with a sense of ethnic primordiality. The indigenous refers to the original, the aboriginal inhabitants of a nation-state that is historically and, in a sense, wrongly identified with another population, the product of a later invasion or colonisation. The ethnification of immigrants and nationals is part of the same process of concretisation of identity. The ethnification surrounding the nation runs parallel to the ethnification of the nation-state itself. The resultant continuum contains an identification with the nation-before-the-nation-state, the nation-state itself, regional subnationals, and the new immigrants. The ethnification of immigrant populations generates the formation of diasporas, the identification with a foreign homeland beyond the borders of the nation-state. The nation-state is thus besieged from within and from without by a general process of fragmentation that polarises as it dissolves the former unity.

The ethnification of the nation is, as I have suggested (Friedman 1994: 233–53), an aspect of a declining hegemonic order in the global system, in which – in lieu of a declining modernism, an identification with an upwardly mobile future for self, society and world – we find a return to roots, to fixed identifications that are immune, in principle, from social change. I have also suggested that the decline in modernism here is countered by a rise of this very same ideological movement in the expanding centres of East Asia. This, I insist, is a statistical process, a tendency and not a simple deterministic situation. The formerly ideal-type, homogeneous Sweden, is today increasingly split by demands for power from the Sami, from certain of the regions, and from immigrant groups; while in the national population there has been a rapid increase in ethnic sentiment. This process is paralleled in various ways in the other nation-states of Europe, and in the increasingly aggressive multiculturalism of the United States.

Cultural/social fragmentation is aided and abetted by grass-roots gut feelings of increasing alienation. To the extent that they appear to some to be the products of state policies of divide and rule, this too is the result of the transformation of the identities prevalent among policymakers, not a mere expression of power itself. The fact that the state is not an autonomous subject but is inhabited by individuals recruited from the wider population is often overlooked by a certain Foucauldian-inspired critique of power. That is, it is not the state as such that produces multicultural ideology, as if it inhered in the nature of power. It was the state that practised assimilation, after all, and in order to understand the establishment of state ideology it is necessary to investigate the changing ideologies of those who inhabit the corridors of power. Here, I suggest, we discover the shared experience and interpretations of social reality which, via a resonance with the larger population, enables such ideologies to function. Multiculturalism, as an abandonment of the ideal of a strong social project and assimilation to that project, is the expression of a broad shift in the 'identity space' of declining Western modernity. This forsaking of modernism, which generates a return to roots, leads to a strengthening of countervailing subnational and ethnic identities. Thus, we have a double process rather than a simple imposition from the top down, as has sometimes been assumed in a certain discourse which I shall discuss below, since it is the expression of a significant social actor in this situation.

HYBRIDISATION AND THE CULTURE OF GLOBAL ELITE FORMATION

There is a fourth process of identification that has not, as far as I know, been given serious consideration, simply because it is enunciated from a position that self-identifies as the subject of the research process, the intellectual elite – or, at least, a fraction of that elite, which I shall call cosmopolitan.

This identity is expressed in the congeries of terms: hybridisation, creolisation, trans-ethnicity, transnationality, hyphenated identities, and so on. It may be expressed in terms of several related logics. The most obvious in ethnic/immigration studies is that ethnicity, in the sense of a homogeneous essential culture attributable to a social group or segment of a population, is a product of top-down classification of the kind that went on in the colonial world. This, as I understand it, was a position adopted by Rex (1973), and became a tradition in this field. It resonates with similar kinds of approaches in Anthropology, and even History. The colonial imposition of categorical identities on 'tribes' and even regions – for example, Melanesia, Polynesia – or the establishment of 'customary' law courts, was part of an ordering of existence that became assimilated into self-identification and then even used as 'nationalist' weapons in the struggle against the colonial powers themselves. This is certainly the case in Melanesia itself, with its vast and variable array of *kastom* movements. Gluckman, Mitchell and Barnes (1949) made similar observations many years ago in South-Central Africa, and today there is an entire school of Subaltern Studies, consisting primarily of historians, who have made this a reputable field of investigation.

Now, for some of these researchers, the question of colonial administrative categories carried over to the imperial centres in the periods of mass immigration has been understood from a modernist perspective, one that stresses the falsity of the categories themselves and assumes that anything there previously – on the ground, so to speak – was assimilated to the new hierarchy. This has given way to an approach which assumes that there was, and continues to be, something else beneath the imposed categories. The most common ways of describing this previous and still extant reality include terms such as fuzzy or porous boundaries, cultural mixture, a general subaltern reality defined in opposition to the categories imposed by colonialism. I do not wish to discuss the value of these propositions, since they are indeed quite variable, but simply to note that the discourse is expressive of a certain position and self-identity. In today's world, this is related to discussions of cultural globalisation in which cultural flows are seen to meet one another and form new combinations, hybrids, which are assumed to be a real historical product of the increasing general globalisation of the world. It is a discourse that is predicated on the presumption of the existance of once pure cultures that may have existed before the age of international capital compressed the globe. It is also a normative discourse in so far as it claims that essentialism must be replaced by concepts of hybridisation and cultural creativity that realise, in the vast array of world cultures, a kind of storehouse of knowledges, foods, clothing, art forms, which are a source of our enrichment. This is a multicultural and constantly mixing world, and those who master it culturally are the cultural 'theorists' who have now begun to define this world for the rest of us.

This position is, as I said, cosmopolitan, but it is a new kind of cosmopolitanism. In the era of a dominant modernism, the cosmopolitan was himself a modernist, one who knew the larger world and understood cultural variation, but one who was primarily a rationalist and a universalist, whose identity was defined in terms of the abstract, the rights of man, not of cultures; science, not wisdom; and rationality without metaphysics. Today's cosmopolitans are cosmopolitans without modernism. They might be called postmodernist in the sense that they identify themselves as encompassing the world's variety and its subsequent mixtures. This encompassment can be carried out only from the top, of course: from a position above any particular cultural world – a rather odd position. But, then, this accounts for the dominance of Cultural Studies in the forefront of the new cosmopolitanism.

The other aspect of the emergence of this identity is that it induces its participants to look elsewhere than the street for its realities. Among those sociologists who have moved in this direction there has been a decided shift to the analysis of literature, of intellectuals, of films, and – not least – of music, where the identification of multiple roots is quite an easy matter. Paul Gilroy demonstrates this movement quite clearly and with brilliant flourish. In *The Black Atlantic* he takes on both essentialism and anti-essentialism in provocative ways, asserting on the one hand a hybrid notion of the Black Atlantic as a 'counter-culture of modernity' (1993: 1), one that expresses an authenticity located not in New York or London but in opposition to a dominant modernity, and that has moulded strands and fragments into something which is shared at the level of the 'structure of feeling' and expressed as a kind of anti-ante modern holism where the aesthetic, the political and the moral are one. His argument is about transnational Blacks, intellectuals all, and it is directed to other intellectuals. It attempts to define Black identity in a new way. The question is for whom, and how? What seems more obvious is that this is a self-identification. It is one based on a kind of ethno-genealogical method which, I shall argue, has little to do with the everyday problems of identity in the street, even as it is part of the same world.

Now, of course, this wariness of nationalism as an underlying basis for racism is present in Gilroy's earlier work, *There Ain't No Black in the Union Jack* (1987), but the same basic argument is expressed here as well:

1. Racism, like other forms of ethnicity, is a product of ethnic absolutism related to the ideology of nationalism.
2. Such ideologies are assimilated into ethnic struggle, and are therefore of the same type as those of the oppressors.
3. The opposite tendency – to invalidate the ethnic as a *mere* mixture – is also wrong as a reaction, since it refuses the commonalities of experience and structures of feeling, as well as non-modern ways of life embodied in such experiences.
4. Real culture is one that is a hybrid diaspora-like structure, but

harbours precisely the pre- and ante/anti capitalist forms that are the basis of opposition and the alternative to modern nationalism.

All this is expressed in real Black oppositional politics today, and not just in music. The form of this opposition is derived by Gilroy from Melucci and Castells, and is post-working-class, where locality, culture and political autonomy are essential replacements for class identity. Against the prevailing ethnic 'absolutism', the cultural nationalism of the European reflected in Black, Red, Polynesian and other 'pure' identities, there is a subaltern hybridity: 'Against this choice stands another, more difficult option: the theorisation of creolisation, métissage, mestisaje, and hybridity' (Gilroy 1993: 2).

The history of Blacks in Britain and in the entire Black Atlantic expresses the kinds of themes indicative of the general fragmentation process of the world system as well as the intellectual cosmopolitan reaction to that process, one that contains a highly ambivalent posture with regard to the ethnification process itself and the desire for something broader, more global, truly cosmopolitan and above it all. This is the hyphenated reality of the postmodern cosmopolitan, a reality that is defined not by the modern, the abstract, but by the plurality of knowledges, of cultures and of their continuous fusion. The metaphor for this position is expressed in the concepts of ecumene, the global village. This is the forging not of a new unity but of a collection of disparate entities under the political umbrella of a super-state, a cultural elite, a council of leaders. The model is not the macro-nation but the medieval Church, the great encompasser. Ecumenical pluralism is the complementary counterpart of fragmented ethnic identities.

In the framework I have suggested, the decentralisation of the global system in political-economic terms leads to the decline of the nation-state and to the kind of regional disorder that simultaneously generates mass migration. The combined internal and external threat to everyday shared experiences and fantasies of the nation leads to increasing racism and a general ethnification of the nation-state: both in the national population and among many immigrants (now transformed into ethnic communities), regions and indigenous groups. The intellectual elite that is positioned above this fragmentation must also define its existence and its world. Hybridisation is a politically correct solution for this group. It is anti-racist, anti-ethnic, and supplies an objective alternative identity which is the postmodernist equivalent of the 'ancient', pre-1980, modernism. The latter combated ethnicity in the name of universalism, the identity of all people and thus of their individual rights. The former does the same in the name of mixture and hybridity, a claim to a humanity so fused in its cultural characteristics that no 'ethnic absolutism' is impossible. This is what I have referred to as cosmopolitanism without modernism: 'A vision of the world in which "race" will no longer be a meaningful device for the categorisation of human beings' (Gilroy 1993: 218).

The reasoning is entirely concrete, and if there is anything universalist here, as some might argue, it is simply the sum total of the particular. But it is the same kind of moral discourse as can be found in modernist versions of the universal liberalism of the past. The positioning of the discourse, of course, has everything to do with its normative moral identity. Cosmopolitanism without modernism is not without modernity as such, but without the rationalist, abstract and developmentalist project of modernism. This position is also entirely opposed to any form of traditionalism and the search for a single set of roots. Gilroy, like others, goes to great lengths to define his hybrid culture as an instrumental part, however subaltern, of modernity; and he argues systematically against attempts to identify the Black Atlantic in terms of an African past.

The problem here is that this position and positioning, which embodies a moral vision of the world, is not self-reflective but entirely transparent and self-evident to itself as a subjectivity. The conditions under which such a hybridisation might occur as a social fact are very far from the pronouncements at hand. The tendency to rootedness, to boundary-making and to opposition to the immediate social environment dictates against such ecumenism, and these tendencies are generated and reinforced by the real fragmentation of the global system.

The same kind of problem exists with respect to the interpretation of ethnicity as game – that is, as an entirely elective practice. It is based on the same kind of positioning, but this is a form of modernism rather than postmodernism. Identity is entirely abstracted from the subject, and reduced to a mere mask or role to be taken on at will. In such a situation identity is no longer a social problem, since it is rendered superficial. In any case, the ability to be able to shift from one identity to the next is similar to hybridisation as a performative phenomenon. Both strategies are dependent upon a radical distanciation of the subject from any particular identity. The inclusive strategy might entail an attempt to define oneself as authentically subaltern, while the latter remains resolutely modernist in treating identity as a role with no roots of its own. For the cosmopolitan modernist, the interpretation of identity as elective is an argument against the depth of such identities and their transformation into mere political instruments. The postmodernist position against ethnicity is based, rather, on the supposed fact of hybridity itself. Writers such as Iain Chambers express a militant attitude against all forms of rootedness:

We are drawn beyond ideas of nation, nationalism and national cultures, into a post-colonial set of realities, and a mode of critical thinking that is forced to rewrite the very grammar and language of modern thought in directing attention beyond the patriarchal boundaries of Eurocentric concerns and its presumptive, 'universalism'. (Chambers 1994: 110)

He refers to the anathema of Yugoslavia as an example of this wrong-headed thinking, based on 'authenticity and national identity' (ibid.). The problem for Chambers is that this mode of thinking, even if it still lingers on, is just plain incorrect. We need to give up roots, and to relish the hybridity of the diaspora. If only we understood how totally mixed we all are, there would be no ethnic strife in the world. The source of the evil of roots is Western nationalism. We need only reject the West and its language of identities to find ourselves once again in the true reality of hybridity. HAVE A NICE DAY!

It is worth recalling here the not-so-recent reconsideration of 'racism' and identity by Lévi-Strauss (1985b) which was so vigorously opposed by UNESCO, whose leadership expected the same approach as the anthropologist had expressed in the 1952 UNESCO text on racism and history. There, while noting the universality of what might be called ethnocentrism, he expressed the belief that the progress of civilisation might be understood as the peaceful combination of the world's cultures in a larger co-operation. This is no longer the case. First, he states – as he implied in his earlier work – that racism is not the same as ethnocentrism, and that the latter is an inescapable tendency that has little to do with learning to think correctly. No intellectual process can eliminate this phenomenon, simply because it has nothing to do with falsity or fallacy. Second, he stresses that strong cultural identities are the source of cultural creativity, and that there is nothing wrong with this as long as it does not lead to racism. He goes even further, suggesting that if cultures exchanged all their elements with one another on a continuous basis, there would no longer be any differences, and thus no mutual attraction.

Now this was – and is – highly politically incorrect in this age of intellectual confusion about the nature of cultural identity. Geertz, in an interesting yet politically fence-sitting reply (1994), criticises Lévi-Strauss's forthrightness, as well as his nationalism. His own point of view is 'postmodern' and multicultural. He believes that we must strive to understand one another's worlds from the inside. But is this a morality that directs us all to become anthropologists? It would imply that everyone should have as much distance from particular worlds as does the ethnographer. Now this, in itself, is enough to defuse any ethnic conflict, by reducing difference to cognitive difference alone. Geertz is highly sensitive to the current massive movement of peoples in the world and their increasing nearness to one another. But this, he argues, makes it ever more imperative that we understand what is going on in other worlds. In an earlier work (1984), he refers to the contemporary world as a collage, or perhaps a pastiche, of mixed-up differences. Here the 'cultural' anthropologist's contribution to the world is precisely his expert knowledge of the other. Now, while Geertz never makes this explicit, there is a logic connecting his view to that of the hybrids. For since the only reality is cultural difference, and the only discourse is its interpretation, then anthropology, at least, is the representation of the multicultural, and the only higher or more abstract level in this discussion, is the totality or collection of cultures, the sum of differences.

Compare this view to that of Bhabha, for whom the transgression of borders is *the* root metaphor. He criticises the concept of the nation and its implied homogeneity, and stresses the importance of the position of the migrant (like himself, of course), a person who is somehow in two places and maintains a double perspective on reality. He uses the notion of cultural hybridity combined with a notion of counter-modernity, and stresses that this is not a normal opposition but apparently a kind of transcendence. The argument is that the migrant must not be placed in one cultural space. This would be tantamount to essentialism, racism, nationalism... all the same. Instead, there is fluidity and an essential (if you will) instability of boundedness. He uses the word 'unhomely' to refer to this situation. Bhabha refers throughout exclusively to literary works, which are the source material for the author's description, or depiction, or 'theory' of social reality in the contemporary world. The question of roots is treated in the same way. We must avoid essentialism at all costs. This implies a position of encompassment in relation to other peoples' identities. The subaltern peoples and voices of the now declining Western hegemony must be acclaimed in their double nature of pre-capitalist, ante- as well as anti-capitalist civilisation, but present as part of the modern world and one of its defining characteristics:

> By disrupting the stability of the ego, expressed in the equivalence between image and identity, the secret art of invisibleness of which the migrant poet speaks changes the very terms of our recognition of the person. (Bhabha 1994: 47)

The language of in-betweenness, even of liminality, dominates and would even seem to organise Bhabha's call to hybridity. Words such as displacement, dis-juncture, tran-sition, tran-scendence are rife in his texts, where the enemy is that which is generally bounded and thus, for him, essentialised. Thus, 'the hideous extremism' of Serbian nationalism is responsible, 'through the death, literal and figurative, of the complex interweavings of history and the culturally contingent borderlines of modern nationhood'. The truth of the cultural mixture characteristic of social reality would seem to go unrecognised by the unenlightened rednecks who dare to invest in their ethnic identity, as if it were all a terrible intellectual error. Applying these views to South African politics, Bhabha celebrates a hybridity that seems to miss all essential political points. But, then, it is based entirely on a passage from one of Nadine Gordimer's novels:

> This halfway house of racial and cultural origins bridges the 'in between' diasporic origins of the coloured South African and turns it into the symbol for the disjunctive, displaced everyday life of the liberation struggle. (Bhabha 1994: 13)

Here we must truly question whether the halfway definition of coloured makes this category any less ethnic, with all its essentialist implications, than any so-called pure category. And what is the programme Bhabha envisaged?

> For a willingness to descend into that alien territory – where I have led you – may reveal that the theoretical recognition of the split-space of enunciation may open the way to conceptualising an *inter*national culture, based not on the exoticism of multiculturalism or the *diversity* of cultures, but on the inscription and articulation of culture's *hybridity*. To that end we should remember that it is the 'inter' – the cutting edge of translation and negotiation, the *in-between* space – that carries the burden of the meaning of culture. It makes it possible to begin envisaging national, anti-nationalist histories of the 'people'. And by exploring this Third Space we may elude the politics of polarity and emerge as others of our selves. (Bhabha 1994: 38)

This is the establishment of a world in which the homogenising tendencies of all identification are eliminated not via modernist anti-cultural identity, but by a postmodernist total fusion of all cultures into a new heterogeneous homogeneity of the 'third space', which, if it is a space, must have boundaries of its own, and thus be based on oppositions to its own others. And, of course, the 'third space' adherents identify themselves against the redneck nationalists, ethnics and indigenes of the world. It is precisely in the metaphor of border-crossing that the notion of homogeneous identity is carried and reinforced, since it is a prerequisite of such transgression. But for whom, one might ask, is such cultural transmigration a reality? In the works of the post-colonial border-crossers, it is always the poet, the artist, the intellectual, who sustains this displacement and objectifies it in the printed word. But who reads the poetry, and what are the other kinds of identification occurring in the lower reaches of social reality?

Border-crossing is the recent metaphor of Chicano Studies in the United States, and an entire literature has been built up around the transnational experience of the migrant. Among the most important literary work that has been discussed, in articles that far exceed the length of that work itself, is Gloria Anzaldúa's *Borderlands/La Frontera: The New Mestiza* (1987), in which the author crosses all boundaries, sexual as well as national, but even more so in her movement between Indian, Mexican and American 'culture'. As self-identified Chicano anthropologist Renato Rosaldo puts it:

> In making herself into a complex persona, Anzaldúa incorporates Mexican, Indian, and Anglo elements at the same time that she discards the homophobia and patriarchy of Chicano culture. In rejecting the classic 'authenticity' of cultural purity, she seeks out the many-stranded possibilities of the borderlands.... She argues that because Chicanos have so long practiced the art of cultural blending, 'we' now stand in a position to become leaders in developing new forms of polyglot cultural creativity. In her view the rear guard will become the vanguard. (Rosaldo 1989: 216)

This is connected to the emergent discourses of the post-colonial and the postmodern which apparently dovetail in the celebration of fragmentation, a dissolution into which concepts such as complexity, chaos, hybridity and the like have been drawn:

> In the present postcolonial world, the notion of an authentic culture as an autonomous internally coherent universe no longer seems tenable, except perhaps as a 'useful fiction' or a revealing distortion.... Rapidly increasing global interdependence has made it more and more clear that neither 'we' nor 'they' are as neatly bounded and homogeneous as once seemed to be the case. (ibid.: 217)

Here coherence, wholeness and authenticity are relegated to the past, both colonial and, even more so, pre-colonial. The myth of anthropological identity is once more stated. The modern world is a cultural mess. The past was truly a mosaic with fixed boundaries, which have, in the mass movement of everything in the age of globalisation, sprung innumerable leaks. This, from a truly global historical view, is absolute nonsense. But it is also misconceived, since it assumes that coherence lies in origins, authenticity, and purity itself. This is a confusion of perspectives – what I have previously called the 'spaghetti principle'. In one – rather trivial – sense, all cultures have always been the product of import and a mix of elements. This was a commonplace for early cultural anthropology, and it is restated with force by Lévi-Strauss in his critique of the chimera of a new multicultural world:

> The term [monocultural] is meaningless, because there never has been such a society. All cultures are the result of a mishmash, borrowings, mixtures that have occurred, though at different rates, ever since the beginning of time. Because of the way it is formed, each society is multicultural and over the centuries has arrived at its *own original synthesis*. Each will hold more or less rigidly to this mixture that forms its culture at a given moment. (Lévi-Strauss 1994: 424; emphasis added)

It is not the origin of its elements but the way they are synthesised that is the specificity of a culture. The use of the concepts 'mixture', 'hybrid' and 'Creole' in such terms simply confuses the fact of geographic origins with the practice of cultural integration, assuming that the former rather than the latter is the defining characteristic of culture. It consists of a diffusionist and ethnically focused form of identification that has little to do with the scientific use of the term in modern anthropology. From the inside of a social world, cultural mixture occurs only as a phenomenon of self-identification. From the outside it is the observer who performs this act of identifying the other 'objectively'. This assumes that ways of doing things, all the forms of social specificity, are products with origins that can remain at home or migrate. I shall hypothesise here that except under very specific circumstances – to be enumerated below – mixed culture is a product of identifications from above/outside the lives of those whose existences are so ordered. And as this outside/above is a social position, the question of class becomes crucial in understanding just what is going on. Briefly, hybrids and hybridisation theorists are products of a group that self-identifies and/or identifies the world in such terms, not as a result of ethnographic understanding, but as an act of self-definition – indeed, of self-essentialising – which becomes definition for others via the forces of socialisation inherent in the structures of power that such groups occupy: intellectuals close to the media; the media intelligentsia itself; in a certain sense, all those who can afford a cosmopolitan identity.

This is well illustrated by the situation in Central America, where mestizo identity has been used as a middle-/upper-class tool against rising Maya identity. Hale refers with some scepticism to the work of Nestor Garcia-Canclini in *Culturas Hibridas*, claiming that 'all cultural identities in Latin America are turning hybrid, and have linked these hybrid cultures to promising new forms of oppositional politics' (1994: 9); but, he adds, 'these new expressions of identity politics are complicit with the policies of elites and the nation-state, that is, the slippage between hybridity and hegemony' (ibid.). An ethnohistorian adds that 'the mestizo concept can be an anti-Indian, psychologically paralysing tool of colonialism' (Sawyer 1993). Hale shows how hybrid ideology has been used to dissipate and disarray the Miskito Indian resistance by 'creolising' them from above, by actively criticising their ethnic essentialism. Hybridisation also opened their bounded social identity in such a way that they could not represent themselves as having any claims as a single group. We are all part-Indian, say members of the elite who have much to lose in the face of minority claims. This is also the case in Guatemala, where the Maya are in the majority but where their politics is defused by elite conversion to hybridity.

THE LOGICS OF IDENTITY
AND IDENTIFICATION

Let me summarise, briefly, the core of my argument. Ethnic purity, racism and hybridity are variations on the same essentialised and fundamentally objectified notion of culture that is continuously reproduced by a specific form of identification, or identity practice, in combination with the general properties of social experience acquired in different positions within the local hierarchies of the global system. The classical notion of culture was not about the identification of origins but about specific relations between elements, symbols, behaviours, institutions, structures of meaning. It was only on the assumption of specific forms of coherence that anthropologists could be concerned with the different 'worlds' that other peoples inhabited. There was another, older museological interest that was paramount among diffusionists, where culture was object, whether thing or practice. In this view, culture was contained in its embodiment rather than its generativity; the meaning was in the object, not in the process of its production. This was an identification of peoples in terms of their origins, a project of ethnic mapping analogous to the project of racial mapping that was part of the self-identification of the colonial centres of the world system. If they are mixed, as I define it, then whatever they think or experience is quite irrelevant. I have defined their identity for them. For Boas and Kroeber, the coherence of a culture was essentially a question of internal construction; but for the museum, there was a conflation of the external and the internal. It is only in this way that hybridity can justify itself. 'I am hybrid' is a statement of self-identification. 'They are hybrid' is a statement of other-identification. It is relevant only as a description of selfhood, unless it can be shown that despite what the locals think, the fact of their hybridity is of great consequence in the organisation of their lives.

The particular form of identification that I have addressed is grounded in the same premises as ethnicity or racism – that is, essentialism. This is not a critique, merely a descriptive statement. Its consequences, however, have a certain critical force. Hybridity is founded on the metaphor of purity. The notion of pure hybridity is a self-contradiction. This becomes evident in situations where it is practised as a group identity. In the United States there is a concerted effort, even a movement, to establish a mixed-ethnic or racial identity, one that is limited to middle-class and especially student groups. Now, there is a basis for this in the practice of many Americans to identify themselves in multi-ethnic genealogical terms: 'I am part-Irish, part-Scot, part-Black, part-Italian' (Waters 1990). These are not hyphenated identities in the social sense, since they are totally individualised, but they resonate with the metaphor for group identity as well. This does not detract from the nature of the identification as such, that is, as genealogical, the passage of substance from one generation to the next.

The mixed-race movement has its own newspapers and local organisations, *Interrace, Bi-Racial Child, Interracial Classified*, among others (Sawyer 1993). The project here is to define a new, unitary group of mixtures for those who feel 'disenfranchised by the current single-race categories' (*New People* 1993: 6, 8). The new mixture has apparently allowed some people to express their 'real' identities (Sawyer 1993: 13), but the logic of identification at group level is expressed in the split of Berkeley's student group, 'Miscellaneous', where Asian-Americans have formed their own group ('hapa forum'), because they feel that they must address their own *particular* issues as opposed to the more general Black-American discourse. The essentialism of identification can easily obliterate all attempts to eliminate purity via hybridity. On-the-ground practices of trans-ethnicity cannot produce anything other than new categories of the same type.

The cosmopolitan of old was a modernist who identified above and beyond ethnicity and particular cultures. He was a progressive intellectual, a believer in rationality who understood cultural specificities as expressions of universal attributes. The new cosmopolitans are ecumenical collectors of culture. They represent nothing more than a gathering of differences, often in their own self-identifications. The old and new cosmopolitanisms are clearly displayed in the difference between authors such as V.S. Naipaul and those closer to Salman Rushdie.

GLOBAL CLASSES AND THE IDEOLOGY OF HYBRIDITY

The ideology of hybridity has clearly gained in popularity, at least in the world of high-culture commentators on popular culture and, of course, in academia. The ecumenical identity harbours its own hegemonic logic in such circumstances, since it consists in an act of both encompassment and fusion. The logics that develop in underclass neighbourhoods are likely to be of a different nature from those that develop among the highly educated world travellers of the culture industries. Both, however, can be understood in terms of their different positions within the global processes of the world arena. These general processes consist of national fragmentation, leading to increasing instability and violence, to move-ments of populations and to the increasing mobilisation of cultural iden-tities, ethnic, regional and national as well as religious and even sexual (gender), age-group and, in principle, every potentially particularist social category in the world system. If this is experienced as postmodern chaos, it is, from a global point of view, quite systemic.

The urban poor, ethnically mixed ghetto is an arena that does not immediately cater to the construction of explicitly new hybrid identities. In periods of global stability and/or expansion, the problems of survival are more closely related to territory and to creating secure life spaces. Class identity, local ghetto identity, tend to prevail, just as the local arena may itself be divided into gang territories. The shift from the mid-1970s to today has been towards an increasing ethnification of such public social arenas, a generalised increase in identity politics that has affected urban ghettos as well as the middle and upper middle classes. In such a process there is little room for the hybrid identification discussed and pleaded for by cultural elites. Even hybridity tends to become ethnic, that is, bounded and oppositional. Ethnification entails the reinforcement of boundaries and of boundedness in a positive feedback process whereby increasing conflict leads to increasing closure, which in its turn leads to increasing conflict.

The global, cultural hybrid, elite sphere is occupied by individuals who share a very different kind of experience of the world, connected to international politics, academia, the media and the arts.[1] Their careers, especially if they were born in the Third World and live in the First, are thoroughly cosmopolitan, but not – as I said above – in a modernist sense. Rather, they are defined in cultural terms, in terms of the combi-nation of differences, often quite reflexively. This era is characterised by the not-so-gradual decline of the nation-state, and it is expressed in a shift from assimilationism to multiculturalism which has a long-term ten-dency to empower ethnic identities: regional and indigenous, but also immigrant minorities. This tendency takes the form of diasporisation, the striking of roots outside the current place of residence – ultimately the formation of 'de-territorialised' identities. The latter is, as I have stressed, the product of a shift in identification rather than an expression of the mere phenomenon of international migration.

The world has, of course, seen innumerable examples of diasporas, but it is only in specific historical conditions that we may speak of a diasporic global structure: an organisation that is a salient component of the world arena. Some decades ago, diasporic identity entailed a political accusation of treachery, a fifth column aimed at penetrating and conquering the nation from within. Today, the diaspora is not only legitimate but a source of liberation for many – liberation from the oppression of the nation-state, of modernity, of mass capitalism. Moreover, it is a source of real power, both political and economic, in the world system. The rise of diasporic identities, just like the rise of all subnational identities, is directly related to the decline of the nation-state itself. I would interpret this process in terms of the decentralisation of capital accumulation, the decline of central or hegemonic powers, and the resultant instability in the global system that has taken the form of fragmenting political identities and allegiances.

The decline of modernity permits the intervention of new interpretations, new identities. At first this was a question of a political equalisation of ethnic groups, but today it has become a celebration of hybridity, the hybridity experienced by the cultural elite itself. This hybridity is quite opposed to the Balkanisation and tribalisation experienced at the bottom of the system. As far as I know, the only places where hybrid identities have been instated and even institutionalised are certain European colonies, in which 'half-castes' and otherwise mixed identities were associated with particular positions in the social order. Where they have been politically dominant, it has often been in situations of anti-colonial struggle, as in the rise of the mestizo identity in Latin America; this has been for limited periods, followed by a demotion of the mestizo to a lower rank. In general, I have argued here that hybridity is always, like all acts of identity, a question of practice, the practice of attributing meaning. It can be understood only in terms of its social context and the way in which acts of identification are motivated.

Cultural theorists and other intellectuals may well take to defining the hybridity of the world they observe, but this would seem to entail two prerequisites:

1. That the world's peoples can be described in terms of culture, culture in the differential sense, that is, as object, substance, essence.
2. Since the world system has played musical chairs with these populations, it has, by definition, done likewise with their cultures. The result is mixture, hyphenation, and so on.

For those intellectuals who subscribe to this view of the world, it creates a self-identification, but it also pretends to describe other people's realities. The objectively 'mixed' cultures of the urbanised sectors of the world system are part of the identity spaces of the identifiers themselves. Those identified, however, have other problems, I suggest, which lead this kind of discourse into a great deal of confusion, not to say conflict, with ordinary people's realities. What is proposed, in a recent article concerning Chinese-Americans, is that the latter are themselves focusing on the wrong issues. By revolting against or trying to purify their identities, certain authors have misunderstood that Chinese-American identity is a particular field of a 'fluctuating composition of differences, intersections and incommensurabilities' (Lowe 1991: 27):

> I stress heterogeneity, hybridity, and multiplicity in the characterisation of Asian American culture as part of a twofold argument about cultural politics, the ultimate aim of that argument being to disrupt the current hegemonic relationship between 'dominant' and 'minority' positions. (ibid.: 28)

Lowe's aims are, first, to attack the dominant discourse, the 'hegemonic' discourse from above which takes Asian-Americans to be a homogeneous minority; second, to contribute to the debate on Asian 'mentality' or ethnicity. She also claims to be aware of the dangers in stressing sameness to the exclusion of differences. These are the differences of class and gender, and even age/generation. In the agonising discussion concerning Asian identities in the United States, there has been much internal critique. She refers to a critique of Amy Tan that claims,

> she has 'feminised' Asian American literature and undermined the power of Asian American men to combat the racist stereotypes of the dominant white culture. Kingston and other women novelists such as Amy Tan, he says, misrepresent Chinese history in order to exaggerate its patriarchal structure. As a result, Chinese society is portrayed as being even more misogynistic than European society. (ibid.: 33)

In her politicking against the opposition between 'nativism and assimilationism', Lowe suggests that the latter 'displaces the challenges of heterogeneity, or subalternity'. In one particular rendition of a film, we are indeed faced with the central question of hybridity. In a discussion of Peter Wang's film *The Great Wall*, we find the following interpretation:

> When the young Chinese Lau finishes the university entrance exam his scholar-father gives him a Coca Cola; children crowd around the single village television to watch a Chinese opera singer imitate Pavarotti singing Italian opera: the Chinese student learning English recites the Gettysburg Address. Although the film concentrates on both illustrating and dissolving the apparent opposition between Chinese and American Chinese, a number of other contrasts are likewise explored: the differences between generations both within the Chao and the Fang families (daughter Lili noisily drops her bike while her father prac-

tices *tai chi*; Paul kisses his Caucasian girlfriend and later tells his father that he believes all Chinese are racists when Leo suggests that he might date some nice Chinese girls). (ibid.: 38)

The point here for the author is that there are other differences; as we have seen, gender, wealth and age play a role in the life-processes of any 'ethnic' group. But while the film itself explores the class, gender and age conflicts that emerge in the transformation of a Chinese community in a new context, this is all reduced to a statement of mixture, as if class, culture and age were of the same order as ethnic identity and, as such, could make it appear more complex. But the film concerns a specifically Chinese (and probably regional) context, in which these other conflicts are clothed and played out. Now, this particular space of identity may not be equivalent to some 'essentialised' model of Chinese culture, but that does not mean it does not have a specificity of its own. The question that is not asked is: 'What is the nature of the changes?' Is it a matter of etiquette, reading one's children's mail, socialising with one's own group?

The politics expressed in this article is that ethnic minorities or 'conglomerates' such as Asian-Americans must maintain their unity in the face of the larger white population, the hegemonic population, at the same time as they challenge that unity by invoking gender, class and age qualities which enable new alliances that ultimately strengthen the minority. Here the ambivalent logic of cosmopolitanism without modernism is clearly expressed. Class, gender and age are all reduced to social constructions, just like ethnicity. They become phenomena of the same order – not in their actual genesis, but in the fact that they are cultural constructs. The first three terms were, for modernists, phenomena produced by social realities, while the last was usually conceived as something more or less imaginary. Today they are equivalent phenomena.

The historical shift in the way the world is identified is noteworthy. The former logics of class and gender were, at least, clearly modernist and universalist. It was a question of the unity of similarities, workers of the world, women and youth. These are transversal identities, transnational and therefore essentially non-cultural in the sense of geographical or even diasporic specificity.[2] The attempt to combine these identities within the category of ethnicity produces the kind of havoc associated actively with the notion of hybridity. Now, without going into the fact that hybrids are, in biological terms, often sterile – clearly an oversight by the self-identified – a hybrid has an internal structure of its own, which is just as unitary as that of any 'purer' organism (whatever that might mean).[3] The ambivalence is so obvious here as to be unavoidable: unity versus confusion; organisation versus juxtaposition. These are the

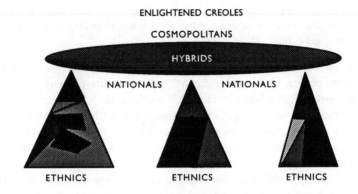

FIGURE 5.1 A hybrid worldview

real terms of this discussion. There is no solution, in so far as all successful identification implies homogenisation.

CONCLUSION

The general argument that emerges from this discussion is that identification is a practice situated in a specific social context, a set of conditions that determine the way in which subjects orient themselves in
relation to a larger reality which they define in defining themselves. The
contrast between hybrid/creole identifications and the essentialisation that
is common to lower-class and marginalised populations, as well as what
are referred to as 'redneck' leaders of ethnic mobilisations, is a contrast
in social position. Thus, I do not offer a critique of hybrid identities.
Their praxis is just as authentic as those that they have tended to criticise. What can be criticised, on the other hand, is the attempt to define
the identities of others in what turns out to be a normative argument. It
is only certain cultural elites that are addicted to such empowerment –
or rather, self-empowerment. In the meantime, the world heads towards
increasing Balkanisation – not because it is led by illiterate peasants who
don't understand that they are all hybrids; not because the 'people' are
misinformed. Experience of the world, however imbued with immediate
interpretations, is neither true nor false; it simply *is*. The on-going history
of the world cannot be interpreted as an intellectual conversation in
which problems can be solved by convincing people that they have got
it all wrong. The absurdity of such a position is a token of the alienation
of its spokesmen and spokeswomen.

NOTES

1. The transcendence of national boundaries by international politicians and bureaucrats was made clear to me recently by such a person, who claimed that the European Union had gone beyond the nation-state, and thus inherently represented a solution to problems of racism and ethnic conflict. This was spoken from a position of interaction among representatives of nation-states around committee room tables, and even more so in cocktail receptions and dinners.

2. Of course, 'non-cultural' is itself culturally specific. I refer only to the internal identification of such categories. The distinction cultural/non-cultural is a cultural property of Western modernity.

3. Now, of course, the metaphor of sterility does not resonate well with the notion of creativity, but it does accentuate the necessity of continuous immigration in order to maintain the population.

REFERENCES

Anzaldúa, Gloria (1987) *Borderlands/La Frontera: The New Mestiza*. San Francisco: Aunt Lute Books.
Bhabha, Homi (1994) *The Location of Culture*. London: Routledge.
Chambers, Iain (1994) *Migrancy, Culture and Identity*. London: Routledge.
Friedman, Jonathan (1994) *Cultural Identity and Global Process*. London: Sage.
Garcia-Canclini, N. (1989) *Culturas Hibridas*. Mexico: Grijalbo.
Geertz, Clifford (1984) 'Anti-anti Relativism'. *American Anthropologist* 86: 263–78.
Geertz, Clifford (1994) 'The Uses of Diversity', in R. Borofsky (ed.) *Assessing Anthropology*. New York: McGraw-Hill
Gilroy, Paul (1987) *There Ain't No Black in the Union Jack*. Chicago: Chicago University Press.
Gilroy, Paul (1993) *The Black Atlantic: Modernity and Double Consciousness*. Cambridge, MA: Harvard University Press
Gluckman, Max, J.C. Mitchell and J.A. Barnes (1949) 'The Village Headman in British Central Africa'. *Africa* 19, 2: 89–106.
Gluckman, Max, J.C. Mitchell and J.A. Barnes (1961) 'Anthropological Problems Arising from the African Industrial Revolution', in A. Southall, (ed.) *Social Change in Modern Africa*. London: Oxford University Press.
Hale, Charles (1994) 'Mestizaje, Hybridity and the New Cultural Politics of Difference in Post-revolutionary Central America'. MS.
Kroeber, Alfred L. (1948) *Anthropology*. New York: Harcourt & Brace.
Lévi-Strauss, Claude (1952) *Race et histoire*. Paris: UNESCO.
Lévi-Strauss, Claude (1985a) 'Preface', in *The View from Afar*. Oxford: Blackwell.
Lévi-Strauss, Claude (1985b) 'Race and Culture', in *The View from Afar*. Oxford: Blackwell.
Lévi-Strauss, Claude (1994) 'Anthropology, Race and Politics: A Conversation with Didier Eribon', in R. Borofsky, (ed.) *Assessing Anthropology*. New York: McGraw Hill.
Lowe, Robert (1991) 'Heterogeneity, Hybridity, Multiplicity: Marking Asian American Differences'. *Diaspora* 1, 1: 24–42.
New People (1993) magazine.
Rex, John (1973) *Race, Colonialism and the City*. London: Routledge & Kegan Paul.
Rosaldo, Renato (1989) *Culture and Truth*. London: Routledge.
Sawyer, L. (1993) 'The Third Category'. MS.
Waters, M. (1990) *Ethnic Options*. Berkeley, CA: University of California Press.

6

'THE ENIGMA OF ARRIVAL':
HYBRIDITY AND AUTHENTICITY
IN THE GLOBAL SPACE

Peter van der Veer

In this chapter I want to explore some recent theoretical developments in Cultural Studies that deal with the specific place of migrants in the production of culture, and valorise hybridity, syncretism, in-betweenness, and the creativity or cultural innovation inherent in migration. Since these theories themselves have been developed through a reading of literary texts written by migrant settlers, I intend to examine two such texts, V.S. Naipaul's *The Enigma of Arrival* and Salman Rushdie's *The Satanic Verses*. As an anthropologist I need first, perhaps, however, to justify my recourse to literary texts as a basis for research on migrant culture, before pointing, in due course, to some of the limitations of this approach.

From its inception, it has been Anthropology's disciplinary privilege to use the concept of culture. This, however, has been a mixed blessing, given the unwieldy nature of the term and its licensing of imaginative musings about more or less anything and everything. Historically, Raymond Williams (1960) reminds us, the use of the term 'culture' in English changed in the course of the Industrial Revolution from the 'tending of natural growth' to 'a whole way of life, material, intellectual and spiritual' by the first half of the nineteenth century. Culture came to be used as a reflection on the momentous societal changes of the period, and – like industry, democracy and class – it received new meanings which reflected on modernity and industrialisation. While Williams restricts his historical analysis to England and English writers, and forgets about empire, for Anthropology, which arose in tandem with imperialism, the use of the concept of culture – holistic, just as Williams indicated

– always had a particular direction: an attempt to locate and define modernity by contrasting it to its non-Western, non-modern Other. Through contrast, Anthropology could illuminate the unique nature of 'modern culture'. It did so not only by positing a universalist notion of culture as a distinguishing feature of the human species but also by conceiving of a plurality of cultures as totalities with clear boundaries, confined to their localities.

Moreover, as Arjun Appadurai has argued, each cultural type tended to be globally located: the honour-and-shame complex in Mediterranean societies, segmentary lineages in Africa, caste in India, and cargo cults in Melanesia. This conceit of Anthropology could, perhaps, be seen as a reflection of the colonial encounter itself, but also, more broadly, of the systematising tendencies of modern thought. The colonial project *located* its subjects by mapping territories and populations in the context of military expansion and political centralisation. The geographical mapping went together with a classification of peoples and customs through censuses and gazetteers. Colonialism also *dislocated* people through its imperial organisation of migrant labour and soldiering. One of the striking examples of colonial dislocation was, obviously, the institution of African slavery, which was succeeded, in the nineteenth century, by the system of Indian indentured labour. It is important to note that these dislocations did not constitute 'free movement', but a 'middle passage' from one boundedness and bondedness to another. Free movement of persons and commodities, a dogma of economic liberalism, was in many places restricted to the enlightened, Western coloniser.

Hence the *location* of culture has been a concern that Anthropology and colonialism had in common, yet post-colonial developments have made culture increasingly difficult to locate. There are three aspects to this difficulty. First, with the crumbling of European colonialism and the subsequent proliferation of nation-states, the national cultures of Western and non-Western societies have acquired, at least in principle, equal status as objects of research. This has enabled the growth of an Anthropology of complex societies, focused on the United States and Europe. The evident complexity of cultural formations in complex societies challenged any unitary view of culture that stressed boundedness, continuity and homogeneity (see also Wicker, Chapter 2 above). Leach's proposal that society and culture were not interchangeable terms, and Barth's that ethnic groups manipulated cultural emblems for collective interests, obviously acquire renewed force when they shift from a focus on rural research among frontier people, far removed from urban centres, to Kachin or Swat Pathans living in London or New York City.

Along with the study of the West has come a shift in anthropological theory from 'system' to 'practice', accompanied by an interest in agency, actors and the actor's point of view. This has resulted in a further dismantling of the notion of the 'cultural whole'. This refocusing has been associated with a distrust of unifying, homogenising forms of anthropological writing, a distrust expressed cogently in a series of reflexively critical anthropological texts of which *Writing Culture* (Clifford and Marcus 1986) is, perhaps, the most outstanding example.

A third feature of this changing intellectual terrain has been the interest in post-colonial migration to the West from the former colonised South. Non-Western cultures are no longer located outside the West, but form an increasingly important social element of the Western cultural scene itself, especially in metropolises like London, Amsterdam, Paris, New York City and Los Angeles. The honour-and-shame complex and all the rest are no longer confined to an elsewhere, outside the West; indeed, there is no easily identifiable 'inside' and 'outside' any more. Along with migration, the study of power relations between a variety of centres and peripheries has challenged the prior stress on national cultures or nationalism, so that anthropologists today increasingly find themselves having to come to grips with the meaning of global culture and transnationalism.

Such highly complex developments in Anthropology form the backdrop to the problem anthropologists face: what to do with the concept of culture in this changing global scene. Rather than address this question in a highly abstract manner, I want to reflect upon the intriguing fact that just when culture has been problematised for anthropologists, it has been hijacked by a relative newcomer to the academy, Cultural Studies. Cultural Studies itself is not a unitary whole. As Stuart Hall suggests, it encompasses multiple discourses and is the product of several historical trajectories. A brief glance at a 1990s' Cultural Studies collection suffices to prove that any serious attempt to describe the discipline is futile. This is particularly true for the American branch of Cultural Studies, which has left even Hall himself speechless ('I don't know what to say about American Cultural Studies. I am completely dumbfounded by it' – 1992: 285).

In this chapter I choose to focus on a specific subcategory of critical theory within Cultural Studies that deals with colonialism and the post-colonial predicament, including migrant culture – both subjects of some interest to anthropologists. The scholars promoting this critical project – Edward Said, Gayatri Chakravorty Spivak, Anthony Appiah, Homi Bhabha, Sarah Suleri – are all exemplars of the very phenomenon of displacement, migrancy, exile and transnationalism that they attempt to understand. Together these scholars form a vanguard of critics of Third

World cultural products (films, art, literature) mostly produced by settler-migrants such as Naipaul, Rushdie or Mira Nair. Distinctively, they bring to bear upon these aesthetic texts a knowledge and cultural experience which, ultimately, also feed back into the texts themselves.

Since the late 1980s, there has been a discernable *rapprochement* between American Cultural Anthropology and this type of Cultural Studies. The very title of collections like *Writing Culture* indicates the interest in the process of writing and in forms of ethnographic narrativisation, an interest that brings these anthropological critics close to literary theory. The subtitle of James Clifford's *The Predicament of Culture*, 'Twentieth-Century Ethnography, Literature and Art', refers to the juxtaposition in the book of chapters on Conrad and Malinowski, Aimé Césaire, museums, and Edward Said. Similarly, a co-authored book by Michael Fischer and Mehdi Abedi (1990) juxtaposes Qur'anic recitation, Irani poster art, Irani migrants in Houston, and the Rushdie affair. It seems evident that Anthropology and Cultural Studies are finding common ground by abandoning the old ideological distinction between 'high' and 'low' culture, between literary production on the one hand, and orality and performance on the other. The collapse of the old distinctions, however, does not revive the old cultural whole. Instead, there is a privileging of the cultural fragment – literary, cinematic, or otherwise.

There is also a shared interest in migration and travel, in movement as opposed to stasis. James Clifford begins his essay 'Travelling Cultures' with a quotation from the Caribbean writer C.L.R. James:

> Time would pass, old empires would fall and new ones take their place. The relations of classes had to change before I discovered that it's not quality of goods and utility that matter, but movement, not where you are or what you have, but where you come from, where you are going and the rate at which you are getting there. (1992: 101)

Clifford argues specifically for a rethinking of anthropology in terms of travel, so that 'constructed and disputed *historicities*, sites of displacement, interference, and interaction, come more sharply into view' (ibid.). The same interest may be found in the postmodern philosophy of Deleuze and Guattari, who propose a new turn in philosophy which they term nomadology. It is a Nietzschean *Umwertung aller Werte*, a nomadic de-territorialisation and deconstruction of the familiar, of the Law of the State, an adventurous guerrilla war against fixed norms, conducted from the periphery of settled societies.

These ideas are developed by the feminist philosopher Rosi Braidotti in an essay entitled 'Nomads in a Transformed Europe: Figurations for an Alternative Consciousness' (1993). Braidotti conceives of herself as a nomad, since she was born in Italy, raised in Australia, educated at the Sorbonne in Paris, and is now teaching in Holland. She celebrates the polyglot, the speaker of many languages, against the God-given seriousness and foundational value of mother tongues:

> In this new Europe that witnesses all of its old problems, in a wave of return of the repressed that is disconcerting, to say the least, in this ethnocentric fortress, the concept of the mother tongue is stronger than ever. It feeds into the renewed and exacerbated sense of nationalism, regionalism, localism, which marks this particular moment of our history. The polyglot surveys this situation with the greatest critical distance; a person who is in-transit between the languages, neither here nor there, knows better than to believe in steady identities and mother tongues. (Braidotti 1993: 32–33)

An anthropologist may be forgiven for expressing some scepticism about this extremely romantic notion of 'nomadism', and some puzzlement about the way this phallocentric trope *par excellence* (from Lawrence of Arabia to Thesiger) acquires a new use in feminist philosophy. Nevertheless, much is clearly expected from living on the margins of society, from migrants who are nomads and who refuse both nostalgia and the comforts of assimilation, who are actively, creatively 'in-between'. And if one looks to at least one indicator of literary success, the nomination for the Booker Prize in Britain, one is indeed struck by the extraordinary contribution of migrants to contemporary English literature.

In English post-colonial literary theory, it is Homi Bhabha (1994) who – somewhat like Braidotti, but more subtly – celebrates,

> the borderline work of culture [which] demands an encounter with 'newness' that is not part of the continuum of past and present. It creates a sense of the new as an insurgent act of cultural translation. Such art does not merely recall the past as social cause or aesthetic precedent; it renews the past, refiguring it as a contingent 'in-between' space, that innovates and interrupts the performance of the present. The 'past–present' becomes part of the necessity, not the nostalgia, of living. (Bhabha 1994: 6)

Bhabha's claims for the role of such art are huge. He speaks about 'cultural interstices that introduce creative invention into existence'; about the 're-creation of the self in the world of travel'; the 're-settlement of the borderline community of migration' (ibid.: 9). He makes claims for a 'political empowerment, and the enlargement of the multiculturalist cause [note that the rebels are not without a cause], coming from posing questions of solidarity and community from the interstitial perspective' (ibid.: 3), and argues that 'this interstitial passage *in-between* fixed identifications opens up the possibility of a cultural hybridity that entertains difference without an assumed or imposed hierarchy' (ibid.: 4).

What I find striking about these statements is that they seem to invoke the traditional romantic trope of the 'self-made individual' who invents himself in the marginality of the American frontier. There is inherent here a notion of almost total innovation, of new subject-formation in 'in-between' sites, inhabited by migrants as pioneer settlers. In an essay with the telling title 'How Newness Enters the World', Bhabha refers to the philosopher Charles Taylor's *Sources of the Self*. Taylor argues that 'the supposition that I could be two temporally succeeding selves is either an overdramatised image, or quite false. It runs against the structural features of a self as a being who exists in a space of concerns.' Bhabha counters that 'such "overdramatised" images are precisely my concern as I attempt to negotiate narratives where double-lives are led in the post-colonial world, with its journeys of migration and its dwellings of the diasporic' (Bhabha 1994: 213). Yet Taylor's aim, arguably, is precisely to show that it is modernity, from Locke and Hume onwards, which defines the modern individual self as neutral, outside any essential framework of moral questions, outside a discursive tradition, outside a narrative which shapes a subject's life as a whole – in relation to a moral idea of the good, achieved in conversation with other selves. Bhabha and Taylor are both, in their different ways, examining the sources of the self. Bhabha emphasises the potential of migrants to reinvent themselves continuously in the post-colonial situation of cultural hybridity; Taylor emphasises the continuity of selfhood in relation to the larger conversations in which it takes part. Since, in modern culture, it is art and literature that are the sites of self-fashioning *par excellence*, I want to examine these issues through a contrastive reading of the two migration novels by Naipaul and Rushdie, both of South Asian origin, both settlers in contemporary Britain.

The title of my chapter is derived from Naipaul's novel about an Indo-Trinidadian novelist, V.S. Naipaul, who rents a house in the English countryside, near Stonehenge, a site that is an almost paradigmatic symbol of prehistoric England. The house is also near Salisbury, which was the first English town apparently known to Naipaul on his faraway tropical island – his third-standard English reader contained a picture of a Constable painting of Salisbury Cathedral. Cultural knowledge about the metropole, acquired in the colonial setting of Trinidad. How casually Naipaul brings up this major theme in his work: the life in a colonial backwater and the desire to arrive (both spatially and socially) in the metropole. But in England one has arrived fully only when one has arrived in what might be quintessential to Englishness, the English landscape.

Naipaul is quite frank about the hardships of coming to England from Trinidad, of having high ambitions to be a writer. He had dreamed of coming to England, 'but my life in England had been savourless, and much of it mean'. Now he seems to have arrived, both as a writer and in the English countryside, but one recalls that the title of his novel is *The Enigma of Arrival*. This title refers to a painting of a wharf by de Chirico, a detail of which appears on the book's cover. Naipaul describes it:

> in the background there are two figures, both muffled, one perhaps the person who has arrived, the other perhaps a native of the port. The scene is of desolation and mystery; it speaks of the mystery of arrival. (Naipaul 1987: 91–2)

And he gives the outline of a story he wants to write, based on the painting:

> The newly arrived person would enter there and be swallowed by the life and noise of a crowded city.... Gradually there would come to him a feeling that he was getting nowhere; he would lose his sense of mission; he would begin to know only that he was lost. His feeling of adventure would give way to panic. He would want to escape, to get back to the quayside and his ship. But he wouldn't know how.... At the moment of crisis he would come upon a door, open it, and find himself back on the quayside of arrival. He has been saved; the world is as he remembered it. Only one thing is missing now. Above the cut-out walls and buildings there is no mast, no sail. The antique ship has gone. The traveller has lived out his life. (ibid.: 91–2)

Here, in effect, is a description of a migrant's nightmare. In a sense, the novel is the fleshed-out version of the story seen by Naipaul in the de Chirico painting. It is a book about death. On the first page we find a dedication: 'In loving memory of my brother Shiva Naipaul, 25 February, 1945, Port of Spain 13 August 1985.' The book ends by recording the period of writing: October 1984 to April 1986. There is almost no mention of Shiva Naipaul, but his absence is marked in the final episode when V.S. Naipaul describes the mortuary rites of his younger sister in Trinidad. Every chapter records a death in Naipaul's environment, ending in the final chapter with the death of his sister. The book itself is a mortuary ritual. And, as always, when one reflects upon the death of others, one realises one's own mortality and makes up the balance of one's life.

Naipaul sees his life as a version of the story told in the de Chirico painting. The steamboat journey from New York to Southampton is full of racial slights; his arrival in London is pathetic; he lives in a poor boarding-house in Earls Court and is very lonely, greatly disappointed in the city he had dreamed of coming to. But the point is that after all these trials, he has now finally arrived in the English landscape. The move to the countryside makes Naipaul nervous:

There was no village to speak of. I was glad of that. I would have been nervous to meet people. After all my time in England I still had that nervousness in a new place, that rawness of response, still felt myself to be in the other man's country, felt my strangeness, my solitude. And every incursion into a new part of the country – what for others might have been an adventure – was for me like a tearing at an old scab. (ibid.: 13)

After a while he meets a farmer, Jack, about whom the narrator fantasises that this man, at least, is genuine, rooted, fitting the landscape: 'I saw him as a remnant of the past (the undoing of which my own presence portended' (ibid.: 19) – very different from the unanchored, uprooted Naipaul, who discovers gradually, however, that Jack himself 'lived among ruins, among superseded things', was a man out of place; that, indeed, his entire image of the unchanging countryside was wrong. Jack dies, his wife leaves for the city; other people come without a shred of feeling for the countryside. The perfection of the countryside, of a well-rooted way of life, disintegrates as soon as he starts to probe it. This disintegration suits the temperament of a man who, as we know from *A House for Mr Biswas*, had, as a child, always lived in great uncertainty, in half-ruined houses, constantly on the move. Perfection might have existed fifty years before, when the estate on which his cottage stands had been created by the wealth of Empire. But he realises that in that period of perfection there would not have been a place for him, the grandson of an Indian indentured labourer.

The arrival of an Indo-Trinidadian novelist in the English landscape makes this landscape appear in a particular light. The estate is not just an estate; it was acquired at the very period in which Naipaul's ancestors were shipped from India to Trinidad to work on rather different estates. Naipaul's reference to Empire is just as casual as Jane Austen's in *Mansfield Park*. As Edward Said argues in *Culture and Imperialism*, the perfection of Mansfield Park involves a plantation in Antigua. Fanny marries her cousin Edmund, the rich heir of Mansfield Park, whose father, Sir Thomas Bertram, has become rich thanks to Empire, to the slave trade. Already, Austen has made a connection between the civility of Mansfield Park and the brutality of Empire, but with Naipaul this connection is evoked more directly, in terms of post-colonial feelings of decline and decay. The owner of the manor suffers from accidia, a word I had to look up in the dictionary. It is a disease of monks in the Middle Ages, caused by solitude and sloth. Such a disease appeals to Naipaul, the writer: a monk in modern times. The descendant of the plantation worker and the descendant of the plantation owner both partake in the decline of Empire.

Decay and decline do not set the tone of the novel entirely, though.

Naipaul confesses a great love for the beauty of the gardens and the landscape; and, in a bitter aside, he remarks:

> That instinct to plant, to see crops grow, might have seemed eternal, something to which the human heart would want to return. But in the plantation colony from which I came – a colony created for agriculture, for the growing of a particular crop, created for the great flat fields of sugar-cane, which were the point and explanation of everything, the houses, the style of government, the mixed population – in that colony, created by the power and wealth of industrial England, that instinct had been eradicated. (ibid.: 215)

Here, however, the colonial rediscovers a human instinct which to this reader, at least, seems more English than universally human. There is a long English literary tradition of devotion to the countryside and to gardening, and Naipaul certainly stands in that tradition. As Raymond Williams argues in *The Country and the City* (1973), the modern English attitude towards the country (which means, in English, both the national territory as a whole and part of the 'land') has to be related to the Industrial Revolution which very early transformed the nature of the rural economy as a result of rapid urbanisation. Dependence on domestic agriculture was very low in Imperial England. In an ironic way, Naipaul's experience shows the other side of the English love for the countryside – its dependence on the colonies. The post-colonial predicament collapses these two sides in a nostalgia for the heyday of Empire, shared by both ex-colonised and ex-colonisers.

The novel's final chapter, appropriately entitled 'The Ceremony of Farewell', describes the mortuary rites performed for his sister Sati. It is a surprisingly mild and rather touching description by this often cynical observer of religion. Moreover, it highlights an important development in contemporary Caribbean Hinduism. The ritual by which the ghost of the deceased is transformed into a benign ancestor has to be performed in the manner prescribed by the ritual manuals. The Brahman priest and his counterpart, the sacrificer [*jajman*] – here husband and sons of the deceased – are entirely immersed in what Naipaul calls 'the physical side of the ceremony'. It has to be done correctly, 'this pressing together of balls of rice and then balls of earth, this arranging of flowers and pouring of milk on heaps of this and that, this constant feeding of the sacred fire' (ibid.: 313). However, there is a new demand for theology here. The husband of the deceased asks whether his wife will return on earth and whether they will be together again, and the priest answers that she might return, but in that case he would not be able to recognise her. Here Naipaul makes the important observation that the rituals had always been partly a mystery, but his family could no longer easily surrender to them. They had been rendered self-conscious by education, travel and history, transformed by wealth. A quest for personal experience and meaning had been added to the earlier emphasis on 'correct practice'.

There is a good deal of nostalgia in this final episode which again celebrates rural life, the countryside. The story is one of progress, social and spatial mobility, accompanied by loss. Progress accompanied by decay – and even a nostalgia for the Empire, all politically very incorrect. But everyone already knows how politically incorrect Naipaul is, so it came as a relief to find in Sara Suleri's *The Rhetoric of English India* (1992) that it is once again OK to read him. Indeed, Naipaul is one of the strongest believers in the Enlightenment tradition, in rationality and modern progress. In a recent lecture to the Manhattan Institute, he rejects religion on the grounds that it prevents people from pursuing knowledge. The alternative to religious tradition, he argues, is the idea of what he calls 'universal civilisation, born in Europe but now truly universal, stripped of its racial taints'. At the heart of this civilisation is the idea of the pursuit of happiness, which contains

> the idea of the individual, responsibility, choice, the life of the intellect, the idea of vocation and perfectibility and achievement. It is an immense human idea. It cannot be reduced to a fixed system. It cannot generate fanaticism. But it is known to exist, and because of that, other more rigid systems in the end blow away. (Naipaul, *New York Times*, 5 November 1990)

Well, at least one thing seems to be clear: this post-colonial writer is not postmodern.

Naipaul, it seems to me, is definitely also not in favour of Bhabha's multiculturalism, but in favour of what multiculturalists would label 'white culture'. Indeed, he could be called an arch-conservative and a protagonist of assimilation in his celebration of the English countryside. Clearly, although it is produced at the cultural interstices, his work runs counter to the very claims made for it by post-colonial Cultural Studies. But this is only one level of Naipaul's work. At another level, he expresses the extent to which his experience of England is inflected through his childhood experiences in Trinidad.

What Naipaul seems to show is the continuity, the wholeness of his life. In the English countryside he sees Trinidad. Death and decay are part of both, and his particular understanding of that decay in England comes from his colonial experience. So, indeed, England is appropriated in a very literal sense. The novel disrupts the fake notion that those English people a migrant may encounter in the countryside are more 'rooted' than the migrant him-/herself. Migrancy, uprootedness and death are common experiences of modernity. This may sound like the ultimate assimilation in the face of death; but again, there is the response to death in Hindu mortuary rites, and a new quest for theological meaning in the old practices. Clearly, I am not claiming that Naipaul is ultimately, beneath it all, a Hindu. This would be an unwarranted, essentialising move. But religion seems to be a habit of the heart which continues to form part of the cultural conversation from which even Naipaul cannot entirely escape. This is a novel not about hybridity but about anxiety and grief as a universal human condition.

Let me now turn briefly to Salman Rushdie's *The Satanic Verses*. It was published a year after Naipaul's novel, in 1988, but it received a great deal more critical attention for well-known reasons. I shall therefore be much briefer here. Naipaul's and Rushdie's works inhabit entirely different worlds. Whereas Naipaul is a modernist, a realist, Rushdie is a post-modernist, a magical realist. Naipaul has a Caribbean-Hindu background; Rushdie an Indian-Muslim one. Yet they also have Britishness and an Oxbridge education in common, and they share a theme: that of South Asia and the South Asian immigration to Britain. But whereas *The Enigma of Arrival* records with great calmness the reflections of a solitary immigrant in the English landscape, *The Satanic Verses* plunges into the cauldron of illegal immigration, racism and anti-racist activism in London. Which is more realistic? Which is more magical? – one may justifiably ask.

The 'carrier' of this theme is one of the key characters in the novel, Saladin Chamcha. When he loses his faith in his father and, thereby, in his religion, he decides to change his identity. He invents himself as an English gentleman, but, typically, can find a living only as an imitator of voices on television, for example in 'The Aliens Show'. Believing that accent conveys social identity, he marries a British wife with an upper-class accent, despite her attempts to get rid of her background. This is the world of make-believe, of an attempt to assimilate, but reality is different, as Chamcha realises when he falls from the sky on the English coast. The story that he has safely floated down from a jumbo jet that has been blown apart above the English Channel is laughed away by the policemen who come to arrest him as an illegal immigrant. Because he has fallen on the coast instead of landing at Heathrow, his carefully constructed identity falls apart. He becomes, quite literally, a devil with goatish features, 'demonised' by the police, who treat him brutally. His wife does not want him back, and so he ends up among 'his own people' in Brixhall (Brixton and Southall), where he witnesses how the police create racial riots. Thatcher's England is a long way from what he had imagined as his new homeland. In the end, he decides to make it up with his father and become Indian again. The migrant has to redefine himself, but it is not entirely a self-definition. Others redefine him, and in many cases in a racist manner.

I would like to draw attention to the fact that Rushdie seems to indicate that the prior self – the relation with one's childhood, with one's father – remains a significant part of the transformation of the migrant. A central element of this prior, original identity – as it were – is religion. And unlike Naipaul, who neutralises his Hinduism by universalising it, Rushdie engages with religious discourse directly by making a comparison between literary and religious inspiration, between Prophet and novelist ('What kind of idea is he?, What kind am I', the text asks – Rushdie 1988: 111). The result of this comparison is that both religion and fiction are portrayed as products of the imagination. Although this is blasphemous from a religious point of view, it does not in itself denigrate Islam; Sara Suleri puts this straightforwardly: 'Rushdie has written a deeply Islamic book' (1992: 191). One might say, indeed, that the book is obsessed with Islam, and wonder why an English novel written for a Western audience is to such an extent about issues that its readers do not have the necessary cultural background to understand. What functions does this exoticism have for a Western audience? Rushdie's previous novel, *Shame*, announced itself as a novel of leave-taking from the East, but *The Satanic Verses* shows, inadvertently, that Rushdie is not yet done with the leave-taking, especially from Islam.

'What does the narrative construction of minority discourses entail for the everyday existence of the Western metropole?' This is the question raised by Homi Bhabha (1994: 223), which he tries to answer in his analysis of *The Satanic Verses*. In his view, the novel deals with the in-determinacy of diasporic identity, and this is the secular, social cause for what has been represented as the 'blasphemy' of the book. 'Hybridity is heresy',

> Blasphemy goes beyond the severance of tradition and replaces its claim to a purity of origins with a poetics of relocation and reinscription.... Blasphemy is not merely a misrepresentation of the sacred by the secular; it is a moment when the subject matter or the content of a cultural tradition is being over-whelmed, or alienated, in the act of translation. (ibid.: 225)

Again, however, one must ask: for whom is it translated, and to what purpose? The angry reactions of South Asian Muslim immigrants expressed their justifiable feelings, I believe, that the novel's passages on the rise of Islam and the Prophet were intended to lampoon their beliefs and practices. These immigrants, who are already socially and culturally marginalised, are thus doubly marginalised in the name of an attack on 'purity' and Islamic 'fundamentalism'. The novel's depiction of the sexual behaviour of the Prophet is felt as a deliberately provocative sneer, and, as we know, Muslims in Bradford responded to this sneer by burning the book. This, in turn, provoked the immense outrage of the secular English elite, and particularly its liberal intelligentsia, an extreme example being Fay Weldon's pamphlet (1989) in which she argues that 'The Bible, in its entirety, is at least food for thought. The Koran is food for no-thought. It is not a poem on which society can be safely or sensibly based'(!). In other words, so-called Islamic fundamentalists are not merely 'purists' who abhor hybridity: they are fundamentally immoral. The upshot of the affair has been not only the threat to the writer's life; just as serious, race relations in Britain and elsewhere in Europe have suffered a considerable setback. If this is how cultural work on the borderline brings newness into the world, we are in for some stormy weather. According to Bhabha, the migrant's survival depends on this form of cultural transition and translation, but one could as well argue that survival depends on the very opposite of this kind of 'newness'.

The celebration of hybridity, syncretism and multiculturalism in Cultural Studies needs to be examined critically. Bhabha's claim that one can bring newness into the world, that one can reinvent oneself when one is writing from the cultural interstices, is a conceit of the literature-producing and consuming world. Literary texts are the very sites of self-fashioning in modern, bourgeois culture. Literature has replaced religious texts as a source of elevated reflection about the nature of the self. Rushdie's thematic takes part precisely in that displacement. What is remarkable, however, is the extent to which his hybrid self-fashioning feeds on Islamic traditions. It is this engagement which leads to a reading of his text not only by those who valorise the invention of culture in art, but also by migrant-settlers who are very differently placed in relation to those traditions.

These Muslim readers are not necessarily fundamentalists at all; their religious ideas are just as hybrid and syncretic as those of the author. They, too, are migrants, but the sources of their identity are authenticated not by profane literary texts but by what are to them sacred religious traditions. It is ironic, therefore, to find that migrants who are at the vanguard of political resistance to the assimilative tendencies of the nation-state, who have their own cultural project for living hybrid cultural lives in a non-Islamic nation – expressed, for example, in a demand for state-funded Muslim schools or the extension of the blasphemy laws – are condemned, while the postmodern hybrid novelist is celebrated by liberals and the state, extolled for his struggle against that very oppositional resistance, against the supposed 'backwardness' of the 'fundamentalist' British Muslim community.

It is also striking that the difference between Naipaul's novel and Rushdie's novel – between the modern and the postmodern, if you wish – is not between an endorsement of Enlightenment values and a critique of them. The difference lies, rather, in the radicality of Rushdie's endorsement of the Enlightenment project – to engage and refashion the religious tradition in which he received his early socialisation, while simultaneously, in his very textuality, constantly to depend on the difference of that tradition. Naipaul emphasises the commonality of the human condition, the fiction of roots. He is an advocate of assimilation to a universal Enlightenment culture which has its origins in Europe, but is now part of world culture. His position resembles that of the historian Arthur Schlesinger in *The Disuniting of America* (Schlesinger 1992). Naipaul does not engage Hindu tradition in order to refashion it. It is part of his childhood upbringing, and he neither rejects nor endorses it. More clearly than any writer I know of, his identity is fashioned by literature, by the production of fiction; as such, his past is only a limited, aesthetic re-source for his narrative.

One could, perhaps, argue that post-colonial Cultural Studies fails to examine critically the status of art and literature in the ideology of modern bourgeois culture, endorsed in its continuous emphasis on individual creativity, invention and the fragmentary nature of culture. Despite their radical stance against racism and discrimination, these scholars leave out of their elaborate analyses the question of how the novel and the novelist are socially situated *vis-à-vis* the constituencies they supposedly represent or write for. The critics thus erase the crucial dimension of power through their very textualisation of it. Both Rushdie and Naipaul embrace Enlightenment traditions. This is not very surprising if one considers that – educated as they were in Oxford colleges – they write English novels for an English-reading cultural elite, by and large living in the West. Most Muslim and Hindu immigrants in Britain are, however, workers. Many live in provincial mill towns in northern England. They have very different class origins, and valorise quite different aesthetic traditions from those of Naipaul and Rushdie, or Bhabha, for that matter (see Werbner 1996). The reading of literary texts as a gateway to the analysis of migrant culture may thus have severe limitations. I am not arguing that such literary texts constitute an invalid tool of cultural analysis; merely that it is crucial to go beyond the analysis of literary discourses and representations to the social, political and economic contexts in which they are embedded. There may be nothing outside the text, as Derrida proposes, but there is certainly something outside the literary text. The Rushdie affair is a painful reminder of that simple but important fact.

The move from a stress on holism to fragment in the interpretation of culture is, in my view, a salutary one. That hybridity, diversity and syncretism are integral dimensions of cultural change is, it seems to me, beyond doubt. It remains important to recognise, however, the tension in modern society between a politics of difference and the totalising cultural project of the modern nation-state; between the drive towards integration, on the one hand, and individualisation and differentiation, on the other. This is reflected in the modern tendency to relegate religious expression to the private sphere, rendering it equivalent to a difference in literary taste. Religious faith and other forms of cultural difference are thus not obliterated, but transformed, and – as Talal Asad (1993: 266) reminds us – comfortably accommodated by urban consumer capitalism. From this perspective, the hybridity celebrated in Cultural Studies has little revolutionary potential, since it is part of the very discourse of bourgeois capitalism and modernity which it claims to displace.

Novelists as different as Naipaul and Rushdie are part of that modernist project. One should, at the same time, recognise that there are alternative projects to the totalising and individualising tendencies of the modern nation-state. These include religious movements, some of them 'fundamentalist'. If one wants to find revolutionary potential in the migrant situation, one can surely find it in these movements. Although they are totalising, their discourses on individuality and hybridity are, of course, rather different. Officially, they emphasise that anti-modern-sounding concept of sacred tradition. Yet this does not, in fact, mean that they are only reactionary or conservative. There are innovative and creative dimensions to these discourses. A truly comprehensive study of migrant culture would need, therefore, to go beyond migrant literary texts, such as those by Naipaul and Rushdie, to examine a wider range of textual interventions, including those articulated by migrant-settlers in a religious idiom, as these are played out in the West.

REFERENCES

Appadurai, Arjun (1986) 'Theory in Anthropology: Center and Periphery'. *Comparative Studies in Society and History* 28: 356–61.
Asad, Talal (1993) *Genealogies of Religion*. Baltimore, MD: Johns Hopkins University Press.
Bhabha, Homi (1994) *The Location of Culture*. London: Routledge.
Braidotti, Rosi (1993) 'Nomads in a Transformed Europe: Figurations for an Alternative Consciousness', in Ria Lavrijsen (ed.) *Cultural Diversity in the Arts*. Amsterdam: Royal Tropical Institute.

Clifford, James (1992) 'Travelling Cultures', in Lawrence Grossberg, Tony Nelson and Paula Treichler (eds) *Cultural Studies*. New York: Routledge: 96–116.

Fischer, Michael and Mehdi Abedi (1990) *Debating Muslims: Cultural Dialogues in Postmodernity and Tradition*. Madison, WI: University of Wisconsin Press.

Hall, Stuart (1992) 'Cultural Studies and Its Theoretical Legacies', in Lawrence Grossberg, Tony Nelson and Paula Treichler (eds) *Cultural Studies*. New York: Routledge: 277–86.

Naipaul, V.S. (1987) *The Enigma of Arrival: A Novel*. Harmondsworth: Viking.

Rushdie, Salman (1988) *The Satanic Verses*. Harmondsworth: Viking.

Schlesinger, Arthur (1992) *The Disuniting of America: Reflections on a Multicultural Society*. New York: W.W. Norton.

Suleri, Sara (1992) *The Rhetoric of English India*, Chicago: University of Chicago Press.

Williams, Raymond (1960) *Culture and Society 1780–1950*. London: Penguin.

Weldon, Fay (1989) *Sacred Cows*. London: Chatto & Windus.

Werbner, Pnina (1996) 'Allegories of Sacred Imperfection: Margin, Hermeneutics and Passion in the Satanic Verses'. *Current Anthropology* 37: S55–S86.

7

ADORNO AT WOMAD:
SOUTH ASIAN CROSSOVERS AND THE
LIMITS OF HYBRIDITY-TALK

John Hutnyk

The more total society becomes, the greater the reification of the mind and the more paradoxical its effort to escape reification on its own. Even the most extreme consciousness of doom threatens to degenerate into idle chatter. Cultural criticism finds itself faced with the final stage of the dialectic of culture and barbarism. (Adorno 1983: 34)

In his essay 'The Culture Industry Reconsidered', Theodor Adorno writes: 'To take the culture industry as seriously as its unquestioned role demands, means to take it seriously critically, and not to cower in the face of its monopolistic character' (Adorno 1991: 88). Thus, while he recognised that 'culture now impresses the same stamp on everything' (Adorno and Horkheimer 1979: 120), Adorno also saw that the standardisation of mass products had even to 'standardise the claim of each one [product] to be irreplaceably unique' (Adorno 1991: 68). These were, however, 'fictitiously individual nuances' (ibid.: 35), examples of the rule of the 'iron grip of rigidity despite the ostentatious appearance of dynamism' (ibid.: 62). Today the multiplication of differences has become repetitive to the point where diversity and difference as commodities seem to offer only more and more of the same. In this chapter I consider this claim in the light of the rise to popularity of 'World Music', in order to evaluate the current vogue for hybridity in culture commentary.

Paul Gilroy writes that the 'hybridity which is formally intrinsic to hip-hop has not been able to prevent that style from being used as an especially potent sign and symbol of racial authenticity' (Gilroy 1993a: 107). In 'so called World Music', he suggests, 'authenticity enhances the appeal of selected cultural commodities and has become an important element in the mechanism of the mode of racialisation necessary to making non-European and non-American musics acceptable items in an expanded pop market' (ibid.: 99). There seems, at first glance, to be a possible convergence here between the critiques of Adorno and Gilroy. The commodification of Black musics proceeds by way of a racialisation that has long been a part of the marketing of Black musics such as jazz, disco and rap to white, Euro-American audiences. Gilroy adds that this has also served as a means of presenting identities for self-confirmation and internalisation to Black communities themselves. If pointing to the artifice of this is 'not enough', as Gilroy suggests, then neither is just dispensing with 'authenticity' debates in order to unblock 'critical theorising' of much consequence either. The point is to take this another step further into a critique of cultural production. But this commodification in cultural production is also something in which we are complicit. For me this complicity begins with attendance as a spectator consuming cultural 'difference' at Womad.

WOMAD

Womad Music Festival, Reading 1994, Adelaide 1994, Morecambe 1995 – huge events no longer confined to llama-wool jumper, bicycle-camping, tea-head greenie hippies and weekend travellers on weekends without a rave, but now successfully drawing in a cross-section of people not immediately or easily consigned to niche-marketing categories. Even with the grab-bag categories it is difficult to specify the world music audience today – beyond the generalities of middle-class (it's expensive to get in), youngish (predominantly below 40) and Western (unlike most specific music genres, say rock or Bhangra, there is no obvious disproportionate cultural or racial audience mix *vis-à-vis* proportional representation in, for example, the UK. Indeed, Womad audiences are significantly diverse). After more than ten years, the product recognition of Womad and the category of world music may not have achieved music industry dominance, but it has captured a significant, and growing, slice of the industry. Bands and musicians from every corner of the world are brought to Europe – on occasion, Australia or Japan – to perform for appreciative audiences. Womad is interesting as a site for the playing out of capitalist cultural production at both ideological and economic registers. The commercialisation of music and the evacuation of politics at such events deserves comment and goes hand in hand (in a pastoral, folksy, face-to-face sense) with an aversion to the technological (or a pastoralising of it) and an absolutist and authentic singularism (not always nationalist) which needs to be unpacked.

World Music has come to be considered by the music industry – its commercial production and promotional arms – as a potentially profitable, and so exciting, expansive and popular way forward in contemporary music. There has been little critical work produced on any aspect of this development at a time when what is required is a multi-perspectival examination of the World Music phenomenon, ranging from a critique of the concepts and terminologies deployed, through the employment practices, marketing of 'Ethnic Identities', commercialisation, and so on, to the attempts at explicit politicisation of Womad audiences by disparate political groupings.

A multi-perspective approach to Womad would enable a focus upon World Music as a kind of commercial aural travel-consumption, where the festival, with its collections of 'representative' musicians, assembled from 'remote' corners of the world, is a (very) late-twentieth-century version of the Great Exhibitions of the nineteenth century. Womad gatherings have for the past decade offered musical 'multiculture' sampled according to the ethnic marketing categories which pass for intercultural relations today. The theoretical importance of an investigation of this would be in the conjuncture of local studies in a global context, addressing the potential for cultural creativity and political activist work within an international media economy. Here I take the first steps towards a study of South Asian music in Britain, as seen in such a context of the World Music phenomenon and the more general commercialisation of the music industry, in order to evaluate present theoretical and critical tools for cultural research.

Although there is space within the Womad ensemble for more 'traditional' forms of South Asian music, such as Bhangra or Qawwali, in the UK today it is post-Bhangra performers who are in the ascendant within the Asian popular music scene. These performers do not all trace their musical heritage back to this popular form of rural Punjabi harvest dance music. Womad is a venue for several different but complementary forms of Asian-influenced musical production, ranging from folk Bhangra to urban punk jungle sounds, yet they can all easily fall into a traditionalism mitigated only by an eclectic global sampling. A comment from Man-tu, one of the Nepali mask-wearing members of the 'trip-hop' band Transglobal Underground, illustrates this: 'World music for me is anything from "Headbutt" [a band which uses bass players, fire extinguishers and shopping trolleys] to Dimi Mint Abba. The term has been misused to refer to anything liked by old hippies in sandals, but to me, it's a street level-vibe.' Natasha Atlas, the front person for Transglobal, wanted to distance World Music from terms like 'traditional', which were 'corny' and 'an imitation of something that belongs in the past'. Yet much of the Womad festival attraction relies exactly upon this 'traditionalism' (or 'primitivism': Hesmondhalgh 1995), placed alongside more explicitly 'contemporary' crossover acts like Transglobal, to sell its global package. (Hesmondhalgh notes a bevy of terms: radical global pop, global techno, ethnic techno, ethno-trance, tribal dance, world house and world dance fusion – his preferred choice – to describe Transglobal Underground). Womad's more explicitly crossover acts often come from the UK, but there is an unacknowledged hierarchy factored into the preferred Womad mix – not too much old style, not too much crossover: what some would call easy listening.

It is through Womad or similar festivals that Asian musics in Britain gain 'mainstream' exposure. Without these events it is likely that the only known Asian performers would be Apache Indian and Sonya Aurora Madan from the indie band Echobelly. Womad brings acts to Britain that would otherwise not be seen, and in this sense it serves a progressive and explorative, innovative role unlike any other organisation in the UK. It achieves this, according to Natasha Atlas, because 'the world is getting smaller'. Hence Atlas wants the music of Transglobal to 'cross over to as many cultures as possible'. Crossover. One of the first impressions of Reading I have is that audiences today are largely uncritical of World Music. On the whole there is a lack of embarrassment or irony in the face of what must be a largely incomprehensible exchange. However much Qawwals, or Bhangra, or whatever, can be described as being able to cross over, it is stretching the notion of the universal language of music and rhythm a little to think that there are no lacunae here.

Surely there is something more to it than intercultural harmony, and surely there are contradictions which might evoke consideration of the politics of difference? How is it that white British performers can wear Nepalese masks on stage, abstracted from their social and cultural context, without critical comment? Such a global sampling has come to be accepted as 'normal', as a part of the benefit of global communications, as a consequence of a 'smaller world', and as something that mass audiences can comfortably appreciate on a sunny weekend (at a reasonable price, where festivals are sponsored by beer corporations). This marked absence of any audience anxiety (at least compared to the anxiety for authenticity of anthropologists and ethnomusicologists) is particularly perplexing at a time of increased awareness of the politics of music in Britain since the introduction of the 1994 Criminal Justice Act and its legislative banning of 'rave' music festivals at which 'music characterised by a succession of repetitive beats' is played (CJA, 50.1; see Sharma, Hutnyk and Sharma 1996).

Womad festival in Reading in 1994 offered the commercialisation of everything: stalls set up in a circle around the perimeter of the festival site sold a smorgasbord of multicultural fast foods (rapid ethnicities of the gullet), political persuasions – from aid for Indian wells to petitions for Tibet (no organised Left parties), campaigns to defend the cassowary from poachers, to John Pilger speaking tours about Indonesian aggression in East Timor – and Womad merchandise (the Womad CD, the Womad book, magazine, T-shirt, cap), as well as sundry other merchandisers – often barely distinguishable from the stalls and displays for various political causes – selling everything from oriental rugs to brass coffee-pots, jewellery, candles, incense, anarcho and techno small-label recordings, and even a weird drumming puppet rhino 'drumming up' support to save soon-to-be-extinct species.

It should not be thought that I am hostile, or mocking attempts to raise awareness about the plight of various mammals designated as aphrodisiacs, meat or game in less liberal cosmologies, nor that the campaign to expose Indonesian military atrocities, as funded, supplied and alibied by Western governments, is without urgency. The problem is that there seemed to be some point of connection and organisation missing in this context, and inappropriate 'appropriations' and half-understood orientations seemed more the norm, despite the best of intentions. No one seemed too embarrassed at the irregular dancing of the waif-like hippie woman spiralling trance-circle-ly in sexy rapture in front of the devotional Islamic Qawwals of Hussain and Party; at the same time, no one seemed to want to join in with her, despite her exhortations to the crowd to 'get up and dance'. The importance of this performance for Hussain and Party, however, is a possible recording contract with Womad's Real World label, and an appreciative audience of Western buyers (a segment of the market not to be ignored). The Bauls of Bengal attracted a similarly curious and appreciative audience – a most cynical understanding of the audience–performance relation here would assess performances only on the criterion of whether or not the crowd can tap their feet and sway to a rhythm. I am particularly interested, and anxious, about the appropriations, and questions of appropriate behaviour, in such a scene where authenticity operates through incomprehension and fracture of context.

Real World record company marketing of essential exoticas is the staple commercial angle of Womad. Working for Real World can be no easy task for the A and R reps and design-wallahs, because of quite inconsistent and differing demarcations of the authentic, and the complications arising from having multiple 'national' musical traditions – so that Bauls of Bengal occupy a genre which sits uneasily alongside Qawwali and UK Asian rap, and no clear-cut resolution into traditional and modern is plausible (not even the 'traditional' classical Indian forms are so neatly traditional in this context). Womad seems to maintain a form of nationalist cultural essentialism that must remain blind to the inconsistencies of its own designations. At this time crossover articulates as 'world music', which in white hands often also loses its political edge. Yet Gilroy also suggests that in the late 1970s it was the reggae of Bob Marley which provided a crossover music able to articulate a critique of colonialism and repression, and which gave young audiences in England a chance to 'make sense of their lives in post-imperial Britain' (Gilroy 1987: 171).

Gilroy suggests that the possibility for some UK post-punk and ska bands to take up this crossover work was short-lived, but perhaps this deserves more careful consideration. The influence of (small) initiatives, such as Public Image Ltd, continues to percolate throughout the scene in the 1990s in diverse forms such as techno, dub, jungle and trip-hop. Understandably, in the context of a book written during the first half of the 1980s, Gilroy seems bitter at the loss of up-front crossover, which gave way, after Marley's death, to 'a new wave of post-punk white reggae musicians' (Gilroy 1987: 171). He directs his barbs elegantly at a target symbolically appropriate for all that came with the election of a Conservative government in Britain – The Police:

> The best known of these [white reggae bands] inverted the preconceptions of Rasta by calling themselves The Police and armed with 'Aryan' good looks and dedication to 'Regatta de Blanc' served, within pop culture at least, to detach reggae from its historic association with the Africans of the Caribbean and their British descendants. (Gilroy 1987: 171)

Whether or not The Police can be held responsible for this disarticulation (William Burroughs was once at an awards ceremony where he was introduced to members of the band; later he quietly advised friends that if they were 'holding any drugs they ought to stash it quick', because he'd 'just found out that those guys over there were cops'), there was a period in which white musical hegemony again asserted itself through appropriation of non-European rhythms. The long tradition of appropriation reaches back to before even the early Beatles and Rolling Stones began playing that devil Negro music unashamed. Nevertheless, whatever the antics of Jagger and Richards & Co., there is reason to think that the protest politics of reggae and punk were not lost for ever in the bland of The Police, and indeed returned with hip-hop, house and techno in another cycle in the late 1980s and early 1990s. Whether or not this is encouraged or corralled on the Womad stage is another matter altogether.

In asking questions about how certain forms of music come to be designated and promoted as 'world music', it is necessary to provide a critique of a number of institutional levels at work conjointly: (a) the commercial manufacture of the genre 'world music' and commercial considerations within the mainstream music industry; (b) the parochialism and biases of the 'mainstream' music industry and its public; (c) the influence of certain individual entrepreneurs, Western or not, with a 'foot in the door' of the music industry; (d) notions of tradition and authenticity, as maintained by the media, and often deployed by 'world' artists themselves; (e) the wider context of international politics, market forces and imperial relations; (f) exoticism, New-Age-ism, the tree-fet-ish lifestyle-hippiedom and feral/folk market opportunism which pro-vides cottage-capitalist support for the 'Womad' sector; (g) cyclical media ethnic feeding frenzy, lack of interesting rock-and-roll, we'll-try-anything-once experimentalism, commodification of everything, and so on; (h) technological development, in the music industry and in communica-tions and transportation, facilitating the performance of those from fara-way locations, their recordings distributed worldwide, their images beamed globally via satellite television.

The political task of a reading of Womad at Reading might include attempts to ascertain levels of educational and organisational impact, against commercial gain and consumption of target audience. The possi-bility of identifying what could be called 'cottage capitalism' throughout the Womad ensemble is real – punters browse past tent-stores and cam-paign tables as they would past display windows in shopping malls. Music from the corners of the world is provided as unique entertainment in the same way as food or clothes work like wallpaper, in endless aural, visual or tasty simulacra. What sort of coherence might be found in the different politics on the display tables remains unclear: some sign a petition or buy a badge to wear upon their lapel, or a scarf or a funny hat. Many more buy funny hats – and express an 'alternative' appearance and a well-cultivated grunge fashion (several varieties thereof). Honest and intense activist commitment also coincides with such lifestyle shop-ping. It could seem that the struggle of musicians and artists from the South to be heard amid this din offers a metaphor for the cacophony of all world struggles drowned out in the on-the-spot reporting of CNN World News – on screen, but not heard.

CNN's reports on Womad 1994 stressed little of the grass-roots politics and made much of the most 'exotic' of the musicians – Hassain Qawwals were shown in detail, with the requisite CNN correspondent speaking over the top of their image. The reporter celebrated Womad as an example of human harmony and togetherness, and the tone was one of tribute to the organisers and the people who attended. The one non-musical aspect of the event mentioned was an aid collection for hospital-ised children in Bosnia. Such liberal music politics and Womad's breadth, from CNN Bosnia relief to cassowary campaigns, has been noted before: 'It is more than a coincidence that the development of charity rock, with its primary focus on Africa [Band Aid, Live Aid, etc.], paralleled the emergence of "world beat", a marketing category dominated by African and African-influenced sounds' (Garafalo 1994: 286).

What this restricted and edited marketing of 'oppositional' cultures does is to bring contradictory impulses into the happy relationship of a capitalism that can sell – and usually neutralise – everything under the sign of value. Everything can be equated to everything else (the beat of authenticity stimulates the rhythm of charity). The efforts of intel-lectuals to facilitate the entry of marginal discourses, like Black musics, into the commercial and public sphere are fraught with exactly this contradiction – one that is shared with both the impulse to charity and the sponsorship of the State, and of CNN itself. Despite all good in-tentions, the consequences are often inevitably incorporation and co-option because there has been no disruption of the overarching system. Another aspect of this double-play is taken up later in this chapter, where I argue that Gilroy overstates the role of performance in his analysis of Black cultural forms (Gilroy 1993a: 75). While his enunciative stress is quite sound against textual narratives, it seems less useful to let this displace attention to mediatised forms of articulation and the role of the technological.

The problem of the privilege of live performance is complicated, since it is often acknowledged that tele-technological flows (of which CNN is part) are essential to Womad's commerical success. Artists do, of course, want to sell their products. A complicated choice is marked out for any evaluation of World Music by – to take one possible formulation of the parameters of this debate among many – Wallis and Malm (1990), who (excerpted in the collection *On Record*) note first of all that:

> Music industry technology has found its way, in a very short time, into every corner of the earth. Both software and hardware can be found in even the remotest village in every country, irrespective of social or economic system. No other technology has penetrated society so quickly – what is more the rate of penetration appears to be accelerating ... [so that we also now see that a] transnational form of nationless culture develops. Through a process of integra-tion and concentration.... At the same time, the amount of music in our

environment has increased to such a level that, even if a saturation point has not been reached, it is getting harder to experience silence! (Wallis and Malm 1990: 161)

They also hold out optimistically against the transnationalization of culture, because:

> This scenario, however bleak it might appear at superficial glance, is not entirely negative. The sound cassette [for example] has given thousands of people the opportunity to hear more music. To a certain extent users can decide what music they want to hear ... cassettes can even be used for recording the sound of the small peoples themselves. The very accessibility of music industry technology has brought about another common pattern of change, particularly noticeable in smaller cultures. It has provided the prerequisite for a counter-reaction against the transnationalization of music – even if no local music cultures have been totally unaffected by international music products. (Wallis and Malm 1990: 161)

Despite some uneasiness about the propriety of metaphors of 'accelerated rates of penetration' and the rather ridiculous ethnographic recovery project phrasing about 'recording the sound of the small peoples themselves', the two poles here set out opposed uses of music technology: both as a force for the homogenisation of culture, and as an opportunity for resistance and creativity. (Evaluations of the project of a group like Arrested Development, or the still more complicated country music of Aboriginal musicians like the Warumpi Band, might complicate this assessment.) The difference here is between the integration and concentration of the music industry to the point of saturation ['any music may now be heard any time anywhere' (Simon Frith, personal communication)] and the counter-reactive possibilities of the cassette, user choice, and local music cultural resistance to transnationalisation.

These two ends of music technology, and the concomitant imbrication of such technologies with socioeconomic and political questions about the technological expansion of the international market and/or the possibilities for autonomy within or against this, have also exercised many writers, critics, and the practitioners themselves. There is still much to be said today for a critique of technologically rampant capitalist expansion. Although nostalgia sits less easily among wary critics, the music-as-alternative narrative is alive and well. Laments for a pre-industrial music manifest themselves in many ways, not least in the rhetoric of Womad, even at the very moment when it is the technological extension of market economies that is the ground of possibility upon which it is staged. Widespread familiarity with 'Indian' music, from Ravi Shanka at Woodstock to Nusrat Fatah Ali Khan on Real World, would not be possible without this extension. The technologies of capitalist music export Hindi film songs to communities in Britain, Canada, the USA, Australia, Fiji, Mauritius, Malaysia, and so on and so on – it is almost a cliché to mention this.

POPULAR CULTURE

The parameters of a discussion of World Music can be recast in terms derived from the much-maligned Adorno if we take up his comments on popular culture. What is important in Adorno's discussion of the culture industry is his interrogation of the relations between mass culture and capitalist imperatives of profit; he notes that with mass production in the culture industry, 'cultural entities are no longer *also* commodities, they are commodities through and through' (Adorno 1991: 86; emphasis added). This comment, in an essay written to 'reconsider' the culture industry argument, maintains an uncompromising and unpopular position that exposes novelty and difference as illusion and commodity fetish (ibid.: 87). There is a homology between a focus upon the skeleton of sameness behind commodity differences and the critique of 'hybridity' which, along with a questioning of the critic's authority to comment, is offered below.

Scott McQuire argues that Adorno and Horkheimer have been used in much recent media theory as 'convenient whipping posts':

> A quick reference to *Dialectic of Enlightenment* today suffices not only to dismiss it, but also to counterpoint the 'advances' of contemporary theory with its (enlightened) concern with popular culture and audience ethnography. (McQuire 1995: 203)

Singled out for attention is the work of Mark Poster, who refers to Adorno's 'revulsion' for popular culture (ibid.: 203). The litany against Adorno has it that he is motivated by a 'disgust for the common' (Poster 1994: 63), sees no worth in the products of mass media, and sees them as homogenising rather than as potentially democratic (I am paraphrasing here). This is to give 'short shrift' to Adorno, as McQuire notes:

> Even in such a pessimistic text as *Dialectic of Enlightenment*, Adorno and Horkheimer are less monolithic in their analysis than Poster suggests. While frequently scathing towards popular culture, they nevertheless grant the culture industry a positive role as the dialectical corrective of 'serious art'. What stalls the dialectic is neither the mass nature nor the technological mediation of the culture industry, but its *gentrification*.... One might well dispute their analysis, but this should not mean simply ignoring their attempt to *relate* these different domains, instead of declaring an absolute preference for one over the other. (McQuire 1995: 204)

Poster fails to understand, McQuire argues, the full significance of his own citation of Adorno and Horkheimer's analysis of 'the twin scourges of the twentieth century': the culture industry and fascism (Poster 1994: 57) – or, in McQuire's gloss, of 'Hollywood and Hitler' – not that Hollywood was fascist but, rather, that it is a mistake to think that fascism was 'simply an exception to the political culture and the political rationality of modernity' (McQuire 1995: 205). Such a discussion plays out across the all-too-easy acceptance of a strict opposition and incompatibility between democracy and fascism, and leads to serious errors 'when relating social and political transformations to transformations in technologies of representation and communication' (McQuire 1995: 205).

The standard reference here is to Hitler's statement that the National Socialists would never have conquered Germany in 1933 without the loudspeaker. Interestingly, Adorno and Horkheimer note that it was by disseminating certain buzzwords like, say, 'Blitzkrieg', that the power of this loudspeaker was brought to people's attention on both sides. They add: 'The blind and rapidly spreading repetition of words with special designations links advertising with the totalitarian watchword' (Adorno and Horkheimer 1979: 165). The point here is that debate about technological change and the music industry's homogenising effects are not simply consequences of cassette availability, of hardware and software, but parameters that need to be placed in political context.

There are reasons to be less sympathetic where Adorno gets denunciative of jazz as a 'cult of the machine', which 'necessarily implies a renunciation of one's own human feelings and at the same time a fetishism of the machine such that its instrumental character becomes obscured thereby' (Adorno 1990: 313). But what is denounced here is not the machine *per se*, but the subjugation of human feeling to instrumental ends. There are, conceivably, other possible instrumental uses for these machines, but it is the domination of the commodity system of the culture industry that is prominent here. Adorno is not denouncing machines or culture but, rather, capitalist production – Poster conflates these.

This conflation is not only a fault of apolitical postmodernists. Reception of Adorno is skewed on all sides, and seems to exact a damning punishment for the presumption of calling entertainment and commodity desire to account – even those arbiters of critical theory fashion who should have been comrades appear keen to dissuade close attention to the specificity of his critique. Jürgen Habermas warns that Adorno and Horkheimer were too Nietzschean (Habermas 1987: 120); translators such as Ashton elide Adorno's Marxism and references to communist co-thinkers from the English version of his *Negative Dialectic* (reading 'exchange system' as 'barter' and turning Adorno's rival Karl Korsch into something of a non-person); and even Fredric Jameson, in his study of Adorno called *Late Marxism* (1990), wants to reconstruct him as an avatar for postmodern times.

By contrast, Robert Young points out (Young 1995: 30) that Adorno's understanding of the relation between high art and popular culture is more complicated; both coexist in a dialectic,

> both bear the stigmata of capitalism, both contain elements of change ... both are torn halves of an integral freedom, to which however they do not add up. It would be romantic to sacrifice one to the other. (Adorno *et al.* 1977: 123; Adorno's letter to Benjamin, quoted in Young 1995: 30)

It may also be a kind of idealism to think that the adding together of these two, plus the removal of the stigmata of capitalism, would bring 'freedom'; but, as with Lukács's notion of free creativity, it allows an opening for evaluations of cultural production in terms of a movement away from the reification and alienation of human production under capitalism, towards liberation. What cultural life would be like after the abolition of the market cannot be specified in advance, but unlike most discussions of culture, which operate an impossible relativism, here is a perspective that provides at least some criteria for making judgements of the avowed 'cultural politics' and egalitarian popular intent that lie behind the idea of Womad as global musical celebration.

So it is possible to ask in a new way (in old Adorno's way): what is the political achievement of a Womad cultural politics that sees people like Nusrat Fatah Ali Khan and Bally Sagoo collaborating on 'crossover' production for the Asian and Western market to a degree of success that attracts the attention of music industry majors like Columbia Records (who offered Sagoo a £1.2 million deal in 1994)? Much of this is attributable to the visibility of these artists provided by the commercial arm of Womad. Is this a part of a dialectical creation of a space for something 'liberatory' that may escape the dominance of commodity fetish forms? There are those who would valorise the success of Bally Sagoo as the creation of an Asian presence or 'space' within mainstream public culture. Here Sagoo's music itself takes on a fetish character – it offers an abstract or spectacular negation of mainstream music and its racially marked exclusions, but it does so through the capital market itself.

While it is still possible to imagine the oppositional use of certain commodities – and the illegal festivals of the anti-Criminal Justice Bill campaign offer an example – the practical and material negation of the social relations of capitalism requires more than this. Sagoo's 'Asian space' is a space wholly within the commodity system, and is not in any way

a dysfunction or disruption of that system. Such dysfunctions there may
be, and the promotion of Asian underground junglist and 'original nutter'
UK Apache may be an example of a performer less easily accommodated
within the music industry machine, but this, too, is insufficient challenge. The potential for any oppositional politics seems wholly curtailed
under the auspices of Columbia, even though the contract signed with
Sagoo included clauses which, according to the artist, guaranteed against
any compromise on 'Asian' content. This ghettoisation of purity and
authenticity serves only to corral the 'ethnically' marked performer yet
again. The *double entendre*, wherein space claimed for cultural expression
becomes a constricted and restrained space within a wider system, is the
recurrent theme of co-option.

HYBRIDITY-TALK

In this context it is instructive to look towards what contemporary commentators might make of it all. Hybridity, diaspora and post-coloniality
are now fashionable and even marketable terms. The authors who deploy
them as key concepts have become the institutionalised social theory
equivalent of household names (and, like household names, they are
marketed and have a brand recognition that is an advertiser's dream). In
many ways they have broken new ground, and forced reconfigurations
and reappraisals that have enlivened and irrevocably transformed academic
debate. Yet at the same time the transformations introduced seem also to
have left the system intact. The point of taking a critical stance towards
the deployment of these terms is not to insist upon true historical ante-
cedents or debates about strict reference that would, for example, trace
the term 'diaspora' back to Jewish, Armenian, Greek, Indian, Chinese,
African or even Black Atlantic units. The point is to question how these
terms gain contemporary currency in the universities, academies, disciplines, history, publishing, political and social forums where things seem
to carry on as if by remote control. Although we see a championing of
experimentation, creative collage and multiple identities, it could be argued that the new contexts remain conventional: the same routines re-
hearsed, well-known tunes replayed – which is to say that the radical
critiques signified by these celebrated names soon turn oxymoronically
into 'new conventions' of scholarship, and our valorisation of these
critiques sometimes comes to nullify critical thinking itself. The same
old record.

Or – perhaps more confusing yet – the celebration of hybrid cultural
activity promotes a seemingly rampant and chaotic mode of creativity.
This in itself would be no problem if it did not also allow an abdication.

In the context of a valorisation of mix, creole, mulatto and mongrel emergence (these are not *quite* the same things), it sometimes happens that a lesser place is accorded to intentional and targeted forms of politicised cultural production, ignoring both resistance to specific structural and institutional constraints and the almost inevitable hegemonic incorporation of random creativity through diffusion and dispersal of difference and its marketability. In this context the *political* work of a band like Fun^Da^Mental (who are regulars at Womad events) or their label-mates Asian Dub Foundation can be obscured by a focus on the hybrid nature of their productions. Yet hybridity-talk in favour of wild creativity and transnational, interracial, intercultural, hybrid mix could become interesting when it is conjoined to a political programme of the kind that Asian Dub Foundation produces (this is discussed below).

For pseudo-progressive, conservative (multiculturalist) forces, the convenience of this moment is clearly the fun and creativity, even radical cool, of fusion forms. What most often seems to be taken from the critical discourse of hybridity and diaspora are those aspects which repackage and reinscribe difference, juxtaposed exotica (hybrid as exotically mixed) and otherness as marketable categories. This is the appeal of someone like Apache Indian. Interestingly, then, hegemony, despite its homogenising cultural reach, now accommodates (circumscribed and carefully marketed) cultural differences. Difference within the system is the condition and stimulus of the market – this necessarily comes with an illusion of equality, of many differences, and, in the bastardised versions of chaos politics which results, the image is of 'crossed' cultural forms merely competing for a fair share. Among things that are forgotten here is that it is often embourgeoisified groups that can avail themselves even of the space to articulate a demand to go to market. In this respect, hybridity-talk might also be suspected of a collusion with State policy-making in that one of the things it can sometimes be is a call for access – a recognition that certain otherwise marginal, overlooked, or previously excluded activities are now creative cultural practices of enough merit also to attract a small share of Arts Council funding, state subsidy, commercial acclaim and critical attention. It is Bally Sagoo who suggests that the day when a Hindi language song gets to number one in the mainstream charts will be the day Asian music arrives (in Sharma, Hutnyk and Sharma 1996).

Hybridity-talk, creole, and so on, seem to imply a bogus notion of the prior and the pure – pre-hybrid cultures. This is a consequence that is inadequately solved by the insistence that all cultures are hybrid, since this is well and good in theory but is not the case in the face of absolutist and essentialist groupings and ideologies. Common parlance assigns

hybrid cultural production to the – usually ethnic – margin, thus implying a wishful vision of future integration into a supposedly homogeneous
Western culture. For too many, South Asia remains a site of mystery,
aroma, colour and exotica, even when it appears in the midst of Britain.
In highlighting such themes, hybridity-talk obscures the aporias of official multicultural policies, and through inaction, in effect, alibis the
overpolicing of inner-urban Britain, excessive and racist immigration
control, and the continued maintenance of white privilege in education,
the workplace, and the public sphere.

Stuart Hall identifies what he calls 'the end of the innocent notion of
the essential black subject', recognising that a politics of representation
has opened up an important, and on-going, debate. If I read his argument correctly, his most crucial point – and the source of my troubles
with it – declares: 'What is at issue here is the extraordinary diversity of
subjective positions, social experiences and cultural identities which
compose the category "black"; that is, the recognition that "black" is
essentially a politically and culturally constructed category' (Hall 1989;
1995; 1996: 443). It seems to me that this point is as important as it is
banal. Was this really something that was not recognised by all except
the most trenchant dogmatic participants in political struggle? In any
case, what now needs to be debated is whether or not this recognition
of the *constructed*-ness of the category 'black' and its political importance
is any less constructed than any other categories, and if so, what it means
to become less 'innocent' and 'essentialist'. What sort of politics flow
from this? – as Hall also asks.

The recognition of diversity that Homi Bhabha has denounced
(Bhabha 1988) as the relativistic tolerance of exoticising multiculturalism
is not that far away here – it could certainly slide into play in the hands
of some commentators who can see a gain in such usages of anti-
essentialism. Furthermore, the slippage from a critique of an innocent
homogenising politics (how innocent actually is this politics – tempered
as it was, or is, in a common experience of racism?) to a further
essentialising refraction is a real possibility. Sanjay Sharma argues that
political identification with the category Black need not mean that being
different, or Asian, or Afro-Caribbean, or a woman, working-class, or
whatever, is incompatible with such a Black politics (see Sharma 1996).
Nor need the politics of Black dissolve on recognition that not all black
people are the same. It is, as Hall notes, still no easier to 'build those
forms of solidarity and identification which make common struggle and
resistance possible' (Hall 1989). Yet the slippage that would make this
task more difficult would be one that extrapolated negatively from pre-
mature declarations of 'the end of the essential black subject' (ibid.),

taken to mean the end of any Black subject position in politics. This latter need not dissolve so fast.

Hall notes that 'some sectors of the mobile (and mobile-phoned) black youth' have taken advantage of Thatcherism and the Enterprise Culture of 1990s Britain, while 'a particular variant of black cultural politics' which had to do with campaigning, representations and media 'has had its cutting edge blunted in the 1990s' (Hall 1995: 16). This rightward shift, which goes along with the general trend of much cultural 'politics' in Western nations, corresponds to the one aspect of multiculturalism that Hall would applaud: 'the racial and ethnic pluralisation of British culture and social life'. This process is 'going on, unevenly, everywhere', and through television and other media the 'unwelcome message of cultural hybridisation' is being brought into 'the domestic sanctuaries of British living rooms' (ibid.: 18). The same process can also be seen going on in youth culture, where 'black street styles are the cutting edge of the generational style wars' (ibid.: 22).

Hall says that 'black popular culture of the 1990s is more internally differentiated, by locality, neighbourhood, generation, ethnic background, cultural tradition, political outlook, class gradation, gender and sexuality than [older] models allow. It is far less "collectivist" in spirit' (Hall 1995: 16), and there can be no doubt that popular culture can be characterised in this way. But when he refers to those many people who 'are still trying to capture its [the dark side of black popular culture] contradictory diversity within older cultural models, honed mainly in the 1970s' (ibid.: 16), the suggestion that the Black politics of the 1970s is superseded does not escape his declaration that he is not trying to periodise. Diversity is now recognised, and older models were inadequate. But surely this does not necessarily mean abandonment of any 'collectivist' spirit, since one can retain this and still be differentiated, by locality, neighbourhood, generation, ethnic background, cultural tradition, class gradation, gender and sexuality – as if it were ever any different in the 1970s. To imply that the 1970s were marked by only a collectivist Black anti-racism would seem to underplay the political and cultural currents that enabled these differentiations to come to notice in the first place.

Gayatri Spivak says that a critique of hybridity is relevant at the present moment because that which hybridity-talk was useful for (for example, fighting the cultural absolutisms of racism in the First World) now tends to inhibit other, also necessary struggles demarcated differently. She suggests that as hybridity implies at its logical extension the hybridity of everything, this means also that contradictions and struggles that were in a certain way prior to those raised around the term still require urgent attention – imperialism, capitalism, exploitation, oppression. She argues that a negative word from sociobiology, hollowed out and reclaimed, is politically useful as a position from which to question the racism of the culturally dominant. But it is 'troublesome since it assumes there would be something that was not hybrid, or if you were to say that hybridity is everywhere, irreducible, then all of the old problems apply' (Spivak, Keele seminar, 1995).

Hybridity-talk is certainly useful in bringing to attention the ways in which cultural constructions can maintain exclusions. But why talk hybridity now rather than a more explicitly radical language? Another way to state this more bluntly is to ask why some 'post-colonial' discursive efforts seem to do very well at avoiding any discussion of Marxism, or indeed can even be considered an elaborate displacement, a way of keeping Marx out of the academy at a time when a materialist method has never been more relevant. The ways in which hybridity displaces other languages and other ways of seeing, and organising, deserves attention. Young's work suggests that something could be said for taking the meanings of hybridity away from the previous century's 'miscegenation' discourses, but this political project seems too often to have given way to an analysis of textual construction. As with Hall, a pro-hybridity stance does not seem to me to offer any guarantees of a revolutionary project, since the place for articulation of hybridity is also a space which already seems all too easily articulated with the market. Hybridity and difference sell; the market remains intact.

My charge against hybridity is thus that it is a rhetorical cul-de-sac which trivialises Black political activity (organisational achievements, history, and so on) in the UK over the past twenty-five years, diverting attention from the urgency of anti-racist politics in favour of middle-class conservative success stories in the Thatcher-with-a-bindi-spot mould. What this means is that rather than continue to fight for solidarity among anti-racists and anti-imperialists, building upon the histories of those struggles of the 1970s and 1980s, the fashion for hybridity theory takes centre stage. Theorising hybridity becomes, in some cases, an excuse for ignoring sharp organisational questions, enabling a passive and comfortable – if linguistically sophisticated – intellectual quietism.

Despite this, some might have thought that a plausible approach would have attempted to make sense of phenomena like World Music, Womad and the new Asian dance musics via an operationalisation of the term 'hybridity', and hybrid cultural production. To ask if hybridity is helpful in elaborating explanations of World or South Asian musics at the same time would offer a chance to make an evaluation of this recently rehabilitated theoretical construct. However, hybridity is inadequate as a description, let alone an explanation, of these musics, and indeed alibis bad examples in a rerun of cultural relativist unities.

Abandoning the operation of hybridity, it would be a more practical political choice to begin with the terms which practitioners, and their audiences, deploy themselves in explanation of what they are doing. Of course, there are obvious problems with this – for example, the way audiences and critics tend to internalise the commentaries provided by practitioners and offered in the music press by A and R reps and artists. Abandoning the theoretical construct of hybridity, or diaspora, or whatever would never guarantee that the analyst is also without baggage or dependencies. The point here is to commit to this political choice. Thus, beginning with the circumstances and struggle of the people involved at least circumvents any notion that an adequate politics can emerge from having the correct 'theory', as some seem to believe.

TECHNOLOGY AND HYBRIDITY

As with the infrastructural facilitation of World Music festivalism like Womad, one of the lines of argument running through the work of Gilroy, Hall and Bhabha attributes significance to the role of technology in the production of hybrid, post-colonial, diasporic, and so on, consciousness. One way to get more specific about these matters would be to examine critically the recent work of the one writer who is, perhaps, the most prominent purveyor of hybridity-talk, Paul Gilroy. Gilroy notes that 'the musical components of Hip-hop are a hybrid form nurtured by the social relations of the South Bronx where Jamaican sound system culture was transplanted during the 1970s', placed in this local setting in 'conjunction with specific technological innovations' and able to 'flaunt and glory in its own malleability' enough to become 'transnational in character' (Gilroy 1993a: 33). At the same time it becomes 'interpreted as an expression of some authentic African-American essence', sprung 'intact from the entrails of the blues' (ibid.: 34). Questioning the assertive nationalism which seems to close down upon diasporic cultural forms leads Gilroy to see 'embarrassing' similarities in the practice of an essentialist Black elite whose racial politics shares something with the 'pseudo-precise, culturalist equations' of the racist Right (ibid.: 34). The employment of hip-hop as symbol of racial authenticity fits a long tradition which uses music in such a register – that Black people have rhythm is a stereotype found at both ends of the political score.

For Gilroy, an investigation of the 'cultural absolutism' and essentialism that attends controversies over the origins of hip-hop has to proceed through examination of the ways in which exclusivist notions of race, ethnicity and culture operate. What he appears to give less prominence to in his evaluation of hip-hop and Black cultural histories, but which underlies much of the *Black Atlantic* argument, is a promise to reveal the transnational and technological co-ordinates within which these histories and identities are now played out. At the end of the book it is the idea of 'global circulation through the most sophisticated means that technological postmodernity can furnish' (Gilroy 1993a: 194) which exercises his thoughts. More work would be required here, as the promise of the technological remains unfulfilled: hybrids, translations and transnationals do not all circulate in an equivalence or at the same speeds. While Gilroy might well note that 'transnational entertainment corporations unwittingly supply a vehicle for circulating [radical Black, tradition recovering, regenerative, etc.] ideas in the form of black popular music' (ibid.:194), it is also the case that the specific technological processes are left somewhat apart from the more literary and folksy interests and concerns of the book. An excellent formulation summarises work which is yet to be done:

> These means of distribution are capable of dissolving distance and creating new and unpredictable forms of identification and cultural affinity between groups that dwell far apart. (Gilroy 1993a: 194)

These two factors – culture and distance – are crucially important. However, Gilroy carries a strong nostalgia for the face-to-face relations of the local community and the dance hall scene (his continued valorisation of call and response restricted to this context rather than followed into technological mediations would count as evidence). It is not clear why he claims that the 'emergent culture of the black image offers no comparable experience of performance with which to focus the pivotal ethical relationship between performer and crowd, participant and community' (Gilroy 1993a: 203). This means that journals like *Black Film Bulletin*, and even Gilroy's own books, as well as numerous documentary, discursive and other mobile mediating forms, are rendered invisible or transparent as constituent parts of identity formation (although they are all possibly more suited to 'ethical' relations than loud, smoke-filled music clubs and such, however fun).

Sidestepping the more mediatised varieties of cultural production and expression that also form a community, Gilroy presents the performer dissolving into the crowd as his favoured example. It is the antiphonal, the communicative, the storyteller role of the musician and active listening that is characteristic and ubiquitous in the cultures of the African diaspora and which, he suggests, may make up the minimal co-ordinates of what should, perhaps, be reserved for the term 'tradition', in that these make diaspora conversations possible (ibid.: 199–200). He says that the idea for much of the book *Black Atlantic* was conceived while 'watching and taking pleasure in the way that African-American and Caribbean singers would win over London crowds and dissolve the distance and difference that diaspora makes' (ibid.: 201). It might be important to remember that these are not exclusively African pleasures – the translating dissolution of distance certainly has its Asian counterparts, Hussain Qawwals at Womad or at the Bradford Mela, for example (for discussion of this, see Kalra and Kaur 1996).

When Gilroy does get around to mentioning Asian musicians, it is in terms that can be read as somewhat begrudging of Asian creativity and participation, though these cannot be ignored:

> In reinventing their own ethnicity, some of Britain's Asian settlers have also borrowed the sound system culture of the Caribbean and the soul and hip-hop styles of black America, as well as techniques like mixing, scratching, and sampling as part of their invention of a new mode of cultural production and with an identity to match. The popularity of Apache Indian and Bally Sagoo's attempts to fuse Punjabi music and language with reggae music and raggamuffin style raised debates about the authenticity of these hybrid cultural forms to an unprecedented pitch. (Gilroy 1993a: 82)

These words do carry a specific tone: reinvention, borrowed, invention, attempts, debates, authenticity, unprecedented … they are hedging words which would probably not be deployed to explain the same processes accompanying junglist innovations in the UK, so why single out Asian cultural production in this way, if not to dismiss it?

Yet Gilroy's politics are usually fine. He wants to 'invert the relationship between margin and centre' in a 'reconstructive intellectual labour' that examines Black cultural history in a way that has 'a great bearing on ideas of what the West was and is today' (Gilroy 1993a: 45). Where such a project gets bogged down for me is in its aversion to any extended investigation of the new global tele-technological cultural conduits within a context of capitalism-in-crisis that recognises 'culture' over and over as hegemony and product. Cultural difference crossed with the new marketing configurations of another round of technological innovation only furthers the reconversion cycle of capitalist production in ways that could be more clearly spelled out. Gilroy continues to identify areas that would begin this critical work, but he never delivers on the technology side.

This does not mean that his work is not the most suggestive we have in the field, especially where he points to current debates about the relationship between politics and aesthetics, or about science and domination, noting that 'few of these debates operate at the interface of science and aesthetics which is the required starting point of contemporary black cultural expression and the digital technology of its social dissemination and reproduction' (Gilroy 1993a: 77). But while I agree that this is an important point, keeping in mind Adorno's critique of the danger entailed in technological enhancement of the commodity system, I do not understand, then, how or why Gilroy immediately needs to differentiate himself from postmodernist textuality by means of what he calls an 'esoteric' interest in 'fleetingly experienced' Black musical forms – most often signalled in his references again to 'antiphony (call and response)' (ibid.: 78). The textuality he avoids is certainly well worth avoiding, but then I think it is through this esoterica that the project of comprehending tele-technological politics and the science/aesthetics nexus is also jettisoned. The question remains:

> How are we to think critically about artistic products and aesthetic codes which, though they may be traceable back to one distinct location, have been changed either by the passage of time or by their displacement, relocation, or dissemination through networks of communication and cultural exchange? (Gilroy 1993a: 80)

Surely it is defeatist to think that technological mediation poses a threat to those long-standing, nurturing alternative Black public spheres; and in a context where both the ghettoisation of Black cultural production, and its extension into all areas of popular culture via the music industry, seem to be stronger than ever, this nostalgia appears to misconstrue what is going on. What is important is to analyse and evaluate the flows of displacement, dissemination, communication, and the hierarchies and exclusions maintained within the political co-ordinates of diasporic engagement with digital capitalism equivalent media.

It could be suggested that an insistence on cultural particularities like the 'democratic moment enshrined in the practice of antiphony' (Gilroy 1993b: 138), the 'oral character of the cultural settings in which diaspora musics have developed', 'traditions of performance' (Gilroy 1993a: 75), and the dance hall scene entails an anti-absolutism that only produces new essences by default and reaction. Gilroy takes pains to point out that he does not want to present the pre-modern as the anti-modern, nor to 'recover hermetically sealed and culturally absolute racial traditions' (Gilroy 1993a: 223). He is for the 'legitimate value of mutation, hybridity, and intermixture' which 'keep the unstable, profane categories of black political culture open' (ibid.: 223), in preference to a reifying cultural or ethnic absolutism that must be rejected. He does want to evaluate not so much the 'formal attributes of these syncretic expressive cultures' but, rather, the problem of how critical '(anti)aesthetic judgements on them can be made' and 'the place of ethnicity and authenticity within these judgements' (ibid.: 75). Authenticity, however, seems already marked out on a dance hall floor that has stronger roots in Africa and Jamaica than in the experiences of Black politics in the UK. In this context, his comments on antiphony as a shrine to 'new, non-dominating social relationships' (Gilroy 1993b: 138) tends towards a celebration of Africocentric particularity, and ignores other cultural possibilities.

Gilroy's reluctance to work with a notion of Black that includes Asian politics in Britain raises difficulties. Examining what he identifies as a 'retreat from a politically constructed notion of racial solidarity' (Gilroy 1993a: 86) in the context of the tele-technological reach of certain intellectual vanguards might indeed produce a different picture. The alleged 'retreat' asserts a 'compensatory recovery of narrowly ethnic culture and identity' (ibid.: 86), and is most clearly visible for Gilroy in the break-up of the unity of the 'commonality' of racial subordination in the UK (for a contrary narrative, see Housee 1995). For Gilroy, this legacy has dissolved as constituent elements of the previously singularly configured peoples of African, Caribbean and Asian descent 'rejected' the 'unifying notion of an open blackness' in favour of 'more particularistic conceptions of cultural difference' (Gilroy 1993a: 86). In another work he places this dissolution under the signs of hybridity and Bhangra when he notes that 'there are now important signs that ... processes of cultural and linguistic syncretism are beginning to take in "Asian" culture too' (Gilroy 1993b: 61). Setting up a hierarchy and history of hybridities, he prioritises Caribbean and African-American hybridity as 'no longer the exclusive raw material for cultural experimentation and synthesis', and to this prior – and, by implication, original and authentic – mixing he announces the emergence of Bhangra which fuses 'traditional Punjabi and Bengali music with Hip-hop, Soul and House' (ibid.: 61). This description of Bhangra could be contested (it emerged well before anyone started talking about house, concurrently with hip-hop, and in a complicated relationship with soul), but it is in the capacity of these new styles to 'circulate a new sense of what it means to be British' that Gilroy finds 'these latest hybrid forms will contribute ... and take their place' (ibid.: 62).

In 'a system of global communication constituted by flows' (Gilroy 1993a: 80), the list of tele-technological co-ordinates in this hybrid, diasporic, globalised and post-colonial world seems often to stand in the place of analysis – but what does repetition of this mantra add? A lot of gee-whiz apocalyptic tone, but little more than lists. This is nowhere more evident than in, for example, James Clifford's surveying of 'diaspora' that recites, on almost every page, the importance of 'a discourse that is travelling or hybridising in new global conditions' (Clifford 1994: 306). This hybridisation travels across 'transnational connections'; telephone circuits; 'technologies of transport, communication, and labour migration; 'airplanes, telephones, tape cassettes, camcorders' (ibid.: 304); 'business circuits and travel trajectories' (ibid.: 305, 306, 309, 311, 328); and then, with Clifford specifically reading Gilroy, 'Gilroy is preoccupied with ships, phonograph records, sound systems, and all technologies that cross' (ibid.: 316) it goes on, and so on right up to the very last line of the article, where 'global technologies' (ibid.: 328) have still not been unpacked beyond this listing.

The question to be asked is whether or not we are in a position to describe and evaluate, not just list, some of these global technological processes. The telematic mantra – of information flow, new media, travelling culture and the internet – is construed as a metonymic list which synecdochically signals both progress and change. Theorists of telematics repeatedly tell us that an intensification, an abstraction and a speeding up of capitalism, financial flows, media, and so on, are the defining characteristics of the current period. Is there really this intensification? A speeding up? How, in the very late twentieth century, might the relative and abstract speeds of capitalism be evaluated? How is this related to processes of cultural hybridity? Is capitalism hybrid now?

MUSICAL ALLIANCES

Does hybridity suggest a political programme? Why has the term achieved such visibility, if not because of its very tameness? Is crossover a marketing niche? Does participation in Womad, or on MTV, entail a sell-out, a betrayal of community and roots, a dalliance with destruction? Aren't cultural producers sometimes both far more politically conservative and market-orientated than hybridity-talk would admit? And aren't some cultural activists far more politically focused, and perhaps even more theoretically astute? *What would a radical hybridity look like?*

This final section presents an introductory discussion of the work of an Asian hip-hop band working in the UK (Asian Dub Foundation) as an example that suggests a way beyond the limits of hybridity-talk as the code for understandings of 'ethnic' popular culture performances. The question to ask here might be something like: does the work of Asian Dub Foundation (ADF) act only as a claim for or defence of a 'cultural' space – in the sense that Gilroy discusses, following Castells, seeing social movements as fragile resistances to domination, not as political programmes? Or is there something in their work which builds alliances across the lines marked out by the critiques of essentialism and absolutism, and which goes beyond hybrid, diasporic, 'world music' politics towards a more 'stable' (Gilroy's term) transnational anti-capitalist, anti-imperialist and, therefore, anti-racist politics? I think so. The task is not only to untangle this politics from hybridity-talk, but also to explicate it in the context of global tele-technological flows.

Questions about the 'hybrid' conditions of production and dissemination/ discussion of Asian musics need to interrogate the media and the forums in which the 'message' of Asian music such as that of Bally Sagoo, Apache Indian and ADF are received: video, television, international satellite, technologies of communication and the ways in which scholarly interest in these technologies rarely moves beyond safe questions about representation. The globalised commercialisation of ethnicity at Womad is an important issue. Is it *post*-colonial? The album, video, music recordings, performances and workshops of ADF escape any easy recuperation into 'world music', hybrid or fusion 'cultural' work, or syncretic post-colonial aesthetics by way of a 'transgressive' assertion of political difference.

In a short video documentary, Smita Malde has shown how ADF emerged from a music technology community workshop in East London. ADF describe their music as neither ethnic, exotic or eclectic (the only E they use is electric – 'Jericho') but, rather, a vehicle for commentary. They are closely involved with anti-racist and self-defence campaigning, especially in East London, and draw on a long tradition of Bengali musical production reaching back to the famous *Joi Bangla, Joi, Joi Karma* formations of the late 1980s and early 1990s (manifest in diverse projects such as music for computer games and anti-Desert Storm/Gulf War agitations). As a part of Nation Records, ADF brings its inner-urban 'dub' consciousness and community activism together in brilliant tunes and sharp lyric lines, all coded around an agitation politics informed by experience and understanding of the multiple oppressions of racism, colonialism and capitalism. They comment on the South Asian presence in Britain: 'We're only here 'cos you were there. Here in England, A global village. Consequences of your global pillage' ('Debris', *Facts and Fictions* 1995).

But ADF is not only about 'conscious lyrics' ('Tu Meri', *Facts and Fictions*), nor only 'Strong Culture', another track title; their work extends to a political programme that asserts the need for new unities and alliances. ADF is visibly and intentionally 'Asian' in identification, *and* involved in Black political groupings (in ways that might be considered 'out of date' by those who want to write obituaries for Black politics). While a focus on hybridity might stop at noting that their video release, *Rebel Warrior*, contains multiple references to, variously, Hindi, Islam, community, and the West, the message extends beyond mere multiplicity. The video, filmed in London, featured schoolyard and campaign scenes that underline an up-front political intent: they point out that confrontation with racist groups cannot be shirked, and requires forces combined to fight. The track is inspired, and celebrates in its chorus, the words of Nizrul Islam's 'Bidrohi', but moves from the Ami Bidrohi of the individual faced with oppression, fighting oppression (*I am the Rebel Warrior*) to combined resistance and a message for all members of the community (A radical fusion ... Unity):

> Repetitive Beats
> beating against your skull
> I'll be striking you down
> to the sound of the war drum
> The doum!
> The doum of the dohl
> taking its toll
> ...
> I am the Rebel Warrior
> I have risen alone
> With my head held high
> I will only rest
> When the cries of the oppressed
> No longer reach the sky
> When the sound of the sword of the oppressor
> No longer rings in battle
> Hear my warcry!
> A radical Fusion
> Strange alliance
> The siren and the flute in unison
> 'Cos that's part of my mission
> To break down division
> Mental compartments
> Psychological prisons
> I'll be sowing the seeds of community
> Accommodating every colour
> every need
> So listen to my message
> And heed my warning
> ...
> Ami Bidrohi! Ami Bidrohi!
> Yes the unity of the Hindu and the Muslim
> Will end your tyranny
> Ami Bidrohi!
>
> ('Rebel Warrior', *Facts and Fictions*, Nation Records 1995)

In this fusion, strange alliance, unity – this combination of the flute and the siren – there is something that would be misrecognised and diminished if it were called hybrid. Hybridity itself stops short of political action, and ADF are well aware of the dangers of such condensations imposed by academic and mainstream categorisations. Yet they recognise the importance of inserting this message into the media flows of MTV, Star TV, pop shows and talkback. Albeit with a cynicism towards the commercial interests of the industry (and its capacity to cannibalise talent), they want to redraw an Asian public culture along explicitly political lines, and in the interests of promoting alliances across differences. This suspicion of the media does not mean cowering before its institutional power, nor merely accepting a proffered space. A similar suspicion of other institutionally authorised makeovers of 'Asian culture' inspires an assertive cultural politics. In another track from *Facts and Fictions*, their most catchy line references just this liberal 'mental prison' that conventional ethnomusicologies, anthro-gazing and social surveillance disciplines operate. In presenting the 'patrons of culture' with 'ethnic' material, they then go further with militant active demands, and they warn the liberals:

> An Asian background
> That's what's reflected
> But this militant vibe
> Ain't what you expected
> With your liberal minds
> You patronise our culture
> Scanning the surface like vultures
> With your tourist mentality
> We're still the natives
> You're multicultural
> But we're anti-racist.
>
> We ain't ethnic, exotic or eclectic...
>
> ('Jericho', *Facts and Fictions*, Nation Records 1995)

Any suggestion that academic work and the constructs it employs are part and parcel of a wider context which includes exploitation, oppression, racism and cultural chauvinism will not be considered new. Multiple differences are catered for (or are reduced to catering at the food stalls of Womad festivals). The danger here is that hybridity and diversity become merely calls for access to the market. Diaspora and transnationalism facilitate circulation and regulation of a global, yet still hierarchical, economy.

Yet within any subsumption of culture into capitalism, the production of escape clauses, nooks and crannies of dissimulation, diversions and dysfunctions offers momentary respites which we should hope to extend, elaborate, valorise – even as so much of this is inevitably absorbed and folded within the factorium (which indeed needs resistances as a kind of motor force). There is in this observation something that goes further than the tainted creativities of hybrid culture studies. Unfixed identities are political; subversion is temporary, alliances are fluid. By new lines of alliance we might refer to those demarcations which are usually accepted and approved, but might be usefully transgressed – the lines that divide music and politics, the white Left and Asian political groups (ADF do this); the lines between Bhangra and post-Bhangra, or between Bhangra and hip-hop, between diaspora and local politics, between technology and tradition, between hybridity and the same. All these are the context in which the politics of *Rebel Warrior* and *Jericho* is part of a resistant social formation generating alliances that remake and renew the possibilities for Left political practice today and (perhaps) grounding differences and knowledges in a political struggle which fosters those lines of escape, new assemblages, wrex mikes, so that these crossed spaces of hybridity and diaspora are open to a politicisation that could blow the complacency of social theory away.

To the extent that Bhangra, jungle, Womad, rave, and even house and techno in clubs, and – very, very maybe – the radical aspects of rock'n'roll, are moments of collective subjectivity resistant or unavailable to commercialisation (and there is nearly always an element, to differing degrees, in each of these forms), these practices can be valorised as counter-hegemonic. Subsequently, these moments suffer the concurrence of entrepreneurialism, industrialisation, bandwagonism, collaboration, opportunism. And the reassertion of hegemonic order is hardly impeded by the almost complete failure on the part of critics and scholars to provide the sort of partisan analysis and vigilance against recuperation to commercialised impoverishment (more or less aided by media filtering and promotion, repressive force, industry priorities and narrow horizons). This is what Adorno called the 'admonitions to be happy voiced in concert by the scientifically epicurean sanatorium-director and the highly-strung propaganda chiefs of the entertainment industry' (Adorno 1974: 38).

In the end it is worth trying to return to Adorno as a way to reconnect capital, hybridity, culture and resistance. Such a return might provide the basis for understanding the cultural politics of hip-hop and the New Asian dance music in the context of the tele-technological formations that Gilroy identifies as important but cannot describe. The key here would be to look at the ways in which the technological facilitates commodification of culture, and also to those who may be capable of offering an oppositional politics. A critique of standardisation, as Adorno presented it fifty years ago, would need to take into account differential production processes and short product runs, just-in-time delivery systems, and niche-marketing strategies, so that the standardisation of everything feared could now be recast in terms of difference and specialisation. Adorno suggests that 'the cult of the new' is 'a rebellion against the fact that there is no longer anything new' (Adorno 1974: 235), since everything is geared towards commodity production.

In a similarly structured 'new' transformation in the sphere of culture, hybridity circulates via tele-technological means (MTV, etc.), carrying the markers of aesthetics and authenticity to forums like Womad, while leaving politics and political differences in the local inner-urban (subcontracting?) enclaves. The ways Womad sanitises difference into so many varied examples of a World Music culture that is everywhere the same fits the scenario Adorno described in the 1950s, when he linked explicitly work practices, and work free time, to the characteristics of commodity culture. Adorno recognises that the culture industry has 'become total – itself a phenomenon of the eversame, from which it promises temporarily to divert people', but this diversion needs to be seen in the context of 'a system where full employment itself has become the ideal', so that 'free time is nothing more than a shadowy continuation of labour' (Adorno 1991: 168–9). Art, for example, becomes only 'one moment of material production' (ibid.: 67), so it is abolished along with conflict, though Adorno suggests that a 'secret omnipresence' of resistance can still be found in the 'romantic deception' of imagining culture outside production. The secret task revealed here would then be to fight for a unity of differences which refuses the show-window limits of cultural authenticity in such hybrid spaces as Womad, since these limits are incompatible with expression of political differences except in so far as these limits are transgressed, and to fight for the expression, and organisational extension, of unity within difference in opposition to capital, *even* in the forums of Womad and telematically transmitted culture.

This current from Adorno might correspond to those thoughts on the constitution of ADF (and other Asian hip-hop bands like Fun^Da^Mental and Hustlers HC) as new assemblages, formations, alliances, or – in a neatly musical metaphor – a new 'composition' of forces refusing commodification and working towards a project of social transformation adequate to the contest with capitalism at this time. The task that remains is to look at how the tele-technological resources used by contemporary activists work; to look to the ways these uses constitute a resistance/refusal in the Adorno sense (rather than simply conceding the 'unwitting' technological facilitation of cultural–political transmission: Gilroy); and to pursue the activist politics of these denizens of 'transl-Asia' (Kalra and Kaur 1996) – not in order to find happy-happy world hybrid forms, but to work for that project of redistributive justice advocated by Old Beardo (Marx) ... [Of course this is just the soundtrack, which is insufficient in itself. Let's dance.]

The duty of the dialectician, as set out here, implies some organisational questions – how an organisational project alongside Adorno would give this critique some kind of grounding; otherwise, this is just a another free-floating intellectual tarot game, ready to be reabsorbed – like our concepts of hybridity, post-colonial and diaspora – back into the culture industry, productive circuits of capitalist culture (studies), Womad stalls, and so on...

In 1967 Adorno wrote: 'Modern bourgeois cultural criticism ... finds a source of comfort in the divorce between "high" and "popular" culture, art and entertainment, knowledge and non-committal *Weltanschauung*' (Adorno 1983: 27). This view of the world seems very happy to identify differences and celebrate multiplicities, but does little in the way of organising political alliances across these differences. It is all well and good to theorise the diaspora, the post-colony and the hybrid; but where this is never interrupted by the necessity of political work, it remains a vote for the status quo. Adorno would name this as the worst of horrors, even in the hands of the best 'dialecticians' (tenured Marxists). To focus on hybridity, and culture, and aesthetic questions, while ignoring (or as an excuse for ignoring) the contextualising conditions in which these phenomena exist (commodity system, political relations, telematics), is to limit rather than extend our project: 'A dialectical theory which is uninterested in culture as a mere epiphenomenon, aids pseudo-culture to run rampant and collaborates in the reproduction of the evil' (ibid.: 28).

NOTE

Thanks to Shirin Housee, Sanjay Sharma and Nikos Papastergiadis for help with the ideas in this chapter, which is based on research funded by the Economic and Social Research Council, UK, as part of a project on 'South Asian Popular Culture: Gender, Generation and Identity' directed by Pnina Werbner. I would also like to thank Laura Turney for editorial work beyond the call of duty, Esther and the Nation crew for music and images, and Simon Frith and Avtar Brah for interventions at just the right time.

REFERENCES

Adorno, Theodor (1973) *Negative Dialectics*. London: Routledge.
Adorno, Theodor (1974 [1951]) *Minima Moralia*. London: Verso.
Adorno, Theodor (1983) *Prisms*. Cambridge, MA: MIT Press.

Adorno, Theodor (1990) 'On Popular Music', in Simon Frith and Andrew Goodwin (eds) *On Record: Rock, Pop, and the Written Word*. London: Routledge: 301–14.

Adorno, Theodor (1991) *The Culture Industry: Selected Essays on Mass Culture*. London: Routledge.

Adorno, Theodor, Walter Benjamin, Ernst Bloch, Bertolt Brecht and Georg Lukács (1977) *Aesthetics and Politics*. London: Verso.

Adorno, Theodor and Max Horkheimer (1979 [1944]) *The Dialectic of Enlightenment*. London: Verso.

Bhabha, Homi K. (1988) 'The Commitment to Theory'. *New Formations* 5: 5–23.

Clifford, James (1994) 'Diasporas'. *Cultural Anthropology* 9, 3: 302–338.

Frith, Simon and Andrew Goodwin (eds) (1990) *On Record: Rock, Pop and the Written Word*. London: Routledge.

Garafalo, L. (1994) 'Culture versus Commerce: The Marketing of Black Popular Music'. *Public Culture* 7, 1: 275–87.

Gilroy, Paul (1987) *There Ain't No Black in the Union Jack*. London: Routledge.

Gilroy, Paul (1993a) *The Black Atlantic: Modernity and Double Consciousness*. London: Routledge.

Gilroy, Paul (1993b) *Small Acts: Thoughts on the Politics of Black Cultures*. London: Serpent's Tail.

Habermas, Jürgen (1987) *The Philosophical Discourse of Modernity*. Cambridge: Polity Press.

Hall, Stuart (1989) 'New Ethnicities', in *Black Film, British Cinema*. ICA Documents 7. London: Institute of Contemporary Arts.

Hall, Stuart (1995) 'Black and White Television', in June Givanni (ed.) *Remote Control: Dilemmas of Black Intervention in British Film and TV*. London: British Film Institute: 13–28.

Hall, Stuart (1996) *Stuart Hall: Critical Dialogues in Cultural Studies*. London: Routledge.

Hesmondhalgh, David (1995) Paper delivered at the International Association for the Study of Popular Music, Glasgow Conference, September.

Housee, Shirin (1995) 'Tales of Trails: From Colonialism to Migrancy'. Paper presented at ICCCR South Asian seminar, Manchester, January.

Jameson, Fredric (1990) *Late Marxism: Adorno, or, The Persistence of the Dialectic*. London: Verso,

Kalra, Virinder and Raminder Kaur (1996) 'New Paths for South Asian Identity and Musical Creativity', in Sanjay Sharma, John Hutnyk and Ashwani Sharma *Dis-Orienting Rhythms: The Politics of the New Asian Dance Music*. London: Zed Books.

McQuire, Scott (1995) 'The Go-for-broke Game of History: The Camera, the Community and the Scene of Politics'. *Arena Journal* 4: 201–27.

Poster, Mark (1994) 'A second Media Age?'. *Arena Journal* 3: 49–91.

Sharma, Sanjay (1993) 'Post Modernism, 'Race' and the Politics of Difference: The Formation of Hybrid South Asian Identities in Britain. Exploring the Emergence and Cultural Politics of a New Asian Dance Music'. M.A. dissertation, Department of Sociology, University of Leeds.

Sharma, Sanjay (1994) 'Who's in the House: The Cultural Politics of the New Asian Dance Music'. Paper presented to the ICCCR South Asia Seminar Series, Manchester, November.

Sharma, Sanjay (1996) 'Noisy Asians or "Asian Noise"?', in Sanjay Sharma, John Hutnyk and Ashwani Sharma (eds) *Dis-Orienting Rhythms: The Politics of the New Asian Dance Music*, London: Zed Books.

Sanjay Sharma, John Hutnyk and Ashwani Sharma (eds) (1996) *Dis-Orienting Rhythms: The Politics of the New Asian Dance Music*. London: Zed Books.

Wallis, Roger and Krister Malm (1990 [1984]) 'Patterns of Change', in Simon Frith, and Andrew Goodwin (eds) *On Record: Rock, Pop, and the Written Word*. London: Routledge: 160-80.

Young, Robert (1995) *Colonial Desire: Hybridity in Theory, Culture and Race*. London: Routledge.

PART TWO

ESSENTIALISM VERSUS HYBRIDITY:
NEGOTIATING DIFFERENCE

8

IS IT SO DIFFICULT TO BE

AN ANTI-RACIST?

Michel Wieviorka

Not so long ago, it was not difficult to distinguish two distinct and opposed discourses in matters of racism – even if the term itself, coined in the interwar years, did not exist. True, at the end of last century in the United States, for example, there were differences of opinion between those who campaigned for, or represented, the cause of Black people – so that William E. DuBois and Booker T. Washington did not defend the same positions; similarly, in France, at the time of the Dreyfus Affair, those who defended Dreyfus were not all of the same mind. Paralleling these differences, considerable variations and internal divisions were evident in the racism or anti-Semitism of the period. But there was a clear distinction between those who supported what was henceforth to be known as anti-racism, on the one hand, and racists and anti-Semites, on the other. (Interesting as this question is, I do not intend here to deal with the question of whether anti-Semitism is a form of racism among others, or whether it is a specific phenomenon that cannot be considered as a subcategory of racism.)

This clear-cut polarity between racists and anti-racists no longer exists, and while it is not difficult to describe recognised, notorious racists or anti-Semites, it must also be admitted that the adjective 'racist' does not refer uniquely to the most blatant and obvious cases. Further still, it is often used to describe people who not only do not consider themselves racist, but also consider that their interlocutors *are* racist – the latter being, however, equally vehement in their rejection of this ascription to themselves. Throughout the world, the old vocabulary of racism has become unacceptable, or almost so. It fuels intense discussions in which those (anti-racists) who are convinced they are acting for a just cause are suspected of the worst prejudices, and anti-racist action is accused, in many cases, of contributing to the very evil it claims to be fighting.

In the United States, a controversy is raging around the verbal restrictions of so-called 'political correctness', the excesses of which should not obscure the fact that it deals with real problems such as multiculturalism and the historical subordination of minority groups (see Barber 1992). Those who think that policies of positive action should be adopted in favour of Black people there are not very far from considering as racist those who plead for broader socialist and welfare policies in the campaign against poverty, a plea constructed as if implying that there was no longer a racism issue in the United States, and that what problems remain are only or mainly social – we shall come back to this point.

In France, since the 1980s and the publication of Pierre-André Taguieff's work (1988), we have seen the development of a critique of anti-racism which began by stressing the drawbacks of anti-racist action, and in particular its inadequacy in the face of contemporary forms of that evil, and then became more radical, at times assuming a passionate and violent tone. It has thus been possible both to say and to write, for example, in the words of Paul Yonnet (1993) – in a book whose ill-concealed Le Penism had repercussions for the publishers, Gallimard, and the journal, *Le Débat*, which sponsored and defended it[1] – that anti-racism is an ideology which has come to the aid of the failing socialist, communist or Marxist ideologues, an instrument manipulated by left-wing actors with no political project; above all, anti-racism has itself been accused of fomenting racism, of precipitating processes leading to the racialisation of society, or exacerbating such processes; of stigmatising people who are not racist with the unacceptable accusation of racism, or restricting to a racial identity individuals who could well invoke quite other identities. The end result of the anti-racists' denunciation of racism, according to the most virulent critics, has been to encourage it, just as the end result of promoting a multicultural society has been to racialise social relations through the construction of groups who define themselves, or are defined, in terms of race.

The present argument has to be understood historically. The 1960s and 1970s were dominated by an anti-racist attitude of suspicion, by the idea that racism had to be hunted down not only in its most obvious and most blatant expressions, but also where it was disguised and concealed in institutional workings; for example, where apparently nobody was racist but the end result was discrimination and segregation (see Carmichael and Hamilton 1967; Friedman 1975: 384–407). The 1980s and, even more so, the 1990s have been dominated by a somewhat different phenomenon, a sort of explosion and dispersal of the problem: racism is said to be everywhere, including among those whose intention it is to combat it; the references are confused while, at the same time, the evil is perceived as gaining ground.

Is it, therefore, so difficult to carry out anti-racist actions? To begin to reply to this question, the best approach is to confront head-on the most sensitive and complex elements in the discussion. We shall consider five of these.

WHAT IS RACISM?

Thirty years ago, the concept of racism did not pose a major problem as such: racism was a way of thinking and acting that referred to the idea of human races, and the differentiation and ranking of groups and individuals in terms of their natural phenotypical or genetic attributes. Racism was in the terminal phase of its classical, biological era. But then the concept exploded, a distinction was made between flagrant and subtle or 'symbolic' racism, institutional racism was discussed and, above all, the idea of cultural racism was developed – sometimes also described as differentialist, or referred to by the term 'neo-racism', or 'new racism' (Wieviorka 1995). At the same time, in current usage, the description 'racist' was used very widely, especially in France, to denounce prejudices or social or generational forms of discrimination (e.g. anti-worker racism, anti-women racism, anti-young people racism, anti-old people racism, etc.).[2] And those who could be suspected or accused of racism began to reverse the accusation or suspicion, as the French experience demonstrates, where even the police, avowed racists, began to speak of 'anti-police racism', and the most radical nationalists denounced the 'anti-French racism' of the socialist Left or the anti-racist movements!

The first task of social science, I believe, is to deconstruct commonsense categories and to set up rigorous analytic concepts in their place. Here, it appears to us that an excessively vague use of the vocabulary of race should be rejected, and that one should resist the extensions which banalise the evil, or remove its specificity, refusing, in consequence, expressions which deform or exaggerate the issues at stake: exploitation of workers, or contempt for and ignorance of old people, however unacceptable, are not 'racisms', and not all expressions of discrimination or segregation are necessarily racist; they may also be social or cultural.

But the fundamental issue posed by the terminology lies in whether it is useful and legitimate to speak of cultural racism (or to use expressions referring to this idea). To speak of cultural racism is to insist on an image of racial difference which is not natural or biological but contained in language, religion, tradition, national origin; it is to stress the fact that for the racist, the culture of the Other, irreconcilable with his own, may constitute a threat to his cultural identity. This poses at least two problems. The first is to comprehend the place of racist fears or hatred when these are articulated against an alien culture. It is not because there are tensions between two cultures that one side or another is racist, and it is not racist to advocate cultural differentialism or relativism, as Claude Lévi-Strauss has argued (see also Friedman, Chapter 5 above). To speak of cultural racism is legitimate if it is being argued that the sources of certain prejudices are cultural, but not if one contends that the definition of 'race' by the racist refers exclusively to cultural characteristics – to customs or religion, for example. To dislike Islam to the point of violence, for example, is racist, if Muslims themselves are constructed as a natural category, and their behaviour, real or imagined, is presented as informed in some way or another by an essence, by innate attributions or an almost genetic cultural heritage.

That contemporary racism should appeal to cultural factors, to the nation, to tradition, to historical or religious identity, and encompass the idea of a natural (or 'racial') substratum, believed by racists to underlie culture, ethnicity and religion, is quite possible, and it is in no way exaggerated in these instances to speak of racism; but we should be careful not to confuse intercultural tensions, abject or violent as they may on occasions be, with racism, which implies, of necessity, an idea of nature. Racism – as we have long known, and as Colette Guillaumin has most eloquently demonstrated (see the discussion in Touraine 1993: 23–41) – is a social construction, a spontaneous or doctrinal representation; in no way can it be based on an external, objective reality of race, even if it is obviously facilitated by a number of – for example – phenotypical characteristics of the racialised group. It is associated with the subjectivity of the actors, and if the latter refer uniquely to nation, religion, traditions and, more generally, to culture, with no references to nature, biology, genetic heritage or blood, it is preferable not to speak of racism.

The second problem posed by the idea of cultural racism is more complex, and demands an incursion into theory. In fact this idea, pushed to the limit, finally differentiates between two sorts of racism. The first, which may be called universalist, postulates essential differences between human races to legitimise prejudices or unequal practices. It is based on a principle of inferiorisation which consists in accepting, and even desiring, the Other within one's own society, but in a position of subordination which enables the latter's exploitation. The second form of racism – cultural or differentialist – believes, by contrast, that the differences between races are the basis for, or lead to, irreconcilable cultural differences, with the result that the culture of the racialised group is perceived to constitute a threat to that of the racialising group. In this perspective, there is no room for the Other within society; he must be kept at a distance, segregated, and in the most extreme cases expelled or eliminated. The distinction between the two modes of racism must be recognised: universalism along with inferiorisation, or differentialisation along with rejection.

But can we deduce from this that each mode forms the basis for a specific type of racism, and that if we pursue this approach even further, we can infer a historical trajectory according to which, in the 1970s, we moved from the first type of racism (that of inferiorisation) to the second (of exclusion)? In fact, I believe not only that we should refuse to go as far as this, but also that we should define racism, in its concrete expressions, as the necessary combination of the two discourses. The discourse based on total inferiorisation is in danger of dissolving problems of racism into the wider problems of domination and social exclusion: hence the main criticism directed at the work of William J. Wilson, for example (Wilson 1977, 1987), is precisely that he declared that for Black Americans in the hyperghetto, racism was declining, and the main problems were now poverty, unemployment, drugs, or urban violence.

A logic of pure differentiation demands that a distance be created between the racialised group and the racialising group, but on this basis attributes to the racialised group a respectable culture, and even tends to suppress the idea of race in relation to it. For example, in research in France a young woman who was vaguely racist complained of the behaviour of Jean-Marie Le Pen, who, according to her, wanted to rid France of its North African immigrants but displayed no hesitation in going to the Maghreb (North Africa) and partying there with the population or the local elites. She had difficulty in accepting a differentialist form of racism, which ceases to be so and accepts differences, even valorising them when the Other is outside the society in which one lives (Wieviorka *et al.* 1992).

Instead of thinking in terms of two racisms, it is therefore preferable to recognise that the phenomenon exists to any appreciable extent only where there is an association of these two main strategies, whose unique combination depends on the specificities of experience, the historical moment and individual preference. South African apartheid long advocated a balance between these two approaches, combining both exploitation and segregation. Nazism was dominated by a differentialist approach, but continually subordinated and exploited Jews, even and including during the very last phases of the 'final solution'. And − to take a final example – several countries in Western Europe, France first and foremost, experienced a period of economic growth during which racism was primarily a strategy legitimising the exploitation of immigrant labour, followed by a new period in which differentialist attitudes tended to dominate, but never acquired a monopoly position.

Let us draw a practical consequence from this statement: if racism is never pure differentialism or pure universalism and inferiorisation, anti-racist action must also learn how to combine countervailing strategies to combat these two approaches by recognising the cultural bases upon which fear or hatred of the Other is constructed. But it must also take into account the social problems which exacerbate these fears – exclusion, frustration or downward social mobility; poverty, unemployment; the social interests of the better-off – all of which encourage the adoption of strategies of social and racial segregation.

IS RACISM ON THE INCREASE?

Robert Miles (1994) quite rightly protests against the weakness of arguments and declarations that we are witnessing a dangerous rise of racism and fascism – of a kind paralleling pre-World War II extreme right-wing movements – in Western Europe. It is true that, overall, the evidence which accompanies these statements is extremely fragile. This is why the criticism cited above – which is, moreover, a classical form of anti-anti-racist criticism – may consist in suggesting that the perspective be reversed: that those who say that racism is increasing tell us more, or invite us to learn more, about themselves than about the phenomenon they refer to.

In France, for example, where the Jewish population has undergone an immense change since the end of the 1960s, it is common to hear Jews referring to the rise of anti-Semitism, and we have seen people mobilising on this basis in mass street demonstrations, in particular at the time of the attacks in the rue Copernic (1980) and the rue des Rosiers (1982), and following the subsequent desecration of the Jewish cemetery in Carpentras (see Wieviorka and Wolton 1987; Wieviorka 1988). But – contrary to the predictions of the vast majority of French Jews – it emerged that the two attacks were perpetrated by Middle Eastern terrorist groups, not by French extreme Right anti-Semitic groups; the desecration in Carpentras has never, at least officially, been cleared up; the way in which Jews reacted to what they interpreted as a rise of anti-Semitism demands some consideration of the way in which they function as a community and of the evolution of the French Jewish community, to explain how it constructs its representation of French

society. On the other hand, it is also an invitation to a deeper consideration of the tools which enable us to measure a phenomenon like anti-
Semitism seriously.

We could continue along these lines here by developing a critique of
representations of the postwar rise of racism in Western Europe. For
example, do opinion polls finding that people questioned admit to being
more racist than in the past tell us about racism, or about the degree of
openness with which people express their attitudes? Do they tell us that
people are more racist today than they were yesterday, or that they are
less hesitant than they were yesterday about giving public expression to
their prejudices? Any explanation probably has to articulate these two
hypotheses. Or, yet again, if statistics show an increase in racist violence,
do they prove that there has been an actual rise in this type of violence,
or provide evidence of a new, totally different phenomenon, and perhaps
even the reverse: of a deliberate desire on the part of the police or racial
victims of violence to make visible and public incidents which were left
unmentioned before – because they were considered banal and tolerable
forms of behaviour; or because political powers exerted no pressure in
this direction on the police; or because the victims knew that it was not
only useless but, perhaps, dangerous for them to appeal to justice or to
the police? As Miles recalls, since Durkheim and his well-known analysis
of suicide, we have learnt not to confuse statistics with the reality of the
phenomenon they claim to be dealing with, and we know that the
figures which indicate a rise in racism may even denote the opposite of
what they suggest: if racial violence seems to be on the rise, is it not
because it is noted as soon as it appears on the scene, recorded, denounced and no longer ignored? Is it not because it is now opposed?

In fact, Miles does not deny the sharp rise in the number of incidents
of racial violence in Western Europe. The statistics from Britain, for
example, are so bad as to beggar any scepticism on this point. Even
given higher rates of reporting and identification of crimes as race-
motivated, there still seems to be a serious rise in such incidents throughout Britain, and the same seems to be true of Germany. What Miles
shows, rightly, is that the institutions of the state and civil society in
Europe are able to mobilise against this violence, legally, politically and
socially, and that they are much stronger than in the past, before World
War II.

All these remarks constitute an appeal for the need to formulate more
appropriate tools for the measurement of racism. This may be a message
to the groups who are victims of racism, who tend spontaneously, just
like those who support them, to amplify the level of threat or of incidents of violence. In some cases it might be more strategic, I suggest, to

be more restrained and objective in making such public statements. A similar criticism can be levelled at the media, which have a tendency, for example, to describe as 'racist' actions that really deserve a different label, or a more complex and refined description.

But let us assume that it is possible to harmonise reliable measuring tools of levels of racism, leaving less room for doubt or uncertainty. The question of estimating the variations in the intensity of racism would nevertheless still not be resolved, for a very simple reason: racism is not expressed in a single and unique fashion, and its concrete expressions are the product of extremely varied combinations of several elementary forms (see Wieviorka 1995, Part II). Now, the development of the elementary forms of racism, in particular contexts, may very well appear to be extremely incoherent. Prejudice, discrimination, segregation, racist doctrines, ideologico-political expressions, and violence do not necessarily have the same time spans, nor the same underlying causes, and may well develop in diametrically opposite directions. How can we speak of the rise or fall of racism if, for example, racial prejudice in public opinion polls is getting stronger, while the statistics for racial violence are clearly on the decrease?

The development of any one of the components of a racist experience does not, therefore, lead to any necessary convergence, a statement that can be formulated otherwise: contrary to an accepted idea, there is no necessary continuity or complementarity between the various elementary forms of racism present within a single experience, or appearing and developing as it evolves. In other words, there is no historical progression according to which – starting with prejudice, for example – we would see racism gradually getting more virulent as it encompasses discrimination and segregation, then grass-roots violence; the next stage would be for the whole of social life to become politicised, while at the same time violence becomes widespread to the point where the State itself becomes racist. In reality, however, the move of racism from infra-politics to politics may well lead to a *decrease* in grass-roots violence, and, conversely, the decline of a racist party may have the paradoxical consequence of precipitating an increase in racist violence – the hypothesis must be made with reference to the national-populist parties, such as the National Front in France and the Northern Leagues in Italy. A complement to this remark is the fact that, contrary to a generally accepted idea, the relation between prejudice and racist actions remains unclear, and is never a foregone conclusion, as Lapiere clearly established in the United States in the interwar period (see Lapiere 1934): one may, indeed, declare publicly that no Asian clients will be admitted to one's hotel or restaurant, while in fact accepting those who come without the slightest difficulty.

Here, also, let us draw the practical consequences from these remarks. We must learn to criticise the information at our disposal, question its pertinence and meaning, while contributing by our demands and our actions to the improvement of the production of knowledge concerning the facts deserving the description 'racist'. We must be careful not to use the adjective 'racist' erroneously, and, by the same token, not to accept passively allegations of this evil. We must recognise that there is no automatic continuity between one elementary form of racism and another, and we must not, for example, infer that anti-Semitic remarks lead directly to the doors of the gas chambers. But, above all, we must realise that the decrease of the evil on one level does not necessarily imply its overall decrease, and that a victory, urgent and necessary as it may be, may very well only constitute the prolegomena to other battles which may turn out to be much more difficult. To put it in concrete terms, using an example which refers to France: we must oppose the National Front, and aim to achieve its political demise. But we must also realise that its decline would probably lead in the long run to the radicalisation of groups and individuals resorting to forms of violence which have to some extent been channelled into political action by this party.

UNIVERSALISM AND DIFFERENTIALISM

There is a structural problem which constantly undermines anti-racist action, and which its protagonists are not always capable of formulating correctly. I refer to the opposition between the contradictory universalist and the differentialist orientations of anti-racist action which are difficult, and perhaps even impossible, to overcome. Racism is capable of amalgamating these two orientations which, as we have just seen, lie at the very heart of its construction. This indicates that racists are not troubled by possible internal contradictions. The specificity of racism is, indeed, its capacity to merge incoherent or heterogeneous affects in a singular hatred of the Other; of wanting, for example, to exploit this hatred and at the same time to eliminate it. But anti-racism cannot function in this way; it does not stand in a perfectly symmetrical relationship to the evil it opposes. It becomes ineffectual and even counterproductive the more it appears to be incoherent and, worse still, incapable of overcoming its contradictions, whereas racism draws its strength from amalgamating the processes it effects.

Universalist anti-racism appeals to reason, the law, the rights of man, citizenship, and equality between individuals. But this orientation, pushed to its limits, implies the refusal to give a public platform to demands emanating from social, cultural, ethnic or self-designated racial groups; it then tends to deny any collective identities that are asserted outside the private sphere, and may even feel threatened by these demands, perceiving them as endangering the legally constituted State or Democracy. As a result, the radical advocates of this orientation are led to condemn those who uphold the right to difference and the recognition of cultural or racial specificities in the public sphere (on this, see Modood, Chapter 9 below). They say that by advocating multiculturalism, we enable groups to represent themselves in public in a way which is not very far from racial, and this leads to the racialisation of social relationships, the exacerbation of interracial shocks and, in the last resort, to the breakdown of public space and democracy.

On the other hand, differentialist anti-racists advocate accepting cultural differences, no matter how small the minority, and consider that it is racist to refuse cultural or racial identities access to the public sphere. There is some truth in their suspicion that, in reality, universalist anti-racists accord legitimacy only to majoritarian representations, and advocate a vision of the world specific to the rulers alone, be they whites, men, or the most powerful nations. Taken to an extreme, such differentialist anti-racism demands that communities be recognised, each with its own unique rules and traditions, and that the demands of each cultural community be given priority over those of the individuals who compose it, and are conceived by differentialists as subordinate to it. This anti-racism considers that those who demand that the laws of the Republic and the legal State have priority over specific customs, or wish only to recognise the rights of individual citizens in the public sphere, are themselves racist.

Presented in this satirical or exaggerated manner, the opposed ideological extremes of anti-racism seem to be organised around an insurmountable contradiction, since any anti-racist position seems to imply its opposite (see Lapeyronnie 1993). And indeed, it is not difficult to find, in several countries, discussions and arguments which can be interpreted in the light of this contradiction: the criticisms and defence by anti-racists of affirmative action in the United States, for example, or the opposed stances of the anti-racists in relation to the Muslim headscarf affair in France, are both illustrations of such anti-racist clashes.

In an imaginary world in which all cultures are homogeneous and distinct from one another, relativism or even ethnocentrism in no way implies the suspicion of racism. But our societies are characterized by the co-presence of many different cultures, and by their fragmentation; cultural differences are produced and reproduced in this context, being subject here and there to ethnicisations and even racialisations which are not necessarily rejected by the members of these groups (see Wieviorka 1993a). Wherever such racialisations are unacceptable, however, this leads to a process of denying, despising or opposing the group. One thus also has to know, as an anti-racist, how to prevent these separate expressions of identity from becoming factors of racial hatred or violence.

This is why rational anti-racism has no choice. It has to navigate between the Scylla of universalism and the Charybdis of differentialism, and to encourage the continual and pragmatic search for an articulation of the two registers. Whether it be a question of public political action, participation in the life of a cultural community or identification with a specific minority identity, anti-racism can avoid defeat (which a liberal train of thought would refer to as the opposite) only by taking as its target the refusal of anything which separates or opposes the universal values of law and reason to the specific values of a given culture. This endeavour may appear theoretically impossible; in fact, experience shows that more often than is believed, it is realistic and efficient (see Wieviorka *et al.* 1992; Wieviorka 1993a; Wieviorka 1993b).

THE SOURCES OF CONTEMPORARY RACISM AND AFFIRMATIVE ACTION

We have stated above that in our opinion racism is the outcome of the association of two main approaches, that of inferiorisation and that of differentiation. This statement can be formulated differently. Indeed, the theme of inferiorisation refers to the presence of the Other in the society in question, and therefore to social relationships of domination or exploitation; whereas the theme of difference refers to the rejection of the Other, and therefore to the idea of the incompatibility of cultures. It is then easy to understand that to speak of a combination of these two discursive strategies is the same as saying that the sources of racism are never purely social, or purely cultural, and that they are always necessarily mixed.

This type of remark enables us, in the first instance, to refute the discussion, still very superficial, which opposes those for whom racism is only a social problem, to be solved through mobilising campaigns against poverty, exclusion or exploitation, or through anti-capitalist struggles (Couper and Martuccelli 1994), against those for whom it is only a cultural problem, linked, for example, to ignorance or slightly exaggerated nationalist sentiments. Racism is at the intersection of these two problems, and the anti-racism which ignores either one or the other would be making a serious mistake.

But is it not reductionist to make a direct connection between racism and its social and cultural causes? Does not the phenomenon have a dynamic and an autonomy of its own? The question is not rhetorical. If racism is a direct product of social and cultural determinations, it could be thought that it could be diminished by acting upon these sources. But while racism may be an autonomous phenomenon, it cannot be stopped by bringing pressure to bear on its causes; it is also necessary to endeavour to stem its dynamic, in particular by administrative measures or regulations that are counteroffensive and not only repressive, that are not restricted to repudiating racist acts but that also, for example, create special opportunities for members of the most deprived minority groups. There is an important discussion here which is taken up by Stephen Steinberg (1993), precisely in relation to the specific dynamic of racism, when he criticises both what he calls the colour-blindness of the Left, on the one hand, and, on the other, the colour-blindness of the Right – the attempt, on the one hand, to stem racism by social policies and, on the other, to confront it with cultural policies. The argument over affirmative action is not only informed by the opposition between universalists and differentialists; it also owes a lot to the opposition between those who think that one should concentrate on attacking racism upstream, at its sources, and those who prioritise a more direct confrontation.

Can we draw any practical consequences from these remarks? Here, considerable caution is advisable. The advocates of direct intervention aimed at countering the inequalities from which the victims of racism suffer – and not only at putting a stop to, or limiting, racial conduct and prejudice – can be considered legitimate, and have a political and intellectual impact, only if they speak in the name of a population which recognises itself in action; in other words, such advocates can function only in a context in which social life is racialised, where groups are willing to define themselves in terms of race, and to demand, on this basis, an end to discrimination and segregation. In this sort of context, more Anglo-Saxon than French, important results can be obtained (see Ezorsky 1991).

But experience demonstrates that it is never the totality of the groups concerned who benefit from affirmative action policy, and that, on the contrary, this type of policy may well introduce internal cleavages in these groups: between the small number who benefit from them, and the remainder who remain deprived. Moreover, many problems are exacerbated or left pending by this type of policy: it often becomes a source of tensions between groups and, in the last resort, it may weaken the institutions that promote such policies, confining communities to definitions that do not correspond to the processes of cultural fragmentation which all groups in our societies are experiencing. By creating a political or an institutional offer, affirmative action policies are an invitation to practices of lobbying in which not all the minorities have comparable resources, and which encourage the emergence of influential individuals who often do not represent much more than themselves. As we saw above, it is difficult to evaluate the intensity of racism seriously: it is even more difficult to evaluate the impact of anti-racist policies. Now, the discussions we have just referred to call for processes of evaluation of the experiments which have been undertaken, and also highlight the actors engaged in the struggle against the evil.

RACISM AND INTEGRATION

In many countries, immigrants are the main victims of racism. They are not the cause but the object, and the idea of a link between their numbers and the intensity of racism is itself questionable. Anti-immigrant racism has been observed in France in places where there are practically no immigrants, if the vote for the National Front is taken as an indication (Mayer and Perrineau 1989), recalling the way in which anti-Semitism can be found without Jews; and at the other extreme, racism may remain limited in situations where there are a considerable number of immigrants.

In situations in which immigrant-origin populations are in the front line whenever the issue of racism arises, the two questions – of immigration and racism – may be merged, or may, by contrast, be kept distinct (Wieviorka 1994). When they are merged, racism and xenophobia are aligned to political positions hostile to immigration, whereas anti-racism is identified with attitudes which are open to immigration, albeit with a measure of tentativeness.

Now, the two issues of racism and immigration call for relatively distinct policies, since racism is a fundamental challenge to the work of the society in question on itself, whereas immigration is a challenge to international relations. Empirically, we see this specificity most clearly where the two issues are relatively distinct because there is a degree of political consensus between the parties in power who are united in opposition to immigration. Racism has more difficulty in rising to the political level in such circumstances than in instances where the political forces adopt different positions. In Great Britain, very little distinguishes the Conservatives from the Labour Party so far as immigration policy is concerned, and while other factors have to be brought to bear on the analysis, this consensus also has to be borne in mind in understanding the tremendous weakness of the racist extreme Right. In France, the Socialist Left is perceived as being favourable to immigration, contrary to the Right, and for the past fifteen years this perception, which is to a large extent unfounded, has constituted a favourable terrain for the National Front.

Infra-political racism is not necessarily less harmful than when the phenomenon is taken over by a party like the National Front, and there is no obvious reason for the British model of anti-racism to be preferable to the French. But it is clear that distinguishing the political discussion on immigration from the question of racism should be encouraged. Indeed, this avoids confusion, and enables the anti-racist actors to concentrate on their object, rather than to get involved in discussions and conflicts which blur the perspective. It releases the question of racism from the setting of immigration, revealing the former while eliminating the latter. To put it bluntly: anything which reinforces the analytical and political distinction between racism and other problems, beginning with immigration, creates favourable conditions for anti-racist action, which may otherwise become bogged down or lose its way down paths where it loses track of the specificity of the issues at stake.

Anti-racist action is therefore faced with fundamental structural difficulties and theoretical problems. It cannot be satisfied either with the easy conscience that moralising speeches or expressions of goodwill induce, or with the idea that racism, which has no scientific basis, ought to decrease with education or with the forward march óf reason. It is at the mercy of all sorts of tendencies and exaggerations, and constantly runs the risk of being inefficient or counterproductive. But what is true for anti-racism is just as true for any collective action, and those who complacently stress the negative effects or the failures of anti-racism are purists whose criticisms, no matter how well-founded they may be, usually hide a refusal or an incapacity to become involved. The criticism of anti-racism is healthy if it is conducted with the aim of enhancing the capacity for action of participants in the intellectual or practical struggle against racism. It must, however, be eliminated if it expresses a nihilism or radical scepticism which amounts to deserting the terrain and leaving it to the forces of evil alone.

Translated by Kristin Couper

NOTES

1. On this controversy, see *Le Débat* 75, May–August 1993.
2. In English, of course, we speak of elitism, sexism, agism, rather than appending the term 'racism' to 'youth', 'age', 'sex', etc. – *Ed.*

REFERENCES

Barber, Benjamin (1992) *An Aristocracy of Everyone: The Politics of Education and the Fortune of America.* New York: Ballantine.

Carmichael, Stokely and Charles Hamilton (1967) *Black Power*. New York: Vintage.

Couper, Kristin and Daniel Martuccelli (1994) 'L'Expérience britannique', in Michel Wieviorka (ed.) *Racisme et xénophobie en Europe*. Paris: La Découverte.

Ezorsky, Gertrude (1991) *Racism and Justice: The Case for Affirmative Action*. Ithaca, NY and London: Cornell University Press.

Friedman, Robert (1975) 'Institutional Racism: How to Discriminate Without Really Trying', in Thomas Pettigrew (ed.) *Racial Discrimination in the United States*. New York: Harper & Row.

Guillaumin, Colette (1972) *L'Idéologie raciste*. The Hague: Mouton.

Lapeyronnie, Didier (1993) 'Peut-il exister une politique antiraciste?', in Michel Wieviorka (ed.) *Racisme et modernité*. Paris: La Découverte.

Lapiere, Richard T. (1934) 'Attitudes versus Actions'. *Social Forces*, 13: 230–37.

Mayer, Nonna and Pascal Perrineau (eds) (1989) *Le Front National a découvert*. Paris: FNSP.

Miles, Robert (1994) 'A Rise of Racism and Fascism in Contemporary Europe? Some Sceptical Reflections on its Nature and Extent'. *New Community* 20, 4: 547–62.

Steinberg, Stephen (1993) 'Racisme et science du faux-fuyant', in Michel Wieviorka (ed.) *Racisme et modernité*. Paris: La Découverte.

Taguieff, Pierre-André (1988) *La Force du préjugé*. Paris: La Découverte.

Touraine, Alain (1993) 'Le racisme aujourd'hui', in Michel Wieviorka (ed.) *Racisme et Modernité*. Paris: La Découverte.

Wieviorka, Michel (1988) (ed.) *Sociétés et terrorisme*. Paris Fayard.

Wieviorka, Michel (1993a) *Racisme et Modernité*. Paris: La Découverte.

Wieviorka, Michel (1993b) (ed.) *La Démocratie à l'épreuve. nationalisme, populisme, ethnicité*. Paris: La Découverte.

Wieviorka, Michel (1994) *Racisme et xénophopbie en Europe*. Paris: La Découverte.

Wieviorka, Michel (1995) (ed.) *The Arena of Racism*. London: Sage.

Wieviorka, Michel, Philippe Bataille, Daniel Jacquin, Danilo Martuccelli, Angelina Peralva and Paul Zawadzki (1992) *La France raciste*. Paris: Seuil.

Wieviorka, Michel and Dominique Wolton (1987) *Terrorisme à la Une*. Paris: Gallimard.

Wilson, William J. (1977) *The Declining Significance of Race*. Chicago: University of Chicago Press.

Wilson, William J.(1987) *The Truly Disadvantaged: The Inner City, the Underclass and Public Policy*. Chicago: University of Chicago Press.

Yonnet, Paul (1993) *Voyage au centre du malaise français*. Paris: Gallimard.

9

'DIFFERENCE', CULTURAL RACISM
AND ANTI-RACISM

Tariq Modood

A NEW RACISM?

During the 1980s, several sociologists and anti-racists discerned the growing presence of a British 'new racism' (Barker 1981; Gordon and Klug n.d.; Gilroy 1987). It was argued that, following the Holocaust and the comprehensive discrediting of nineteenth-century scientific racism, racism based upon biological theories of superior and inferior races was no longer intellectually and politically viable as a public discourse. In-stead, what had emerged was a racism based upon cultural differences, upon the 'natural' preference of human beings for their own cultural group, and the incompatibility between different cultures, the mixing or coexistence of which in one country, it was alleged, was bound to lead to violent social conflict and the dissolution of social bonds. It was a racism which was said to have been first articulated in the speeches of Enoch Powell in the late 1960s, was nurtured in the New Right intellectual circles of the 1970s, burst into prominence in the early 1980s with the publicity accorded to the polemical output of writers associated with the radical right-wing journal *The Salisbury Review*, and was then disseminated by many newspaper columnists and leader writers in both the broadsheets and the tabloids.

Several commentators have seen that this 'new racism' is not peculiar to the English New Right, but is part of a much larger intellectual and political movement. Étienne Balibar, for example, has argued that it is part of 'a racism in the era of "decolonisation", of the reversal of population movements between the old colonies and the old metropolises' (Balibar 1991: 21). It has developed in a way that gives expression to the perceived problem of assimilating or integrating culturally primitive and backward peoples into modern civilisations; into, for example, the France of the 'land of the Rights of Man' (ibid.: 24). He sees its prototype in modern anti-Semitism, of which he writes:

> Admittedly, bodily stigmata play a great role in its phantasmatics, but they do so more as signs of a deep psychology, as signs of a spiritual inheritance rather than a biological heredity. (ibid.: 24)

Such an interpretation of racism, Balibar points out, is particularly helpful in explaining the French colonial oppression of Muslims and contemporary Muslimophobia, and he borrows a term from Pierre-André Taguieff to identify it as 'differentialist racism'. David Goldberg, too, is surely right in his judgement that '[s]ince World War II, and especially in the past fifteen or twenty years, the cultural conception of race has tended to eclipse all others. It has become paradigmatic' (Goldberg 1993: 71).

A culturalist racism, then, should not be supposed to have originated with the British New Right. It has a much greater international and historical depth. It could indeed be said that in the long history of racism, it is nineteenth-century biologism that is the exception, and certainly Europe's oldest racisms, anti-Semitism and Islamophobia, are culturalist (Ballard 1996). Even the contemporary version of culturalist racism identified as 'new racism' certainly predates the speeches and writings of New Right politicians and intellectuals, who in fact gave an ideological expression to an extreme version of a common-sense or folk racism that has been around for some time. It is surely as old as the New Commonwealth immigration and settlement in Britain against which it was directed and which gave rise to its development, although it has become more explicit as the presence of these settlements, and the multicultural challenge they pose, has become more evident. I shall call this folk sentiment, as well as the culturally grounded, differential treatment, practices, policies and ideologies which it has given rise to or is part of, 'cultural racism', to distinguish it from biological racism, which it presupposes.

While biological racism is the antipathy, exclusion and unequal treatment of people on the basis of their physical appearance or other imputed physical differences – saliently in Britain their non-'whiteness' – cultural racism builds on biological racism a further discourse which evokes cultural differences from an alleged British or 'civilised' norm to vilify, marginalise or demand cultural assimilation from groups who also suffer from biological racism. Postwar racism in Britain has been simultaneously culturalist and biological, and while the latter is essential to the racism in question it is, in fact, the less explanatory aspect of a complex phenomenon. Biological interpretations have not governed what white British people, including racists, have thought or done; how they have stereotyped, treated and related to non-whites; and biological ideas have had increasingly less force both in the context of personal relationships and in the conceptualisation of groups. As white people's interactions with non-white individuals increased, they did not become necessarily less conscious of group differences but they were far more likely to ascribe group differences to upbringing, customs, forms of socialisation and self-identity than to biological heredity.

A central feature of this combined racism was that the non-white presence in Britain was conceived of in terms of a double contrast. The first, a contrast between White/European/British and 'coloured'/Black/non-European, was a distinction based on skin colour. A further subdivision – of the 'coloured' group into Asians and West Indians – was also essential to the identification and definition of racial groups, and constituted the second dualism. As I shall soon show, these dualisms exist in common-sense or folk typologies as well as in the New Right discourse. But before we explore these contrasts, let us briefly consider what kind of anti-racist response was made to them.

ANTI-RACISMS AND ASIAN IDENTITIES

There have, in fact, been two different anti-racisms, an earlier and a later version. The early response – exemplified by the Campaign Against Racial Discrimination (CARD) in the 1960s, and influenced by the American Civil Rights Movement under the leadership of Martin Luther King Jnr – was to repudiate biological racism by arguing that all human beings are equal, irrespective of colour, and are entitled to the same civic rights within the nation-state. This colour-blind humanism gave way – again, first in the United States and more gradually in Britain, where it became prominent in the 1980s – to two forms of colour-conscious anti-racisms. One form consisted in the recognition of the essential need to monitor the socioeconomic disadvantages of non-whites, and the structural bias against them, in all the public institutions of a white society, in order to identify discrimination and measure both inequality and the extent of progress made towards its elimination.

The second form of anti-racism consisted in raising black consciousness, in getting black people to emphasise their blackness and pride in their roots, their solidarity with other black people and their struggles, and to organise as black people in mutual self-help and collective empowerment (Malcolm X 1966; Cleaver 1968; Blauner 1972). This movement was, in effect, to create a new black identity or black political ethnicity. The result was that the racists' first contrast, the black–white opposition, was accepted, even sharpened by racism-awareness, but re-interpreted. When this American anti-racist movement was pursued in Britain, it highlighted a problem, for in Britain there was also a second cleavage: a West Indian–Asian dualism. Despite the different political and cultural histories that this cleavage represented, British anti-racism, having accepted the first opposition between black and white, continued to deny any political or anti-racist strategic significance to this internal division (see, for example, Gordon and Klug n.d.: 23). I have argued in a series of articles that this denial has been a politically naive sociological falsification which has had a deleterious effect upon the ability of Asians to mobilise for anti-racist struggles (Modood 1992, 1994). Since the source of my feeling that British anti-racism has not taken sufficiently seriously the existence and nature of cultural racism is not merely socio-logical, but a matter of personal experience as an Asian living in Britain, it may be helpful to say a little about that starting point.

The effect of these anti-racisms upon Asians (initially, to be told – or to argue – that there were no real black–white differences, and later that 'colour' was the basis of ethnic pride and political solidarity) was to create a schizophrenic contradiction in many Asians' sense of identity. For during the period in which these were the dominant public anti-racist views, young British Asians were being brought up by their families and communities to feel that we *were* different *qua* Asians and *qua* specificities of religion, language, caste, national/regional origins, and so forth. We came to notice over time that it was our continued cultural differences that were resented by many of the British as alien, and made us a target of harassment and attack. Initially, the migrant generation were unsure of how long they expected to be in Britain; many expected and wished to return to their homelands in due course, and few sought any public policy of multiculturalism; but the general feeling was that even if our modes of living were to be modified through a process of settling into, and adaptation to life in Britain, some essential core of continuity had to be maintained. This was not, it must be stressed, a crudely conservative view; Asian parents knew, even if they did not always relish the prospect, that changes would occur if their children and grand-children were to be accepted, as indeed they wished them to be, by white British people, and to succeed in the new society.

Different parents, different Asian communities, had different views on the pace of change and what should and must not be changed. In my family, national origins (Pakistan) and language (Urdu) were considered to be of lesser importance and hence detachable from the core values, which was defined as Islam (for an account of my father's Islam, see M.S. Modood 1990). This did not mean a rigid 'fundamentalist', anti-Western, anti-modernist religiosity (it particularly did not mean this in the 1960s and 1970s), but it did mean that the new ways of living, the gradually becoming a part of British society, had to be ultimately justified in terms compatible with a Muslim faith and the welfare of Muslim people. The ultimate form of 'selling out', of self-abnegation, I was taught, was to be a traitor to Islam and to be indifferent to the fate of Muslims.

Of course, only about half of the South Asians in Britain are Muslim, and not all Muslims are equally committed to a Muslim identity (which is certainly open to a number of interpretations). Some Pakistanis see their cultural heritage and Pakistani identity as being inseparable from – and hence not of lesser value than – their Muslim lifestyle. Some valorise only their Punjabi or North Indian cultural identity, while others valorise their common past struggle against British imperialism. My point is not to reduce the complexity and range of identities and commitments in the South Asian communities to the religious, though I do believe that religion is much more central to British Asian ethnicity than many anti-racists would like to acknowledge. My point is that South Asian immigrants to Britain believed, and taught their children to believe, in the uniqueness of their culturally distinct beliefs and practices, and felt that this cultural heritage was of value and under threat (Modood *et al.* 1994).

The threat did not come just from racism. It also arose from the fact of migration and settlement in a society very different from the one in which one had roots – in which, for example, religion played a very different role in structuring collective identities. Yet the anti-racisms of both the earlier and the later periods ignored these issues, and with them the significance of Asian ethnicities. This meant that one was denied a language in which to debate cultural difference and the extent to which Asian cultural differences were increasingly being racialised; a language in which to give expression to ethnicity while seeking, at the same time, to oppose racist stereotyping and public expressions of contempt, as well as right-wing 'culturalist' constructions of identity; a form of words to express loyalty to one's own minority community within a public discourse of equality and civic integration.

In some ways, the second form of anti-racism was an advance on the first in that it brought issues of representation as well as policy under critical political scrutiny; it was a less defensive anti-racism which did not assume that cultural homogeneity was a prerequisite of common citizenship. It highlighted the crucial issue of identity. Yet from an Asian point of view, the black consciousness movement was in other ways less preferable to the earlier civic anti-racism, for the assertive identity it promoted to unite the victims of racism focused on colour. Ironically, this was at a time when it was cultural racism that was on the increase, eclipsing other forms, and when Asians were asking themselves what were the core identities they felt were under threat and most worth preserving, and hence were least interested in defining themselves in terms of a global colour identity.

The second anti-racism, therefore, excluded Asians and other victims of racism who did not see their primary identity and incorporation into British society in terms of colour; or at least, it was an anti-racism that was insensitive to the concerns and vulnerabilities of such groups. Yet the secondary status of Asians in anti-racism went further. For as I have suggested, there was one ethnic identity with which this second anti-racism was compatible – indeed, they usually went hand in hand. This was black consciousness or a black pride movement where 'black' meant African roots and origins in the enslavement of African peoples in the 'New World'. Hence the 1980s anti-racism consisted of (in the case of white people, a solidarity with) an oppositional blackness based on an inversion of the racist white–black/coloured divide, together with a cele- bration of the positive elements of the black diasporic African heritage of struggle, and of the achievements of the contemporary bearers of that heritage. There was tension between these two versions of blackness – political solidarity of all non-whites, and a black diasporic African eth- nicity – but no real anti-racist criticism of what was perceived as a natural and benign conflation. Yet my experience in racial equality work was that the assertion of any other non-white minority identity – Asian, Indian or Muslim – was condemned as culturalism, as racism(!) or as divisive of the anti-racist effort and minority unity (Modood 1994). This created an anti-racism that failed to acknowledge the existence of cultural racism, and therefore to contend with the specificities of anti-Asian racism. An absurd situation had emerged in which anti-racists were en- couraging self-pride and assertiveness in the racially subordinated, but were intolerant of Asians defining themselves, their circumstances, frus- trations and aspirations, except in approved ways.

In fact this opposition to Asian ethnicity has been anomalous within the broader left-wing politics of the last two decades, in which the soli- darities of class or social citizenship have been superseded by an ideal of equality based on the view that 'a positive self-definition of group differ- ence is in fact more liberatory' (I.M. Young 1990: 157). It is a politics that has informed not just black power anti-racism but the gay pride movement and, above all, radical feminism. Those elements of the Old Left that thought such politics divisive have found themselves having to accommodate it or risk irrelevance. Yet the intolerance of Asian self-definition did not come only or even primarily from the Old Left; the charge that Asian self-definition is divisive is heard as frequently from advocates of the politics of difference (Gilroy 1987).

THE COMPLEXITIES OF RACISM

More recently – not unrelated to a hypothesising of the existence of a new racism, and partly following the lead of some in the field of Cultural Studies (e.g. Gilroy 1987, 1990) – a reappraisal of anti-racism as a strategy and mode of discursive representation has been initiated. One of the arguments for a reappraisal is that contemporary racism was, but no longer is, a unitary phenomenon: that Britain has become 'multi-racist'. Support for this diversity is evidenced by the fact that white people who are racist towards some ethnic groups can nevertheless admire other ethnic groups because of, for example, aspects of their subcultural styles:

> Most typically, of course, many White working-class boys discriminate posi-tively in favour of Afro-Caribbean subcultures as exhibiting a macho, proletar-ian style, and against Asian cultures as being 'effeminate' and 'middle-class'. Such boys experience no sense of contradiction in wearing dreadlocks, smok-ing ganja and going to reggae concerts whilst continuing to assert that 'Pakis Stink'. (Cohen 1988: 83)

Les Back found these insights confirmed in his ethnographic study of a large South London council estate in 1985–87 (Back 1993). He observed among the young whites on the estate a 'neighbourhood nationalism', side by side and in tension with a British nationalism. While the latter was understood as a preserve of whites, the former was based on racially mixed groups of friends and the prestigious position of black youth cul-tures and styles in the area, and embraced blacks as well as whites. The Vietnamese on the estate were, however, excluded from both these local patriotisms, and therefore incurred 'the full wrath of the new racism which defines "outsiders" in terms of "cultural" difference' (ibid.: 228). Back believes that this situation is interestingly new. Indeed, it is relatively new in terms of British sociology and anti-racist discussions. I would suggest, however, that, like the 'new racism' itself, these inconsistent and differential racisms are as old as the immigration and settlement they are attempting to make sense of and live with.

British race relations policies and anti-racisms are premised on the assumption that the problem is of an exclusionism typified by the notice that some landladies in the 1950s put in their front windows: 'No Coloureds' (the fuller version being 'No Irish, No Coloureds, No Dogs') (Cohen 1988: 14); notices evoking memories for those newly arrived immigrants like my father of signs outside the clubs of the British in India: 'No Indians, No Dogs'. The imagined solution to this exclusionary tendency is symbolised by the black-and-white handshake that serves as the logo of the Commission for Racial Equality. But neither the problem nor the solution was ever quite so simple. The 'No-Coloureds' racism was not unitary: racists always distinguished between the groups they rejected, and while the likelihood of someone who discriminated against one group discriminating against other groups was probably high, the culturally constructed grounds of rejection varied depending upon the immigrant group.

Alastair Bonnett cites a BBC interview with some 'Teddy Boys' just after the 1958 racist attacks in Notting Hill (Bonnett 1993: 19–20, using an interview transcript in Glass 1961). He observes that while there is a reductionist, homogenising racialism, 'They're all spades' – it is constantly qualified, as particular groups (notably Jamaicans and Maltese) are identified and 'extricated from the "racial"/colour based logic involved in drawing a clear line between "spades" and "us"' (Bonnett 1993: 20). My own memories of my secondary modern, working-class school in North West London in the second half of the 1960s are very much in line with Back's South London observations, making doubtful the suggestion that he has discovered a new phenomenon. While there was indiscriminate racist name-calling, the black and white boys had interracial friendships and a respect for each other, focused, above all, on football, which was greater than either had for Asian boys. The school roll included many skinheads and other adherents of the cult of Paki-bashing who appeared to me at the time to have a very clear perception of an elemental difference between 'Pakis' (a.k.a. Indians and Asians) and 'non-Pakis'. The contrast that Cohen referred to, cited above, between 'pushover' Asians and 'hard' West Indians was certainly in place, though the more recent contrast between academic, obedient Asians and disruptive, dull (male, but not female) Afro-Caribbeans was, with Asians still struggling with the English language, as yet in its infancy. Mac an Ghail, on the basis of observation in a Midlands working-class secondary school in the 1980s, has argued that this pair of stereotypes is fostered by (racist) teachers (Mac an Ghail 1988). I certainly do not remember it being confined to the teachers, or actively led by them (see also Gillborn 1990; Willis 1977).

This perception of 'coloured immigrants' as coming not in one but in two kinds, 'black'/'Jamaican'/'West Indian'/'Afro-Caribbean' and 'Paki'/

'Indian'/'Asian', is not confined to schools, youth or the working class. Despite the way in which anti-racists represent racist discourse, the actual speeches and literature of, say, Enoch Powell, the National Front, the Conservative New Right or the British National Party constantly make this distinction, and this is evident even in the quotes that some anti-racists use (e.g. Gordon and Klug n.d.: 17–19; Gilroy 1987: 45–6). In the only in-depth research of how racial stereotypes work in job selection (Jenkins 1986), Richard Jenkins undertook a study of middle managers across a range of public- and private-sector organisations. Through interviews, he identified eight stereotypes in what the managers said (the percentage indicates the number of times this comment came up in the interviews):

1. West Indians are lazy, happy-go-lucky, or slow   43%
2. Asians are hard workers   34%
3. Asians are more ambitious and academic   14%
4. West Indians are aggressive and excitable   12%
5. West Indians mix better with whites   13%
6. Asians are clannish and don't mix   13%
7. West Indians have a chip on their shoulders   11%
8. Asians are lazy, less willing   11%

None of these stereotypes is about – to use the managers' favoured term – 'coloured people' as such. What emerges once again are two groups, and what is interesting is that there is only one stereotype, 'laziness', that applies to both (points 1 and 8), and even there, the votes cast suggest contrast rather than similarity. In this respect racism, especially British racism, is quite different from sexism. Of course there are stereotypes about different kinds of women: for example, the bossy, the demure, and the man-hater. But – unlike the case with non-whites – there are some fundamental stereotypes about women *as such*: they are less rational, more emotional; physically weak and lacking in toughness; more caring, and so on. While the managers' categories could exist only in the context of a society in which racism was present, it would be quite wrong to suppose that stereotypes such as these are confined to a special group of people: racists, or white people. A Runnymede Trust survey found that about the same number (nearly 50 per cent) of Afro-Caribbeans as whites assented to the proposition 'Asian people work harder than white people' (the Asian figure was nearly 70 per cent); similarly, about 15 per cent of whites and nearly the same number of Asians agreed with the proposition 'White people are more intelligent than black people' (Amin and Richardson 1992: 44).

These fundamentally contrasting images and generalisations about Asians and West Indians are not hidden away in private conversations, to be teased out through subtle research. They are commonly found in the mass media, especially in the tabloid press. Alastair Bonnett has interestingly brought out how, in the 1980s, even among opponents of non-white immigration such as the *Sun*, there is a softening of a blanket rejectionism as worthwhile qualities are found in one or other minority group (Bonnett 1993: 25–9). Usually such positive qualities are attributed to one group but not to the other, so that the two groups are not just distinguished, but implicitly contrasted. From the examples Bonnett offers, two sets of contrasts can be identified: one favouring Afro-Caribbeans, the other Asians.

1. Asians are law-abiding, hard-working, resourceful and respectful of traditional family values; blacks lack the discipline and structures to resist an inner-city underclass culture of drugs, vice, crime and violence.
2. Asians have a profoundly alien culture; they do not share and do not want to share the Judaeo-Christian outlook and/or a democratic individualism; black people, typified by the celebration of the boxer Frank Bruno as a 'Great Briton', are patriotic Britons who enrich a shared popular culture and bring honour to national sporting teams.

Bonnett goes on to point out that while these sweet–sour contrasts are based on very old, long-standing stereotypes and cultural relationships, they nevertheless more than hint at a new right-wing redefinition of Britishness by de-emphasising 'whiteness' in favour of characteristics such as 'law abiding', 'family-loving', 'individualism', and so on, which minorities may already have or can learn (or be taught) to emulate. It is a vision that claims to be colour-blind, while it propagates a culturally intolerant British nationalism, suggesting that contemporary racist sentiment is capable not just of the kind of 'neighbourhood nationalism' of a working-class council estate but of effacing colour racism while reinforcing cultural racism at a macro-level (not that cultural intolerance is confined to the Right; see Weldon 1989). Moreover, as Bonnett also notes, in the late 1980s and early 1990s a third racialised grouping emerged in public discourse as a target for racist graffiti and attacks, a group apparently particularly suited to focus the unease evoked by alien cultures and their seeming lack of respect for, and incompatibility with, the British way of life. I refer here, of course, to Muslims. As I argue elsewhere, I believe that Muslimphobia is at the heart of contemporary British and European cultural racism (Modood 1990, 1992).

THE RISE OF CULTURAL RACISM

The implications of the development of a seemingly 'colour-blind' nationalism, which appears to be gaining support, need to be spelled out. While it is just possible that it will give us a post-biological racist cultural intolerance, it is much more likely that the hostility against perceived cultural difference will be directed primarily against non-whites rather than against white minorities. That is to say, even if it should be the case that colour racism may become negligible in its own right, it is still possible for it to operate in conjunction with cultural racism. What we would have is a situation in which colour racism is triggered by, and becomes potent only in combination with, cultural antagonisms and prejudices. It is by no means an impossible development for colour prejudice to decline, while discourses attacking the collective cultures of minority groups rise. At this point, cultural racism would have come into its own. In my view it is quite possible that we shall witness in the next few decades an increasing de-racialisation of, say, culturally assimilated Afro-Caribbeans and Asians, along with, *simultaneously*, a racialisation of other culturally 'different' Asians, Arabs and non-White Muslims.

Having anything but a European physical appearance may be enough in contemporary European societies to make one a possible object of racist treatment (not that only European societies can be racist; see, for example, Dikötter 1990). But such phenotypical racism can also be the foundation of a more complex form of racism. I am not, however, arguing that wherever there is biological racism there must be cultural racism too, or that cultural exclusionism occurs only in the context of racism, or should be re-labelled 'racism'. Ethnic hierarchies and religious discrimination, for example, can and do exist in all-white or all-black societies – in societies where groups are not differentiated by physical appearance. My argument is that racialised groups which have distinctive cultural identities, or a community life defined as 'alien', will suffer an additional dimension of discrimination and prejudice. The hostility against the non-white minority is likely to be particularly sharp if that minority is sufficiently numerous to reproduce itself as a community, and has a distinctive and cohesive value system which can be perceived as an alternative, and possible challenge, to the norm. It is particularly important to recognise that racism constitutes opposition to, discrimination against, not just individuals but, above all, communities or groups.

Racism normally makes a linkage between a difference in physical appearance and a (perceived) difference in group attitudes and behaviour. In contemporary settings this linkage is not usually crudely genetic or biological, but is likely to rest on history, social structure, group norms, values and cultures. The causal linkage is unlikely to be perceived as scientific or determining but as probabilistic, and therefore allowing of exceptions. Thus, European people can have good personal relations with certain non-white people and yet have stereotypes about the groups those persons are from, believing that the groups in question have major adjustment problems (chips on their shoulders, etc.). These whites are likely to deny that they are racists ('my best friend is black...'). Indeed, this denial can be genuine, for it is possible not to be a racist in individual relationships or in the context of shared cultural assumptions, yet be a racist in one's attitudes towards groups. Such collective racism can be overridden in the course of interracial friendships and shared lifestyles where a non-white friend, for example, can demonstrate that he or she is the exception to the stereotype; yet on the other hand, it is also clear that despite such one-to-one relationships, stereotypes may continue to be held by the white friend (and, of course, not only by whites) to apply to the group as a whole.

Cultural racism is likely to be particularly aggressive against those minority communities that want to maintain – and not just defensively – some of the basic elements of their culture or religion; if, far from denying their difference (beyond the colour of their skin), they want to assert this difference in public, and demand that they be respected just as they are. Some of the early researchers on racial discrimination in England were quite clear about the existence of a colour and cultural component in racial discrimination, yet thought the former much the more important. A leading study by W.W. Daniel, for example, concluded:

> The experiences of white immigrants, such as Hungarians and Cypriots, compared to black or brown immigrants, such as West Indians and Asians, leaves no doubt that the major component in the discrimination is colour. (Daniel 1968: 209)

This was further confirmed for Daniel by the finding that West Indians experienced more discrimination than Asians, and he takes the view that people who physically differ most from the white population were discriminated against most; therefore, he argues, 'prejudice against Negroes is most deep-rooted and widespread' (ibid.: 209). In contrast, he thought that lighter-skinned Asians suffered from some discrimination for cultural reasons, but that this would tend to decrease for British-educated second-generation Asians. While his prediction appears, on the surface, reasonable, it overlooked the increasing significance that cultural racism was to play in determining attitudes to ethnic minorities.

The annual Social Attitudes Survey, which began in 1982, has consistently recorded, as have other surveys, that the English think there is more extreme prejudice against Asians than against Afro-Caribbeans. The differences are minor, though widening: in 1991, 58 per cent of whites thought that there was considerable prejudice against Asians, and 50 per cent against West Indians (K.Young 1992: 181). The more detailed breakdown, available in the 1986 survey report, shows that the difference is mainly accounted for by those under the age of 35 and those in social classes III (manual), IV, V and other (Airey and Brook 1986: 163). In other words, anti-Asian racism appears to be on the increase. Perhaps an even better measure of the difference between attitudes to these two major ethnic groups can be found among the white respondents who admitted to being prejudiced themselves: 14 per cent said they were prejudiced against Asians as against only 5 per cent against black people; the figures for the under-35s were 20 per cent and 5 per cent respectively, and the factorial difference was even greater in the North and Midlands (ibid.: 164). A Policy Studies Institute survey conducted in 1994 found that all ethnic groups believe that prejudice against Asians in general, and Muslims in particular, is much the highest of all ethnic, racial or religious prejudices, and it is believed by Asian people themselves that the prejudice against Asians is primarily a prejudice against Muslims (Modood *et al.* 1997).

These survey findings are confirmed by several qualitative or personal accounts – for example, by Dervla Murphy in her documentation of racism in Bradford and Birmingham (Murphy 1987), and by the Scottish-Nigerian writer Adewale Maja-Pearce in his travels around Britain (Maja-Pearce 1990). Both found that white people expressed more hostility towards Asians, especially Pakistanis, than any other group (see Murphy 1987: 214). Maja-Pearce was indeed moved to write: 'This obsessive hatred of people from the Indian subcontinent is paralleled in recent [pre-Bosnia] history by a well-known event in central Europe' (Maja-Pearce 1990: 72). Part of the explanation for the failure of Daniel's prediction may be found in Michael Banton's observation, made just a decade later:

> the English seemed to display more hostility towards the West Indians because they sought a greater degree of acceptance than the English wished to accord; in more recent times there seemed to have been more hostility towards Asians because they are insufficiently inclined to adopt English ways. (Banton 1979: 242)

INDIRECT DISCRIMINATION

My attempt thus far to establish that there is such a thing as 'cultural racism' has focused on stereotypes, prejudices and discourse, on perceptions and attitudes which are not only part of a climate of opinion but lead to direct acts and practices of racial discrimination in areas of social life such as employment, housing, schools, social services, electoral politics, and so on. There is also, however, a dimension of indirect discrimination involved in this racism. I take my idea of indirect discrimination from the British Race Relations Act (1976). A practice or policy may make no reference to race or ethnic groups, but may nevertheless disproportionately disadvantage some groups more than others. For example, a company policy that gives preference in filling jobs to local people is formally non-racist (and even may date from the time when Britain was not multiracial), but if the local population happens to be predominantly white, the policy disadvantages minority groups. If there are no countervailing justifiable reasons in favour of this policy – related, for example, to the efficiency of the business – then this constitutes indirect discrimination.

It should be clear that many kinds of non-racist forms of socioeconomic inequalities, especially forms of class exclusivity – for example, a bias in favour of Oxbridge graduates for certain kinds of elite jobs – are *prima facie* cases of indirect racial discrimination (see, for instance, Commission for Racial Equality 1987). Cultural differences too, however, can be the basis for unintended discrimination. Every society has ways of doing things – customs, norms, cultural preferences and rewards – which reflect a majority view, or that of a particularly prized cultural group. Membership of a non-dominant cultural group can deprive one of, say, excellence in the dominant language and its modes of representation, or access to certain useful social networks. A member of any group which has failed to master or accept the established norms may find it systematically and cumulatively more difficult to meet the target those norms underwrite. Such norms may vary from the unwillingness to engage in the social drinking of alcohol to wearing what counts as acceptable, professional and appropriate clothing, to accent or manner of speech. To be disadvantaged because of one's religion or culture is to suffer discrimination. The English custom that requires staff to work on Fridays, the day of collective worship for Muslims, while recognising that it is unreasonable to demand work on Sundays, may have no justifiable grounds other than local custom. What is taught in schools, the character and delivery of medical and social services, the programme schedules of television and radio, the preference for certain forms of entertainment and culture, can all be sites of culture-blind indirect discrimination.

I cannot possibly pursue here the different kinds of issues that have arisen in these different fields and that, together, give substance to what I might call the outer, indirect part of the concept of cultural racism. A very good example of a debate about the kind of ethnocentrism I have in mind has been raging in American academia and elsewhere, regarding the demands by feminists and ethnic minority activists that university curricula and intellectual canons reflect a multiculturalism appropriate to the country as a whole, encompassing groups which have been historically marginalised and culturally denuded, 'written out' as agents (as opposed to objects) of intellectual inquiry (for an attempt to moderate the debate, see Barber 1992). My own focus has been on how South Asians, and especially South Asian Muslims, have been marginalised and written out of equality debates and anti-racist perspectives.

A MORE PLURAL ANTI-RACISM

I am aware that the concept of cultural racism as elaborated here will seem perverse to some. It will seem yet another example of what Robert Miles calls an 'inflation of the meaning of racism' (Miles 1989) created by bringing together two things – racism proper and cultural prejudice or ethnocentricism – that are apparently quite distinct, thereby obscuring the real nature of racist thinking and practices. Against that I would argue that while it is true that there is no logical connection between cultural prejudice and colour racism, by the same token there is no logical connection between racial discrimination and class inequalities, yet when the two do come together, the concept of racial disadvantage is a good one to describe the situation. Or again, there is no necessary connection between racism and sexism (for the opposite view, see Balibar 1991: 49), but we know they can be connected, and when they are, a distinctive phenomenon is created in the form of stereotypes about submissive Asian women or the strong black woman who cannot keep her man (Anthias and Yuval-Davis 1992: 125). Similarly, there may be only a contingent, matter-of-fact connection between colour prejudice and cultural prejudice, true for only certain times and places; nevertheless, when the two kinds of exclusionism and oppression come together, we have a distinctive phenomenon worthy of its own name and conceptualisation.

In this conceptualising, far from obscuring racism, we learn something about it: namely, that – contrary to just about everybody who writes about racism, including those who emphasise the specificities of different kinds of racisms and its articulations with nation, gender, class, and so on (Miles 1989; Anthias and Yuval-Davis 1992) – contemporary British racism is not dependent upon any (even unstated) form of biological determinism. True, there is always some reference to differences in physical appearances and/or a legacy of the racism of earlier centuries, but the reference is not necessarily to a deep biology; minor phenotypical differences are all that is required to mark out racial groups, stereotype them and treat them accordingly. Being able to pick individuals out on the basis of their physical appearance and to assign them to a racial group may be an essential aspect of the definition of racism, but physical appearance stands only as a marker of race, not as the explanation of a group's behaviour. Racists impute inferiority, undesirability, distinctive behavioural traits, and so on, to a group distinguished by their appearance; but this does not imply an assumption on their part that the behavioural qualities are produced by biology rather than by history, culture, upbringing, by certain norms or their absence.

In the extreme case, cultural racism – as I have argued above – does not necessarily hinge on colour racism, merely a colour racism *at the point* of cultural racism. Ironically, then, it is not the contemporary racists who make biology the cause of culture, but those anti-racists who define the 'new racism' as the view exposed by some anti-racists 'that there are biologically-determined differences between groups of people which are so fundamental as to lead to unbridgeable gaps in culture and lifestyle' (Gordon and Klug n.d.: 22). Perhaps the tactic of understating the cultural dimensions of racism is intended to have a simpler thesis to refute, and to focus energy and debate merely on colour racism. But if so, it is to fail to oppose racism and to create the basis of a movement which all racially victimised groups can identify with.

For if the New Right's 'new racism' of Enoch Powell and the *Salisbury Review* did anything, it was to make explicit and to elaborate a *cultural* determinism, without apparent biological claims, the purpose being to raise doubts about the possibility of assimilating cohesive 'alien' minorities into the nation, and to challenge the feasibility of the reformist goal of a pluralist, multicultural British nationality. To interpret a thesis of cultural determinism directed at phenotypically identified groups as a disguised form of biological determinism, as some anti-racists have done, is to understate its persuasiveness for those who are unmoved by a crude biologism. An anti-racism narrowly focused on colour racism is, therefore, at best a partial, at worst a misdirected, riposte to the New Right and the complex and damaging racism in contemporary Britain. It is an anti-racism which, by failing to meet discourse with counter-discourse, fails also to connect with many British South Asians' anxieties and energies.

The growing calls to revise and update anti-racism by pluralising the concept of political blackness are to be welcomed (Hall 1988: 28; Parekh 1994: 102). An element of this project depends on the argument that a 'black' political identity does not compete with or replace other identities – for example, 'Asian'; for, it is argued, different identities refer to different aspects of a person's subjectivity, or are emphasised in different situations – say, one in politics, the other to do with culture. As no one has yet given this idea any content, I am unsure what is being proposed. Who, for example, is to decide what is a political situation and what a cultural one? As a matter of fact, most of the minority of Asians who think of themselves as 'black' think this in relation not to specific contexts but to what they perceive as a pervading fact of social existence (Modood *et al.* 1997). Moreover, is 'blackness' really available to Asians when some of the most thoughtful and acclaimed contributions to the development of 'blackness' are not about downgrading the cultural content but about increasing the reference to African roots and the Atlantic experience (Gilroy 1987; 1993)? Can political blackness, emotionally and intellectually, really hope to replace an ethnic blackness, with all its powerful resonances and appeals to self-pride, with a notion that is supposed to unite in certain limited contexts for pragmatic purposes? It is because I think that 'blackness' contains so much of the history, sorrow, hopes and energy of descendants of African enslavement in the Atlantic world that I do not think it can be turned into a politics that is neutral between different non-white groups. It cannot have the same meaning for, or equally give strength to, those who can identify with that history and those who cannot.

There is in racial discrimination and colour racism quite clearly a commonality of circumstance among people who are not white. It is partly what gives sense to the term 'ethnic minorities' and to suggestions for a 'rainbow coalition' (Modood 1988: 402). The question is not whether coalitional anti-racism is desirable, but of what kind. My personal preference and commitment is for a plural politics that does not privilege colour identities. We must accept what is important to people, and *we must be even-handed between the different identity formations*. Political blackness is an important constituent of this pluralism, but it cannot be *the* overarching basis of unity. The end of its hegemony is not without its problems and dangers, but is not to be regretted. A precondition for creating/re-creating a coalitional pluralism is the giving up of the corrupting ideal of a solidaristic monism.

A new public philosophy of racial equality and pluralism must aspire to bring into harmony the pluralism and hybridity that exist on the ground, not to pit them against themselves by insisting that some modes of collectivity trump all others. That was the error of the anti-racism of the 1980s.

REFERENCES

Airey, Colin and Lindsay Brook (1986) 'Interim Report: Social and Moral Issues', in Roger Jowell *et al.* (eds) *British Social Attitudes.* SCPR: Gower.

Amin, Krutika and Robin Richardson (1992) *Politics for All: Equality, Culture and the General Election 1992.* London: Runnymede Trust.

Anthias, Floya and Nira Yuval-Davis (1992) *Racialised Boundaries: Race, Nation, Gender, Colour and Class and the Anti-Racist Struggle.* London and New York: Routledge.

Back, Les (1993) 'Race, Identity and Nation within an Adolescent Community in South London'. *New Community* 19: 217–33.

Balibar, Étienne (1991) 'Is There a 'Neo-Racism?', in Étienne Balibar and Immanuel Wallerstein, *Race, Nation, Class: Ambiguous Identities.* London: Verso: 17–28.

Ballard, Roger (1996) 'Islam and the Construction of Europe', in W.A.R. Shadid and Van Koningsveld (eds) *Islam, Hinduism and Political Mobilization in Western Europe.* Kok Pharos.

Banton, Michael (1979) 'It's Our Country', in Robert Miles and Annie Phizacklea (eds) *Racism and Political Action in Britain.* London: Routledge: 223–46.

Barber, Benjamin R. (1992) *An Aristocracy for Everyone: The Politics of Education and the Future of America.* New York: Ballantine.

Barker, Martin (1981) *The New Racism: Conservatives and the Ideology of the Tribe.* London: Junction Books.

Blauner, Robert (1972) *Racial Oppression in America: Essays in Search of a Theory.* New York: Harper & Row.

Bonnett, Alastair (1993) *Radicalism, Anti-Racism and Representation.* London and New York: Routledge.

Cleaver, Eldridge (1968) *Soul on Ice.* New York: McGraw-Hill.

Cohen, Philip (1988) 'The Perversions of Inheritance: Studies in the Making of Multi-racist Britain', in Philip Cohen and Harbajan S. Bains, *Multi-Racist Britain.* London: Macmillan.

Commission for Racial Equality (1987) *Chartered Accountancy Training Contracts: Report of a Formal Investigation into Ethnic Minority Recruitment.* London: CRE.

Daniel, W.W. (1968) *Racial Discrimination in England.* London: Penguin.

Dikötter, F. (1990) 'Group Definition and the Idea of "Race" in Modern China'. *Ethnic and Racial Studies* 13: 420–31.

Gillborn, David (1990) *'Race', Ethnicity and Education: Teaching and Learning in Multi-Ethnic Schools.* London: Routledge.

Gilroy, Paul (1987) *There Ain't No Black in the Union Jack: The Cultural Politics of Race and Nation.* London: Hutchinson.

Gilroy, Paul (1990) 'The End of Anti-Racism'. *New Community* 17: 71–83.

Gilroy, Paul (1993) *The Black Atlantic: Modernity and Double Consciousness.* London: Verso.

Glass, R. (1961) *London's Newcomers: The West Indian Migrants.* Cambridge, MA: Harvard University Press.

Goldberg, David T. (1993) *Racist Culture: Philosophy and the Politics of Meaning.* Cambridge, MA and Oxford: Blackwell.

Gordon, Paul and Klug, Francesca, n.d. (probably 1986) *New Right New Racism.* London: Searchlight.

Hall, Stuart (1988) 'New Ethnicities', in Kobena Mercer (ed.) *Black Film, British Cinema.* London: Institute of Contemporary Arts; also in J. Donald and A. Rattansi (eds) (1992) *'Race', Culture and Difference.* London: Sage.

Jenkins, Richard (1986) *Racism and Recruitment.* Cambridge: Cambridge University Press.

Mac an Ghail, Mairtin (1988) *Young, Gifted and Black.* Milton Keynes: Open University Press.

Maja-Pearce, Adewale (1990) *How Many Miles to Babylon?* London: Heinemann.

Malcolm X (1966) *The Autobiography of Malcolm X*, written with Alex Hailey. New York: Hutchinson/Collins.

Miles, Robert (1989) *Racism.* London and New York: Routledge.

Modood, M.S. (1990) 'My Faith: A Personal Statement', in Frances Gumley and Brian Redhead (eds) *The Pillars of Islam.* London: BBC Books.

Modood, Tariq (1988) '"Black", Racial Equality and Asian Identity'. *New Community* 14, 3: 297–404.

Modood, Tariq (1990) 'British Asian Muslims and the Rushdie Affair'. *Political Quarterly* 61, 2: 143–60; also in J. Donald and A. Rattansi (eds) *'Race', Culture and Difference.* London: Sage.

Modood, Tariq (1992) *Not Easy Being British: Colour, Culture and Citizenship.* Stoke-on-Trent: Trentham for the Runnymede Trust.

Modood, Tariq (1994) 'Political Blackness and British Asians'. *Sociology* 28, 4.

Modood, Tariq, Richard Berthoud, Jane Lakey, James Nazroo, Patten Smith, Satnam Virdee and Sharon Beishon (1997) *Ethnic Disadvantage in Britain: The Fourth National Survey of Ethnic Minorities.* London: Policy Studies Institute.

Modood, Tariq, Sharon Beishon and Satnam Virdee (1994) *Changing Ethnic Identities.* London: Policy Studies Institute.

Murphy, Dervla (1987) *Tales from Two Cities.* London: John Murray.

Parekh, Bikhu (1994) 'Minority Rights, Majority Values', in D. Milliband (ed.) *Reinventing the Left.* Cambridge: Polity Press.

Weldon, Fay (1989) *Sacred Cows.* London, Chatto Press.

Willis, Paul (1977) *Learning to Labour.* Aldershot: Gower.

Young, Iris Marion (1990) *Justice and the Politics of Difference.* Princeton, NJ: Princeton University Press.

Young, Ken (1992) 'Class, Race and Opportunity', in Roger Jowell *et al.*, *British Social Attitudes*, 9th Report. Aldershot: SCPR.

10

CONSTRUCTIONS OF WHITENESS
IN EUROPEAN AND AMERICAN
ANTI-RACISM

Alastair Bonnett

INTRODUCTION

It would be hard to imagine someone writing a book about what it means
to be white. Most white people don't consider themselves to be part of a
race that needs examining. They are the natural order of things. (Saynor
1995)

As James Saynor's remark implies, within White-dominated societies,[1]
and among White people, Whiteness remains a relatively underdiscussed
and underresearched 'racial' identity. Indeed, while the history and categorisation of 'non-Whiteness' has frequently been subject to debate, it
is only in the past few years that a comparable discussion has begun on
the subject of Whiteness. One of the most important consequences of
this relative invisibility has been the naturalisation of Whiteness for White
people; whiteness tends to be far more visible to non-Whites – for
example, to African-Americans (see hooks 1992; Erikson 1995; and on
British Asians, see Puar 1995). Within the vast majority of texts that
draw on the notion of 'racial' difference, Whiteness is positioned as
existing outside the political and economic forces that seem to shape
other racialised identities. As Dyer (1988: 46) notes:

> It is the way black people are marked as black (are not just 'people') in repre-
> sentation that has made it relatively easy to analyse their representation, whereas
> white people – not there as a category and everywhere as a fact – are difficult,
> if not impossible, to analyse *qua* white.

174   DEBATING CULTURAL HYBRIDITY

The naturalisation of Whiteness has not been limited to racist discourses. In this chapter I will show that the reification of Whiteness is also a central current within English language anti-racist thought and practice. I shall, in addition, be suggesting that this process has deleterious consequences for the anti-racist project. More specifically, I argue that the reification of Whiteness has enabled people of European extraction to imagine that their identity is stable and immutable and, relatedly, to remain unengaged with the anti-racist historicisation (and de-naturalisation) of 'racial' meaning.

As my title indicates, I shall be focusing on the European (more specifically, British) and North American anti-racist debate. The active and diverse anti-racist traditions within these societies are currently experiencing a series of intellectual and practical crises and opportunities. Traditional anti-racist paradigms are being challenged by a variety of forces, including a so-called 'new ethnic assertiveness' (Modood 1990a), conservative anti-anti-racism and postmodern critical interventions (for discussion, see Bonnett 1993a; Rattansi 1992). Ali Rattansi (1992: 52–3) has argued that 'if anti-racism is to be effective' it will be 'necessary to take a hard and perhaps painful look at the terms under which [it has] operated so far'. More specifically, Rattansi calls attention to anti-racists' inadequate and simplistic modes of 'racial' representation. Unprepared to acknowledge the 'contradictions, inconsistencies and ambivalences' within White and non-White identities (ibid.: 73), orthodox anti-racism appears ill-equipped to engage creatively with the fluid and complex forces of the racialisation process. This chapter represents an attempt to engage and move forward the debate around 'racial' representations within European and American anti-racism.

My account begins with an assessment of the emergence of a White 'racial' identity during the nineteenth and twentieth centuries. It is argued that the era witnessed the development of an increasingly fixed and narrow vision of the boundaries and meaning of the term 'White'. Second, I analyse some instances of the reified nature of Whiteness implicit in contemporary British and North American anti-racism. These include 'White' in anti-racist nomenclature; Whiteness versus the 'new ethnic assertiveness'; and essentialist interpretations of the attributes of White identity. Having introduced the way anti-racism often erases and reifies Whiteness, I turn to a review of recent anti-racist activism and writings that appear to offer an alternative approach. In particular, I address two forms of what I shall term 'White Studies': first, the literature of 'White confession'; and second, historical 'geographies' of Whiteness. As we shall see, although both discursive forms articulate problematic notions of Whiteness, I want to suggest that the historical geography approach does point towards the possibility of more nuanced, and hence strategically and theoretically more useful, anti-racist reading of Whiteness. The chapter concludes with an assessment of the practical and theoretical implications of anti-essentialist readings of Whiteness.

THE CREATION OF A WHITE 'RACIAL' IDENTITY

Reference to a White 'racial' identity is a relatively recent phenomenon. Indeed, as we shall see, the ubiquitous contemporary usage of the category 'White', as referring only to 'Europeans' and their descendants, does not appear to have been firmly established until the present century. Before the emergence of the 'race' concept in the late eighteenth and early nineteenth centuries (Banton 1977, 1987), the notion that a group of people were 'white' did not imply that they belonged to a discrete biological entity with a set of immutable 'racial' attributes. Rather, the term's most common meaning referred simply to an individual's or group's skin colour. The *Oxford English Dictionary* (1989) offers examples of the use of white (referring to 'Whiteness or fairness of complexion') in this sense from the early thirteenth century (see also Snowden 1983 for earlier examples). This largely descriptive use of the term continued to be influential well into the period of European colonial expansion. Thus we find, as a recent study by Reid shows (1994: 274–5), that Portuguese 'conquistadors routinely described their Gujerati or Arab antagonists as "white", as well as the Chinese and Ryukyuans'. The *OED* offers a similar example from a travel book published in 1604. Grimstone's *D'Acosta's History of the Indies* describes 'a part of Peru, and of the new kingdom of Grenado, which ... are very temperate Countries ... and the inhabitants are white'.

Other, more familiar uses of the category, which centred on notions of ethno-religious lines of descent, were also, however, developing as the West expanded its imperial dominion. Thus, for example, the first usage of White as an 'ethnic type (chiefly European or of European extraction)' that the *OED* cites, and which is not specifically applied to a non-European group, is the distinction made by the English cleric C. Nesse in 1680, between 'the White Line, (the Posterity of Seth)' and 'the black line, the Cursed brood of Cain'. Here Whiteness is being associated with a moral lineage, an association that was inevitably strengthened by the intellectual conflation of 'Europe' with 'Christendom' that had developed from the late medieval period onwards (Hay 1957; den Boer 1995). Thus a triple conflation of 'White', 'Europe' and 'Christian' arose that imparted moral, cultural and territorial content to Whiteness.

The development of 'racial' science at the end of the eighteenth century may be seen to have lent further authority to a number of the central categories employed within the ethno-religious tradition, and further subverted the development of 'multiracial' uses of 'White'. However, the completion of this process is comparatively recent. Throughout the eighteenth and nineteenth centuries diverse readings of Whiteness continued that transcended the narrowly 'Eurocentric' vision of the category with which we have become so familiar in our own century. David Roediger's historical studies (1992, 1994) of the consolidation of White 'racial' identity in the United States provide ample testimony to the instability of the term in nineteenth-century America. He explains how Irish and Italian immigrants were initially not deemed to be White, and had to struggle to establish themselves as a 'natural' part of the White labour fraternity. Within the nineteenth and even early twentieth centuries, the mismatch between 'European' and White may also be observed working in the other, more traditional direction: through the use of 'white' to label groups associated with non-European areas of the world. This usage achieved a rather tense marriage with 'racial' science in the English school textbook *A Geography of Africa* (Lyde 1914: first published 1899). 'The non-European population' of Africa, the book explains, 'belongs mainly to one of two races, the White and the Black' (Lyde 1914: 2). Among the 'Whites' of Africa Lyde includes 'Arabs and Abyssinians ... Berbers and Tuaregs, Masi and Somalis' (ibid.).

Although, of course, Whiteness is still subject to rearticulation and resignification, the twentieth century has seen the category become increasingly synonymous with 'European'. Indeed, the two words appear to be used interchangeably in the majority of English-language 'race' commentaries. Clearly, this process makes the notion of 'non-White Europeans' a problematic one (Bonnett 1993b). It is interesting to note in this regard that – as Elba (1990) reports – in the United States the phrase 'European American' is beginning to be used as a more ethnically resonant substitute for 'White'. Although this trend derives from an assumed equivalence of the two categories, it may eventually lead to White being seen as an archaic and offensive 'racial' descriptor (like 'yellow', 'red', 'brown' and, to a lesser extent, 'black'). At the present time, however, this speculation merely serves to highlight the extraordinary resilience and ubiquity of the term.

Although a full explanation of the consolidation of a 'European' meaning for White in the twentieth century lies beyond the scope of this chapter, the importance of one causal factor – the influence of the American 'race relations' paradigm – appears relatively clear. In American 'racial' discourse, a highly dualistic vision of 'racial conflict' between 'Blacks' and

'Whites' has been a long and firmly established structuring dynamic of the 'race' debate. As the cultural and economic power of America has spread across the world, these constructions have come to be diffused across the globe (adopted, but also sometimes adapted – for example, through British political uses of Black; see Modood 1990b).[2] Thus, although Whiteness is far from being simply an American invention, its continuing ubiquity, restrictive interpretation and conceptual opposition to Blackness may be understood to have been either introduced and/or consolidated in numerous different nations through the cultural and economic influence of the late twentieth century's principal hegemon.

We have seen that White is neither an eternal nor an immutable category. As this suggests, the contemporary meaning of Whiteness is not necessarily stable or permanent but, rather, a site of change and struggle. What is particularly striking, however, is the failure of anti-racists to engage with this site of potential contestation.

ANTI-RACISM AND THE REIFICATION
OF WHITENESS

If a White 'racial' identity has become both increasingly ubiquitous and narrowly defined, a similarly static and uncritical understanding of Whiteness has permeated the anti-racist project.

I am not, of course, claiming here that the supposed attributes of White 'racial' consciousness have not been examined by anti-racists (for they have at some length; see, for example, Katz 1978; Wellman 1977). Rather, I am seeking to show that Whiteness has tended to be approached by anti-racists as a fixed, asocial category rather than a mutable social construction. In other words, anti-racists have, for the most part, yet to become aware of, and escape from, the practice of treating Whiteness as a static, ahistorical, aspatial, objective 'thing': something set outside social change, something central and permanent, something that defines the 'other' but is not itself subject to others' definitions.

It is my contention that reifying myths of Whiteness subvert the anti-racist struggle. They create an essentialising dynamic at the heart of a project that is necessarily critical not only of 'racial' stereotypes, but of the 'race' concept itself. They also lead towards the positioning (or self-positioning) of White people as fundamentally outside, and untouched by, the contemporary controversies of 'racial' identity politics. For within much contemporary anti-racist debate, Whiteness is addressed as an unproblematic category (albeit with negative attributes), a category which is not subject to the constant processes of challenge and change that have characterised the history of other 'racial' names. This process enables

white people to occupy a privileged location in anti-racist debate; they
are allowed the luxury of being passive observers, of being altruistically
motivated, of knowing that 'their' 'racial' identity might be reviled and
lambasted but never actually made slippery, torn open, or, indeed, abolished.

To exemplify these points, I will offer three instances of the erasure
and objectification of Whiteness within anti-racism:

1. 'White' in anti-racist terminology

Anti-racists have often sought to show that language matters. Writers as
diverse as Gilroy (1987) and Modood (1988) have insisted that 'racial'
terms are neither politically neutral nor static; that they have contested
histories. Not unrelatedly, anti-racists have tried to encourage the use of
'racial' nomenclature that embodies political reflexivity and discourage
expressions that appear imposed, outmoded, offensive and/or phenotypically reductive.

However, there is one exception to this linguistic sensitivity. 'White'
tends to be excluded from anti-racists' list of acceptable or debatable
'racial' nouns (see, for example, ILEA 1983; Gaine 1987). Indeed, in the
majority of anti-racist work the meaning of Whiteness appears to be
considered beyond dispute: its boundaries are obvious. Thus the reification
of Whiteness is enacted as an erasure: Whiteness is simply left out.

For a typical example we may turn to the highly influential anti-racist
policy documents published by the Inner London Education Authority
(ILEA) in 1983. These documents made liberal use of the concept of
Whiteness. Thus, for example, in *A Policy for Equality: Race* (1983), references are made to the fact that 'white people have very much to learn
from the experiences of black people' (1983: 5) as well as to the way
'racism gives white people a false view of their own identity and history'.
In all this the ILEA implies that there exists 'a white community', a
distinct and obvious group of people who have their 'own identity and
history'. The reification inherent in such interpretations is cemented into
unassailable common sense by this particular document's 'Note on
Terminology'. The note begins with the somewhat cryptic clause 'The
following terms are used:'. Beneath the authority's colon we find explanations of the meaning of three 'racial' adjectives – 'Afro-Caribbean',
'Asian' and 'black'. There is no entry on 'white'. It is the only 'racial'
noun mentioned in the main text whose meaning is not explained. Thus
White is allowed to 'speak for itself'. It is permitted the privilege of
having an obvious meaning; of being a normal rather than an exceptional case; of being a defining, not a defined, category.

2. *Destabilising Blackness/stabilising Whiteness*

Much recent concern has been expressed in Britain about the meaning and boundaries of Blackness. A number of writers, including Tariq Modood (1988, 1990b) and Ali Rattansi (1992), have made an important intervention into British anti-racism by arguing that the anti-racist practice of defining South Asian people as Black denies the variety and multifaceted nature of the cultural identities of this group.

Yet these attempts to destabilise the homogenising currents within anti-racism have been fragmentary and partial. It is only certain specific 'communities', such as South Asians and Muslims, that are being dis-embedded from the monoliths of orthodox anti-racism. The corollary of Blackness – Whiteness – has been left entirely undisturbed. Thus we find that even within an article entitled 'Beyond Racial Dualism' (in Modood 1992), the mythologies of Blackness are attacked, whilst those of White-ness are left undiscussed (see also Modood, Chapter 9 above). Only one half of the dualism is surmounted: Whiteness remains intact, while Blackness is demolished.

This selectivity is, I would submit, a potentially disastrous facet of contemporary discourses that seek to reflect and/or reiterate the so-called 'new ethnic assertiveness' (Modood 1990a). It is important not to forget that, within Britain, anti-racists' constructions of Blackness were designed to serve an important purpose: to establish and support a 'community of resistance' within and against a White racist society. In other words, 'Black' was a politically self-conscious category necessitated by the existence of a naturalised and unselfconscious 'whiteness'. The close links established between Blackness and a militant, relatively unethnicised, identity may be seen to have made the term incapable of incorporating, and sustaining, divergent ethnicities in the same way as Whiteness appears to do. How-ever, this vulnerability is rooted in the anti-essentialist tendencies inherent within any project that attempts to privilege political over 'natural' soli-darity (see also Hutnyk and Werbner, Chapters 7, 13 in this volume). It is, then, a somewhat savage irony that it is 'Black', a relatively sophisti-cated and 'self-knowing' construction, rather than 'white', the unself-comprehending identity that forced 'Black' into existence, that is on the receiving end of so many contemporary attempts to destabilise 'racial monoliths'.

3. *'White racism' as an essentialist category*

As I have implied, anti-racists have often implicitly, and even explicitly, placed a myth of Whiteness at the centre of their discourse. This myth views 'being White' as an immutable condition with clear and distinct

moral attributes. These attributes often include: being racist; not experiencing racism; being an oppressor; not experiencing oppression; silencing; not being silenced. People of colour are defined via their relation to
this myth. They are defined, then, as 'non-Whites': as people who are
acted upon by Whites; people whose identity is formed through their
resistance to others' oppressive, silencing agency (this construction is discussed in Modood 1990b).

To exemplify this point I will turn to a recent Canadian anti-racist
text. In 1994, a Toronto-based private anti-racist consultancy called the
Doris Marshall Institute produced an address on 'Maintaining the Tensions
of Anti-racist Education' in the journal *Orbit*. About a third of the piece
is devoted to a commentary on the relationship between a White member
of the group and the commissioning of the article. 'The editors of *Orbit*',
notes the Institute (DMI 1994: 20), 'approached Barb Thomas, one of
the core members of the Doris Marshall Institute (DMI), to write an
article on our approach to anti-racism education.' However, this decision
was in error, notes the Institute, because:

> Barb is a white woman who does not experience racism. There is a mounting,
> legitimate critique of white people getting the space, resources and recognition
> for anti-racism work. (1994: 20)

The Doris Marshall Institute goes on to explain that the role of anti-
racism is to strengthen 'the voices and leadership of persons of colour'
and to

> insist that white people take responsibility for confronting racism and assist
> white people in this when necessary, and challenge speakers and writers to
> make explicit their voices and locations and what their limits and possibilities
> are. (1994: 20–21)

It is being argued here that the 'limits and possibilities' of a racialised
subject's engagement with anti-racism are established by her or his experiences of racism. Although this proposition has a certain superficial
straightforwardness (but see Miles 1989; and Fuss 1990), it relies on a
number of essentialist demarcations and categorisations. More specifically, the experiences of 'white people' are presented as manifest and
unchanging. The characteristics of Whiteness are removed from social
context and set outside history and geography.

It is important to note that this process does not occur simply because
racism is being associated by anti-racists, such as the Doris Marshall Institute, with 'white' racism against 'people of colour'. This conflation
clearly removes from view many forms of racialised ethnic and religious
antagonism and disadvantage. However, to recognise the diversity of racism

and of White experience is not necessarily to deconstruct Whiteness. The problem with the Doris Marshall Institute's interpretation is not merely their lack of sensitivity to the plurality of Whitenesses but, more fundamentally, their faith in Whiteness as a common-sense, obvious and discrete entity at the heart of 'racial' history. Whiteness is thus employed as both the conceptual centre and the 'other' of anti-racism; the defining, normative term of anti-racist praxis and theory. As this implies, to define Whiteness, to acknowledge its contingent, slippery constructions, would radically destabilise orthodox anti-racism. It is towards studies that appear to promise such a transformation that I now turn.

CHALLENGES AND REAFFIRMATIONS OF ANTI-RACIST ORTHODOXY WITHIN 'WHITE STUDIES'

Some recent examples of anti-racist work seek explicitly to raise the issue of Whiteness within anti-racist debate. This sensitivity to the existence of a White 'racial' identity should not, however, be confused with an anti-essentialist agenda. A divergence between the two tendencies is particularly apparent in the form of White studies I discuss first, the literature of 'White confession'.

Confessions of a White anti-racist

The recent flurry of interest in Whiteness in both Europe and America has generally been viewed as a new and original phenomenon. However, there are a number of pathways within this work, some of which are relatively well-worn. The most significant of these more travelled routes is the literature and practice of White confession.

This paradigm, which seeks to enable and provoke Euro-Americans to confront/realise/admit to their own Whiteness, represents a reworking of the 'consciousness-raising' or 'awareness-training' forms of anti-racism that rose to prominence in the 1970s and early 1980s. These approaches were characterised by their interest in the way so-called White people develop 'racial' prejudices (see, for example, Wellman 1977; Katz 1978). More specifically, they tended to suggest that 'Whites' need to 'face up to' their own, and other 'White' people's, racism in order successfully to expunge it from their psyche.

Over the past decade, a number of well-known critiques of the individualistic, moralistic character of 'Racism Awareness Training' (RAT) have undermined its authority as a management and counselling resource (Sivanandan 1985; Gurnah 1984). However, its confessional dynamic remains a potent force within anti-racism, including White studies. At its crudest the confessional approach erases all questions relating to the contingent, slippery nature of Whiteness. Instead, a moral narrative is offered based on the presumed value of 'White' 'self-disclosure' (see, for example, Chater 1994; Camper 1994). Thus in her article 'Biting the Hand That Feeds Me: Notes on Privilege from a White Anti-Racist Feminist', Nancy Chater attempts to expose her own and other 'White' feminists' 'Whiteness' to anti-racist critique. Drawing on that most reifying of reflexive devices, 'speaking as a...', followed by a keyword mini-autobiography, Chater explains that 'as an anti-racist white feminist' she inevitably has

> to confront the ready potential of speaking or acting in ways that are based on or slide into arrogance, moralising, self-congratulation, liberal politics, appropriation, careerism or rhetoric. (Chater 1994: 100)

Thus, Whiteness is defined as referring to a 'racial' group characterised by its moral failings; a community which is exhorted to be watchful of the reactionary tendencies apparently inherent in its anti-racist practice. Chater goes on prescriptively to sketch a number of ethical dilemmas faced by 'White' anti-racist feminists. In particular, she suggests that such people need continually to monitor their seemingly innate capacity to silence non-Whites, and to acknowledge their own embeddedness within a 'racial' elite. 'White' feminists should also avoid assuming 'an edge of moral or intellectual superiority over and distance from other white people, especially those displaying a lack of politicised awareness of racism' (ibid.: 101). In other words, Chater is suggesting that so-called 'Whites' should not – indeed, cannot – escape being part of 'their racial group', or its attendant political conservatism.

I am not suggesting here that Chater's prescriptive strategies are necessarily wrong, and that anti-racists should ignore or contradict her advice. What I wish to draw attention to is the process of category construction that structures her argument – more specifically, the process whereby Whiteness assumes a fixed and pivotal role as both a 'racial community' and a 'site of confession'. These locations establish Whiteness as an arena not of engagement with anti-racism but of self-generated altruistic interest for 'others' as well as for 'White people's' own moral well-being. Indeed, it is tempting to argue that White confessional anti-racism establishes Whiteness as the moral centre of anti-racist discourse. For while non-White anti-racists are cast as taking part in an instrumental politics of 'resistance' and 'self-preservation', 'White anti-racism' is continually elevated to a higher ethical terrain, removed from the realm of co-operation and participation to the more traditional (colonial, neo-colonial and anti-racist) role of paternalistic 'concern'.

The essentialising tendencies within Chater's text find echoes in other, more theoretically nuanced work. For although, as we shall see, the development of historical geographies of Whiteness has enabled a decisive move away from the reifying traditions outlined above, even some of its most adept adherents sometimes slip into moralising and confessional modes of analysis and address.

Thus, for example, Helen charles writes of the importance of 'Coming out as white'. Explaining that 'it is negatively exhausting teaching "white women" what it is like to be black', she notes: 'I feel it is now time for some verbal and textual "outness"' amongst White women (charles 1992: 33). The implicit parallel charles is making between queer activists' 'outing' of closet homosexuals is an instructive one. It suggests that Whiteness is being interpreted as a fixed disposition; a 'trait' that needs to be admitted to and exposed. And once uncovered, Whiteness may, presumably, be 'lived openly'. The association of Whiteness with what is conceived to be a psychosocial proclivity (i.e. sexuality) undermines the anti-essentialist advances that have been made in recent 'White' studies. More generally, I would conclude that the confessional approach forms a destabilising and unhelpful tendency set against the more rigorously sociological trajectory being developed in other parts of the field.

Historical geographies of Whiteness

Against the major tendency of anti-racists to reify Whiteness, a genuinely new and original counter-tendency may be emerging. The writers and activists within this group offer an interpretation of Whiteness characterised by three things:

(a) An analysis of the historical and geographical contingency of Whiteness.
(b) A critique of the category White, as currently constructed and connoted, as racist (but not necessarily a belief that all those people commonsensically assumed to be, or labelled, 'White' are, *ipso facto*, racist).
(c) A sensitivity to the hybrid nature of contemporary 'racial' identities.

The critical focus of this group is upon the racialisation process that produces Whiteness. Their political problematic is how this process may be simultaneously recognised without being reproduced. Thus the existence of Whiteness as a social fact is acknowledged, dissected and resisted.

However, there is considerable diversity within this school. Two broad tendencies may be discerned. The first attempts to subsume the analysis of Whiteness within a class analysis of the racialisation process. The second stresses the plural constitution, and multiple lived experiences, of those to whom Whiteness has been ascribed.

Theodore Allen (1994), David Roediger (1992, 1994), Noel Ignatiev (1995) and the contributors to the journal *Race Traitor* (subtitle: *Treason to Whiteness is Loyalty to Humanity*) may be placed firmly within the former camp. Each traces Whiteness as a project of American capitalism and labour organisations, and each explicitly calls for its 'abolition'.

These scholars and activists view White identity as the self-interested creation of racialised capitalism; an ideology that offers false rewards to one racialised fraction of the working class at the expense of others. Thus it is argued that the task of anti-racists is not to encourage so-called White people to confess to their 'own identity' but to enable them politically and historically to contextualise, then resist and abandon, 'Whiteness'. The editors of *Race Traitor* (1994a, 1994b) explain their project in the following terms:

> Two points define the position of *Race Traitor*: first, that the 'white race' is not a natural but an historical category; second, that what was historically constructed can be undone. (*Race Traitor* 1994: 108)

Whiteness is presented here as an entirely oppressive identity. 'We will never have true democracy', explains Rubio in the same journal, 'so long as we have a "white community"' (1994: 125).

However, the political conclusions of these historical studies derive, in the main, from a relatively limited reading of the synchronic social context of Whiteness. For although Whiteness is seen as – to use Allen's words – 'the overriding jetstream that has governed the flow of American history' (1994: 22), it is analysed as if it were almost entirely a product of class, and particularly labour, relations. Thus, although a precise and useful account of the construction of Whiteness emerges from these texts, it is not one that readily opens itself to dialogue with other histories or struggles.

Moreover, within this body of work there is an unhelpful romanticisation of Blackness. Indeed, *Race Traitor*'s project is not merely to destroy Whiteness but to enable Whites to 'assimilate' Blackness. Of course, Blackness, too, is seen as a social construction, but it is construed as a construction that needs to be supported and reproduced. The editors argue:

> When whites reject their racial identity, they take a big step towards becoming human. But may that step not entail, for many, some engagement with blackness, perhaps even an identification as 'black'? Recent experience, in this country and elsewhere, would indicate that it does. (*Race Traitor* 1994: 115)

This formulation is clearly based upon a series of assumptions concerning the meaning of Blackness. It implies that the romantic stereotype of the eternally resisting, victimised 'Black community' needs to be further strengthened in order to create a suitable location for escapees from Whiteness. Thus Black people are condemned to reification as the price of White people's liberation from the racialisation process.

The somewhat clumsy political strategies of the White abolitionists are, it seems to me, a disappointing conclusion to their work. However, this failure is less apparent in other historical geographies of Whiteness. In particular, Ruth Frankenberg's study *The Social Construction of Whiteness* provides a number of insights into the slippery, incomplete and diverse nature of a White 'racial' identity. Frankenberg draws from her interviews with thirty White Californian women a complex portrait of the

> articulations of whiteness, seeking to specify how each is marked by the interlocking effects of geographical origin, generation, ethnicity, political orientation, gender and present-day geographical location. (Frankenberg 1993: 18)

Thus, for example, in a chapter entitled 'Growing up White: The Social Geography of Race', Frankenberg explores her interviewees' childhood experiences of Whiteness. For some, Whiteness was always something explicit, and physically and morally separate from non-Whiteness. 'I grew up in a town', explains one respondent, where 'everyone was aware of race all the time and the races were pretty much white people and Black people' (1993: 51). However, for another women, as Frankenberg notes, '"white" or "Anglo" merely described another ethnic group' (1993: 65). One interviewee, enculturated within a 'mixed' Mexican and White community, explains that she

> never looked at it like it was two separate cultures. I just kind of looked at it like, our family and our friends, they're Mexicans and Chicanos, and that was just a part of our life. (1993: 66)

Unfortunately, Frankenberg does not engage with the ambiguities of 'Hispanic' identity. Thus, for example, she ignores the surely pertinent fact that – as Henwood (1994: 14) notes – in 'the 1990 Census half of all Hispanics reported themselves as white, a little under half as "other", and a few as black, native, or Asian'. Despite this absence, however, Frankenberg's discussion of the multiple and shifting boundaries of Whiteness is of immense value. It also provides a number of interesting points of contact with other studies of the hybrid nature of 'racial' subjectivities. In particular her work invokes parallels with the creative appropriation and intermixing of ethnic identities observed by a number of commentators of contemporary youth cultures (for example, Hebdige 1979; Ross and Rose 1994; Jones 1989).

Simon Jones, in his ethnographic study of White Rastafarians in Birmingham (Jones 1989), looks at a 'White community' that self-consciously splices its own Whiteness with styles and ideologies associated with Rastafarianism. This escape, as Jones notes, draws on a correlation of Whiteness with boredom and passivity and of Blackness with rebellion and the exotic. It is an 'escape', then, based on certain familiar clichés of Whiteness and Blackness. Despite this reliance, however, the process of becoming and socially interacting as a White Rastafarian inevitably opens up the fluidity of 'racial' identity, creating incomplete, impermanent and explicitly constructed moments of appropriation and cultural 'play'.

Another moment of hybridity is addressed by Jeater in her account of the 'multiracial' anti-racist politics of late-1970s inner London. At that time, recalls Jeater,

> We all began to celebrate the complexities and interdependencies of our cultural heritages. White people like myself ... who grew up listening to reggae music and who perhaps took part in the urban uprisings against the state, were as much a part of this project as everyone else ... the cosmopolitanism and the dynamic interactions of cultural traditions created a real sense that the world was there to be forged in new ways. (Jeater 1992: 118–19)

Such moments of crisis and youth revolt provide, perhaps, the clearest indications of the possibility of the deconstruction of 'racial' categories, of creative hybridity. As the work of the historical geographers of Whiteness cited above implies, however, the 'confusion', and intermixing, of 'racial' signs and boundaries is not restricted to moments of youthful transgression. Disruptive and mutant forms of 'White' identity have a long and varied lineage. Both such histories and contemporary analyses provide a useful resource for anti-racist engagements with White identity.

CONCLUSIONS: ENGAGING WHITENESS

This chapter has focused on one of the most intractable and, I believe, counterproductive of anti-racism's traditional monoliths. It has argued that anti-racism has objectified Whiteness, and that this process has been perpetuated within confessional approaches to anti-racism. As we have seen, however, the past few years have also witnessed signs of a new willingness to look at the historical and geographical contingency of Whiteness. This latter body of work enables a reconceptualisation of Whiteness as a diverse and mutable social construction. Clearly, this trajectory also implies a new level of sophistication in both the recognition of and resistance to Whiteness.

I wish to conclude by engaging with the debate around the meaning, as well as the political and social implications, of an anti-racist and anti-essentialist perspective on White identity.

Within the academic field of 'racial' studies, most of the English-language debate about the merits and demerits of anti-essentialism has focused on Black identity. More specifically, controversy has been aroused by the work of poststructuralist African-American writers (for example, Gates 1986, 1988; Baker 1986; Appiah 1985; see also Fuss 1990; Abel 1993) who have seemed to undermine the meaning and political coherence of Blackness. To deconstruct Blackness, it has been argued, is politically naive. 'It is insidious', notes Joyce (1987a: 341; see also Joyce 1987b), 'for the Black literary critic to adopt any kind of strategy that diminishes or ... negates his blackness.' As Fuss (1990: 77) points out, critics such as Joyce charge that 'to deconstruct "race" is to abdicate, negate, or destroy black identity'. Identifying poststructuralism with White critics, Fuss argues:

> In American culture, 'race' has been far more an acknowledged component of black identity than white; for good or bad, whites have always seen 'race' as a minority attribute, and blacks have courageously and persistently agitated on behalf of 'the race'. It is easy enough for white poststructuralist critics to place under erasure something they *think* they never had to begin with. (Fuss 1990: 93)

In the eyes of some critics the gulf between the deconstructive and essentialist positions has been bridged by the development of 'a strategic use of positivist essentialism in a scrupulously visible political interest' (Spivak, quoted by Fuss 1990: 31; see also Baker 1986). Such a position enables minority groups to 'preserve' identities that facilitate struggle, resistance and solidarity while maintaining a critique of reified notions of 'race'. Asked to expand upon the implications of strategic essentialism, the term's progenitor, Spivak, comments: 'The only way to work with collective agency is to teach a persistent critique of collective agency at the same time.... It is the persistent critique of what one cannot not want' (1990: 93).

Spivak's allusion to 'what one cannot not want' reinforces the impression that this is a debate formulated entirely around the perceived interests of oppressed groups (more specifically, African-Americans). As this implies, the question of when we should stick to Blackness and when we should critique it cannot simply be transposed by analogy on to questions of Whiteness. Given the exclusionary and normative nature of its development, any form of essentialist 'sticking to' Whiteness is not a viable anti-racist position. As we have seen, Whiteness has developed, over the past two hundred years, into a taken-for-granted experience structured upon a varying set of supremacist assumptions (sometimes cultural, sometimes biological, sometimes moral, sometimes all three). Non-White identities, by contrast, have been denied the privileges of normativity, and are marked within the West as marginal and inferior.

Unfortunately, those seeking to develop arguments for – or counter-arguments against – a politically engaged anti-essentialism have rarely considered the implications of these positions for White identity (though see Abel 1993). Thus, some of the most important questions for an anti-foundationalist anti-racism have remained undiscussed. Perhaps the most pertinent of these is how Whiteness can be made visible, exposed for critical inspection, while at the same time opened as a myth, either a racist or even a 'Black' construction that needs to be, if not abolished, permanently caged between inverted commas. In other words, we need to ask how the enormous power of Euro-American institutions and social dynamics can be acknowledged and confronted at the same time as the essentialist pretensions of Whiteness are denied.

It is important to note that the central tension at work within these questions is not between essentialism and anti-essentialism. Acknowledging the social power, the social existence, of Euro-American hegemonies is not the same as claiming (however ironically or self-consciously) that Whiteness – read as a possessive label of that power – is a fixed or natural category. As this implies, the position that bridges the tension outlined in the questions I ask above may more usefully be termed strategic decon-struction than strategic essentialism. The problematic of strategic decon-struction is not when and how to 'stick to', 'preserve' or 'save' Whiteness, but when and how Whiteness should be opened up, torn apart, made slippery, and when and how it should be revealed and confronted.

One possible route out of this dilemma is to view Whiteness as a political category. Ever since James Baldwin's provocative assertion 'As long as you think you are white, there's no hope for you' (quoted in Roediger 1994), a political reading of Whiteness has remained a minor theme within the most incisive anti-racist work. In the mid-1980s Clark and Subhan suggested, but did not develop, the notion that 'both in global terms and in the British context ... White as a political term is a term for the oppressor' (n.d.: 33). The recent development of historical geographies of Whiteness has provided this position with fresh potential. Thanks to the research of critics such as Roediger, the ideological contours of Whiteness can be rigorously mapped and historically con-textualised. This work offers a substantive empirical and theoretical base for anti-racist rearticulations of Whiteness from a natural to a political category. Anti-racists may then assess how individuals, institutions and states embrace, overthrow or reflexively monitor their Whiteness.

Political Whiteness may most usefully be viewed as an intellectual resource, rather than a universal solution. In certain circumstances it may provide an appropriate way of approaching a 'White' identity that is able to remain both theoretically and practically apt. In other contexts, however, political Whiteness may distort the nature of anti-racist alliances, offering White people nothing but a sense of negation, expressed through indulgent guilt complexes that erase the multiple and fragmented ethnicities that overlap with Whiteness. As many commentators have observed (e.g. Macdonald et al. 1989; Cohen 1992), one of the most important tasks of contemporary anti-racism is to engage so-called 'White' people, to bring them 'inside' the anti-racist project. This implies that the notion of political Whiteness should be set within a wider and more sophisticated anti-racist project that enables the historical and personal experiences of Euro-Americans to be explored with people of all 'races'. Such a process could provide Euro-Americans with a stake in anti-racism, as a project that talks to and about them, while weakening the common-sense, normative nature of 'White' identity.[3]

A central aspect of any such enterprise would be the opening up of both the mutative, contingent history of 'racial' identities and the possibility of their creative collision and hybrid reconstitution in the future. Hybridity in this sense – as Bhabha (1990) explains – does not merely refer to a marriage of traditions (though see Young 1995). Rather, it

> is the 'third space' which enables other positions to emerge. This third space displaces the histories that constitute it ... [and] gives rise to something different, something new and unrecognisable, a new area of negotiation of meaning and representation. (Bhabha 1990: 211)

Anti-racists need simultaneously to recognise and resist Whiteness while enabling and analysing its hybrid supersession. Whiteness has traditionally been the invisible centre of the 'race' equality debate. It is now time to draw it into an explicit *engagement* with the anti-racist project.

NOTES

This chapter incorporates sections previously published in *New Community* 22, 1: 97–110 ('Anti-racism and the Critique of White Identities', 1996).

  1. In this chapter the initial letter of 'racial' terms is capitalised in order to signify that such expressions are being employed as sociopolitical rather than biological categories. Lower-case initial letters are used only in quotations or to signal the term's employment as a natural, as opposed to a social, construct.

2. The most distinctive usage of 'Black' in the United Kingdom is as a 'pan-racial' label for those who seek to resist, and/or the victims of, White racism. This usage draws from established anti-colonial and anti-imperialist solidaristic discourses, as well as the practical benefits many Black Britons have perceived within a political and broad-based anti-racist alliance (see Sivanandan 1982).

3. This approach may also provide a way of engaging those so-called White people who have begun to construct a mythical history of themselves as belonging to an increasingly beleaguered ethnic minority. Charles Gallagher's recent interviews on American college campuses have indicated how the invisibility of Whiteness is fading for many, only to be replaced by the desire to find 'a legitimate, positive narrative of one's own whiteness ... accomplished by constructing an identity that negated white oppressor charges and framed whiteness as a liability (Gallagher 1995: 177). The irony of such narratives is that as they seek to connote an interest in Whiteness, they expose their ignorance about and disinterest in the actual historical development of White identity. Perhaps, however, by challenging such 'defensive Whites' to make good their professed curiosity about Whiteness – and drawing their particular experiences and anxieties into a wide-ranging and liberating history of the construction and mutual dependency of 'racial' categories – they, too, may be drawn into the anti-racist and anti-essentialist project.

REFERENCES

Abel, Elizabeth (1993) 'Black Writing, White Reading: Race and the Politics of Feminist Interpretation'. *Critical Inquiry* 20, 3: 470–98.

Allen, Theodore (1994) *The Invention of the White Race: Volume One: Racial Oppression and Social Control*. London: Verso.

Appiah, Anthony (1985) 'The Uncompleted Argument: DuBois and the illusion of race'. *Critical Inquiry* 12, 1: 21–37.

Baker, Houston Jr (1986) 'Caliban's Triple Play'. *Critical Inquiry* 13, 1: 182–96.

Banton, Michael (1977) *The Idea of Race*. London: Tavistock.

Banton, Michael (1987) *Racial Theories*. Cambridge: Cambridge University Press.

Bhabha, Homi (1990) 'Interview with Homi Bhabha: The Third Space', in J. Rutherford (ed.) *Identity: Community, Culture and Difference*. London: Lawrence & Wishart: 207–21.

Boer, Pim den (1995) 'Essay 1: Europe to 1914: The Making Of An Idea', in K. Wilson and J. Dussen (eds) *The History of the Idea of Europe*. London: Routledge: 13–82.

Bonnett, Alastair (1993a) *Radicalism, Anti-racism and Representation*. London: Routledge.

Bonnett, Alastair (1993b) 'Forever White? Challenges and Alternatives to a "Racial" Monolith'. *New Community* 20, 1: 173–180.

Camper, Carol (1994) 'To White Feminists'. *Canadian Woman Studies* 14, 2: 40.

charles, Helen (1992) 'Whiteness – The Relevance of Politically Colouring the "Non"', in A. Phoenix and J. Stacey (eds) *Working Out: New Directions for Women's Studies*. London: Falmer Press: 29–35.

Chater, Nancy (1994) 'Biting the Hand That Feeds Me: Notes on Privilege from a White Anti-racist Feminist'. *Canadian Woman Studies* 14, 2: 100–104.

Clark, Gillian and Nazreen Subhan (n.d.) 'Some Definitions', in K. Ebbutt and B. Pearce (eds) *Racism in Schools: Contributions to a Discussion*. London: Communist Party of Great Britain.

Cohen, Phil (1992) 'It's racism what dunnit': Hidden Narratives in Theories of Racism', in J. Donald and A. Rattansi (eds) *'Race', Culture and Difference*. London: Sage.

Dyer, Richard (1988) 'White'. *Screen* 29, 4: 44–64.

Doris Marshall Institute (1994) 'Maintaining the Tensions of Anti-racist Education'. *Orbit* 25, 2: 20–21.

Elba, Richard (1990) *Ethnic Identity: The Transformation of White America*. New Haven, CT: Yale University Press.

Erikson, Peter (1995) 'Seeing Whiteness'. *Transition* 67: 166–85.

Frankenberg, Ruth (1993) *The Social Construction of Whiteness: White Women, Race Matters*. Minneapolis, MN: University of Minnesota Press.

Fuss, Diana (1990) *Essentially Speaking: Feminism, Nature and Difference*. London and New York: Routledge.

Gaine, Chris (1987) *No Problem Here: A Practical Approach To Education and 'Race' in White Schools*. London: Hutchinson.

Gallagher, Charles (1995) 'White Reconstruction in the University'. *Socialist Review* 24, 1/2: 165–87.

Gates, Henry Jr (ed.) (1986) *'Race', Writing and Difference*. Chicago: University of Chicago Press.

Gates, Henry Jr (1988) *The Signifying Monkey*. Oxford: Oxford University Press.

Gilroy, Paul (1987) *There Ain't No Black in the Union Jack: The Cultural Politics of Race and Nation*. London: Macmillan.

Gurnah, Ahmed (1984) 'The Politics of Racism Awareness Training'. *Critical Social Policy* 11: 6–20.

Hay, Denys (1957) *Europe: The Emergence of an Idea*. Edinburgh: Edinburgh University Press.

Hebdige, Dick (1979) *Subculture: The Meaning of Style*. London: Methuen.

Henwood, Doug (1994) *The State of the U.S.A. Atlas: The Changing Face of American Life in Maps and Graphics*. Harmondsworth: Penguin.

hooks, bell (1992) *Black Looks: Race and Representation*. Toronto: Between the Lines.

Ignatiev, Noel (1995) *How the Irish Became White*. New York: Routledge.

Inner London Education Authority (ILEA) (1983) *Race, Sex and Class: 3. A Policy for Equality: Race*. London: ILEA.

Jeater, Diane (1992) 'Roast Beef and Reggae Music: The Passing of Whiteness'. *New Formations* 18: 107–21.

Jones, Simon (1989) *Black Culture, White Youth: The Reggae Tradition from JA to UK*. London: Macmillan.

Joyce, Joyce (1987a) 'The Black Canon: Reconstructing Black American Literary Criticism'. *New Literary History* 18, 2: 335–44.

Joyce, Joyce (1987b) '"Who the cap fit": Unconsciousness and Unconscionableness in the Criticism of Houston A. Baker, Jr. and Henry Louis Gates, Jr.'. *New Literary History* 18, 2: 371–84.

Katz, Judy (1978) *White Awareness: Handbook for Anti-racism Training*. Norman, OK: University of Oklahoma Press.

Levine, Judith (1994) 'The Heart of Whiteness: Dismantling the Master's House'. *Voice Literary Supplement* 128: 11–16.

Lyde, Lionel (1914) *A Geography of Africa: Fifth Edition Containing Problems and Exercises*. London: Adam & Charles Black.

Macdonald, Ian *et al.* (1989) *Racism, Anti-racism and Schools: A Summary of the Burnage Report*. London: Runnymede Trust.

Mason, Peter (1990) *Deconstructing America: Representations of the Other*. London: Routledge.

Miles, Robert (1989) *Racism*. London: Routledge.

Modood, Tariq (1988) '"Black", Racial Equality and Asian Identity'. *New Community* 14, 3: 397–404.

Modood, Tariq (1990a) 'British Asian Muslims and the Rushdie Affair'. *Political Quarterly* 61, 2: 143–60.

Modood, Tariq (1990b) 'Catching up with Jesse Jackson: Being Oppressed and Being Somebody'. *New Community* 17, 1: 85–96.

Modood, Tariq (1992) *Not Easy Being British: Colour, Culture and Citizenship*. Stoke-on-Trent: Trentham Books for the Runnymede Trust.

Puar, Jasbir (1995) 'Resituating Discourses of "Whiteness" and '"Asianness" in Northern England'. *Socialist Review* 24, 1/2: 21–53.

Race Traitor: Treason to Whiteness is Loyalty to Humanity (1994a) *Race Traitor* 3. (Published at P.O. Box 603, Cambridge, MA, 02140, USA).

Race Traitor (1994b) 'Editorial: When Does the Unreasonable Act Make Sense?' *Race Traitor* 3: 108–10.

Rattansi, Ali (1992) 'Changing the Subject? Racism, Culture and Education', in A. Rattansi and D. Reeder (eds) *Rethinking Radical Education: Essays in Honour of Brian Simon*. London: Lawrence & Wishart: 52–95.

Reid, Anthony (1994) 'Early Southeast Asian Categorisations of Europeans', in S. Schwartz (ed.) *Implicit Understandings: Observing, Reporting, and Reflecting on the Encounters Between Europeans and Other Peoples in the Early Modern Era*. Cambridge: Cambridge University Press: 268–94.

Roediger, Dave (1992) *The Wages of Whiteness: Race and the Making of the American Working Class*. London: Verso.

Roediger, Dave (1994) *Towards the Abolition of Whiteness: Essays on Race, Politics, and Working Class History*. London: Verso.

Ross, Andre and Tricia Rose (eds) (1994) *Microphone Fiends: Youth Music and Youth Culture*. London: Routledge.

Rubio, Phil (1994) 'Phil Rubio Replies'. *Race Traitor* 3: 124–5.

Saynor, James (1995) 'Living in Precarious Times'. *The Observer*, 27 August.

Sivanandan, A. (1982) *A Different Hunger: Writings on Black Resistance*. London: Pluto Press.

Sivanandan, A. (1985) 'RAT and the Degradation of Black Struggle'. *Race and Class* 26, 4: 1–33.

Snowden, Frank (1983) *Before Color Prejudice: the Ancient View of Blacks*. Cambridge, MA: Harvard University Press.

Spivak, Gayatri Chakravorty (1990) 'Gayatri Spivak on the Politics of the Subaltern'. *Socialist Review* 20, 3: 81–97.

Wellman, David (1977) *Portraits of White Racism*. Cambridge: Cambridge University Press.

Young, Robert (1995) *Colonial Desire: Hybridity in Theory, Culture and Race*. London: Routledge.

ETHNICITY, GENDER RELATIONS

AND MULTICULTURALISM

Nira Yuval-Davis

In this chapter I examine critically some of the ways in which gender relations affect and are affected by ethnicity, culture, racism and anti-racism, and how these relate to strategies of negotiating difference such as multiculturalism, identity politics and coalition politics. In conclusion I argue for a 'transversal politics', a model of political work thus named by Italian feminists which reflects anti-racist feminist analysis and practice in recent years in several different countries. Before engaging more deeply with the substantive issues and theoretical arguments, however, several conceptual definitions central to my argument are called for.

RACIST DISCOURSE, ETHNIC PROJECTS
AND CULTURAL RESOURCES

Racist discourse is defined (following Anthias and Yuval-Davis 1984, 1992; Yuval-Davis 1991, 1992a) as involving the use of ethnic categorisations (which might be constructed around biological, cultural, religious, linguistic or territorially based boundaries) as signifiers of a fixed, deterministic genealogical difference of 'the Other'. This 'Otherness' serves as a basis for legitimising exclusion and/or subordination and/or exploitation of the members of the collectivity thus labelled.

Ethnicity relates to the politics of collectivity boundaries, dividing the world into 'us' and 'them' around, usually, myths of common origin and/or common destiny, and engaging in constant processes of struggle and negotiation. These are aimed, from specific positionings within the collectivities, at promoting the collectivity or perpetuating its advantages by means of access to state and civil society powers. Ethnicity, according to this definition, is, therefore, primarily a political process which constructs the collectivity and 'its interest' – not only as a result of the general positioning of the collectivity in relation to other collectivities, but also as a result of the specific relations of those engaged in 'ethnic politics' with others within that collectivity (Yuval-Davis 1994).

Gender, class, political and other differences play a central role in the construction of specific ethnic politics, and different ethnic projects of the same collectivity can be engaged in intense competitive struggles for hegemonic positions. Some of these projects can involve different constructions of the actual boundaries of the collectivity – as, for example, has been the case in the debate about the boundaries of the 'Black' community in Britain (Sivanandan 1982; Modood 1988; Brah 1991; see also in this volume Modood [Chapter 9], Hutnyk [Chapter 7] and Werbner [Chapter 13]). Ethnicity is not specific to oppressed and minority groupings. On the contrary, one of the measures of the success of hegemonic ethnicities is the extent to which they succeed in 'naturalising' their ideologies and practices to their own advantage.

Ethnic projects mobilise all available relevant resources for their promotion. Some of these resources are political, others are economic, and yet others are cultural – relating to customs, language, religion, and so on. Class, gender, political and personal differences mean that people positioned differently within the collectivity could sometimes, while pursuing specific ethnic projects, use the same cultural resources for promoting opposed political goals (for example, using various Qur'an surahs to justify pro- and anti-legal abortion politics, as was the case in Egypt, or using rock music to mobilise people for and against the Extreme Right in Britain). At other times, different cultural resources are used to legitimise competing ethnic projects of the collectivity – for example, the Bundists used Yiddish as 'the' Jewish language – in an ethnic–national project whose boundaries were East European Jewry, while the Zionists (re)invented modern Hebrew (until then used mostly for religious purposes) in order to include in their project Jews from all over the world. Similarly, the same people can be constructed in different ethnicist–racist political projects in Britain as 'Paki', 'Black', 'Asians', or 'Muslim fundamentalists'.

Given this multivocality of ethnic emblems and resources, it is clear why ethnicity cannot be reduced to culture, and why 'culture' cannot be seen as a fixed, essentialist category. As Gill Bottomley proposes when she discusses the relationship between ethnicity and culture: 'Categories and ways of knowing ... are constructed within relations of power and maintained, reproduced and resisted in specific and sometimes contradictory ways' (Bottomley 1991: 305). More specifically, she claims:

> 'Culture', in the sense of ideas, beliefs and practices that delineate particular ways of being in the world, also generate conscious and unconscious forms of resistance – to homogenisation, to devaluation, to marginalising by those who fear difference. (Bottomley 1991: 12)

WOMEN AND CULTURE

The insight above is extremely important when we come to look at the contradictory relation between women and culture. Women, who are usually marginalised by hegemonic ethnic projects, often find ways of resistance – 'patriarchal bargaining' is how Deniz Kandiyoti (1988) describes these survival strategies of women within the constraints of specific social situations. As the women from Women Against Fundamentalism called out when they counter-demonstrated against the anti-Rushdie Islamist demonstration in London in 1989: 'Our tradition – resistance, not submission!' On the other hand, the compliant behaviour of women can fulfil crucial roles in hegemonic ethnic projects. Collectivities are composed, as a general rule, of family units. A central link between the place of women as national reproducers and women's subjugation can be found in the different regulations – customary, religious or legal – which determine the family units within the boundaries of the collectivity and how they come into existence (marriage), or reach their end (divorce and widowhood). Women need not only to bear, biologically, children for the collectivity, but also to reproduce it culturally. The question of which children are considered legitimate members of the family and/or the collectivity plays a crucial role in this.

However, there are several other dimensions to the roles women play in the cultural construction of collectivities. The mythical unity of ethnic 'imagined communities', which divides the world between 'us' and 'them', is culturally maintained and ideologically reproduced by a whole system of diacritical emblems, which Armstrong (1982) calls symbolic 'border guards'. These 'border guards' can identify people as members or non-members of a specific collectivity. They are closely linked to specific cultural codes, styles of dress and public conduct, as well as to more elaborate bodies of customs, literary and artistic modes of creativity and, of course, language. Symbols of gender play a particularly significant role in this articulation of difference.

Just outside Cyprus airport there is a big poster of a mother mourning her child – Greek Cyprus mourning and commemorating the Turkish invasion. In France, it was La Patrie, a figure of a woman giving birth, that personified the revolution; in Ireland, Mother Ireland; in Russia, Mother Russia; and in India, Mother India. Women often come to symbolise the national collectivity, its roots, its spirit, its national project (Yuval-Davis and Anthias 1989; Yuval-Davis 1993). Moreover, women often symbolise national and collective 'honour'. Shaving the heads of women who 'dare' to fraternise – or even to fall in love – with 'the enemy' is but one expression of this. In a television programme on Dutch television in February 1994, a young Palestinian man boasted proudly that he had killed his female cousin (who was married and a mother of two) because she had co-operated with the Israelis, and thus brought dishonour on the family. Forced veiling or insistence on particular styles of dress and behaviour are milder forms of the same construction of women. Women's distinctive ways of dressing and behaving very often – especially in minority situations – come to symbolise the group's cultural identity and its boundaries.

Because of this construction of womanhood as epitomising the collectivity, systematic rapes have become part of warfare, as in Bosnia. In the Geneva Convention, rape is still defined (although women's human rights' organisations have been campaigning against this) not as a war crime or a form of torture, but as a 'crime against honour'. And it is not the woman's honour that is being referred to, but that of her family and her collectivity. Making videos of such rapes in order to screen them on Serbian television and other TV stations has been the ultimate grotesquery associated with this practice.

The other side of this coin is that wars are declared and fought for the sake of 'womenandchildren' (as one word, in Cynthia Enloe's usage; see Enloe 1990). Protecting the honour and welfare of the collectivity's women and children – who, traditionally, are left at the rear while the men fight on the battlefront – is the most common justification for men's obligation to fight and kill – and be killed. (The recent incorporation of women into the militaries might, however, help to shift the traditional grounds of legitimation of organised violence somewhat [see Yuval-Davis 1992c; 1997: ch. 5]).

Women, however, are not only accorded the task of symbolising their nation or ethnic collectivity; they are often also usually expected to reproduce it culturally. As Floya Anthias and I have written (Anthias and Yuval-Davis 1984; Yuval-Davis and Anthias 1989), women are often the ones chosen to be the intergenerational transmitters of cultural traditions, customs, songs, cuisine, and, of course, the mother tongue (sic!). This is especially true in minority situations in which the school and the public sphere present different hegemonic cultural models to that of the home. Often, wives of immigrants are at least partially excluded from the public sphere because of legal restrictions, a lack of work opportunities or linguistic inadequacies, while at the same time they are expected to remain the primary bearers of a distinctive 'home' culture. This is one of the main reasons that stronger social control is likely to be exercised on girls than on boys, especially among the children of immigrants. The importance of women's culturally 'appropriate behaviour' can gain special significance in 'multicultural societies'.

MULTICULTURALISM

Trinh Minh-ha has commented (1989: 89–90) that there are two kinds of social and cultural differences: those which threaten and those which do not. Multiculturalism is aimed at nourishing and perpetuating the kind of differences which do not. As Andrew Jakubowicz concluded in relation to the Australian policies of multiculturalism:

> Multi-culturalism gives the ethnic communities the task to retain and cultivate with government help their different cultures, but does not concern itself with struggles against discriminatory policies as they affect individuals or classes of people. (1984: 42)

Carl-Ulrik Schierup (1995) has claimed that multiculturalism is an ideological base for transatlantic alignment aimed at the transformation of the welfare state. This alignment aspires to be the hegemonic credo in the contemporary era of postmodern modernity. He argues, however, that the paradoxes and dilemmas of existing multiculturalisms confront its ideological framework with similar problems to the ones that 'real socialisms' present to 'Socialism'.

Multiculturalist policies have been developed in Britain in order to accommodate the settlement of immigrants and refugees from its ex-colonial countries, and have broadly followed forms of legislations and political projects which were developed for this purpose in the USA, as well as other ex-imperial settler societies such as Canada and Australia. In all these states there is a continuous debate about the limits of multiculturalism between those who want a continued construction of the national collectivity as homogeneous and assimilatory, and those who have been calling for the institutionalisation of ethnic pluralism and the preservation of the ethnic minorities' cultures of origin as legitimate parts of the national project. A controversial related question is the extent to which the conservation of collective identities and cultures is important in itself, or only because of the collective will that promotes this preservation, and whether projects aimed at the conservation of cultures can avoid the reification and essentialisation of these cultures. As Floya Anthias has put it:

> Debates on cultural diversity confuse culture and ethnicity.... Is it the boundaries that should be kept or the cultural artifacts that act as their barbed wire? However, the question is not just about homogeneity, but also about western cultural hegemony. (1993: 9)

In Australia, for instance, the call of those who have objected to multiculturalism has been for an 'Anglomorphic society', even if the members of the Australian national collectivity are not of Anglo-Celtic origin, as this quotation from Knopfelmacher (1984; see also Yuval-Davis 1991: 14) demonstrates: 'With anglomorphy firmly established in Australia and stable as a rock, the "British" character of the country is independent of the "race" of the immigrants.' In the USA, the ideological target has been the American 'melting-pot', but those who object to multiculturalism in the American context emphasise the primacy of its European cultural heritage: 'Would anyone seriously argue that teachers should conceal the European origins of American civilisation?' (Schlesinger 1992: 122). Collective cultural identity rather than the ethnic origin and colour of collectivity members seems to be the crucial factor in these constructions.

It would be a mistake, however, to suppose that those who advocate multiculturalism assume a civil and political society in which all cultural identities would have the same legitimacy. In Australia, for instance, the government's document on multiculturalism emphasises 'the limits of multi-culturalism' (Office of Multicultural Affairs 1989), and in all states in which multiculturalism is an official policy there are cultural customs (such as polygamy, using drugs, etc.) which are considered illegal as well as illegitimate, giving priority to cultural traditions of the hegemonic majority. Moreover, in multiculturalist policies the naturalisation of a Western hegemonic culture continues, while the minority cultures become reified and differentiated from what is regarded by the majority as normative human behaviour.

John Rex describes multiculturalism as an enhanced form of the welfare state in which 'the recognition of cultural diversity actually enriches and strengthens democracy' (1995: 31). This happens for three basic reasons: because the values of specific cultures might be intrinsically of value, and might enrich society; because the social organisation of minority communities provides them with emotional support; and because it also provides them with more effective means of getting further resources and defending their collective rights. The question arises, however, concerning the nature of these collective rights, and what specific provisions the state needs to make towards individuals and collectivities in its heterogeneous population. Jayasuriya has pointed out that two separate issues are involved here: 'One is the centrality of needs in the collective provision of welfare and the other is the difficult question of boundaries of need in claiming for one's right' (1990: 23).

The most problematic aspects of these questions become apparent when the provision relates not to differential treatment in terms of access to employment or welfare but to what has been defined as the different cultural needs of different ethnicities. These can vary from the provision of interpreters to the provision of funds to religious organisations. In the most extreme cases – as in the debates around Aboriginals, on the one hand, and Muslim minorities following the Rushdie affair, on the other – there have been claims for enabling the minorities to operate according to their own customary and religious legal systems. While the counter-arguments have ranged from the fact that this would imply a *de facto* apartheid system to arguments about social unity and political hegemony, those who support these claims have seen them as a natural extension of the minorities' social and political rights. This raises the question of how one defines the boundaries of citizens' rights. Jayasuriya (1990) distinguishes between needs – which are essential, and therefore require satisfaction by the state – and wants, which fall outside the public sector and are to be satisfied within the private domain in a voluntary way.

The differentiation between public and private domains plays a central role in delineating boundaries of citizenship in the literature, although not enough attention is being given to the fact that the public domain contains both the state domain and the domain of civil society. Turner (1990), for instance, has anchored his typology of citizenship in the extent to which the state enters or abstains from entering the private domain. As the examples above show, however, the dichotomous construction of private/public spheres is culturally specific, as well as gender-specific in itself (Yuval-Davis 1991, 1992b, 1997). The whole debate on multiculturalism stumbles on the fact that the boundaries of difference, as well as the boundaries of social rights, are determined by specific hegemonic – perhaps universalistic, but definitely not universal – discourses. And as we saw above, universalist discourses which do not take into account the differential positionings of those to whom they refer often cover up racist (and I would add sexist, classist, ageist, disablist, etc.) constructions.

One of the primary examples for a multiculturalist perspective which reifies and homogenises specific cultures is the book published in 1993 by UNESCO called *The Multi-Cultural Planet* (Laszlo 1993), in which the world is divided into culturally homogeneous regions, such as 'the European culture' (but also 'the Russian and East European culture', 'the North American culture', 'the Latin American', 'the Arab', 'the African', etc.), among which dialogues and openness should be developed.

Although multiculturalism is generally hailed by its promoters as a major anti-racist strategy, it has been criticised from the Left for ignoring questions of power relations, accepting as representatives of minorities people in class and power positions very different from those of the majority members of that community, and being divisive by emphasising the differential cultures of members of the ethnic minorities, rather than what unites them with other Blacks who share with them similar predicaments of racism, subordination and economic exploitation (Bourne and Sivanandan 1980; Mullard 1980). Other critiques from the Left have been directed against both the 'multiculturalist' and 'anti-racist' positions (Rattansi 1992; Sahgal and Yuval-Davis 1992).

These critiques have pointed out that in both approaches there is the inherent assumption that all members of a specific cultural collectivity are equally committed to that culture. They tend to construct the members of minority collectivities as basically homogeneous, speaking with a unified cultural or racial voice. These voices are constructed so as to make them as distinct as possible (within the boundaries of multiculturalism) from the majority culture, so as to make them 'different'. Thus, within multiculturalism, the more traditional and distanced from the majority culture the voice of the 'community representatives' is, the more 'authentic' it would be perceived to be within such a construction. Within 'anti-racism', a similar perspective also prevailed. The voice of the 'Black' (of the all-encompassing binary division black/white) has often been constructed as that of the macho liberatory hero, rejecting all which might be associated with White Eurocentric culture.

Such constructions do not allow space for internal power conflicts and interest differences within the minority collectivity: conflicts along the lines of class and gender as well as, for instance, politics and culture. Moreover, they tend to assume collectivity boundaries which are fixed, static, ahistorical and essentialist, with no space for growth and change. When such a perspective becomes translated into social policy, 'authenticity' can become an important political tool with which economic and other resources can be claimed from the state on the grounds of being 'the' representative of 'the community' (Cain and Yuval-Davis, 1990). As Yeatman observes:

> It becomes clear that the liberal conception of the group requires the group to assume an authoritarian character: there has to be a headship of the group

which represents its homogeneity of purpose by speaking with the one, authoritative voice. For this to occur, the politics of voice and representation latent within the heterogeneity of perspectives and interests must be suppressed. (Yeatman 1992: 4)

This liberal construction of group voice, therefore, can inadvertently collude with authoritarian fundamentalist leaders who claim to represent the true 'essence' of their collectivity's culture and religion, and have high on their agenda the control of women and their behaviour.

Multiculturalism, therefore, can often have very detrimental effects on women in particular, as 'different' cultural traditions are often defined in terms of culturally specific gender relations, and the control of women's behaviour (in which women themselves, especially older women, also participate and collude) is often used to reproduce ethnic boundaries. An example of such a collusion, for instance, is the case in which the judge refused a request for asylum to an Iranian woman who had had to escape from Iran after refusing to veil because 'this is your culture' (case recounted by the solicitor Jacqui Bhabha). Another is the placement of a young Muslim girl, who had fled her parents' home because of their restrictive control of her behaviour, in another Muslim home, even more pious, against her wishes and the advocacy of the Asian Women's Refuge (case recounted by Southall Black Sisters).

A contradictory multiculturalist practice is described by Jeannie Martin (1991): the practices of 'ethnic families' are weighted against a 'good society' model, which becomes identical with some unspecified Anglo-family norm, 'on behalf of ethnic women', focusing on 'atavistic practices such as clitoridectomy, child marriages, etc.', as the 'limits of multicultural diversity'. Martin describes this approach as typical of the 'ethnicists' among the multiculturalist theorists in Australia, and points out that what motivates them is not a real concern for women – because the ethnicists assume that women's subordination is part of the natural order of things in which the family is at the forefront. Rather, this is a device for establishing ranking among men of diverse backgrounds, based on the degree of their deviation from the Anglo-model – constructed as the ideal, positive model.

An alternative dynamic model of cultural pluralism to the multiculturalist ones has been developed by Homi Bhabha (1990, 1994a, 1994b). Abolishing the division of space/time and structure/process, and emphasising the constantly changing and contested nature of the constructed boundaries of the national 'imagined community', and of the narratives which constitute its collective cultural discourses, Bhabha notes the emerging counter-narratives from the nation's margins – by those national and cultural 'hybrids' who have lived, because of migration or exile, in more than one culture. Such 'hybrids' both evoke and erase the 'totalising boundaries' of their adoptive nation. Such counter-narratives do not, of course, have to come from immigrant minorities. The growing voice of Indigenous People, for example, is an instance of a counter-narrative which is heard from within. So too, of course, counter-narratives about the boundaries of 'the nation' have disintegrated the former Yugoslav and Soviet nations; and while not being as radical in other national communities, the construction of the nation and its boundaries are a matter of constant debate everywhere. It is important to note in this context what Homi Bhabha fails to consider: that 'counter-narratives', even if they are radical in their form, do not necessarily have to be progressive in their message. As Anna Lowenhaupt Tsing (1993: 9) claims, such counter-narratives have to be situated 'within wider negotiations of meaning and power at the same time as recognising local stakes and specificities'.

Another danger in Bhabha's approach is that it may interpolate essentialism through the back door – that the old 'multiculturalist' essentialist and homogenising constructions of collectivities are attributed to the homogeneous collectivities from which the 'hybrids' have emerged, thus replacing the mythical image of society as a 'melting-pot' with the mythical image of society as a 'mixed salad'. Characteristic of such a position has been, for example, the description by Trinh Minh-ha of herself, in a recent conference on Racisms and Feminisms in Vienna (October 1994), as standing 'on the margin, resisting both the majority culture and that of her own group'.

It is against this construction of essentialist fixed constructions of cultures, nations and their boundaries, and the reduction of ethnicity to 'culture', that transversal politics have been developed.

FEMINISM, MULTICULTURALISM AND IDENTITY POLITICS

The feminist version of 'multiculturalism' developed as a form of 'identity politics' which replaced earlier feminist constructions of womanhood, informed primarily by the hegemonic experiences of white, middle-class Western women. Despite the politically important introduction of the differentiation between sex and gender – the former described as a fixed biological category, the latter as a variable cultural one – the feminist technique of 'consciousness-raising' assumes, as a basis for political action, a *de facto* fixed reality of women's oppression that has to be discovered and then changed, rather than a reality which is being created and re-created through practice and discourse. Moreover, it is assumed that this reality of women's oppression is shared by all women, who are perceived to constitute a basically homogeneous social grouping sharing the same interests. Women's individual identities have come to be equated with women's collective identity, whereas differences, rather than being acknowledged, have been interpreted by those holding the hegemonic power within the movement as mainly reflections of different 'stages' of 'raised consciousness'.

Although the fallacy of this position has been acknowledged to a large extent by many activists and scholars in the various women's movements in recent years, the solution has often been to develop essentialist notions of difference such as, for example, between Black and White women, middle-class and working-class women, or Northern and Southern women. Within each of these idealised groups, the assumptions about 'discovered' homogeneous reality usually continue to operate. 'Identity politics' tend not only to homogenise and naturalise social categories and groupings, but also to deny shifting boundaries of identities and internal power differences and conflicts of interest. On the other hand, as Daiva Stasiulis and I have pointed out (1995), there are also serious problems with the analyses of many postmodernist feminists who have developed alternative non-essentialist deconstructionist approach to grapple with the notion of 'difference' (e.g. Gunew and Yeatman 1993; Larner 1993; Nicholson 1990; Young 1990). By using terms such as 'contingent identities' and 'hyphenated feminisms', they virtually dispense with notions of asymmetrical and systemic power relations (Fuss 1989; Stasiulis 1990: 294; Yuval-Davis 1991, 1994).

It is important to emphasise that postmodernist deconstructionist approaches are not necessarily immune to *de facto* essentialist constructions, as Paul Gilroy (1994) has pointed out. These often occur when notions of 'strategic essentialism' of the Gayatri Spivak variety are evoked: while it is acknowledged that such categories involve 'arbitrary closures' for the sake of political mobilisation, these categories become reified via social movements and state policy practices.

Rejecting such reified constructions of categories does not negate the primary importance that considerations of individual and collective positionings, power relations both within and in relation to other collectivities, and the cultural, political and economic resources which they carry, should have in the construction of any political alliances.

TRANSVERSAL POLITICS

Transversal politics are based on dialogue that takes into account the different positionings of women, or people in general, but does not grant any of them *a priori* privileged access to the 'truth'. In 'transversal politics', perceived unity and homogeneity are replaced by dialogues that give recognition to the specific positionings of those who participate in them, as well as to the 'unfinished knowledge' (to use Patricia Hill Collins's term [1990]) that each such situated positioning can offer.

Central to transversal politics are the processes which the Italian feminists from Bologna's Women's Resource Centre have called 'rooting' and 'shifting'. The idea is that each participant in the dialogue brings with her the rooting in her own grouping and identity, but tries at the same time to shift in order to put herself in a situation of exchange with women who have different groupings and identities.

Transversal politics are not just coalitions of 'identity politics' groups which assume that all members of such groups are equally positioned and culturally, socially and politically homogeneous. Gender, class, race, ethnicity, location, sexuality, stage in the life cycle, ability, and all other dimensions of specific positionings are taken into consideration, as well as the particular value systems and political agendas of the participants in the exchange.

In another place (Yuval-Davis 1994) I have explored in detail a variety of approaches to coalition politics, and brought two very different examples of transversal politics. The first example is that of the London-based group Women Against Fundamentalism (WAF). WAF includes women from a variety of religious and ethnic origins (Christians, Jews, Muslims, Sikhs, Hindus, etc.). Many of the members also belong to other campaigning organisations, often with a more specific ethnic affiliation: Southall Black Sisters (SBS), the Jewish Socialist Group, and the Irish Abortion Support Group. However, except for SBS – which had an organisational and ideological initiatory role in establishing WAF – women come there as individuals rather than as representatives of any group or ethnic category. On the other hand, there is no attempt to 'assimilate' the women who come from the different backgrounds. Differences in ethnicity and point of view – and the resulting different agendas – are recognised and respected. But what is celebrated is the common political stance of WAF members, as advocating 'the Third Way' against fundamentalism and against racism. At the same time, WAF campaigns on, for instance, state religious education, or women's reproductive rights, have been informed by the differential experiences of the group's women, given their different positionings and backgrounds. Inderpal Grewal and Caren Kaplan (1994) describe the Asian Women's Shelter group in San Francisco as having very similar political dynamics in its work to those of WAF.

The other example of transversal politics in action is described in my article, 'Women, Ethnicity and Empowerment' (1994). It refers to a meeting that took place in Bologna in 1992 between Italian, Israeli and Palestinian feminists. Although since the 1980s there had been many dialogue groups which had brought Israelis and Palestinians together, such meetings very often seemed to bear some of the worst characteristics of identity politics – participants perceived one another as 'representatives' of their national collectivities, thus forming an internally homogeneous delegation. These meetings frequently deteriorated into mutual collective guilt invocations that only helped to reify national boundaries. The aim of the Italian feminists who invited both the Israeli and the Palestinian women to participate in the meeting (as well as Algerian, Black British feminists and myself as outside supporters) was to break out of this pattern, and – given the responses of many of the participants afterwards – they largely succeeded.

The boundaries of the different national groupings at the meeting were determined not by an essentialist notion of difference but by a concrete and material political reality. The Israeli group, for instance, included both Jewish and Palestinian women citizens of Israel. Also, the women involved in the different groups were not perceived simplistically as representatives of their groupings. While their different positionings and backgrounds were recognised and respected – including the differential power relations inherent in their corresponding affiliations as members of Occupier and Occupied collectivities – all the women who were sought and invited to participate in the dialogue were committed to refusing 'to participate unconsciously in the reproduction of existing power relations', and 'to finding a fair solution to the conflict' (Italian letter of invitation, December 1990). The Italian feminists who organised the meetings between the Palestinian and Israeli women also later supported similar dialogues developed between Serbian, Croatian and Bosnian women in the former Yugoslavia, under the umbrella name Women in Black.

Two things are vital in developing the transversal perspective: first, that the process of shifting should not involve self-decentring, that is, losing one's own rooting and set of values. As Elsa Barkley Brown has pointed out: 'one has no need to "decentre" anyone in order to centre someone else; one has only to constantly pivot the centre' (1989: 922). It is vital in any form of coalition and solidarity politics to keep one's own perspective on things while empathising and respecting others. In multiculturalist types of solidarity politics there can be a risk of uncritical solidarity. This was very prevalent, for instance, in the politics of some sections of the Left with regard to the Iranian revolution or the Rushdie affair. They regarded it as 'imperialist' and 'racist' for the West to intervene in 'internal community matters'. Women are often the

victims of such a perspective, which allows the so-called (male) representatives and leaders of 'the community' to determine policies that
ultimately concern women, their well-being and their physical safety.

Secondly – and following from this first point – the process of shifting should not homogenise the 'other'. Just as there are diverse positions
and points of view among people who are similarly rooted, so there are
among the members of the other group. The transversal coming together
should not be with the members of the other group *en bloc*, but with
those who, in their different rooting, share compatible values and goals
to one's own. Transversal politics do not assume that the dialogue lacks
boundaries, and that each conflict of interest is reconcilable. However,
the boundaries of such a dialogue are determined by the message rather
than the messenger. The struggle against oppression and discrimination
might (and mostly does) have a specific categorical focus, but is never
confined just to that category, which can thus avoid reification.

A word of caution, however, is required here. A transversal politics is
not always possible, as the conflicting interests of people who are situated
in specific positionings are *not* always reconcilable. When solidarity *is*
possible, however, it is important that it is based on transversal principles.

REFERENCES

Anthias, Floya (1993) 'Rethinking Categories and Struggles: Racism, Anti-racisms
    and Multiculturalism'. Paper delivered at the European workshop on Racism
    and Anti-Racist Movements, University of Greenwich, September 1993.
Anthias, Floya and Nira Yuval-Davis (1984) 'Contextualising Feminism: Ethnic,
    Gender and Class Divisions'. *Feminist Review* 15: 62–75.
Anthias, Floya and Nira Yuval-Davis (1992) *Racialised Boundaries: Race, Nation,
    Gender, Colour and Class and the Anti-Racist Struggle*. London: Routledge.
Armstrong, J. (1982) *Nations before Nationalism*, Chapel Hill, NC.: University of
    North Carolina Press.
Balibar, Étienne (1992) 'Paradoxes of Universality', in David Goldberg (ed.) *Anatomy
    of Racism*. Minneapolis, MN: University of Minnesota Press.
Barkley Brown, Elsa (1989) 'African-American Women's Quilting: A Framework
    for Conceptualising and Teaching African-American Women's History'. *Signs*
    14, 4: 921–9.
Bhabha, Homi (ed.) (1990) *Nation and Narration*, London: Routledge.
Bhabha, Homi (1994a) *The Location of Culture*, London: Routledge.
Bhabha, Homi (1994b) 'Subaltern Secularism'. *Women Against Fundamentalism
    Journal* 6.
Bhabha, Jacqui (1994) Personal legal notes.
Bottomley, Gill (1991) 'Culture, Ethnicity and the Politics/Poetics of Representa-
    tion'. *Diaspora* 3: 303–20.
Bourne Jenny and A. Sivanandan (1980) 'Cheerleaders and Ombudsmen: The
    Sociology of Race Relations in Britain': *Race & Class* 21, 4.

Brah, Avtar (1991) 'Difference, Diversity, Differentiation'. *International Review of Sociology* New Series 2: 53–72.

Cain, Harriet and Nira Yuval-Davis (1990) '"The Equal Opportunities Community" and the Anti-Racist Struggle'. *Critical Social Policy*, Autumn.

Enloe, Cynthia (1990) '"Womenandchildren": Making Feminist Sense of the Persian Gulf Crisis. *The Village Voice*, 25 September.

Fuss, Diana (1989) *Essentially Speaking: Feminism, Nature and Difference*. New York: Routledge.

Gilroy, Paul (1994) *The Black Atlantic: Modernity and Double Consciousness*. London: Verso.

Grewal, Inderpal and Caren Kaplan (1994) 'Introduction: Transnational Feminist Practices and Questions of Postmodernity', in I. Grewal and C. Kaplan (eds) *Scattered Hegemonies*. Minneapolis, MN: University of Minnesota Press: 1–35.

Gunew, Sneja and Anna Yeatman (eds) (1993) *Feminism and the Politics of Difference*. St Leonards, NSW: Allen & Unwin.

Hill Collins, Patricia (1990) *Black Feminist Thought: Knowledge, Consciousness and the Politics of Empowerment*. Boston, MA: Unwin Hyman.

Jakubowicz, Andrew (1984) 'State and Ethnicity: Multiculturalism as an Ideology'. *Australia and New Zealand Journal of Sociology* 17, 3.

Jayasuriya, L. (1990) 'Multiculturalism, Citizenship and Welfare: New Directions for the 1990s'. Paper delivered at the 50th Anniversary Lecture Series, Dept of Social Work and Social Policy, University of Sydney.

Kandiyoti, Deniz (1988) 'Bargaining with Patriarchy'. *Gender and Society* 2, 3.

Knopfelmacher, Prof. (1984) 'Anglomorphism in Australia'. *The Age*, 31 May, Melbourne.

Larner, Wendy (1993) 'Changing Contexts: Globalisation, Migration and Feminism in New Zealand,' in S. Gunew and A. Yeatman (eds) *Feminism and the Politics of Difference*. Sydney: Allen & Unwin.

Laszlo, Ervin (ed. for UNESCO) (1993) *The Multi-Cultural Planet*. Oxford: One World.

Martin, Jeannie (1991) 'Multiculturalism and Feminism', in G. Bottomley, M. de Lepervanche and J. Martin (eds) *Intersexions*. Sydney: Allen & Unwin: 110–31.

Minh-ha, Trinh T. (1989) *Woman, Native, Other*. Bloomington, IN: Indiana University Press.

Modood, Tariq (1988) '"Black", Racial Equality and Asian Identity'. *New Community* 14, 3: 397–404.

Mullard, Chris (1980) *Racism in Society and Schools*. London: Institute of Education, University of London.

Nicholson, Linda J. (ed.) (1990) *Feminism/Modernism*, New York: Routledge.

Office of Multicultural Affairs (1989) *National Agenda for a Multicultural Australia*. Canberra: AGPS.

Rattansi, Ali (1992) 'Changing the Subject? Racism, Culture and Education', in J. Donald and A. Rattansi (eds) *'Race', Culture and Difference*. London: Sage.

Rex, John (1995) 'Ethnic Identity and the Nation State: The Political Sociology of Multi-Cultural Societies'. *Social Identities* 1, 1: 21–41.

Sahgal, Gita and Nira Yuval-Davis (eds) (1992) *Refusing Holy Orders: Women and Fundamentalism in Britain*. London: Virago.

Schlesinger, Arthur M. Jr (1992) *The Disuniting of America: Reflections on a Multi-cultural Society*. New York: W.W. Norton.

Sivanandan, A. (1982) *A Different Hunger*. London: Pluto Press.

Schierup, Carl-Ulrik (1995) 'Multi-culturalism and Universalism in the USA and EU Europe'. Paper delivered at the *Nationalism and Ethnicity* workshop, Bern, 2–4 March.

Stasiulis, Daiva K. (1990) 'Theorising Connections: Race, Ethnicity, Gender and Class', in P. Li (ed.) *Race and Ethnic Relations in Canada*. Toronto: Oxford University Press.

Stasiulis, Daiva and Nira Yuval-Davis (eds) (1995) *Unsettling Settler Societies: Articulations of Gender, Ethnicity, race and Class*. London: Sage.

Tsing, Anna Lowenhaupt (1993) *In the Realm of the Diamond Queen*. Princeton, NJ: Princeton University Press.

Turner, Bryan (1990) 'Outline of a Theory of Citizenship'. *Sociology* 24, 2.

Yeatman, Anna (1992) 'Minorities and the Politics of difference'. *Political Theory Newsletter* 4, 1: 1–11.

Young, Iris Marion (1990) *Justice and the Politics of Difference*. Princeton, NJ: Princeton University Press.

Yuval-Davis, Nira (1991) 'Ethnic/Racial and Gender divisions and the Nation in Britain and Australia", in Richard Nile (ed.) *Immigration and the Politics of Ethnicity and Race in Australia and Britain*. London: Institute of Commonwealth Studies: 14–26.

Yuval-Davis, Nira (1992a) 'Zionism, Anti-Zionism and the Construction of Contemporary "Jewishness"'. *Review of Middle East Studies* 5: 84–109.

Yuval-Davis, Nira (1992b) 'Secularism, Judaism and the Zionist Dilemma'. *WAF: Journal of Women Against Fundamentalism* 3: 8–10.

Yuval-Davis, Nira (1992c) 'The Gendered Gulf War: Women's Citizenship and Modern Warfare', in H. Bresheeth and N. Yuval-Davis (eds) *The Gulf War and the New World Order*. London: Zed Books: 219–225.

Yuval-Davis, Nira (1993) 'Gender and Nation'. *Ethnic and Racial Studies* 16, 4: 621–32.

Yuval-Davis, Nira (1994) 'Women, Ethnicity and Empowerment'. Special issue on 'Shifting Identities, Shifting Racisms', in K. Bhavnani and A. Phoenix (eds) *Feminism and Psychology* 4, 1: 179–98.

Yuval-Davis, Nira (1997) *Gender and Nation*. London: Sage.

Yuval-Davis, Nira and Floya Anthias, (eds) (1989) *Woman – Nation – State*. London: Macmillan.

12

DOMINANT AND DEMOTIC DISCOURSES OF CULTURE: THEIR RELEVANCE TO MULTI-ETHNIC ALLIANCES

Gerd Baumann

INTRODUCTION

Assuming that the forging of multi-ethnic alliances must entail a process of negotiating 'cultural' and 'community' differences, it is worth asking how such differences are conceived in the first place. In this chapter I propose that there are two constructions involved. One conceptual praxis – here called the dominant discourse – imagines differences of 'culture' to be homologous with differences of 'ethnic' identity and often of 'community', defined on quasi-biological lines. In doing so, this discursive praxis reduces both culture and 'ethnic' difference to reified essences. It cannot, however, in any simple way be rubbished as 'false' or 'plain reificatory', for it forms part of the discursive competence of citizens from 'ethnic' minorities themselves, and continues to function as one element in the negotiation of difference. To validate and describe it as such, however, has little to gain from an uncritical acceptance of its dominant status and hegemonic effectiveness. Rather, it needs to be studied as the counterpart to an equally effective alternative discourse, here called the demotic.

Where the dominant discourse views 'culture' as the reified possession of 'ethnic' groups or 'communities', the demotic discourse questions and dissolves this equation between 'culture', ethnos, and 'community'. On the basis of this dual discursive competence, 'culture' and 'community' are rendered into terms of active negotiation and debate, the social processes that underlie the forging of multi-ethnic 'communities of action' out of reified 'communities' of 'culture'. The documentation of the demotic alongside the dominant discourse thus has an immediate bearing, I suggest, on understanding how multi-ethnic alliances actually proceed in the negotiation of 'cultural' or 'community' differences as locally perceived.

The empirical evidence for these propositions was collected during seven years of resident research in Southall, a multi-ethnic suburb of London.[1] The town numbers some 60,000 people of internally diversified South Asian, Afro-Caribbean, Irish and English backgrounds. The obvious starting point for fieldwork in such a setting would have been a 'community study': selecting one 'community', preferably religious, national or 'ethnic', and describing it, so far as was analytically defensible, as an autonomous local 'culture'. Yet what struck me most forcefully over the first year or so of research was the multitude of crosscutting social and cultural cleavages. Tracing religious cleavages, Southall was a town of Sikh, Hindu, Muslim, and various Christian 'communities'. Tracing linguistic cleavages, it was a town of Punjabi, Gujerati, Urdu, and several English-speaking 'communities'; tracing the cleavages of their migratory histories, Southallians of different religions and languages, national and regional 'communities' could yet again form different 'communities', such as East African-Asian as opposed to subcontinental-Asian. The multitude of crosscutting cleavages rendered Southall a palpably plural society, and to do justice to this plurality meant ranging across the categorical divides of seemingly autonomous 'communities' of 'culture'.

Equally importantly, it was Southallians themselves who could be seen to distance themselves, in a variety of contexts, from the 'community' paradigm. The more one listened, the more there seemed to be 'communities' within 'communities', as well as 'cultures' across 'communities'. The equation between 'community' and 'culture', dominant as it is in much public discourse about 'ethnic' minorities, disintegrated the more I got to know local people. As I have indicated, Southallians indeed replicated the equation between a 'community' and 'its' 'culture' in a number of contexts. Yet in others, the same Southallians could dissolve the dominant equation by statements such as: 'In our community, we don't have a culture'; 'Of course we have a culture, but we're not a community'; or 'That [other] community is really part of our culture'. In analysing such data, it thus became necessary to take a deliberate look at the genesis, the salient features, and the limitations of the dominant discourse itself. This may briefly be summarised by deconstructing the concept of culture.

THE DOMINANT DISCOURSE

Ethnographers' uses of the word 'Culture' have established one essential point of consensus: 'Culture' is not a real thing, but an abstract and purely analytical notion. In itself, 'it' does not 'cause' behaviour, but denotes an abstraction from it, and is thus neither normative nor predictive but a heuristic means towards explaining how people understand and act upon the world. As a deliberate abstraction its use is in conceptualising that ever-changing 'complex whole' (Tylor 1958) through which people engage in the continual process of accounting, in a mutually meaningful manner, for what they do, say, and might think. Culture thus exists only in so far as it is performed, and even then the ontological status of the term is that of a pointedly analytical abstraction. This ethnographic insight has been clarified, and enshrined even against the Boasian heritage of American anthropology, by a new consensus against essentialist approaches to culture (Barth 1994; Keesing 1994; Sahlins 1994; Vayda 1994).

Outside the academy, however, the word was borrowed and assigned a new and far more concrete meaning in the discourse of what Rothschild has described as 'ethnopolitics' – that is, the process of

> mobilising ethnicity from a psychological or cultural or social datum into political leverage for the purpose of altering *or reinforcing* ... systems of structured inequality between and among ethnic categories. (Rothschild 1981: 2; emphasis added)

In this process, ethnopolitical activity

> stresses, ideologises, reifies, modifies, and sometimes virtually re-creates the putatively distinctive and unique cultural heritages of the ethnic groups that it mobilises. (ibid.: 3)

Ethnic labels are thus validated as referring to actual 'ethnic groups', and these 'groups' are defined with reference to a homogeneous and discrete 'culture' they are assumed, *ex hypothesi*, to share. An early example of this new public and political use of 'culture' was the Black Consciousness Movement in the United States. Whereas the Civil Rights Movement demanded equal individual rights for all citizens, regardless of who they were, the Black Consciousness Movement addressed its constituents not as citizens, but as a distinctive collectivity – a 'community' with its own 'culture'. In this new political discourse, in which civil rights are contested on the basis of 'ethnic' and 'cultural' identities, 'culture' as an academic abstraction, referring to a perpetually changing process of 'meaning-making', is replaced by 'culture' as a reified entity that has a definite substantive content and assumes the status of a 'thing' that people 'have', 'belong' to or 'are members of'.

In this new context, the word 'culture' can no longer function as a purely analytical abstraction; it has to be 'filled with traits' – that is, specified as a substantive heritage that is normative, predictive of individuals' behaviour, and ultimately a cause of 'why' those who 'have' it behave as they do. Kapferer (1988) has described such processes with regard to the rise of extreme nationalism as 'the reification of culture, the production of culture as an object in itself' (1988: 97), and has shown how selected established patterns and traits are 'systematically removed from their embeddedness in the flow of daily life, fashioned into symbolic things, and placed in a stable, dominant, and determinate relation to action' (ibid.: 210).[2]

Such a reification of culture must appear necessary, moreover, if the word is to serve in the contestation over a new kind of rights: a category of rights more collective in conception than the traditionally individualist Civil Rights, but far more exclusive in character than universal Human Rights. These 'community' rights are claimed – or, indeed, denied – on the basis of membership in a collectivity defined by 'its' 'culture'. Vertovec (1992) rightly stresses the element of political contestation when he describes how 'Trinidad Hindu culture was made an object in itself so as to articulate a shared ethnic identity in the face of potentially intensified patterns of ethnic inequality and resource competition' (Vertovec 1995).

As for Britain, one may see a condensed example of this reified view of 'culture' in the phrase 'between two cultures'. The image it evokes is not of young people performing culture as a process of making sense of each other and of adult others, but of a culture-less flock lost between two immovable objects named 'cultures'. The political consequences of such an essentialist approach to 'cultural' and 'community' difference have been documented in rare detail by Kalka (1991), whose data originate from the London borough situated immediately north of Southall. The deliberate transformation of local politics into a contestation between putatively discrete 'communities' of 'culture' led to acrimonious 'ethnic' rivalries and highly divisive debates, while 'the majority of Asian residents in the borough were totally unaware of the struggle conducted presumably on their behalf' (Kalka 1991: 219).

To note reificatory assumptions in a public discourse is not to call that discourse false and, as it were, be done with it. For analytical purposes, of course, reification makes no sense. In Whitehead's well-worn phrase, it involves the 'fallacy of misplaced concreteness'. In a discourse of political contestation, however, reification may be desirable, and even seem necessary, to effect mobilisation. This mobilisation of all those who are deemed to 'have the same culture' is helped by the appeal, reassuring or challenging, to form part of a predefined 'community'.

I need not recapitulate here the semantic intricacies of the word 'community'.[3] Suffice it to say that in the dominant discourse, 'community' can function as the conceptual bridge that connects 'culture' with 'ethnos'. It can lend a spurious plausibility to the assumption that 'ethnic' minorities must, by the very fact of the 'ethnic' bond itself, share the same 'culture'. This slippage is all the easier since 'culture' appears already as a reified entity, and it is a general propensity of reifying thought that 'through reification, the world of institutions appears to merge with the world of nature' (Berger and Luckmann 1967: 108). Thus 'culture', and especially 'ethnic culture', can indeed appear as 'a universal mandate of natural laws, as the necessary consequence of biological ... forces' (ibid.).

Not all public discourse about minority 'communities', defined by their reified 'cultures', needs to invoke this assumed cultural imperative explicitly. Its evocation is evident, none the less, in innumerable examples, for it offers two strategic advantages: substantively, it appeals to a popular biological reductionism; and formally, it allows for discursive closure.

An appeal to biological reductionism is not surprising, of course, when we are examining a dominant discourse used about 'ethnic' minorities. It is still a popular assumption, found as easily among anthropology students as in mass media across the globe, that ethnos – much like 'tribe' – and, indeed, like the scientifically discredited notion of 'race' – designates a biological fact. These purportedly 'natural' cleavages between humans are easily and widely associated with cleavages of 'culture'. The tenacity with which even the term 'race' continues to dominate many informants' ideas of biology as the foundation of cultural diversity is evidence, if any were needed, for the persistent appeal of common-sense biologism: the expectation that cultural differences are founded in natural ones. This biologism is understandable, and even the ethnographic record of pre-colonial times is replete with peoples who regarded their own kinship systems, incest prohibitions, family structures, political, economic and religious conventions as 'natural'. It is thus not surprising that even notional collectives such as 'ethnic minorities' should be credited with that reassuring quality of being, at once, both natural and cultural entities. From the stylisation of 'ethnic' categories into 'communities', defined by a reified 'culture', protagonists of the dominant discourse can thus progress to a portrayal of minorities as forming ethnic-cum-cultural 'communities'.

At this point, discursive closure is complete. The two key terms mutually reinforce each other, for those defined as 'ethnic' minorities must form a 'community' based on their reified 'culture'; and their 'culture' must appear in reified form, because they are, after all, a 'community'. In cases where a reified minority 'culture' can be equated with a particular 'ethnic group', the circular discourse can seek added plausibility from popular forms of biological reductionism. It can thus reduce all the cultural complexities, both within 'communities' and across whole, plural societies, to an astonishingly simple equation: 'Culture = community = ethnic identity = nature = culture'.

I shall end here my short – and, by necessity, summary – sketch of the dominant discourse without interrogating the possible causes of its hegemonic position.[4] For our present purposes – that is, in relation to discussing multi-ethnic alliances – it will be clear that we need to go beyond this dominant discourse, even though it may well be used among 'ethnic' minorities themselves. Gilroy (1992) has addressed this salient overlap in his critique of the 1980s 'anti-racism' movement. He notes the elaboration of 'new forms of racism [which ...] are distinguished by the extent to which they identify race with the terms "culture" and "identity"' (Gilroy 1992: 53). In other words – and if I understand Gilroy rightly – the terms 'culture' and 'identity' may function as surreptitious code words for 'race'. Gilroy indeed pursues his argument down to the meaning of 'culture'. The argument is that both the New Right and the anti-racist movement have converged on 'a belief in the absolute nature of ethnic categories ... compounded firstly by a reductive conception of culture and secondly by a culturalist conception of race and ethnic identity' (ibid.: 50).

Such a critical appraisal of the dominant discourse cannot, however, absolve the ethnographer from studying its manifestations. Speaking of my own data, Southallians, too, use the dominant discourse whenever their judgements of context or purpose make it seem appropriate. It would be naive to pitch a Southall demotic discourse against the dominant one, and presumptuous for an ethnographer to adjudicate their relative merits. There are, at any rate, perfectly good reasons why people should reify the culture that, in other contexts, they are aware of re-making, reshaping, and re-forming. Culture-making, after all, is not an *ex tempore* improvisation but a project of social continuity placed within, and contending with, moments of social change. Southallians engage the dominant discourse as well as the demotic one. They reify 'cultures' while at the same time making culture. Even when they explicitly engage the demotic discourse, the faultlines of the dominant one are effective and, more than that, empirically visible. Thus, the patterns by which, say, Sikh or Afro-Caribbean Southallians, 'whites' or Muslims remap their 'cultures' and 'communities' are, and remain, distinctive to an observable degree. My argument is thus not, in summary, to rubbish the dominant discourse as a piece of reificatory obfuscation, but to study it as the counterpart to an equally effective alternative discourse, which I have here called the demotic.

THE DEMOTIC DISCOURSE

Where the dominant discourse equates 'culture' with 'ethnos' or 'ethnic community', its demotic counterpart disengages these very conceptions. Ideas of 'culture' and 'community' are thus rendered negotiable in the social process. To show this demotic discourse in practice would, of course, require an ethnographic detail for which this brief chapter does not allow (see Baumann 1996). It may be useful, however, to hint at some general patterns of the demotic discourse as they emerge in those of Southall's 'communities' of 'culture' that the dominant discourse identifies most easily. In most general contexts, Southallians tend to identify three 'communities' on quasi-'racial' lines: 'Asians', 'Caribbeans' and 'whites'. The first category, 'Asian', is widely subdivided, however, into three 'communities' defined by their religion: Sikh, Hindu and Muslim. Southallians are aware, of course, that there are 'Black' people who are Muslim, and, indeed, 'Asians' who are Christian. The division into five 'communities', however, is regarded as a practical shorthand in most general contexts. Taking these five 'communities' at face value, and abstaining from any critical scrutiny of this local version of the dominant discourse, let me summarise how the dominant equation of 'community' and 'culture' can be disengaged. As I have hinted already, this disengagement tends to take different forms, and privilege different concerns in different 'communities'.

Among 'members' of 'the Sikh community' – locally the most influential both in numbers and in political and economic weight – there were strong dynamics leading towards forging new 'communities' on the basis of congregation and caste interacting with perceptions of class. Among Hindu Southallians, by contrast, one could observe claims of a Hindu 'culture' encompassing people and ideas of other 'communities' (Dumont 1980), especially – but not only – Sikhs of the lower castes. Muslim Southallians were clearly aware that the local 'Muslim community' was divided into a variety of contending 'cultures', categorised according to languages, regions and national loyalties. 'Members' of Southall's 'Afro-Caribbean community' could view the dominant equation between 'community' and 'culture' as altogether inappropriate for people who had been denied their 'culture' for so long. The predominant phrasing of the demotic discourse here was orientated towards the 'making' of a 'culture' for the 'Afro-Caribbean' or 'African-Caribbean' community. Among the approaches explicitly aimed at 'finding', and thus consciously creating, a new common 'culture', special weight was given to four contending approaches: a religious, a historical, a pan-Africanist, and an expressive-musical. 'White' Southallians, finally, tended to be equivocal about their 'community' status. Irish Southallians endorsed the existence of an 'Irish culture', but widely denied the existence of an 'Irish community'; and English Southallians tended to cultivate a 'minority consciousness' without explicit reference to an 'English culture'. Both Irish and English Southallians attempted various forms of personal, religious or political identification with the 'cultures' of surrounding 'communities'.

What all these manifestations of the demotic discourse have in common is one basic skepsis: 'culture' and 'community', or 'ethnos' and 'culture', are disengaged from each other, and their dominant equation is denied in appropriate contexts. This may, incidentally, make it desirable not to speak of 'a' demotic discourse in the singular, but to speak of demotic discourses in the plural. The generic term to designate all demotic discourses as locally engaged would then have to be of a higher order of generality: for instance, demotic discursive competence. It seems slightly scholastic, however, to engage in terminological quibbles here. My point concerns the recognition of a demotic discursive praxis which differs from the dominant one, and its implications for an understanding of multicultural alliances.

Southallians of all 'cultures' and 'communities' are thus able, and motivated in chosen contexts, to disengage the dominant equation and to rethink, or pragmatically redefine, the relationship between 'community' and 'culture'. This does not mean, of course, that the dominant discourse is thereby revoked altogether. Southallians continue to engage it, depending on their judgements of context and purpose. What the data show, however, is a dual discursive competence. In certain contexts, Southallians engage the dominant discourse; in others, they deny its essential equation. This dual discursive competence turns 'culture' and 'community' themselves into terms of multi-ethnic debate. Their definitions and boundaries become the object of questioning and plural reinterpretation, and spark off argument even in the public domain. These arguments, and the dual discursive competence they rely upon, have an immediate bearing on the forging and functioning of cross-'community' and multi-ethnic alliances; for these, after all, involve the creation of a new 'community of action' that brings together people of different 'cultures', however defined or even reified.

From the Southall data, such processes can be shown in a variety of ways: the – originally anti-racist – subsumption of 'Asians' into a unified

'Black community' faltered locally because South Asian Southallians could not accommodate their conception of 'Asian culture' within the idea of a 'Black community'. The 1980s controversy about religious assemblies in schools pitched advocates of 'community worship' against protagonists of a multi-ethnic, consciously multiculturalist 'multi-faith' worship. Both cases can be read as contestations between the dominant discourse of 'communities of culture' and the demotic discourse of 'culture' as the result of both 'community' and cross-'community' negotiation. Similar constellations can be seen in Southallians' use of 'community' rituals to address cultural 'others' (Baumann 1992). Given the complexity of these local debates, however (see Baumann 1996), I shall limit myself here to a more manageable example, and raise some points on the conception of a cross-'community' 'Asian culture'. Across the categorical distinctions of religion, region and nationality among South Asian Southallians, one can observe both a conscious aspiration towards and a vociferous critique of the idea of a comprehensively 'Asian culture'. The debate about an 'Asian culture' can thus be seen as a negotiation of cross-'community' alliances which draws on Southallians' dual command of the dominant as well as the demotic discourse.

AN ETHNOGRAPHIC EXAMPLE: NEGOTIATING AN 'ASIAN CULTURE'

One of the most convincing – because unsought-for – signs that teenage Southallians of South Asian backgrounds have begun to construct a comprehensively 'Asian community' with its own 'Asian culture' arose in discussions about 'arranged' and caste-endogamous marriages (C. Ballard 1979; R. Ballard 1972). It was remarkable how many young Southallians saw 'arranged marriages' and the strictures of caste as a part of 'Asian culture' rather than a specifically Hindu, Muslim or Sikh 'culture'. It is widely considered an 'Asian custom' or 'rule' that 'Asians' should marry within their religious 'community' and their caste. This way of speaking enables South Asian Southallians to discuss their views as 'young Asians' together; and thus it contributes to their discovery of a shared 'Asian identity'. This commitment to a comprehensively 'Asian culture' marks a point of convergence that noticeably removes juveniles from the under-standings of the term 'culture' observed among children. While their younger siblings largely predicated their 'culture' concept on their religion, South Asian Southallian adolescents have come to see their own identity as 'young Asians' in town. Their discourse of 'culture' and 'community' can be seen to widen, with time, to include this new, secular, cross-religious, cross-caste, and sometimes political discourse of an 'Asian' identification.

To speak of an 'Asian culture' in the dominant sense of a unified 'community' heritage is, of course, implausible, as all Southall children know. It would demand blindness to the enormous diversity and the momentous contention that have long characterised the subcontinent. In Britain, at any rate, 'Asian' as a term to designate a shared 'culture' signifies a new departure, rather than a tradition or heritage. This departure is consciously innovative, although one should be wary here of playing a sociological 'generation game', as if the forging of post-immigration 'Asian culture' were the preserve of youngsters alone. Mannheim (1982) has shown up the spuriousness of using 'generation' as a sociological category. There is, however, an articulate awareness among young South Asian Southallians that being 'young and born here' involves them in, and qualifies them for, the conscious creation of a comprehensively 'Asian culture'.

To characterise this evolving 'Asian culture', three elements spring to teenagers' minds. They concern classification as 'Asians' by others, be they 'white' or Afro-Caribbean; an aspiration, like Afro-Caribbeans, to achieve a unity within that imposed classification; and a wish, like the 'other two cultures', to express this unity symbolically, often through music. A few words should be said about each of these dimensions of an 'Asian culture' increasingly recognised as a unifying factor by the young.

The endorsement of an 'Asian' 'community of culture' can be seen as a response to classification by others. The young Southallians who, in their teens, begin to apply the term to themselves are far less likely to have heard it from their parents than from Afro-Caribbean and 'white' peers at school, from teachers, and notably from television (Gillespie 1995). Sometimes, this inclusive self-categorisation as 'Asians' can begin to take on a political significance. In this sense, they explain that 'Asians should unite' in the face of discrimination and racism, as Afro-Caribbeans are seen to have done. Reference is sometimes made to the 'Southall Riots' of 1979 and 1981, when 'Asian youth united and took the lead' in protesting their common grievances. But this is rare, and an explicitly political approach tends to develop only later in adolescence. For the vast majority of young Southallians, though, politics is far less interesting than having fun with chosen peers. And as among so many youth whom anthropologists have studied, it is music that plays an eminent part in their expressive and symbolic peer culture.

Probably the greatest boost to a comprehensively 'Asian' cultural consciousness that my fieldwork could document was the 're-invention' (Baumann 1990) of Bhangra, a traditional Punjabi folk dance, music and song form. It was turned, from the late 1970s onwards, into a genre of amplified, 'modernised' pop music, to listen to on records or dance to at discos and parties. One can hardly overestimate the popularity of Bhangra among young South Asian Southallians during the 1980s. The adaptation of Bhangra that complements traditional lyrics and drum rhythms with electronic keyboards and guitars, synthesisers and new 'sampling' and 'scratching' techniques of recording is indeed largely a local invention. It was known originally as 'The Southall Beat', championed by the local groups Alaap, Heera and Holle Holle, and popularised further by some sixty West London groups. What is of greatest interest here is its expressive and symbolic contribution to young Southallians' conceptions of a new 'Asian *culture*'. I have found this expressed time and again by Southall youngsters, and most concisely by a musician interviewed in Southall's *Ghazal and Beat* music monthly; Komal, one of the lead singers of the group Cobra, characteristically refers to the impetus towards *cultural* unity and autonomy that many South Asian youth received from, and then defined in contradistinction to, young Afro-Caribbeans:

> I can remember going to college discos a long time ago, when all you heard was Reggae, Reggae, Reggae. Asians were lost, they weren't accepted by whites, so they drifted into the black culture, dressing like blacks, talking like them, and listening to reggae. But now *Bhangra* has given them 'their' music and made them feel that they do have an identity. No matter if they are Gujeratis, Punjabis or whatever – *Bhangra* is Asian music for Asians. (Dewan 1988: 8)

The internal divisions by region could be multiplied, of course, by those of religion and intra-religious traditions, caste, migratory history, class, and numerous other factors. Yet the idea of Bhangra as an 'Asian music for Asians' consciously replaces these internal divisions by a shared external distinctiveness. Most Southall parents I spoke to had precious little use for a comprehensive 'Asian culture', but tended to define their cultural distinctiveness with regard to far more particularist pre-emigration heritages. These can be upheld without any recourse to a category of 'Asian culture', implying that Sikhs, Hindus and Muslims, Punjabis, Gujeratis and Bengalis were 'the same'. Yet this is precisely what growing numbers of Southallian teenagers wish to see among themselves. They tend, to an overwhelming majority, to marry 'within' their own 'communities' of religion, as well as caste. Those who do not tend to leave Southall. Yet the discovery of an 'Asian' 'culture' among the young presents an apt example of the processes by which 'culture' and 'community' become objects of debate and terms of cross-'community' exploration.

Such exploratory new uses of the idea of 'culture' carry within themselves the potential for contestation about culture itself. A second example may serve to bring out this potential. It is taken from Southall's socialist and feminist 'communities', and I refer to them here for a number of reasons. They are, of course, relatively small local minorities; yet it is decidedly strange to read so many 'community studies' in which no one local seems capable of fundamental dissent, and everyone seems engaged in reproducing the same, indiscriminately shared, 'ethnic culture'. This lacuna is a direct result, of course, of the dominance of the dominant discourse. Secondly, I take it as read that socialist or feminist convictions can establish alternative cultures – that is, comprehensive systems of meaning-making with and about 'others'. Finally, even relatively small networks of dissenters can influence ideas of 'culture' and 'community' prevalent around them – as is shown, for instance, in Pryce's (1979) exceptionally pluralist 'community study' of Afro-Caribbeans in Bristol. As I have shown elsewhere (Baumann 1996), the counter-cultures of Southall socialists and feminists contribute to the agenda that Southallians at large have to face. In the present case, these agendas are concerned with a critique of 'Asian culture' from what the dominant discourse would call 'within'.

An initiative named 'Southall Monitoring Group' provides support and case work for victims of racially motivated violence, runs workshops and public campaigns, and monitors the activities of police as they affect 'minorities'. The group's network of supporters includes Southallians of all 'ethnic' and religious 'communities', and the political orientations they share are broadly 'Left' and sometimes Marxist. This orientation necessitates a reassessment of '[traditional] cultures' and their heritage. An example from the pen of the group's full-time co-ordinator is given in the following quote, in which he takes issue with the idea of 'preserving Asian culture': does this project, he asks, 'also include the preservation of practices such as dowry deaths, sati (bride burning), killing of "untouchables", retention of the caste system' (*The Gazette*, 5 August 1988: 10)?

Such criticism of 'traditions' is seen by many South Asian Southallians as discrediting their 'culture' in an already hostile environment, and the political dilemma it poses is obvious enough. It appears even more clear-cut when 'Asians' are not only the victims of racist attacks but are themselves among the perpetrators of other violent acts, some directed against women.

A partly overlapping network of Southallian socialists and feminists supports a group named 'Southall Black Sisters' which is pledged to confront these issues. Unlike the Monitoring Group, Southall's Black Sisters face the problems of reassessing their 'community's cultural heritage' in sharply pointed ways. The problem of critiquing 'Asian culture' would be easy, of course, if South Asian Southallian feminists could limit their criticism to a populist chastising of individual violators; yet a feminist analysis obliges them to challenge institutions fundamental to many Southallians' heritages, such as 'arranged marriages' and the dowry system:

> within the Asian community our priorities remain to challenge head-on practices such as domestic violence, arranged marriages, the dowry system and sexual abuse in the family. If we do not confront these patriarchal structures and forces we will be guilty of colluding with them. (*Southall Black Sisters* 1986: 2)

Such open criticism of 'traditional Asian culture' is apt to incur the wrath of established 'community leaders' intent upon the good reputation of 'their' communities. Thus, Southall's most powerful South Asian 'community' organisation, the Indian Workers' Association, addressed a letter to the Borough Council responsible for funding both the Black Sisters and the Monitoring Group. I quote it from a leaked version whose authenticity I see no reason to doubt. I have taken the liberty of highlighting passages that caricature the dominant discourse:

> We *on behalf of the community* would like to inform you that both these groups play a negative role through their activities in Southall ... their *whole life style*, activity, and involvement is totally *alien* to the *customs, language, tradition* and *culture* of *the* black community. [emphasis added]

The dilemma of the two sides facing each other here is rooted in the dominant discourse itself. 'Community leaders', working on the premiss of having to 'represent' whole ethnic-cum-cultural 'communities', must underpin their efforts by demanding and gaining respect for the 'culture' concerned. This 'culture' must be represented as a monolithic body of lifestyles and convictions, hallowed by 'custom' and shared among all 'their' constituents. Those, however, whose culture entails a reassessment of the status quo, and implies an appreciation of culture as continually remade, must then be disowned. They are, in effect, declared 'aliens' in relation to the reified 'culture' that 'community leaders' are supposed to represent. The dilemma of the other side is equally poignant. Those whose chosen culture of conviction does not allow them to endorse some of their 'ethnic' culture's traditions and values must say so even in the face of a general public that may well be ignorant, lacking in respect, or ill-intentioned. The tensions documented in a letter such as this are far more than the result of personal animosities or local-level politicking. They are an index of a dialectic that applies far more widely: that between 'culture' as reified in the dominant discourse, and culture performed as a process of negotiation within, about and across 'ethnic communities'. This dialectic needs, I think, to be reflected in our under-standing of 'ethnic cultures', and has an immediate impact on the analysis of multi-ethnic alliances.

CONCLUSIONS

An analysis of multi-ethnic alliances cannot usefully start from the assumptions of the dominant discourse. To treat 'ethnic communities' as self-evident, quasi-biological collectives of a reified 'culture' amounts to an implicit denial of the culture-making processes within 'ethnic com-munities' themselves. Multi-ethnic alliances are clearly not a matter of 'community of culture A' allying itself with 'community of culture B'. Rather, it is the conception, and the making, of culture itself that multi-ethnic alliances must renegotiate. If multi-ethnic alliances succeed in forging 'communities of action' out of 'communities' of reified 'cultures', then a rethinking of the culture concept is crucial. I have suggested that there are two culture concepts at work, and that they can be located in two different discourses. The dominant discursive praxis, reificatory and often biologistic as it is, forms part of the multi-ethnic equation. Yet so does the demotic discourse of culture with which people engage at the same time, and which is used to contest culture as a process of negotia-tion within, about and across their 'ethnic' identifications. To delegitimate the dominant discourse would be presumptuous; to continue to ignore the demotic would be an implicit denial both of the culture-making processes among 'ethnic' minorities and of the cultural potential of multi-ethnic alliances. At the risk of overstating the argument, one may well think of 'the negotiation of difference in multi-ethnic alliances' as a negotiation of the dialectic between dominant and demotic discourses of culture as locally engaged.

NOTES

1. In addition to part-time resident fieldwork (1986–90), this comprised a period of fifteen months of full-time research, made possible by a grant from the Leverhulme Trust, London. I am most grateful to its Chairman and Trustees, as to Professor Adam Kuper, who, as my Head of Department at Brunel University, has been most generous in his organisational support and intellectual guidance. I fur-ther thank Peter van der Veer and my new colleagues at Amsterdam, as well as the editors of this volume, for their most helpful and supportive critical feedback. This chapter presents a synopsis of arguments specified further in a monograph in press (Baumann 1996), and I thank Cambridge University Press for permission to use some of the material here.

2. On the tendency to reify 'minority' cultures in Britain, see Brah (1987), who critiqued the representation of women of South Asian backgrounds:

Many of the contemporary academic, political and popular discourses ... operate within a totally reified concept of culture as some kind of baggage to be carried around instead of a dynamic, and potentially oppositional, force which stands in a complex relationship with the material conditions of society. (Brah 1987: 44)

Phoenix (1988) moves in much the same direction in her critique of academic studies of 'black' teenage motherhood, and draws attention to the way in which 'narrow definitions of culture' are but translations of an ideology of 'race' into a discourse of reified 'culture' (1988: 153–9). Keesing (1994) has suggested that this 'conception of culture [which] almost irresistibly leads us into reification and essentialism' (1994: 302) is based on an ethnocentric construction of 'radical alterity – a culturally constructed Other radically different from Us' (ibid.: 301). He seems to forget, though, that people may reify their 'own culture' as readily as they reify 'other cultures'. Van der Veer (1994) indeed traces Indian communalist conflicts to 'the basic ... fallacy of both sociological and [non-academic] communalist versions [... which] portrays Muslim and Hindu values as reified systems' (1994: 29).

3. Unlike the word 'culture', 'community' has never held a privileged place in the vocabulary of social scientists. On the contrary, among academics it has had a decidedly bad press. It is usually traced to the German sociologist Tonnies (1887), who tried to use it as an analytical abstraction in an essentially evolutionist account. Hillery (1955) researched a grand total of ninety-four meanings attributed to the term by sociologists, and the word appears quite clearly as a common-sense term with no theoretical potential for analytic use. Macfarlane (1977) has forcefully advocated that it be abandoned altogether. More recently, the anthropologist Anthony Cohen (1985) has, in one brilliant short treatise, stripped away whatever substantive meaning one might have attributed to the word, and shown 'community' to be a contextually contingent 'symbolic construction'. This does not, of course, detract from its potential in political contestation and, indeed, confrontation, as Ignatieff (1992) observed in connection with the Rushdie affair, when

the only thing on which anti-Islamic liberals and their fundamentalist opposite numbers agreed was that there was such a thing as a "Muslim community". "It" was either a threat to liberal civilisation as we know it, or "it" was a resurgent faith on the march. At the height of the affair, Muslims in Britain could be forgiven for wishing no one had ever thought them a community at all. (Ignatieff 1992: 17)

The word remains attractive, however, even to the detractors of 'ethnic' minorities, because it appears to value people as members of a special collective. What is special about this collective, in the case of 'ethnic' minorities, is that they are readily presumed to share a 'culture' in its reified form.

4. For a discourse to be recognised as dominant, one would expect it to show five features that are, in practice, interdependent: its conceptual make-up should be economical, not to say simple; its communicative resources border on monopoly; it should be flexible of application, and should allow for the greatest ideological plasticity; finally, it should lend itself to established institutional purposes.

REFERENCES

Ballard, Catherine (1979) 'Conflict, Continuity and Change: Second-generation South Asians', in Verity Saifullah Khan (ed.) *Minority Families in Britain: Support and Stress.* London: Macmillan: 209–29.

Ballard, Roger (1972) 'Family Organisation among the Sikhs in Britain'. *New Community* 2, 1: 12–33.

Barth, Fredrik (1994) 'A Personal View of Present Tasks and Priorities in Cultural and Social Anthropology', in Robert Borofsky (ed.) *Assessing Cultural Anthropology.* New York: McGraw-Hill: 349–61.

Baumann, Gerd (1990) 'The Re-Invention of *Bhangra*: Social Change and Aesthetic Shifts in a Punjabi Music in Britain'. *The World of Music* (Berlin), 2: 81–98.

Baumann, Gerd (1992) 'Ritual implicates "Others": Rereading Durkheim in a Plural Society', in Daniel de Coppet (ed.) *Understanding Rituals.* London and New York: Routledge: 97–116.

Baumann, Gerd (1996) *Contesting Culture. Discourses of Identity in Multi-Ethnic London.* Cambridge: Cambridge University Press.

Berger, Peter and Thomas Luckmann (1967) *The Social Construction of Reality: A Treatise in the Sociology of Knowledge.* London: Penguin.

Brah, Avtar (1987) 'Women of South Asian Origin in Britain: Issues and Concerns'. *South Asia Research*, 9, 1: 39–54.

Cohen, Anthony (1985) *The Symbolic Construction of Community.* Manchester: Manchester University Press.

Dewan, Veeno (1988) 'Upcoming: Cobra'. *Ghazal and Beat* 4: 8. Southall, Middlesex: Derbar Publishers.

Dumont, Louis (1980) *Homo Hierarchicus: The Caste System and its Implications.* Augmented English translation. Chicago: University of Chicago Press.

Gillespie, Marie (1995) *Television, Ethnicity, and Cultural Change.* London: Routledge.

Gilroy, Paul (1992) 'The End of Antiracism', in J. Donald and A. Rattansi (eds) *'Race', Culture and Difference.* London: Sage in association with the Open University.

Hillery, G.A. Jr (1955) 'Definitions of Community: Areas of Agreement'. *Rural Sociology* 20.

Ignatieff, Michael (1992) 'Why "Community" is a Dishonest Word'. *The Observer*, 3 May: editorial page.

Kalka, Iris (1991) 'Striking a Bargain: Political Radicalism in a Middle-Class London Borough', in Pnina Werbner and Muhammad Anwar (eds) *Black and Ethnic Leaderships in Britain: The Cultural Dimensions Of Political Action.* London: Routledge: 203–25.

Kapferer, Bruce (1988) *Legends of People, Myths of State: Violence, Intolerance and Political Culture in Sri Lanka and Australia.* Washington, DC: Smithsonian Institution Press.

Keesing, Roger (1994) 'Theories of Culture Revisited', in Robert Borofsky (ed.) *Assessing Cultural Anthropology.* New York: McGraw-Hill: 301–10.

Macfarlane, Alan (1977) 'History, Anthropology and the Study of Communities'. *Social History* 5: 631–52.

Mannheim, Karl (1982) 'The Problem of Generations', in Chris Jenks (ed.) *The Sociology of Childhood: Essential Readings*. London: Batsford Academic and Educational Press: 256–69.

Phoenix, Ann (1988) 'Narrow Definitions of Culture: The Case of Early Motherhood', in S. Westwood and P. Bhachu (eds) *Enterprising Women. Ethnicity, Economy, and Gender Relations*. London: Routledge: 153–79.

Pryce, Ken (1979) *Endless Pressure. A Study of West Indian Life-Styles in Bristol*. Bristol: Bristol Classical Press.

Rothschild, Joseph (1981) *Ethnopolitics: A Conceptual Framework*. New York: Columbia University Press.

Sahlins, Marshall (1994) 'Goodbye to Tristes Tropes: Ethnography in the Context of Modern World History', in Robert Borofsky (ed.) *Assessing Cultural Anthropology*. New York: McGraw-Hill: 377–94.

Southall Black Sisters (1986) Southall Black Sisters Annual Report. Typescript.

Tylor, Edward Burnett (1958 [1871]) *Primitive Culture*. New York: Harper Torchbooks.

Van der Veer, Peter (1994) 'The Foreign Hand: Orientalist Discourse in Sociology and Communalism', in Carol Breckenridge and Peter van der Veer (eds) *Orientalism and the Postcolonial Predicament*. Philadelphia, PA: University of Pennsylvania Press: 23–44.

Vayda, Andrew (1994) 'Actions, Variations and Change: The Emerging Anti-Essentialist View in Anthropology', in Robert Borofsky (ed.) *Assessing Cultural Anthropology*. New York: McGraw-Hill: 320–29.

Vertovec, Steven (1992) 'Community and Congregation in London Hindu Temples: Divergent Trends'. *New Community*, 18, 2: 251–64.

Vertovec, Steven (1995) 'Hindus in Trinidad and Britain: Ethnic Religion, Reification, and the Politics of Public Space', in Peter van der Veer (ed.) *Nation and Migration: The Politics of Space in the South Asian Diaspora*. Philadelphia, PA: University of Pennsylvania Press: 132–56.

13

ESSENTIALISING ESSENTIALISM, ESSENTIALISING SILENCE: AMBIVALENCE AND MULTIPLICITY IN THE CONSTRUCTIONS OF RACISM AND ETHNICITY

Pnina Werbner

FEAR OF ESSENTIALISM

Essentialism, it seems, has become the bogey word of the human sciences, an accusation generating a virtual 'paranoia' (Fuss 1990: 1). Against essentialism, social constructionists stress the contingent, fractured, ambivalent and reflexive nature of culture and identity as these are played out in the context of power and domination.

In the study of racism and ethnicity, the founding assumption of anti-essentialism has been the fluidity, hybridity and openness of national culture and diasporic collective identities. Yet the scholarly fear of essentialism has also inspired a growing interest in the *sites* of essentialism – in the question of who essentialises whom, when and for what purposes.

Such constructionist questions highlight the paradoxical fact that, as Fuss puts it, 'there is no essence to essentialism' (1990: xii). Equally significant is a growing sense that constructionism has gone too far – in denying the ontological grounds of experience as a source of cultural meaning, and particularly so with regard to the 'phenomenology of embodiment' (Shilling 1993: 80), here considered as it relates to the experience of racial violence and suffering and the collective identities this experience generates.

Although the rise of organised racial violence in Europe during the 1990s has been a much-publicised social fact (see Bjorgo and Witte 1993; Witte 1994; Bjorgo 1995), there has been a tendency to gloss over the increase in racial violence in Britain itself, most scholars preferring, instead, to focus their deconstructive gaze on the stereotypes and textual narratives of racialising discourses. Nevertheless, the figures add up to a depressing record: in Britain in 1992–93, for example, there were 8,000 officially recorded incidents of racial violence, a figure which disguises the extent of the violence, thought to have been a multiple of this number (*Runnymede Bulletin*, September 1993). In September 1993, a candidate from the British National Party, the neo-Nazi fascist party, was for the first time elected as a municipal councillor in a London borough (he later lost his seat). An anti-racist demonstration against the BNP, which demanded the banning of explicitly racist political parties, ended in violence with a large number of policemen and demonstrators injured. Since 1992 the number of recorded incidents has risen; there has been an increase in vigilante activism of ethnic minority youth, minor 'race' riots in Bradford and Brixton, and further evidence of unwarranted police violence against members of minority groups.

Such processes of escalating racial and xenophobic violence in Britain appear to generate contradictory social trajectories. On the one hand, the pathways of mediated alliances and crosscutting ties between the majority and ethnic minority groups, which might counter the growing cycle of violence, become increasingly fragile. In Gregory Bateson's terms, we may say that violence generates counter-violence in a schismogenetic process of communal polarisation (on schismogenesis, see Bateson 1958 [1936]: 175–97).[1] On the other hand, opposing this trend, anti-racist movements mobilise an increasingly broader and more committed spectrum of ethnic groups for joint action against this escalating violence (see Miles 1994a).

In this chapter I analyse the experiential consequences of ethnic violence as a social force which absolutises ethnic identities. My argument starts from the premiss that violence is performative and exemplary: an extreme act of symbolic communication which generates a transformation in human relationships. The moral philosopher Emmanuel Levinas contrasts violence with altruism, which he defines as the human recognition of personal responsibility to an other in his or her difference. Unlike altruism, violence, he argues, denies otherness its legitimate right to exist and to be different. For Levinas, 'face', the acceptance of human alterity, contrasts with the 'silence' of violence, which is the turning away of face, a silence which is the denial of otherness (Levinas 1987).

In the following analysis, I build on Levinas's contrast to argue for a critical difference between processes of objectification and reification: between 'ethnicity' as a shifting, hybridised politics of identity or collective self-representation, and 'racism' or xenophobia – ethnic absolutism – as a progressively essentialising politics of violation and absolute negation of alterity. My argument responds in part also to a contemporary debate in Britain about anti-racism and multicultural identities. It is a debate which has highlighted some of the intractable dilemmas inherent in the multicultural privileging of singular, discrete and exclusive ethnic or racial identities in the public sphere.

At issue are problems of both representation and self-representation. The distinction is critical, for it raises questions about the moral and political right to represent a cultural other. Increasingly, the tendency has been to label all collective representations – whether of ethnic and religious groups, or classes and nations – as misplaced essentialisms (so that as anthropologists we can no longer study a 'society', a 'community', a 'culture' or a 'people'). Yet this indiscriminate accusation of essentialism, applied uncritically to all objectifications of collective agents, has tended, I shall argue here, to obscure processes of collective representation and self-representation which are *not* essentialist. To appreciate this further, I turn first to a consideration of the meaning of essentialism.

To essentialise is to impute a fundamental, basic, absolutely necessary constitutive quality to a person, social category, ethnic group, religious community, or nation. It is to posit falsely a timeless continuity, a discreteness or boundedness in space, and an organic unity. It is to imply an internal sameness and external difference or otherness.

The charge of essentialism attaches to any form of analysis which may be said to obscure the *relational* aspects of group culture or identity, and to valorise instead the subject in itself, as autonomous and separate, as if such a subject could be demarcated out of context, unrelated to an external other or discursive purpose (see Rorty 1992). The charge of essentialism is also levelled at structuralist analyses that highlight the internal coherence of symbolic patterns or social systems, and at phenomenological ones that stress the emotional power of distinctive cultures to define experience: the social force of taken-for-granted sentimental cultural attachments.

As a political performance, essentialising is defined as a form of displacement, 'which serves to disguise and distort the real thing', in Edward Said's terms (Said 1985: 22), to obliterate people, he says, as 'human beings' (ibid.: 27). Representation as distortion is seen here as a mode of silencing and suppressing the voices of oppressed subgroups. In this respect essentialism is a performative act, a mode of action.

Attempts to avoid essentialising the social collectivities we study lead, however, to a series of conundrums. If to name is to re-present, to imply a continuity and discreteness in time and place, then it follows that all collective namings or labellings are essentialist, and that all discursive constructions of social collectivities – whether of community, class, nation, race or gender – are essentialising. If Western Orientalism constructed a false non-Western Other, the Saidian critique of Orientalism runs the danger of constructing false counter-Occidentalisms of the West (Clifford 1988: 259, 262 *passim*; Carrier 1995: 1–3 *passim*). Since any objectification of a group or collectivity necessarily implies a continued unity in time and space, and a measure of integration, it would seem to follow that all forms of objectification essentialise.

In seeking a way out of this apparent aporia, Dominguez suggests that ethnographic writing should focus not on groups but on the process of objectification itself: the way collectivities describe, redescribe and argue over who they are (Dominguez 1989: 38; see also Yuval-Davis and Baumann in Chapters 11 and 12 above). Her work, like that of other feminists and post-colonial critics, reiterates that who has the right to objectify is itself a political question, because objectification implies 'a semiotic appropriation of self by the other' (ibid.: 166) and, by implication, a silencing of the other.

The issue is not, we need to remember, merely discursive, a linguistic paradox disclosing the limits of language. Policy decisions, state fund allocations, racial murders, ethnic cleansing, anti-racist struggles, nationalist conflicts or revivals, even genocide, follow on essentialist constructions of unitary, organic cultural collectivities.

The very heterogeneity of that list points, however, to the tangled issues I want to address here: citizenship rights and multiculturalist agendas are as much dependent on collective objectifications as are racist murders or ethnic cleansing. It is therefore critical to establish clearly the difference between modes of *objectification* and modes of *reification*. I want to suggest that reification is representation which distorts and silences, and hence is essentialist in the pernicious sense implied by this term. In this chapter I explore the difference between such reifications and normal ethnicity – a mode of *objectification* that, unlike xenophobia, ethnicism or racism, is, I suggest, a rightful performance or representation of multiple, valorised and aestheticised identifications.

That the problem of collective objectification is political, and not merely theoretical, is underlined by the energy devoted by ethnic activists and academics in Britain to arguing about the moral appropriateness of group labels. Such labels seem to capture the essence of a group, and this has lead to fierce debates about what ethnic minorities should call themselves, and be called. Label after label is rejected. First, the label of 'migrant' was rejected, then of 'immigrant', then of 'black', then of 'Asian' (see also Modood and Bonnett, Chapters 9 and 10 above).

PUBLIC ARENAS AND THE SELF-IMAGINING
OF COMMUNITY

The argument about ethnic naming highlights the fact that it is not only Western representations of the Other which essentialise. In their performative rhetoric the people we study essentialise their imagined communities in order to mobilise for action. Within the spaces of civil society, the politics of ethnicity in Britain are not so much imposed as grounded in essentialist self-imaginings of community. Hence, ethnic leaders essentialise communal identities in their competition for state grants and formal leadership positions. But – equally importantly – such leaders narrate and argue over these identities in the social spaces which they themselves have created, far from the public eye. Hence much of the imagining that goes towards mobilising ethnic or religious communities in Britain occurs in *invisible* public arenas, before purely ethnic audiences (on the significance of such popular cultural public arenas in India and more generally, see Freitag 1989).

In other words, self-essentialising is a rhetorical performance in which an imagined community is invoked. In this regard, the politics of ethnicity are a positive politics: they serve to construct moral and aesthetic communities imaginatively.[2] These moral and aesthetic communities are not fixed: they overlap and vary in scale. They emerge situationally, in opposition to other moral and aesthetic communities. Seen over time, this multiplicity of contingent, shifting and emergent collective identities enact a composite, unreflective, 'natural' and changing hybridity. The politics of race, extreme nationalism or xenophobia, by contrast, are a violent politics. The communities essentialised by the perpetrators of violent acts of aggression are not imagined situationally but defined as fixed, immoral and dangerous. In being demonised, they are reified.

Violence is an act which demands retribution. It creates, as Kapferer argues, its own 'meaning' and 'order', in which ethnic identities 'flash off' each other (Kapferer, forthcoming). It is performative, a 'display' of self-sufficient autonomy and rejection of otherness which becomes in time routine practice, grounded in common-sense social constructions. Through this process, the signifying practices of racial violence come to be constitutive of self and identity – as happens, for example, among white working-class adolescents (see Hewitt 1986; Rattansi 1995). Unless it is checked, violence generates an escalating cycle of fear and counter-violations, leading to an unbreachable moral chasm. To achieve this end, xenophobic actors 'theatricalise' and 'ritualise' violence, in order to destroy the natural syncretisms, hybridities and multiple affiliations of everyday life and 'magnify' cultural differences (Tambiah 1986: 117).

It was such a cycle which led to the racialisation of British Muslims in the course of the Rushdie affair. The emotionally charged development of the *Satanic Verses* affair can thus serve to illuminate the schismogenetic nature of essentialism as a social process grounded in violence.

AGONISTIC MORAL PANICS:
THE SATANIC VERSES

The Satanic Verses was a politically polemical novel inserted into an already charged political field. The field was marked by a cycle of agonistic moral panics, which generated a chain of essentialisms and counter-essentialisms.

Moral panics demonise tangible surface targets through a process of 'displacement' (see S. Cohen 1972: 9). In a moral panic, underlying social contradictions converge on apparently concrete causes. As moral panics overlap, as the 'demons proliferate', the sense of threat reaches a point of crisis in which ordinary people begin to fear 'the breakdown of social life itself, the coming of chaos, the onset of anarchy' (Hall *et al.* 1978: 322–3) – in short, apocalypse, which only an 'exceptional' response can forestall.

The historical roots of the Rushdie affair in Britain can be traced to British and American imperialism in Iran, an intervention which violated Iranian national integrity. Supported by the West, the Shah of Iran's modernisation drive attacked not only political freedoms but Islam as the national religion, evoking instead a pre-Islamic Persian history, dating back 2,500 years to Cyrus the Great (see Lewis 1975).

The Shah's deliberate attack on Islam generated the first moral panic, led by the Islamic clergy, which ultimately sparked the Iranian revolution. The Iranian revolution led to the second moral panic, this time in the West, which was fuelled by a fear of a violent, fanatical 'Islamic fundamentalism'. Rushdie, and secular Muslim intellectuals like him, shared that fear, as other Islamic countries like Pakistan began, following the Iranian revolution, to abolish hard-won civil liberties, and especially the rights of women (see Mumtaz and Shaheed 1987).

Both moral panics generated essentialist definitions of opponents. Iranians, in their fear, demonised the Shah and essentialised America as 'The Great Satan'. The West, and urbanised liberal Muslims in Islamic countries, demonised the Ayatollah Khomeini and essentialised the Muslim hordes. *The Satanic Verses* can be seen as a cultural response to this real sense of fear experienced by a Muslim cosmopolitan elite.

The publication of the novel sparked a new moral panic. Muslims globally perceived it as a public symbolic violation, a Western and Zionist conspiracy to defame and mock Islam and its sacred symbols. In Britain the moral panic was a tangible symptom of the contradictions Pakistani immigrants were experiencing between their aspirations as economic migrants and the cultural alienation which permanent settlement implied (see P. Werbner 1996a). The fact that the book seemed to mock and deride Islamic culture and values made it a symbol of racism, of the humiliation Pakistanis experience daily as black victims of racial abuse and discrimination.

Hence a novel which might at another time have passed unnoticed came to be displaced as the devilish locus of a moral panic. The author was literally demonised in the Islamic press and cinema, his slanted eyes and long ears lending themselves to the creative imagination of Muslim cartoonists. A literature defending Muslim interpretations of the book emerged (see, for example, Ahsan and Kidwai 1991). A deep sense of hurt pride and offence generated a campaign against the author, even before the Ayatollah's *fatwa*.

The violent response of Muslims to the author and the book triggered a British and Western counter-moral-panic. This last in the cycle of agonistic moral panics displaced and essentialised local British Muslims as folk devils. It papered over the contradiction in Britain between the 'nation', invoked as an expression of a shared, unified and homogeneous culture and history, and the multicultural, multi-racial nature of contemporary British society. British Muslims came to epitomise the danger to the nation as a moral community, to freedom of expression, to physical safety, to universal cultural *communication* between all citizens. 'Islamophobia' – the fear of Muslims – became a direct expression of this moral panic.

Muslim and English moderates attempted to dissipate the panic by refocusing attention on the blasphemy law and its bias in favour of Christianity. Indeed, the whole debate has consisted of such refocusings, each side foregrounding and essentialising different dimensions of the cycle of agonistic panics and counter-panics (on this process in scientific discourse more generally, see Strathern 1991).

As the affair continued, it became clear that Muslim religious feelings were not protected under the British blasphemy law. British Muslims discovered that their religion could be violated and mocked without the law affording them any protection. In response, in a schismogenetic process of polarisation, they essentialised English society as hostile and unfeeling. At the same time, they reconstituted themselves as a community of suffering.

RACISM AND AMBIVALENCE

A digression is in order here: my claim that racism reifies and absolutises cultural difference is challenged by a contemporary stress on the inherently ambivalent nature of relations between racist and racialised, coloniser and colonised, in which 'fear and desire double for one another and play across the structures of otherness' (Hall 1992: 256). In the postmodern world, Rattansi argues, 'racist identities are decentred, fragmented by contradictory discourses and the pull of other identities ... [they are] not necessarily consistent in their operation across different contexts and sites' (Rattansi 1995: 70). For the racist, 'the racist object is not only disgusting and hateful, but powerful, fascinating, erotic and possessing qualities admired by racist subjects' (ibid.: 74). This seems to accord with Fanon's claim that the ambivalence of racist (or colonial) 'desire' is mirrored by the racialised subject's dream of dispossessing and replacing his oppressor: 'there is no native who does not dream at least once a day of setting himself up in the settler's place' (Fanon 1967: 30). Hence the colonial situation is characterised by a continual fluctuation between attraction and repulsion (Young 1995: 61).

Reflecting on such ambivalent desires, it might seem that racist subjectivities are fractable, situational and partial, not unlike any other collective identities. There are, in other words, 'no watertight definitions to be had of ethnicity, racism and the myriad terms in between.... Indeed, all these terms are permanently in-between, caught in the impossibility of fixity and essentialism' (Rattansi 1995: 53). The dangers of such a thesis are obvious: in conflating the multiplicities and hybridities of everyday ethnicity with the ambivalences of racism or ethnicism, ethnic sentiments are, in effect, criminalised, while racist motivations are, by the same token, exonerated. All is ambivalence.

At first glance, Hall's or Rattansi's views merely echo the stress on ambivalence in the encounter between racist and racialised in the work of Homi Bhabha. Like Bhabha, Rattansi's psychoanalytic focus on sexuality importantly recognises the emotional roots of identity. Yet he fails, like Bhabha, to appreciate the critical difference between racism and everyday ethnicity — that is, between reification and objectification. There are important parallels between my critique of his approach here and the criticisms levelled by some post-colonial writers at Bhabha's reading of Fanon.

According to JanMohamed (1985), Bhabha fails to recognise that Fanon viewed the colonial conflict as an irreducible Manichaean struggle. Indeed, reading *The Wretched of the Earth* one cannot escape the progression Fanon traces from the moment of colonial repression and mutual envy and/or desire to the polarised liberatory violence of the nationalist movement (the point stressed by Parry 1987) pitched against the utter brutality of colonial counter-violence (Fanon 1967).

For Gates, reviewing this argument, it simply reflects the porousness of Fanon's work which makes it amenable to multiple, positioned, critical readings (Gates 1991: 458). From my perspective, what Fanon importantly recognised is that all relations between racists and victims, colonisers and colonised, are imbricated in violence. This is ultimately what differentiates racism, ethnicism or xenophobia from banal, everyday ethnicity, however competitive, interested and ethnocentric identity politics may be. In a racist relationship desire and attraction are schismogenetically transformed into an impulse to violate, to rape and to molest. The key is to be found in the process itself, which is enunciatory, performative and dynamic, not static and logocentric.

The interpretative differences between Fanon-gazers are thus also differences in the interpretation of racism itself; a question of what happens when words become acts. My proposal is that violent acts erase the ambivalences of racism to reveal a 'Manichean world' (Fanon 1967: 31). In this sense the 'third space' of pre-revolutionary, blurred and compromised identities which Fanon describes – a site where racist and racialised mirror and are drawn towards each other, inversely and perversely – is *from the start* a space of distorted specularities: *a pathological space.*

One should be careful not to conflate spatial metaphors of heterotopia, cultural ambivalence, multiplicity or hybridity which may denote quite different relations.[3] In Bhabha's own work, an optimistic evocation of an 'intervening space' in which a 'new transnational and translational sense of the hybridity of imagined communities' will replace the polarising violence associated with ideas of a 'pure, "ethnically cleansed" national identity' (1994: 5) is ambiguously located *vis-à-vis* his analysis of the 'splitting' of the colonial space of consciousness in a 'Manichean delirium'; 'a paranoid fantasy of boundless possession' (ibid.: 43–5) in which the ambivalent figure of the deracinated *évolué*, doubly, *neurotically*, as I read it, different according to Fanon, occupies a liminal space betwixt-and-between colonised and coloniser.

In my reading of Bhabha, the *post*-colonial space of the migrant he evokes is marked ambiguously both by pathological ambivalence and violence and by multiplicity: of split subjects and identities which deny the possibility of 'claiming an [authentic and whole] origin for the self', since the diasporic sense of self is necessarily disrupted by a consciousness of difference (1994: 47): one 'is continually positioned in space between a range of contradictory places that coexist' (ibid.). The mistake Bhabha makes is to conflate the third space of multicultural multiplicity with the Fanonian, pre-revolutionary, perverted and fear-driven space of colonial specularities (ibid.: 50–51). This conflation obscures the specificity of the redemptive project undertaken by Third World and Black writers: to write the counter-narratives of the margins, not merely in order to unsettle 'any simplistic polarities and binarisms' (ibid.: 53) – the task of remaking the nation in its complex cultural and ideological heterogeneity – but, above all, in order to expose the violence and suffering generated by the encounter. This is Paul Gilroy's central point (1993): that black aesthetics and polemics were produced by the engagement with the darker, destructive side of modernity. Unlike Gilroy, however, both Bhabha and Rattansi fail in the final analysis to distinguish clearly between the interruptive juxtapositions which objectify hybridised ethnic and cultural differences and the violating ambivalences of racism.

THE EMERGENCE OF A COMMUNITY OF SUFFERING

By contrast to everyday ethnicity, ethnicist or racial violations create communities of suffering. Counterposed against the self-declared ethnic 'purity' of the racists, a community of suffering is often a hybrid assortment of Others. The 'Muslims' racialised in the aftermath of the Iranian revolution or of the Rushdie affair, form a composite unity of nationalities and ethnicities. To understand how such a community of suffering emerges, we need to consider the ontological structure of racism as violence, and to examine the specificities of its violations. By doing so, we can begin to disclose how these generate the creative cultural narratives of communities of suffering.

Violence and violation are, of course, pervasive in Britain, as they are in other industrialised societies. Every year there are thousands of cases of domestic violence, violent robbery and homicide. Racism, xenophobia or extreme nationalism differ, however, from these other acts of violence in being directed against individuals by virtue of their (ethnically, biologically or culturally marked) group memberships. The violence is directed symbolically against the whole group by violating individual members of it. From this perspective, ethnic violence ('ethnicism') – even between groups putatively of the same 'race', as in Sri Lanka, Bosnia or Zimbabwe – is a form of racism, since what is critical is the way in which groups are essentialised violently in order to subordinate or exclude them permanently. It makes little difference, in this respect, whether such groups are marked out by colour, language, religion, territory, or claimed common origin.[4]

FIGURE 13.1   Racist violations and anti-racist movements

Target: the individual	Emergent movements
Body 'Face' Economic rights Political rights	Joint supra-ethnic/racial civil rights movements and the creation of a 'new' common identity
Target: aesthetic and moral community	Emergent movements
Communal icons Communal 'face' Communal property Communal cultural rights	Separate cultural movements; multicultural alliances; cultural/racial separatism

Racial or xenophobic attacks are meant to be exemplary. The message of the attackers is clear: these immigrants, black people, Muslims, don't belong here. They must go or be eliminated. In this sense violence is a 'theatrical' locutionary act, an act of public communication. Hence, although racial violence seems to be haphazard and uncontrolled, in reality it is systematic.

As in tribal feuds, continuing violence comes in time to be perceived as an essential feature of intergroup relations. Where aggression goes unpunished, it comes to be legitimised ideologically.

In order to highlight the systematic nature of racial, xenophobic or quasi-nationalist violations, I turn now to a consideration of the dimensions of personhood and sociality that racism as violation invariably targets. Against the trend, I am arguing for the need to go beyond the recognition that there are many historically contingent racist discourses (P. Cohen 1988), and to seek the ontological structure of racism in the violations which repeat themselves *across* these and make the experience of racism ontologically comparable in the perception of its victims.[5] My focus is particularly on the *materiality* of racism, its embodiment, which is revealed graphically in the objects that racism targets:

1. the human *body* (through torture, death, rape, physical mutilation, slavery);
2. individual and group *property* (through dispossession of land, personal property, corporate possessions, national estates);

3. sacred *communal symbols* (through physical destruction or desecration of places of worship, of religious and cultural icons, of aesthetic works, or by suppressing language);

4. group *political autonomy* (by jailing, exiling or executing leaders and dismantling regimes, and by attacks on vulnerable members of the group, such as women and children).[6]

Effectively, then, ethnic violence targets the body, the body politic, the material bases of physical and sociopolitical reproduction, and the emblematic representations of subjectivity, personhood and society.

Everyday, banal racism, the kind most often encountered in Western democracies, replicates this series in parallel acts of sometimes invisible aggression:

1a. against the person or subject (through verbal insults and abuse, and deliberate social exclusion);

2a. against equal opportunities and *citizenship rights* (in housing, employment, education, etc.);

3a. against sanctified *cultural icons* (via slurs and attacks on a group's culture by the media, or public political demands that the group assimilate or 'integrate');

4a. through a silencing of *group voices* in the public sphere; this was a pertinent feature, of course, of the Rushdie affair.

As a quotidian enactment, racists try to force the redefinition of social situations as confrontations between culturally or biologically marked collective actors. This contrasts with the normal political process of collective boundary construction which is fundamentally recursive and situational, reliant on the sited play of different subjective identities. Racism is thus a vortex which swallows up all other identities. In so doing it violates 'normal' expectations of sociality by generalising all situations that include cultural Others as Manichaean.

Because racism and xenophobia are ontologically structured in violent polarising acts, this makes the *experience* of racism ontologically comparable in the perception of victims *across cultural communities* and beyond the historical specificities of particular racisms. The early politics of the British Black anti-racist movement exemplify this hybrid transcendence of migrant identities. As Sivanandan recalls:

> We learnt ... to weave from the differing but common traditions of our anti-colonial struggle a common struggle against racism. We related to both the struggle back home and the struggle now, the struggle of Gandhi and Nehru, of Nkrumah and Nyerere ... a beautiful massive texture. (Sivanandan 1990: 66)

The vital sedimented memory of common suffering and resistance is the shared 'text' for future cultural creativity. Involved here is far more than a mere 'invention of tradition'; at stake is the imaginative rewriting of the experience of those who 'suffered the sentence of history – subjugation, domination, diaspora, displacement' (Bhabha 1994: 172), a memorialising of 'a solidarity founded in victimisation and suffering' (ibid.: 191). In sum, the moral fable of collective suffering is an allegory that can travel, as exemplified by Black slaves' aesthetic reworking of the myth of Exodus (Gilroy 1993: 207–8).

Racism, xenophobia or quasi-nationalism are the very opposite of altruism and moral proximity, as Bauman has argued (Bauman 1989; 1992: 47–53). It is the inversion of the moral community (and hence of ethnicity); a denial of 'face' in Levinas's terms (Bauman 1992); an act of violent 'silencing' in Foucauldian terms. The 'silences' arising from violent group subordination need thus to be distinguished from the 'silences' of quotidian ethnicity: a recursive and reiterative process through which multiple identities are selectively highlighted – now figure, now 'silent' ground. To pursue this statement further, I turn now to an analysis of the 'silences' of ethnicity.

MORAL COMMUNITIES

Like communities of suffering, moral communities disguise their composite multiplicity under a semblance of unity. Indeed, the challenge for the moral community is to transcend its internal cultural, political and gendered differences. Hence, although British Pakistanis are most known for their violent public protests in the aftermath of the publication of *The Satanic Verses*, in reality their main work of community formation has been hidden, virtually invisible, and has taken place in the spaces they have created for themselves. It is in these public arenas that Pakistanis mobilise to celebrate or fund-raise, and in which – to echo Clifford Geertz – they tell themselves stories about themselves.

The fundamental notion of public service for Pakistanis is *khidmat*, service rendered selflessly with no expectation of return. *Khidmat* is a form of unilateral giving, a sacrificial offering in the sight of God, an expression of public responsibility. The limits of the moral community are the limits of such unilateral giving or, alternatively, of sharing. *Khidmat* is thus an embodied, metonymic act of *identification* which expresses personal commitment stemming from a shared identity. During the 1990s, for example, Pakistanis, along with other British Muslims and concerned citizens, were engaged in a major philanthropic fund-raising drive throughout Britain to raise medical aid and food for the Muslims in

Bosnia. The drive included voluntary functions, concerts and political meetings, as well as the organisation of convoys of food, clothing and medicine across Europe to Bosnia.

Much of this fund-raising is highly politicised and competitive, yet even at its most agonistic, philanthropic giving of this type constitutes a symbolic statement about the recognised limits of trust. The category encompassing donors and recipients is, from this perspective, imagined as a moral community. Through his/her donations, an individual expresses membership in a circle composed of mutually trusting others.

But most importantly for the argument put forth here, rather than *khidmat* signifying identification with a single, essentialised community, giving enables subjects to reach out to a variety of overlapping and pro- gressively widening imagined moral communities – from a circle of known intimates to the whole ethnic or religious community, including many unknown persons, and finally, to a scattered diaspora or the national homeland (see P. Werbner 1990). Hence the other is transmuted, through giving, into an extension of the self.

Unilateral giving grounds hybrid identities in dialogical relations, by connecting the self to significant others. In claiming public recognition, moral communities assert a beneficent equality rather than superior moral worth, positioning themselves within a system of named moral commu- nities. Giving (like racial violence) is performative – a symbolic, indeed theatrical, gesture. But unlike violence, it is a gesture of reaching out, of responsibility and identification, signalling moral commitment or 'proximity' in the sense suggested by Levinas. Identities, in other words, are lived not only discursively, but through gestures of identification or rejection.

Anthropologists in recent years have increasingly recognised the dialogic nature of community. A moral community is not a unity. It is full of conflict, of internal debate about right and wrong (on this feature of Muslim society, see, for example, Fischer and Abedi 1990; Bowen 1989; P. Werbner 1996b, 1996c; and more generally on internal moral arguments of identity, Paine 1989; Dominguez 1989; R. Werbner 1991). Such debates imply fierce competition for leadership. They also involve competition for the right to name: Who are we? What do we stand for? What are we to be called? Are we Muslims? Democrats? Pakistanis? Socialists? Blacks? Asians? The power to name, to inscribe, to describe, to *essentialise*, implies a power to invoke a world of moral relationships, a power underlined in the myth of Genesis. Naming constitutes a forceful act of leadership in its own right.

Solidarities are not givens but achievements, usually ephemeral. Yet they are imaginatively critical moments: anti-essentialist arguments attacking the false construction of 'culture', or 'community', fail to recognise the importance for participants in moral debates of an imaginative belief in the reality of such achieved solidarities (see Friedman 1992; Friedman and Baumann, Chapters 5 and 12 above). Strategic essentialising has to be grasped as a reality beyond a constructivist historiography of subaltern consciousness (Spivak 1987: 205): in fact, the subaltern *does* speak, even if her or his voice does not always reach 'us' – does not necessarily *seek* to reach us. The performance of identity outside and beyond the official public sphere, in alternative public spaces (Gilroy 1993: 200), precedes and anticipates any public action in the larger national arena.

In Britain, diasporic public arenas are spaces in which local-level community leaders engage in moral arguments and dialogues among themselves, in front of local audiences. In such meetings, leaders promote not only 'ethnic' but a variety of civic values – democratic, nationalist, religious. Their speeches stress that people are locked in moral interdependency; that – as one local-level Pakistani leader put it – 'A person cannot exist outside the community, as a wave cannot exist outside the ocean.' The rhetoric of such organic leaders evokes vivid images and tropes, appealing (in the case of Pakistani settlers) to Punjabi and Islamic cultural idioms and moral ideas in order to score points and move their audiences. In their performative rhetoric local leaders evoke not only moral communities but aesthetic communities as well.

THE AESTHETIC COMMUNITY

If the moral community is constituted through acts of giving, the aesthetic community is defined by cultural knowledge, passion and creativity. This is particularly important in the case of South Asians in Britain, for whom language and popular culture cut across different South Asian national and religious affiliations to create a broader, hybridised unity (on this, see Hutnyk and Baumann, Chapters 7 and 12 above). Aesthetic communities have their cultural experts: their orators, poets, priests, musicians, saints and intellectuals. Their members share common idioms of humour, love, tragedy, popular culture, festivals, cricket and myths of the past: of national or religious exemplary heroes, of great battles and victories, of oppression and freedom. They share aesthetic ideas of spatial separations between the profane and the sacred, sensuality and spirituality, 'fun' and sobriety. To perpetuate and reproduce these, Asians, Pakistanis and Muslims in Britain incorporate themselves in a myriad of associations: literary societies, religious organisations, orders and sects, sports clubs, women's cultural associations, and so forth.

In their artistic celebrations and rituals Pakistanis perform implicit acts of identification with several different aesthetic communities. As immigrants they evoke nostalgically their Pakistani homeland and the villages of the Punjab, Sindh or the Frontier; they cite the poetry of their national poet, Muhammad Iqbal, which is laced with heroic images of rivers, eagles, and metaphors of a Muslim nation. The moral lessons they draw are Islamic, but also Western-democratic. The aesthetic community is intertwined with the moral community. Ideas about purity and pollution, good and evil, sin and redemption, articulate the two. In their symbolic and rhetorical performances Pakistanis *fuse* their complex identities as Punjabis, Pakistani nationals, socialists, democrats, British citizens, Asians and Muslims. This fusing of discrete identities appeals to the deepest sentiments of their audiences, to their nostalgic yearning for another place with its smells and physical sensations, to their religious faith and to their sense of national loyalty. Paradoxically, such fusings of different identities undermine singular, essentialist self-representations while at the same time they infuse them with emotive power (see P. Werbner 1996c).

In practice, then, the moral and aesthetic imaginings of ethnic diasporic communities shift continuously between poles of objectification and reification. This is reflected in the politics of ethnicity and multi-culturalism in the public sphere.

In Britain, ethnic participation in the wider public sphere concerns two key orientations: a demand for ethnic rights, including religious rights, and a demand for protection against racism. Different identities and identifications *empower* these two orientations, pointing to the critical difference in Britain between the politics of ethnicity and the politics of race. Very generally, the politics of ethnicity in the public sphere are focused on cultural rights, public consumption in the voluntary sector and the allocation of state resources and jobs (see P. Werbner 1991a). Within this context, ethnic identities are evoked situationally, depending on the source and purpose of funding, the specific activities of voluntary organisations and the constellation of groups seeking representation, grants or posts. In their negotiation with the local state, ethnic identities are highlighted pragmatically and objectified relationally and contingently.

By contrast to ethnic politics, the politics of race create fixed, opposed groups confronting each other across a moral chasm, a 'dominant cleavage' (Gluckman 1940, 1956; Rex 1986).[7] Despite the common view that constructions of community by the state and local state reify cultural categories, the reality is more complex. Fictions of unity in the public sphere are generated within a bureaucratic moral economy based on attempts to fit the specificities of each case into a framework governed by notions of 'equity' and redistributive 'fairness'. The very multireferentiality of the term 'community' and its application enables the state and local state to respond flexibly to competing ethnic demands for public resources and positive action. This ambiguity allows for contextual redefinitions rather than fixed reifications. The moral economy of state allocations on a tight budget is thus quite rational: it attempts to allow for the special needs of ethnic minorities while selecting the *largest* possible constituency, defined (variably) by race, language, religion, national origin or neighbourhood, capable of managing the allocation amicably, without too much internal conflict. The welfare state thus constantly attempts to match scarce resources with claimed and perceived needs and collective group 'labels'. As a result, public fictions of communal unity vary situationally, and are constantly evolving through negotiation and dialogue between administrators and ethnic representatives (see P. Werbner 1991a). This familiar feature of ethnic politics differs radically from the essentialising processes of public reification which mark fixed cultural exclusions and subordination, often violently enacted.

The morally paramount division generated by the violations of racism might be expected to encompass and subsume all other cultural and religious divisions in a single community of suffering. Yet in contemporary Britain, the seeking of common aesthetic and moral narratives by the victims of racism has turned out to be highly problematic. Whereas racists essentialise and reify their victims differentially, these victims of racism struggle to find a shared, unitary identity they can all agree upon.

ESSENTIALISING SILENCE

Anti-racist discourses do not simply mirror differentialist racist discourses, each racism with its 'own' anti-racism. Because racial violence is an embodied, material attack suffered across racialised groups, it creates the potential ground for a mobilisation of broad, inter-ethnic alliances. Such alliances include also members of the majority group who are concerned with the broader defence of the nation-state's civic culture or citizenship identity (see also Rex 1992: 54).

Given their common experiences of racism and the shared sentiments these generate, anti-racists as a community of suffering can, potentially, evolve their own counter-discourses and self-identifications in the political arena. By doing so, they can transcend their particular ethnicities, class origin or gendered identities to forge new moral and aesthetic communities imaginatively.

But, paradoxically, racism, whether random or perpetrated by the state and police, violates *selectively*: Bangladeshis in London suffer more street violence, blacks are subjected to more police harassment, immigration controls affect Asians more; black women are doubly marginalised; the cultural icons of particular groups are desecrated differentially. This differentialism drives a wedge between ethnic groups. It was highlighted by the Rushdie affair, which separated Muslims as a community of suffering from the secular 'black' community.

The paradox that racism not only unites victims but also divides them culturally has been highlighted by a political and academic debate between anti-racists regarding the validity of their shared identification as 'black', Black being originally used as the banner of a social movement of doubly oppressed workers within the broader socialist radical camp (on this debate, see Sivanandan 1990: 77–123; Anthias and Yuval-Davis 1992: 7, 132–56; Brah 1992).

In its heyday, as we have seen, the black solidarity movement denied the significance of ethnic cultures, focusing singularly on the colonial and class struggle. Along with this focus came a sustained critique of anthropological studies of ethnicity, which were attacked for being divisive, apolitical and essentialising. Ethnicity, it was argued, colluded with the capitalist and bourgeois domination of a divided black working class. 'Culture' in this neo-Marxist critique was not ethnic but working-class and popular (see Hebdige 1979). Anthropology, in stressing the uniqueness of ethnic cultures, failed to recognise the class and racial dimensions of immigrant existence in Britain (CCCS 1982).

The Manichaean world imagined by the movement essentialised all whites as racists. At the same time the subtle racism of differentialist discourses projected a distorted ethnicism. Instead of demonising Britain's ethnic minorities as non-human, the New Right stressed the virtues of English national cultural solidarity and the dangers inherent in multi-culturalism. Rather than blatant colour racism, members of this new social movement stereotyped the cultures of Britain's various ethnic minorities as inferior or primitive. They appealed to the virtues of Englishness and the moral superiority of English culture, with its tried and tested democratic, liberal and enlightened values. They attacked the obdurate unwillingness of immigrants to assimilate and embrace this culture wholly (for a discussion, see Miles 1989; see also Gilroy 1990 for a neo-Marxist reponse).

In the light of these developments, anti-racism as a mode of correcting false fictions of otherness was increasingly acknowledged as a devastating failure, not only by conservative critics but by radical activists themselves (see, for example, P. Cohen 1988; Gilroy 1987; Murphy 1987; Modood 1988). One challenge to the radical position took the form of a rejection by Asian intellectuals of a unitary 'black' label.

In a series of articles culminating in his contribution to this volume (Chapter 9 above), Tariq Modood argued that a 'black' identity is being 'coercively' imposed on Asians against their will; as such it disempowers – and, indeed, harms – them. There is a difference, Modood argues, between a 'mode of oppression' – a negation – and a 'mode of being' – a positive, empowering cultural and psychological force which enables a group to 'resist its oppression'. Indeed, he claims, not all racist violations are the same. The most virulent white English hostility is reserved for communities which reproduce their cultural distinctiveness. The manufacture of a black identity out of black American, African and Afro-Caribbean history, Modood continues, serves to marginalise 'Asians' in relation to Afro-Caribbeans not only culturally, but economically and politically.

In the face of such arguments, and the evident vitality of Asian cultural creativity in Britain, Stuart Hall, in similar vein, revises an earlier position which attacked 'ethnicity studies' (CCCS 1982). He reflects that 'we always reconstructed' the 'great collectivities' of class, race and nation: 'more essentially, more homogeneously, more unified, less contradictorily than they ever were, once you actually got to know anything about them' (1991: 46). Asian people, he continues,

> when they came using their own resources of resistance, when they wanted to write out their own experience and reflect their own position, when they wanted to create, they naturally created within the histories of the[ir] language, the[ir] cultural tradition ... (ibid.: 56)

The problem with this debate is that it appears to replace one reification ('black') by another ('Asian'). The latter, in turn, disguises morally and culturally divisive oppositions among Asians between religious, nationalist and linguistic groups: Muslims, Hindus and Sikhs, Indians, Pakistanis and Bangladeshis, Punjabis, Gujeratis and Sindhis. Asianness, like blackness, is locked in a misplaced concreteness. It is not, after all, primarily *Asian* collective sacred icons and cultures which are violently targeted by racists in Britain, but the discrete national and religious icons of subgroupings within the broader South Asian collectivity. As we have seen, the most violent racism at present is directed against British Muslims. When, however, the primary battle is for state allocations or posts, the basic relationship which is publicly represented is not racial, but *ethnic*. Here the dynamics of fission and fusion rather than of a single dominant cleavage are the main operator, the 'voices' and 'silences' the product of relationally objectified ethnic segmentary oppositions rather than of violent, reified suppressions.

Stuart Hall's discussion of the ambivalences of the politics of representation fails to distinguish between these two silences. His discussion is nevertheless insightful because it discloses, perhaps unintentionally, the ontological and phenomenological dimensions of the segmentary principle of fission and fusion (that is, of situational objectifications). Opposites, Hall argues, not only repel, but are also attracted to one another; they bear the trace of their resemblance, articulated in an encompassing term of identification which, in turn, 'silences' those differences. The relationship between communal representations or identities, seen thus, he continues, is inherently dynamic and 'positional'. Its further complexity lies in the way multiphrenic, overlapping identities are managed in practice, or singular identities highlighted in political contestations.

But such 'silences', the silences of ethnicity, are – and this is a key point in the present argument – quite different from the violently produced silences of racism. Ethnicity does not deny proximity and alterity; it merely highlights difference. Ethnicity is an argument with other opinions – a dialogical heteroglossia in Bakhtinian terms. The violent silences of suppressed voices denied a political presence in the public sphere are generated by a denial of otherness – a denial of 'face' and 'opinion' in Levinas's terms. The two silences – of ethnicity and racism/ethnicism – are thus quite different; indeed, opposed. There is no 'becoming' in the silence of racism, because no proximity or commonality is acknowledged. Such a silence is the silence of tyranny, of absolute 'I'-ness or ipseity (see Levinas 1987: 18–23; 47–53). Thus Hall is right to argue for the need to '*decouple*' ethnicity from racism in the analysis of 'Englishness' (1992: 257), but he is wrong to equate the ambivalences of ethnicity with those of racism.

There is also a third, related, class of silences, which I shall call 'methodological silences'. These silences are discussed by Strathern (1991) in her application of chaos theory and fractal graphics to problems of social scale. Methodological silences are constituted by the gaps created by our scientific discourses, the 'remainder' these discourses generate. As Strathern points out, no representation, however complex and apparently exhaustive, is ever complete; there are always, in principle, further gaps to be filled, described or explained. In this sense all knowledge is partial, and replete with silences. As we produce knowledge, 'we become aware of creating more and more gaps' (Strathern 1991: 119). Discussing black people, we become aware of ignoring Asians; discussing Asians, we ignore Muslims; and so forth, right down to the individual, the self, and the divided self.

There are, then, at least three types of 'silence', which differ, *in principle*, from each other, and parallel different forms of essentialism. The voices of ethnic and subethnic groups, like the voices of individual subjects, are not necessarily silenced by violent suppression; they are given expression at different scales of action, in particular contexts, in front of different audiences. By contrast, minorities which are oppressed, marginalised and 'silenced' seek to make their voices heard from the widest public platforms: the national media, a canonical national high culture, and economic and political debating forums. It is in these contexts that national images and public agendas are formulated which affect the destiny of these groups.

Feminists have been key advocates against the rising tide of multiculturalism represented by Modood and others (e.g. Ballard 1992). As Yuval-Davis reiterates in Chapter 11 of this volume, feminists evoke the voices of ethnic minority women in Britain, silenced by the valorisation of essentialised definitions of cultural communities. They argue that to recognise the separate rights of such communities is to promote patriarchal values which deny Muslim or black women the equality and 'voice' due to them as British citizens (see the contributions to Sahgal and Yuval-Davis 1992; Murphy 1987; Yuval-Davis 1993; Ali 1992; also Goering 1993). Fixed public communal labels necessarily ignore the internal differentiations within cultural communities, the multicultural and hybrid identities of its members. To empower specific named collectivities legally or financially at the expense of others is to privilege a particular, situationally defined and objectified collectivity as an essentialised, *reified*, discrete continuity.

In arguing against such 'organic' political evocations of community – that is, community as an essentialised *Gemeinschaft* – Anthias and Yuval-Davis go even further: they deny the very utility of the term itself (Anthias and Yuval-Davis 1992: ch. 6, especially 163; Yuval-Davis 1993: 3; see also Eade 1991). This rejection must also be seen in the light of the hitherto almost fixed association 'community' has acquired in the sociological imagination with Tonnies' ideal typification as a traditional, face-to-face collectivity of consociates, bound in amity (see Hetherington 1993). The liberating impact of Benedict Anderson's notion of 'imagining' has been to release this restricted notion of 'community' from the prisonhouse of sociological language. Anderson traces the transformation of 'community' as a sociospatial collectivity of contemporaries (*not* consociates) who perceive themselves as sharing similar, synchronised everyday lives. The release of the term from its common-sense sociological straitjacket reveals its refractive and situational features. Like *cieng* (meaning 'home') among the Nuer, 'community' evokes sited meanings and values *contextually*.

A recognition of the sited nature of 'community' serves only, however, to underline the fundamental aporias of the politics of representation: a public identity has ontological connotations – it is constitutive of self and subjectivity through its ethical and aesthetic evocations. It is empowered, empowering and passionately defended. Multiculturalism empowers morally and aesthetically imagined communities, not oppressed class fractions.

Yet the immediate thrust of multiculturalism is towards a fragmentation of solidarities, so that the politics of representation become the politics of proportional representation, percentage politics. The clash of interests between disadvantaged groups exposes the moral hollowness of ethnic claims (Werbner and Anwar 1991; Anthias and Yuval-Davis 1992).

Such cultural fragmentation is impotent to contend with powerful organised racist violence. Effective anti-racist struggles depend on the evolution of common, unitary narratives and the *suppression* of cultural differences between victims of racism. The search thus continues for a powerful *hybridising*, essentialising allegory which can mobilise a wide constituency of anti-racists positively, as label after label, narrative after narrative, is rejected.

CONCLUSION

My aim in this chapter has been to recover the performative and processual dimensions of racism and ethnicity; to move away from a logocentric emphasis on racism as discourse to an understanding of the embodied materiality of racism (or ethnicism) as experience, and its polarising force. Just like racism, ethnicity, too, is materially embodied and grounded in sentiment. But whereas racism negates and violates (however ambivalently), ethnic identities are performed through gestures of identification, of reaching out. These two modes of relatedness marking alterity need thus to be theorised in terms of the systematically contrasting ways in which they deploy essentialist and non-essentialist representations and self-representations in the public domain. Even when racism highlights its ambivalences by masquerading as ethnicity (as do 'New Right' differentialist discourses), its intentions remain self-evidently aggressive, transgressive and absolutist: racism draws a line; it essentialises alterity.

By contrast to racial politics, the politics of ethnicity depend on scale and situation. The highlighting of a particular ethnic, as against racial, collective identity in the public domain generates a field of relevant oppositional identities at a particular social scale. This is because collective identities are defined within moral and semantic social worlds of oppositions and resemblances. There is no collective identity in and for itself, as a positivity without an implied negation. Bureaucratic fictions of unity essentialise, but they do so by objectifying communities situationally and pragmatically, in relation to notions of redistributive justice. This objectification is quite different from the violent essentialising of racism, or the mobilising, strategic essentialising of self-representation. Self-essentialising as a mode of reflexive imagining is constitutive of self and subjectivity. It is culturally empowering. But it is not, unlike racist reifications, fixed and immutable.

We are confronted with a duality: while ethnic identities are always positioned, and situationally grounded, racialised identities are fixed by a single dominant opposition, highlighted and elaborated above all others in response to physical and moral violations (see, for example, R. Werbner 1991; Kapferer 1988). This is because the politics of representation or identity are most critically divisive and overarching when they recall past violations and evolve into a politics of moral accountability. In such a politics, history is invoked as a charter of injustice still awaiting restitution (on such a politics, see R. Werbner 1995). For Muslims in Britain, the Rushdie affair is experienced as a festering open wound, an unpaid debt that demands redress and moves them to claim a separate anti-racist identity in the public sphere. But where racism is recognised as violating a whole spectrum of minority groups, the shared embodied materiality of their suffering creates potential ground for common oppositional fables and a genuine cultural fusion in broader alliances, as they come to realise the reality of a major radical, unbridgeable moral breach. By contrast, ethnic competition generates fission and fusion, and situational oppositions.

My argument, I believe, goes beyond the recognition of 'unity in diversity' or even of a 'universal diversity' – the assumption that political struggle does not have to be uniform or united, but must recognise continued differences of interest and positioning: 'otherwise any notion of solidarity would be inherently racist, sexist and classist' (Anthias and Yuval-Davis 1992: 197; see also Yuval-Davis, Chapter 11 above). In asking what impels people towards solidarity against the disruptive power of difference, I suggest that it is because racism and xenophobia are (at least for some, if not all, members of racialised minorities) materially *embodied*, and experienced as personal or collective violation – and hence suffering – that persons quite differently positioned are able to interpret and fabulate this experience ideologically, aesthetically and morally as essentially unitary, *across* gender, class and ethnic differences; to create, in other words, a 'new' identity.

The result is that in modern, ethnically diverse nation-states there are continuous centrifugal and centripetal pressures: on the one hand, to assert and elaborate particular identities; on the other, to create broader, more universalistic alliances.

Hence, not all collective cultural representations and self-representations in the public sphere are essentialising in the same way. To lump all forms of objectification together as essentialist is, from this perspective, to essentialise essentialism. It is to conflate two opposed relational fields – of objectification and reification.

This is precisely, however, what many discussions of racism and ethnicity in Britain tend to do. This tendency is exacerbated by the sometimes exclusive focus on the ideological dimensions of ethnicity and racism.[8] Yet contrary to the view of some scholars, otherness or alterity exists within a complex field of relations. There is no fixed divide between self and other. Instead, alterities form a continuous series on a rising scale: from the divided or fragmented self to major collective cleavages between ethnic groups or nations.

Against the ideological and logocentric stress in scholarly discussions of racism, I have argued here that collective constructions of racism and ethnicity are forms of polarising or recursive symbolic action, part of a host of other acts, played out in public arenas, all of which aim to effect change, transform, attack, or elicit support. The verbal rhetoric of racism or ethnicity is performative and strategic rather than descriptive and representational, a political weapon in a public struggle for state resources, citizenship rights or a universal morality.

NOTES

This chapter draws on work in progress and earlier work by the author listed below, and is part of a forthcoming book provisionally entitled *Diaspora and Millennium: Islam, Identity and the Aesthetics of the Religious Imagination.* An earlier version was presented as a Keynote Address to the Swiss Ethnological and Sociological Associations' joint Annual Conference on 'The Other in Society: Migration and Ethnicity', at Berne University in October 1993, and has been published in the proceedings of that conference (Wicker *et al.* 1996). It was also presented to Keele University's Department of Sociology and Social Anthropology, and at an ICCCR seminar at Manchester University. I would like to thank the participants in the seminar for their helpful and incisive comments. Special thanks are due to Bobby Sayyid and Nick Lee for their insightful suggestions in revising this draft.

1. Gregory Bateson has argued that there are two forms of schismogenesis, based on complementary and symmetrical oppositions, both of which lead through a dynamic process of mutual opposition towards greater differentiation of value and a progressive exaggeration of difference and antagonism, unless they are checked by counter-tendencies. See Nuckolls (1995) for an interesting recent discussion of Bateson's work.

2. Bauman (1992) attributes the notion of an aesthetic community to Kant, citing Lyotard (1988). The notion of an aesthetic community is more distinctively grounded, however, in postmodernist theory than in a Kantian universalist aesthetics

(see Geertz 1993: ch. 5, for a superb account of what makes for an aesthetic community).

3. Kevin Hetherington has developed the Foucauldian notion of 'heterotopia' (Hetherington 1996).

4. Hence Anthias and Yuval-Davis (1992: 12) argue perceptively that racism is a

discourse and practice of inferiorising ethnic groups.... Ethnocentrism occurs when one's own culture is taken for granted as natural, and is characteristic of all ethnicities to a greater or lesser extent. Xenophobia, or the dislike of the stranger or outsider, on the other hand, becomes racism when there are power relations involved.

5. Stuart Hall has stressed the historical specificities of racism. No doubt, he says,

there are general features of racism. But even more significant are the way in which these general features are modified and transformed by the historical specificities of the contexts and environments in which they become active. (Hall 1986: 23)

He goes on to deny the

misleading view that because racism is everywhere a deeply anti-human and anti-social practice, that therefore it is *the same* – either in its forms, its relations to other structures or processes, or its effects. (ibid.)

The view presented here is that while this is undoubtedly the case, the ontological features of racism as violence need to be analysed in their generality, across these differences.

6. Racist ideologies, myths and fantasies focus on this same substantive structural constellation which constitutes the violence in the first place, as Philip Cohen (1988) shows.

7. The breach is the outcome of the 'success' or profitability of violence for its perpetrators, which marks the start of a fundamentally different relationship between two groups. It also creates an impetus to rationalise and justify the new relationship from the perspective of the oppressor. From the point of view of its victims, the historical act of violence becomes the basis, as mentioned, for a politics of moral accountability (see R. Werbner 1995). For the violators, politics are henceforth determined by a structure of fear.

8. The focus on discourse is very general, and in the post-colonial critical literature follows Said's use of Foucault. Robert Miles, from a more orthodox Marxist perspective, also privileges discourse in his definition of racism (Miles 1989, 1994b). I would agree with Anthias and Yuval-Davis's critique of this limitation (1992: 11).

REFERENCES

Ahsan, M.M. and A. R. Kidwai (1991) *Sacrilege versus Civility: Muslim Perspectives on the Rushdie Affair*. Leicester: The Islamic Foundation.

Ali, Yasmin (1992) 'Muslim Women and the Politics of Ethnicity and Culture in the North of England', in Gita Sahgal and Nira Yuval-Davis (eds) *Refusing Holy Orders*. London: Virago: 101–23.

Anderson, Benedict (1983) *Imagined Communities*. London: Verso.

Anthias, Floya and Nira Yuval-Davis (1992) *Racialized Boundaries: Race, Nation, Gender, Colour and Class and the Anti-Racist Struggle*. London and New York: Routledge.

Ballard, Roger (1992) 'New Clothes for the Emperor: The Conceptual Nakedness of the Race Relations Industry in Britain'. *New Community* 18, 3: 481–92.

Bateson, Gregory (1958 [1936]) *Naven*. Stanford, CA: Stanford University Press.

Bauman, Zygmunt (1989) *Modernity and the Holocaust*. London: Routledge.

Bauman, Zygmunt (1992) *Intimations of Postmodernity*. London: Routledge.

Bhabha, Homi (1994) *The Location of Culture*. London: Routledge.

Bjorgo, Tore (1995) *Terror from the Extreme Right*. London: Frank Cass.

Bjorgo, Tore and Rob Witte (eds) (1993) *Racial Violence in Europe*. London: St Martin's Press.

Bowen, John R. (1989) '*Salat* in Indonesia: the Social Meanings of an Islamic Ritual'. *Man* (n.s.) 24: 299–318.

Brah, Avtar (1992) 'Difference, Diversity and Differentiation', in J. Donald and A. Rattansi (eds) '*Race*', *Culture and Difference*. London: Sage in association with the Open University: 126–45.

Carrier, James G. (ed.) (1995) *Occidentalism: Images of the West*. Oxford: Clarendon Press.

Centre for Contemporary Cultural Studies (CCCS) (1982) *The Empire Strikes Back: Race and Racism in 70s Britain*. London: Hutchinson.

Clifford, James (1988) *The Predicament of Culture: Twentieth-Century Ethnography, Literature, and Art*. Cambridge, MA: Harvard University Press.

Cohen, Philip (1988) 'The Perversion of Inheritance: Studies in the Making of Multi-Racist Britain', in Philip Cohen and Harwant S. Bains (eds) *Multi-Racist Britain*. London: Macmillan Educational.

Cohen, Stanley (1972) *Folk Devils and Moral Panics: The Creation of Mods and Rockers*. London: MacGibbon & Kee.

Dominguez, Virginia (1989) *People as Subject, People as Object: Selfhood and Peoplehood in Contemporary Israel*. Madison, WI: University of Wisconsin Press.

Eade, John (1991) 'The Political Construction of Class and Community: Bangladeshi Political Leadership in Tower Hamlets, East London', in Pnina Werbner and Muhammad Anwar (eds) *Black and Ethnic Leaderships in Britain*. London: Routledge.

Epstein, A.L. (1978) *Ethos and Identity: Three Studies in Ethnicity*. London: Tavistock.

Evans-Prichard, E.E. (1948) *The Nuer*. Oxford: Clarendon Press.

Fanon, Frantz (1967 [1961]) *The Wretched of the Earth*. London: Penguin.

Fischer, Michael, M.J. and Mehdi Abedi (1990) *Debating Muslims: Cultural Dialogues in Postmodernity and Tradition*. Madison, WI: University of Wisconsin Press.

Freitag, Sandra (1989) *Collective Action and Community: Public Arenas and the Emergence of Communalism in North India*. Berkeley, CA: University of California Press.

Friedman, Jonathan (1992) 'The Past in the Future: History and the Politics of Identity'. *American Anthropologist* 94, 4: 837–59.

Fuss, Diane (1990) *Essentially Speaking: Feminism, Nature and Difference*. London: Routledge.

Gates, Henry Louis Jr (1991) 'Critical Fanonism'. *Critical Inquiry* 17: 457–70.

Geertz, Clifford (1993 [1983]). *Local Knowledge*. London: Fontana.

Giddens, Anthony (1987) 'Nation States and Violence', in *Social Theory and Modern Sociology*. Oxford: Polity Press.

Gilroy, Paul (1987) *There Ain't No Black in the Union Jack*. London: Hutchinson.

Gilroy, Paul (1993) *The Black Atlantic: Modernity and Double Consciousness*. London: Verso.

Gluckman, Max (1940) *Analysis of a Social Situation in Modern Zululand*, Rhodes-Livingstone Paper 28, Manchester.

Gluckman, Max (1956) *Custom and Conflict in Tribal Africa*. Oxford: Blackwell.

Goering, John (1993) 'Reclothing the Emperor while Avoiding Ideological Polarisation: A Comment on Roger Ballard's Essay'. *New Community*, 19, 2: 336–47.

Hall, Stuart (1986) 'Gramsci's Relevance for the Study of Race and Ethnicity'. *Journal of Communication Inquiry*, 10, 2: 5–27.

Hall, Stuart (1991) 'Old and New Identities, Old and New Ethnicities', in A.D. King (ed.) *Culture, Globalisation and the World System*. London: Sage.

Hall, Stuart (1992 [1988]) 'New Ethnicities', in James Donald and Ali Rattansi (eds) *'Race', Culture and Difference*. London: Sage Publications in Association with the Open University.

Hall, Stuart *et al.* (1978) *Policing the Crisis: Mugging, the State and Law and Order*. London: Macmillan Educational.

Hebdige, Dick (1979) *Subculture: The Meaning of Style*. London: Methuen.

Hetherington, Kevin (1993) 'The Contemporary Significance of Schmalenbah's Concept of the Bund'. *Sociological Review* 42, 1: 1–25.

Hetherington, Kevin (1996) 'New Age Travellers: Heterotopic Places and Heteroclite Identities'. *Theory, Culture and Society* 13, 4: 33–52.

Hewitt, Roger (1986) *White Talk, Black Talk: Inter-Racial Friendship and Communication amongst Adolescents*. Cambridge: Cambridge University Press.

JanMohamed, Abdul R. (1985) 'The Economy of Manichean Allegory: The Function of Racial Difference in Colonialist Literature'. *Critical Enquiry* 12, 1.

Kapferer, Bruce (1988) *Legends of People, Myths of State: Violence, Intolerance and Political Culture in Sri Lanka and Australia*. Washington, DC: Smithsonian Institution Press.

Kapferer, Bruce (forthcoming) *The Feast of Fear*. Chicago: University of Chicago Press.

Levinas, E. (1987) *Collected Philosophical Papers*, trans. Alphonso Lingis. Dordrecht: Martinus Nijhoff Publishers.

Lewis, Bernard (1975) *History: Remembered, Recovered, Invented*. Princeton, NJ: Princeton University Press.

Lyotard, Jean-François (1988) *Peregrinations: Law, Form, Event*. New York: Columbia University Press.

Miles, Robert (1989) *Racism*. London: Routledge.

Miles, Robert (1994a) 'A Rise of Racism and Fascism in Contemporary Europe? Some Sceptical Reflections on its Nature and Extent'. *New Community* 20, 4: 547–62.

Miles, Robert (1994b) *Racism after 'Race Relations'*. London: Routledge.

Modood, Tariq (1988) '"Black", Racial Equality and Asian Identity'. *New Community* 14, 3: 397–404.

Modood, Tariq (1994) 'Political Blackness and British Asians'. *Sociology* 28, 4: 859–76.

Modood, Tariq (1996) 'If Races do not Exist, Then What Does? Racial Categorisation and Ethnic Realities', in Rohit Barot (ed.) *The Racism Problematic: Contemporary Sociological Debates on Race and Ethnicity*. London: Edwin Mullen Press.

Mumtaz, Khawar and Farida Shaheed (1987) *Women of Pakistan: Two Steps Forward, One Step Back?* Lahore: Vanguard Books.

Murphy, Dervla (1987) *Tales from Two Cities*. London: John Murray.

Nuckolls, Charles W. (1995) 'The Misplaced Legacy of Gregory Bateson: Toward a Cultural Dialectic of Knowledge and Desire'. *Cultural Anthropology* 10, 3: 367–94.

Paine, Robert (1989) 'Israel: Jewish Identity and Competition over Tradition', in Elizabeth Tonkin, Maryon McDonald and Malcolm Chapman (eds) *History and Ethnicity*. ASA Monograph 27, London: Routledge.

Parry, Benita (1987) 'Problems in Current Theories of Colonial Discourse'. *Oxford Literary Review* 9, 1 & 2.

Rattansi, Ali (1995) 'Western Racisms, Ethnicities and Identities in a "Postmodern" Frame', in Ali Rattansi and Sallie Westwood (eds) *Racism, Modernity and Identity: on the Western Front*. Cambridge: Polity Press.

Rex, John (1986) 'The Role of Class Analysis in the Study of Race Relations: A Weberian Perspective', in John Rex and D. Mason (eds) *Theories of Race and Ethnic Relations*. Cambridge: Cambridge University Press.

Rex, John (1992) *Ethnic Identity and Ethnic Mobilisation in Britain*. Monographs in Ethnic Relations, 5. CRER for the ESRC.

Rorty, Richard (1992) 'The Pragmatist's Progress', in *Umberto Eco: Interpretation and Overinterpretation*. Cambridge: Cambridge University Press.

Sahgal, Gita and Nira Yuval-Davis (eds) (1992) *Refusing Holy Orders: Women and Fundamentalism in Britain*. London: Virago.

Said, Edward W. (1985 [1978]) *Orientalism*. London: Penguin.

Shilling, Chris (1993) *The Body and Social Theory*. London: Sage.

Sivanandan, A. (1989) 'All that Melts into Air is Solid: The Hokum of New Times'. *Race and Class* 31, 3:1–30.

Sivanandan, A. (1990) *Communities of Resistance: Writings on Black Struggles for Socialism*. London: Verso.

Spivak, Gayatri C. (1987) *In Other Worlds: Essays in Cultural Politics*. New York and London: Methuen.

Strathern, Marilyn (1991) *Partial Connections*. Savage, MD: Rowman & Littlefields.

Tambiah, S. J. (1986) *Sri Lanka: Ethnic Fratricide and the Dismantling of Democracy*. London: I.B. Tauris.

Werbner, Pnina (1990) *The Migration Process: Capital, Gifts and Offerings among British Pakistanis*. Oxford: Berg.

Werbner, Pnina (1991a) 'The Fiction of Unity in Ethnic Politics: Aspects of Representation and the State among Manchester Pakistanis', in Pnina Werbner and Muhammed Anwar (eds) *Black and Ethnic Leaderships in Britain: The Cultural Dimensions of Political Action*. London: Routledge: 113–45.

Werbner, Pnina (1991b) 'Factions and Violence in the Communal Politics of British Overseas Pakistanis', in Hastings Donnan and Pnina Werbner (eds). *Economy and Culture in Pakistan: Migrants and Cities in a Muslim Society.* London: Macmillan: 188–215.

Werbner, Pnina (1991c) 'Introduction', in Pnina Werbner and Muhammad Anwar (eds) *Black and Ethnic Leaderships in Britain: The Cultural Dimensions of Political Action,* London: Routledge: 15–37.

Werbner, Pnina (1996a) 'Allegories of Sacred Imperfection: Magic, Hermeneutics and Passion in *The Satanic Verses'. Current Anthropology* 37, February, Special Issue: S55–S86.

Werbner, Pnina (1996b) 'The Making of Muslim Dissent: Lay Preachers and Hybridised Rhetoric among British Pakistanis'. *American Ethnologist* 23, 1: 102–22.

Werbner, Pnina (1996c) 'The Fusion of Identities: Political Passion and the Poetics of Performance among British Pakistanis', in Lionel Caplan, David Parkin and Humphrey Fisher (eds) *The Politics of Cultural Performance.* Providence, RI: Berghahn Publishers: 81–100.

Werbner, Pnina and Muhammad Anwar (eds) (1991) *Black and Ethnic Leaderships in Britain: The Cultural Dimensions of Political Action.* London: Routledge.

Werbner, Richard P. (1991) *Tears of the Dead.* Washington, DC: Smithsonian Institution Press.

Werbner, Richard P. (1995) 'Human Rights and Moral Knowledge: Arguments of Accountability in Zimbabwe', in Marilyn Strathern (ed.) *Shifting Contexts.* ASA Monograph. London: Routledge.

Werbner, Richard P. (1996) 'Introduction: Multiple Identities, Plural Arenas', in Richard Werbner and Terence Ranger (eds) *Postcolonial Identities in Africa.* London: Zed Books.

Wicker, Hans-Rudolf, Jean-Luc Alber, Claudio Bolzman, Rosita Fibbi, Kurt Imhoff and Andreas Wimmer (1996) *Das Fremde in der Gesellschaft: Migration, Ethnizität und Staat.* Zurich: Seismo.

Witte, Rob (1994) (ed.) *Racist Violence and Political Extremism.* Special Issue of *New Community* 21, 4.

Young, Robert (1995) *Colonial Desire: Hybridity in Theory, Culture and Race.* London: Routledge.

Yuval-Davis, Nira (1993) 'Gender and Nation'. *Ethnic and Racial Studies* 16, 4: 621–32.

PART THREE

MAPPING HYBRIDITY

14

TRACING HYBRIDITY

IN THEORY

Nikos Papastergiadis

In the last decade there has been barely a debate on cultural theory or postmodern subjectivity that has not acknowledged the productive side of hybridity, and described identity as being in some form of hybrid state.[1] This is a radical inversion of the historical status that has trailed this concept. For as long as the concepts of purity and exclusivity have been central to a racialised theory of identity, hybridity has, in one way or another, served as a threat to the fullness of selfhood. The hybrid has often been positioned within or beside modern theories of human origin and social development, mostly appearing as the moral marker of contamination, failure, or regression. Yet one of the 'achievements' of poststructuralist theory was to liberate the subject from notions of fixity and purity in origin. And in a social context where the political structures for mobilising and integrating emancipatory projects were also fragmenting, it was almost a form of succour to remind ourselves of our 'multiple subjectivities'. Can we now have the confidence that hybridity has been moved out from the loaded discourse of 'race', and situated within a more neutral zone of identity?

The contemporary discourses of cultural criticism and critical theory have embraced a number of models for representing the supposed 'newness' of postmodern identity: along with the concept of hybridity there is the cyborgian fantasy of fusion between man and machine, as well as the morphing of one object into another. This incorporation of the concept of hybridity into the mainstream cultural discourse has raised new problems. Hybridity has served as the organising principle for international cultural initiatives, and entered the programmes of local social movements.

Despite its historical association, which bears the dubious traces of colonial and white supremacist ideologies, most of the contemporary discussions on hybridity are preoccupied by its potential for inclusivity. The dark past of hybridity rarely disturbs the more cheerful populist claims. One of the aims of this chapter is to contextualise the various trajectories of thought and traditions in which hybridity has been inserted.

A quick glance at the history of hybridity reveals a bizarre array of ideas. Hybridity has shadowed every organic theory of identity, and was deeply inscribed in the nineteenth-century discourses of scientific racism. Whether it highlighted physiological or cultural difference in identity, it served primarily as a metaphor for the negative consequences of racial encounters, or a set of mercurial metaphors. For even when the scientific basis of racism had been discredited, racist practices were not abandoned but rehoused in the discourse of social types. Indeed, the enigmatic 'nature' of the hybrid may still lurk within the contemporary uses of hybridity as a model for cultural identity. Cultural critics like Jean Fisher stress that the concept is too deeply embedded within a discourse that presupposes an evolutionary hierarchy, and that it carries the prior purity of biologism (Fisher 1995). Gayatri Spivak feels that the preoccupation with hybridity in academic discourse has tended to gloss persistent social divisions of class and gender.[2]

The current use of hybridity may be motivated by a perverse pleasure of taking a negative term and transform it into a positive sign: 'to wear with pride the name they were given in scorn' (Rushdie 1988: 93). Why should the nineteenth-century eugenicists be allowed to retain a patent on hybridity? Should we use only words with a pure and inoffensive history, or should we challenge essentialist models of identity by taking on and then subverting their own vocabulary?

The positive feature of hybridity is that it invariably acknowledges that identity is constructed through a negotiation of difference, and that the presence of fissures, gaps and contradictions is not necessarily a sign of failure. In its most radical form, the concept also stresses that identity is not the combination, accumulation, fusion or synthesis of various components, but an energy field of different forces. Hybridity is not confined to a cataloguing of difference. Its 'unity' is not found in the sum of its parts, but emerges from the process of opening what Homi Bhabha has called a third space within which other elements encounter and transform each other (Bhabha 1994).

CULTURAL HYBRIDS AND NATIONAL RECONCILIATIONS

Hybridity evokes narratives of origin and encounter. Whenever the process of identity formation is premissed on an exclusive boundary between 'us' and 'them', the hybrid, born out of the transgression of this boundary, figures as a form of danger, loss and degeneration. If, however, the boundary is marked positively – to solicit exchange and inclusion – then the hybrid may yield strength and vitality. Hence the conventional value of the hybrid is always positioned in relation to the value of purity, along axes of inclusion and exclusion. In some circumstances, the 'curse' of hybridity is seen as a mixed blessing.

For Octavio Paz, Mexican national identity is undeniably hybrid. With considerable melancholy, however, Paz situates this hybridism in the damaged maternal representations of the 'Malinche complex' and the *chingada*, the violated woman. The people of Mexico are all children of a primal violation, that of conquest. Malinche represents the Indian woman who gave herself to the conquistadors. Cortez took her as his mistress; by learning his language she became both his lover and his guide. She revealed everything until there was nothing else to take, then she was abandoned.

The ancestral drama for Mexico is thus poised between a traitor and a violator. The father wrapped in the cloak of the conqueror escapes the moral gaze, but the mother, as *chingada* who is left to give birth to the hybrid nation, is seen as a victim who facilitated violence. The identification of Malinche with the *chingada* reinforces the dominant ideology of rape as it shifts moral attention away from the man, and focuses on how she provoked her own violation. The figure of the mother as *chingada* reduces her to abject passivity; an inert heap of bones, blood and dust. All identity is gutted. The mother is maligned for her submission; her wounds are reminders that the children are the 'fruit of violation'. Disgust and self-hate compound and provoke further bitterness: 'Mexican people have not forgiven *La Malinche* for her betrayal' (Paz 1967: 77).

Paz sees in this rejection of the violated mother by the unforgiving child both a cry for purity in origin and a demand for another mother who would rather die than suffer contamination. Rejecting Malinche, the Mexican rejects hybridity in the past, and refuses engagement with difference in the present. This rejection of the violated mother serves as a negation of origin by preferring the phantasmagoric exile of solitude and the impossible nostalgia of the uncontaminated womb. With stern invocations, Paz turns back to his people, urging them to face up to the traumas of the 'fallen' mother and to embrace the ambivalence of Malinche.

Racial classifications and the mythology of white supremacy reached their zenith in the justifications of slavery and imperial conquest. Notions of superiority were often premissed on alterity, exclusivity and purity. The comforts of ideology, however, failed to constrain a parallel ideology of conquest through sexual penetration. Hence the paradox of conquest: distanciation *and* penetration. In Latin America, desire and disavowal were most palpably embodied by the presence of hybrids. The unspeakable distaste for – and yet undeniable presence of – hybrids is reflected by the compulsive classifying of the gradations of blackness. Each word carried a different status and specified the elements in the union.[3] These names included mulatto, half-breed, half-caste, mixed breed, quadroon, octoroon, sambo, mango, mestizo. Up to one-sixty-fourth black could be distinguished (Williamson 1980: xii). In Brazil, despite its cultural hybridity, it took time before the word hybrid was not spoken as a curse. Gilberto Freyre's celebrated account of Brazilian culture, *The Masters and the Slaves*, begins with the confession: 'Of all the problems confronting Brazil there was none that gave me so much anxiety as that of miscegenation' (1946: xx).[4] The rest of the book, as is foretold in an introductory anecdote, seeks to give light to the shadowy status of the hybrid:

> Once upon a time, after three straight years of absence from my country, I caught sight of a group of Brazilian seamen-mulattoes and cafusos crossing Brooklyn Bridge. I no longer remember whether they were from São Paulo or from Minas, but I know that they impressed me as being the caricatures of men, and there came to mind a phrase from a book on Brazil by an American traveller: 'the fearful mongrel aspect of the population'. That was the sort of thing to which miscegenation led. I ought to have had someone to tell me what Roquette Pinto had told the Aryanizers of the Brazilian Eugenic Congress in 1929; that these individuals whom I looked upon as representative of Brazil were not simply mulattoes or cafusos but *sickly* ones. (Freyre 1946: xx)[5]

In the early records of colonial encounters, the ambiguity surrounding hybrids was wrapped in ambivalence. On the one hand, hybridity was blamed for causing bad health. The symptoms included fatigue and indolence. Economic inertia, moral decadence and even syphilis were also effects that hybrids supposedly brought to the New World. But, on the other hand, Freyre reports that the coloniser's and the priest's preferred mistress was the mulatto, and he provides countless examples of their desire for the 'lascivious hybrid woman'. For Freyre, the negative associations given to hybridity were not the result of a deeply internalised ideology of purity but, rather, a confusion of subject positions. The disastrous consequences of the first contact, he argued, had been falsely projected on to the offspring. Freyre believed that once the genuine causes of disease and disorder were identified, the hybrid's advantage would be restored and would establish a firm grounding for a 'racial democracy'. Moral repugnance would dissolve as the society was enlightened by its own potentialities. In this new, celebratory myth, which was defined in opposition to the polarities of race relations in the USA, hybrids were conceived as lubricants in the clashes of culture; they were the negotiators who would secure a future free of xenophobia.

Freyre had found a resolution to his anxiety over miscegenation; he would no longer see himself as belonging to a civilisation whose origin was 'sickly'. He became convinced that a hybrid society creates a new social order through the principle of synthesis and combination of differences. Nevertheless, he retained uncritically the hierarchy that privileged the white race through its association with the positive of public versus private, culture versus nature, masculine versus feminine, throughout his celebration of hybridity.

Freyre's Eurocentrism stopped him from questioning the paradigms of savagery and primitivism. The conceptual world of the Other was rarely entertained; it was simply their virility and domesticity that was embraced. This is no coincidence, for the model that Freyre is expounding is ambiguously drawn from European modernism, while his narrative of incorporation is coded in terms of a sexualised arousal and submission. The shock of the Other serves to stimulate seduction, and to quicken consumption; via ingestion and absorption. The useful is extracted; the rest is excreted. The modernist in the 'New World' cannibalised the Other, but something troublesome always remained. The hybrid social space that Freyre evokes still privileges the coloniser's aspirations – even as it incorporates the most 'useful' and 'desirable' elements from the 'savage' and the 'slave'. It was also clear, however, that a hybrid society which admits to the vagaries of its origin and does not seek to define itself through 'absolute ideals' and 'unyielding prejudice', a society that proclaims a loose and open-ended cultural identity, while opening a space for tolerance towards difference, does not necessarily guarantee a universal extension of social justice.

So although Freyre seems to have demonstrated that a hybrid society is not necessarily one in decay or invariably riven by conflict, his anxiety over miscegenation is still evident in his proclamation that the hybrid is not a disavowal of European identity: '[It] tends to become more and more extra-European though in no sense anti-European' (Freyre 1974: 87). The hybrid is transformed into a sign for the extension of the European spirit. The mixing of blood shifts from being a stain or a stigma to an aesthetically pleasing and virile combination. Yet the success of the hybrid depends on a particular recipe: potency is secured by the implanting of the white seed in the nurturing indigenous womb. A modernist fantasy of appropriation through insemination is repeated throughout Freyre's narrative of the assimilation between European culture, Indian domesticity and Negro virility.

By privileging the role of mixture, Freyre's account of cultural development clearly distances itself from the nineteenth-century theories of natural law, evolution and racial purity that dominated the Romantic constructions of nationhood. Hybridity succeeds not in its blind conformity to the European model but in the application of European systems and ideals in a 'New World'. Progress in the 'New World' is marked by the dialectic of adaptation and transformation. The hybrid's progress is therefore linked to a Eurocentric model of maximisation. Mixture is celebrated in Freyre's narrative, but at a secondary level, because it is through mixture that a new order can be realised that will integrate and maximise the Eurocentric 'spirit'. Mixture overtakes purity because it can outperform it. Once again, hybridity is justified not by 'love of humanity' but by the logic of maximisation.

The limitations in Freyre's model of hybridity can be further exposed by considering his acknowledgement of a methodological debt to Picasso (Nunes 1994: 20). The ambivalence of hybridity in early modernism is seldom examined in terms other than a celebration of the Western capacity for integrating the 'raw' forms of the Other into the dynamic body of metropolitan culture. The difficulties of conceptualising hybridity can be witnessed in an essay by the Marxist art critic Max Raphael, where he sets out to examine the means by which Picasso contributed to a major 'break' in the European tradition. Raphael argues that Picasso's affinity for 'Negro Art' represented a potential trespass of what was conceived as the border between reason and non-reason,[6] while also signifying a reversal in the exchange of cultural influence from the periphery to the centre. Despite its limitations, his account of this process of incorporation into modern art does, at least, outline a dynamics of transformation and redemption:

> The integration of Japanese art was the loophole by which traditional [European] artistic rationalism found its way to an artistic sensualism closer to nature. The incorporation of Negroid art, on the other hand, turns against rational and sensory contents in favour of metaphysics and the irrational, and at the same time creates a new, completely Non-European rationalisation of form. (Raphael 1980: 130)

Thus he suggests that the integration of 'Japanese' art and 'Negroid' art follows the same principle but proceeds through diametrically opposed categories: 'Japanese' art enters through the door of European rationality in order to beckon the West towards its own objectives – that is, to find its way back to nature; 'Negroid' art, by contrast, is projected into the anarchic zone of irrationality. The presence of the two forms is at first perceived as both indigestible and incomprehensible. Yet it is this confrontation with otherness, albeit via latent or marginal concepts, that yields a new form. In both cases the foreign is incorporated in order to confirm or extend conventional European values. Raphael argues that Picasso, in incorporating foreign elements, fails to question the ruptures within metropolitan culture because he leaves the prior distinction between spiritual value and material production untouched. Picasso's example provides a template upon which Raphael can thereby address what he regards as the contradictions between early modernity and colonialism:

> Psychically emptied and over-rationalized, man discovers in the natives of his colonies a vast traditional domain, and this discovery accelerates his own rapid and continuing flight from Reason. But it also consolidates his humanity in the face of the machine, and activates his hitherto passive mysticism. (Raphael 1980: 131)

His account of the reconciliation of the modern split between body and soul proceeds not through a critique of the existing relationship between material production and spiritual value, in which the modern self is already inscribed, but through an argument about the consumption of the idealised Other. Raphael argues that the non-European forms were assimilated back into the European tradition through the mediation of historically prior traditions. The reactivation of latent forms is the lever which allows the entry of the Other, and facilitates a form of moral and normative rejuvenation.

> European art assimilated Negroid influences by introducing: (1) the principle of corporeality, and hence, the Greek tendency, during the period of Cubist objects; (2) the mysticism of the soul, and hence, the Gothic, during the period of the Cubist field. (Raphael 1980: 142)

This critique of the utilisation of non-Western elements in Picasso's art gives us an indication of an underlying pathos in the motivation to incorporate foreign elements, and also a surprising insight into the simplicity with which the foreign was understood within modern culture. I say that this insight is surprising because most critics associate the concept of modernity with an increasing complexity in the structures of everyday life, and assume that the cultural processes that accompany such structures are equally sophisticated. As Don Miller wryly observes: 'An idea like "simple modernity" would be seen as a blatant contradiction' (Miller 1992: 120). But this is precisely what we do witness in the cultural dynamics that Raphael traces. He argues that the West's success in material production was achieved at the expense of hollowing out Western spiritual values. However, the turn to primitivism in modern art was not a wholesale critique of material production, but simply another extension of the prevailing logic of appropriation and displacement. In primitivism we witness not only the commodification of other spiritual values but also the domestication of this otherness as it is translated back into the familiar Western forms of 'corporeality' and 'mysticism'.

By demonstrating Picasso's paradoxical appeal to Western reason and non-Western spirituality, in his shift from realism to abstraction, Raphael attempts to probe at the very flaws in modern rationality, as well as to address the unresolved paradoxes between form and content in modernism. His account of Picasso's achievement is significant not just for its evaluations but also for its construction of a model of cross-cultural assimilation. According to the dynamics of this model, for the Other to be domesticated it must also be doubled; it must have one face that turns inwards, conveying a sense of belonging, and another that turns to the exterior, pointing to the beyond. It is this duality, he suggests, which secures a sense of extension and bridging; thus, for every foreign element to be accepted, there must be both a centrifugal and a centripetal force; a narcissistic sense of inclusion and a transgressive sense of extension. If the non-Western is to enter the West, it must do so in the guise of the cultural hybrid: the non-western-Westerner.

HYBRIDITY IN COLONIALISM

The clash of cultures that colonialism invariably provoked, rather than producing a neat bifurcation between coloniser and colonised, encouraged the formation of new cultural hybrids. Ashis Nandy's account of the levels of consciousness which at first sustained and then undermined the colonising project stresses that the conventional binarism that represented the colonised as victim and the coloniser as victor overlooks the fact that both were caught up as players and counter-players in a single dominant model. Shifting his attention away from the obvious sites of conflict and violence, Nandy focuses on the actual interfaces, processes of negotiation and means of resistance expressed by urban Westernised Indians and the degrees of degradation experienced by the English coloniser. Agency is never the monopoly of one player, he suggests, for both are locked in a dyadic relationship in which the coloniser becomes a self-destructive co-victim (Nandy 1983: xv).

Colonialism produced new losses and gains, allowed new forms of identity to ascend, and debased or crushed others. This trajectory was always, at least, dual. It was one of the peculiar features of English colonialism that the subjects who induced the greatest discomfort and were the victims of the most bitter attacks were the hybrids. The repulsion that was genuinely felt towards them was, according to Nandy, deeply connected to the repression of the antonyms and oppositional dualisms that jostled for position in the coloniser's sexual identity and political ideology. Perhaps no other figure articulated these contradictions so exquisitely as did Rudyard Kipling. The very man who so persistently crisscrossed the tremulous line between 'Westernised Indian' and 'Indianised Westerner' was also the one who insisted that 'West' and 'East' could never be reconciled. For Nandy, Kipling displayed the qualities of the hero who 'interfaced culture' and kept open the feminine side in masculinity, while also being able simultaneously to despise the effeminate hybrid who lacked a clear sense of self. Kipling's capacity to project his own self-hatred is thus taken as an index of the underlying repressions in colonialism:

> Kipling distinguished between the victim who fights well and pays back the tormentor in his own coin and the victim who is passive–aggressive, effeminate and fights back through non-cooperation, shirking, irresponsibility, malingering and refusal to value face-to-face fights. The first was the 'ideal victim' Kipling wished to be, and the second was the victim's life Kipling lived and hated living [as a schoolboy in England]. If he did not have any compassion for the victims of the world, he did not have any compassion for a part of himself either. (Nandy 1983: 68)

The conflict of interests between coloniser and colonised was also a conflict between the parts and processes of identity. It promoted a self-image and form of consciousness that was defined in opposition to the putative characteristics of the 'Eastern man', and exaggerated the qualities of masculinity, hardness, distanciation and responsibility. A self was fashioned that was not only more congruent to the needs of the colonial machine but intolerant of the inherent sexual as well as cultural mixtures in one's self and in others. The acknowledgement of his own androgynous biculturalism was – according to Nandy – Kipling's most disturbing dilemma, and his solution, which accords with the dominant model, was to opt for absolute choice. He should be *either* Western *or* Indian. It was inconceivable to be *both*, for the path of progress was opposed to such meandering oxymorons and perambulating paradoxes.

While a reordering of the coloniser's consciousness and a distanciation from that of the colonised was central to the success of the colonial project, it was also – as Nandy suggests – the cause of the rigidity that ultimately facilitated its own demise. Kipling could never reconcile *both* his Western *and* his Indian selves, yet in everyday life such conjunctions were both practical and continuous with the syncretic processes which constructed Indian identity. The relentless quest for purity and the historical burden of superiority never allowed Kipling to grasp the resilient dynamism of hybridity, so he remained slightly detached from even his most beloved subjects. By contrast to the attitude of colonisers, crucial to the transformative processes of Indian tradition was a willingness to engage critically with the other: 'to capture the differentia of the West within its own cultural domain' (Nandy 1983: 76).

Kipling's personal failures are history lessons for Nandy, because each expression of moral repugnance and political outrage was so utterly framed by Enlightenment ideals of development through determinate sequences. Surveying the culture as if caught in the 'backward innocence of childhood', the Indian identity slipped in and out of any determinacy. It was this indeterminateness which Kipling hated, yet it was the key to Indian survival under colonialism, and to the creative space that ensured cultural transformation.

For Nandy, all encounters produce change. The perversity of colonialism is thus measured not just in terms of the extreme exploitation of the Other but also in the contortions and constrictions of the self that were necessary to enforce such a relationship. Nandy explains this process of cultural co-optation in two ways. First, he demonstrates the homology between sexual repression and political dominance which led to an internalisation of self-images of masculinity and hardness as the appropriate 'manly' modes of colonial rule. Second, he reveals that the Indian's initial identification with the aggressor was not just an attempt to seek salvation by means of mimicry but a resurrection of latent self-images which could be made compatible with the ideology of colonialism.

A version of Indian hyper-masculinism would thus not only mirror back the ruler's own self-redefinition but also serve as a 'new, nearly exclusive indicator of authentic Indianness' (Nandy 1983: 7). Under colonialism both the ruler and the ruled produced new self-images which were selectively drawn from earlier forms of social consciousness. Colonialism found legitimacy because it elicited a set of codes that were common to both cultures, and because it was thereby able to privilege components that were previously subordinant or recessive in these cultures. The seeds of this foundational colonialism were already contained in the consciousness of both parties, and central to its legitimacy was the valorisation of the pure and the denigration of the hybrid – that is, of sexual and spiritual androgyny.[7]

Nandy's account of the colonial modes of exchange through the psychic mechanisms of projections and introjections, and his celebration of the 'superior' resilience of hybridity, leave one central question un-answered: does the encounter with the Other presuppose a replaying of old identities or the invention of new ones? Nandy systematically elabo-rates the principles of exchange as a rupture in prevailing cultural codes and priorities, and the establishment of new modes of self-presentation and social management. The rupture is seen not as a total upheaval but as a radical shift of emphasis, which leads to the highlighting of aspects of the self that had been kept dark, and a promotion of previously reces-sive components of culture.

Although there is no explicit theory of hybridity in Nandy's narra-tive, this process of rupture and regrounding outlines the dynamism of exchange. Nandy is able to link the denials and repressions in, say, Kipling's consciousness to both an inability to keep the contradictory forces in play and a tendency to create a distorted and untenable self-image. Similarly, he praises the 'Indian's' humble capacity to include aspects of the Other without losing his or her original cultural checks and balances. However, in order to consolidate the argument that distanciation inevitably leads to atrophy and identification secures survival, one also needs a closer theory of the dynamics of exchange. Moreover, to understand both the disturbing anxiety generated by cultural hybrids and the productive and enabling force of hybridity there needs to be a closer scrutiny of the creation of differences, precisely when there is a renewed circulation of equivalences, or an exaggerated outburst of hostility towards the 'intimate enemy'. For this theorisation of difference we must turn elsewhere, and move on from the history of culture to consider the semiotics of culture.

THE SEMIOTICS OF HYBRIDITY

Bakhtin's attention to the mixture of languages within a text, which both ironises and unmasks authority, demonstrates a new level of linking the concept of hybridity to the politics of representation (see Young 1995: 20–22). The language of hybridity becomes a means for critique and resistance to the monological language of authority. The hybrid text always undoes the priorities and disrupts the singular order by which the dominant code categorises the other. In Bakhtin's theory the 'doubleness' of the hybrid voices is composed not through the integra-tion of differences but via a series of dialogical counterpoints, each set against the other, allowing the language to be both the same and different. This clearly constitutes a turning point in the debates on hybridity. This turning point is most evident in the current appeal of Bakhtin's theory of heteroglossia and the carnivalesque. However, while there has been a greater appreciation of the subversive potential of language, the attention to difference within literary and critical theory has been mostly confined to an analysis of its products rather than an engagement with its processes. To overcome this limitation it would be useful to turn to the work of Yuri Lotman, a Russian semiotician who both drew on Bakhtin's theory of hybridity and extended it into the semiotics of culture. If the concept of hybridity is to go beyond a mere celebration or denigration of difference, then Lotman's theory, which outlines the dynamism of difference within culture, might provide a valuable framework.

Lotman's approach to the semiotics of culture goes beyond the conventional concerns with the use of signs for communication of content. In his work, culture is defined as a system that mediates the individual's relationship to his or her context, the mechanism for processing and organising surrounding signs. The way we deal with inputs, how decisions are made, priorities established, behaviour regulated, models envisaged and questions posed in the 'communicating dialogue' with the outside world is all expressive of a particular sense of culture. This dialogue always comprises relatively individualised languages which are in a state of interdependence, and are transformed by their specific historical conditions. Lotman stresses this interdependence and avoids any movement towards analytical abstraction, for culture is never a mere summation of separate and discrete languages. In Lotman's theory the form of culture is defined via references to motion rather than by comparison to a static or bounded object; hence it is seen to be more like a river with a number of currents moving at different rates and intensities. The aim is to see how culture operates as a whole, in a state of constant 'creolisation', or what he calls the 'semiotic physiology' as opposed to the 'atomistic approach'.

The name Lotman gives to this dynamic process of influence, transformation and coexistence within the space of culture is the semiosphere (Lotman 1991: 123). The semiosphere is the totality of semiotic acts: from squeaks to sonatas, from blips on the radar to burps at the dinner table. It also includes all acts past and present, possessing a 'memory which transforms the history of the system into its actually functioning mechanism, ... the mass of texts ever created and ... the programme for generating future texts' (Lotman and Uspenskij 1984: xii). While the value and position of elements within a language shift and change, and the set of languages within a cultural field intersect, fragment, diversify or realign, the whole of the semiotic space remains constant. Thus the semiosphere refers to the totality of the cultural system, and also to the condition for the development of culture.

To illustrate the heterogeneity of elements and the diversity of functions within the semiosphere, Lotman uses the example of the museum as a model for the possibility of representing and containing difference within a system. The museum, he argues, is a single space containing exhibits from different periods; each exhibit bears inscriptions in languages which may or may not be decipherable. There are instructions, explanations, guides, rules and plans which, to some degree, regulate the responses of visitors and staff. Within this single space, Lotman stresses, we have to remember that all the elements are dynamic, not static, and that the correlations between terms are constantly changing. In a context where the construction of the museum as an encyclopaedic repository of culture's diversity is deeply contested, this may seem like a flawed example. Nevertheless, it remains a paradigmatic instance of staging difference within contemporary culture.

Within the model of the museum we can at least see how Lotman's conception of the semiosphere recognises oppositions and tensions, for it does not presuppose either that this binarism leads to a single point of antagonism, or that positions are mutually exclusive and immutable. His representation of the system of communication recognises that binarisms constantly undo their own fixity. It describes a system in which there is a constant conflict between resolute and opaque codes, compatible and contradictory practices. The relationship between centre and periphery in the semiosphere is not explained by either the functionalist paradigm of mechanical integration or the dialectical model for the overcoming of antagonisms but, rather, by a stress on the dynamics of contestation over the *fit* between the language of the code and the language of practice. At one stage Lotman tries to evoke the incalculable flux of intellectual energy within the semiosphere by saying that it 'seethes like the sun' (1991: 150). However, with this metaphor, which suggests both organic thrust and chaotic dispersal, there is the sense that the principle of power cannot be contained neatly in the acts of cultural exchange.

The structure of the semiosphere is thus crowded, possessing languages with different levels and forms of representation. Lotman consciously idealises the opposition between centre and periphery in terms of codification and indeterminacy in order to articulate the constant tension in the definition of norms, customs and laws which are generated to legitimise the extension of one language over the whole semiosphere. He is astutely conscious of the counterproductive consequences of a hegemonic language. In the semiosphere, the expansion of one language is achieved only by its rigidification and its severance from the milieu of dynamic interaction. To expand in a unified manner is to become more and more prone to disintegration. For the periphery never passively accepts conversion, and it is this tension between the code of the centre and its (in)ability to reflect the practices in the periphery that produce a dissenting language. Lotman describes the contradictions that await 'the proselytising mission' of the centre thus:

> If in the centre of the semiosphere the description of texts generates the norms, then on the periphery the norms, actively invading 'incorrect' practice, will generate 'correct' texts in accord with them. Secondly, whole layers of cultural phenomena, which from the point of view of the given metalanguage are marginal, will have no relation to the idealised portrait of that culture'. (Lotman 1991:)

This uneven terrain of cultural production and the stochastic distribution or multi-vectorial transmission of culture are also stressed by Michel Serres. In his complex analyses of cultural dynamics he persistently questions the transparency of the laws of determinism and challenges the conventional passage from the local to the global (1982: 80). The productive tension between local and global, noise and dialect that Serres notes is similar to Lotman's tracking of the flux of energy that follows every crisscrossing of a boundary. For Lotman, the semiosphere is in a constant state of hybridity. It always oscillates between identity and alterity, and this tension is most evident at its boundaries: 'Every culture begins by dividing the world into "its own" internal space and "their" external space. How this binary division is interpreted depends on the typology of the culture' (Lotman 1991: 131).

An archetypical example of this type of differentiation between US and THEM, a relationship of non-relationship whereby the exterior Other is defined by the logic of the inversion, is the designation of the Other as barbarian. The crucial marker is, in this instance, language: a Barbarian was simply a person who did not speak Greek. However, the Other that is within the semiosphere is not perceived by such an *a priori* categorisation, but identified through the processes of translation. The construction of the exterior Other by the logic of inversion is designed to preclude dialogue, whereas the presence of an other who speaks different languages within the semiosphere interacts through translation, and thus facilitates both dialogue and transformation. Because the different languages within the semiosphere do not have mutual semantic correspondences, translation presupposes asymmetry. Once the external Other's utterances stop sounding like muttering '*bar bar bar*', and he or she is deemed to speak Greek properly, he or she is no longer just a Barbarian. But this difference, as Lotman emphasises, has to be perceived as both necessary and desirable, for the precondition for dialogue is the mutual attraction of the participants. Lotman outlines the mechanisms by which dialogue occurs in the context of difference – that is, how information is generated from the tension between a language and its contact with a foreign text – and he describes this process of interaction in five stages. This enables us, I suggest, to reflect on Raphael's and Nandy's accounts of the encounter with an Other.

First, a text arrives from the outside; it appears in its original form, in its own language. Its strangeness is intact.

Second, a transformation at both ends begins to occur – that is, the imported text and the receiving culture begin to restructure each other. The foreign text is idealised because it offers the local culture the opportunity to break with the past. Here the foreign text is imbued with salvific qualities. However, there also emerges a counter-tendency whereby the foreign text is linked to a submerged element in the receiving culture; the foreign thus activates a dormant component, and is therefore interpreted as an organic continuation or a rehabilitation of the familiar culture.

Third, there emerges the tendency to deprecate the source of origin from which the text came, and emphasise that the true potential of the text is realised only if it is integrated into the receiving culture. Reception has not only led to transformation but is also a form of transcendence. Before, it was debased and distorted; now it has the grace of truth and universality.

Fourth, after the imported text has been fully assimilated, its distinctive presence has been dissolved, and has led to the production of a new model. Now that the receiver has internalised the text and restructured its own axioms and values, the local becomes producer of the new and original texts.

Fifth, the receiver is now a transmitter – or, in Lotman's words, it 'issues forth a flood of texts directed to other, peripheral areas of the semiosphere' (Lotman 1991: 147).

Lotman was conscious that this dialogue – or what he calls this process of 'infection' – could be realised only under favourable historical, social and psychological conditions. But Serres adds another dimension which locates the interruptive moment and the potential for innovation not singularly in the dialogue between the interlocutors, but in what he sees as the alliance against a disruptive third man:

> Such communication (dialogue) is a sort of game played by two interlocutors considered as united against the phenomena of interference and confusion, or against individuals with some stake in interrupting communication. These interlocutors are in no way opposed, as in the traditional conception of the dialectic game; on the contrary, they are on the same side, tied together by a mutual interest: they battle against noise.... They exchange roles sufficiently

often for us to view them as struggling against a common enemy. To hold a
dialogue is to suppose a third man and to seek to exclude him: a successful
communication is the exclusion of the third man. The most profound dialectical problem is not the Other who is only a variety – or a variation – of the
same, it is the problem of the third man. (Serres 1982: 66–7)

Where Lotman defines the semiosphere as the resultant and the condition of possibility of the system of communication, Serres invokes the
interruptive third man – or what he also referred to as the parasite.
Lotman's theory acknowledges the fluidity and perpetuity of cultural
interaction. Serres highlights the previously unacknowledged vectorial
counter-forces of a third element which emerges whenever two subjects
enter into a dialogical relationship. Both approaches break with functionalist models for understanding the incorporation of difference in terms
of either assimilation or amalgamation. Both theorists are intensely conscious of the role of the hybrid and creolised, and draw attention to the
splitting, the interference in the dissemination of languages, leading us
towards a re-evaluation of the position, role and function of the stranger,
yet both theories say little about the precondition of desire in mutual
attraction, or the disposition to delegate the stranger to the position of
the third man. Are these structural questions simply left as the invisible
bias of history?
    The problem with the semiosphere is that it does not directly address
the politics inherent in making the distinctions between language and
silence, coherence and babble, comprehension and confusion; the determining patterns of selection that influence which languages will be learnt
and what thresholds between the axioms of transparency and opaqueness
in language will be sustained in order to stimulate particular forms of
knowledge and to permit the emergence of particular claims. In other
words, it does not address the politics by which the margin is hierarchised,
appropriated, tokenised or fetishised in order to serve the interests and
maintain the order constructed by the centre. For all his attention to the
fluid dynamics of the semiosphere, Lotman appears to have overlooked
the specific forces of access and exclusion. The levels of travelling and the
process of transmission discount any degree of loss or mutation in the
course of the journey. Meaning begins only once the text enters the space
of the semiosphere; but what traces are there of the meanings prior to this
encounter? The arrival of a foreign text is never a perfect isomorph of
another culture; it, too, is formed by the travails of travelling.
    From this perspective it appears that the primary tendency within the
semiosphere is towards the acculturation of the foreign text and subtle
modification of the dominant language. However, in order to witness
the innovative potential of the foreign text, or the restructuring of the

dominant language according to the laws of the Other, we will have to measure the resilience of the foreign code and examine the impact resulting from the insertion of the foreign text. If the interruptive force of hybridity is ultimately smoothed over, as it is incorporated into the semiosphere, then we must question whether this theory of dynamic transformation is sufficiently attentive either to the concept of difference or to the contemporary crisis within culture.

HYBRIDITY IN POST-COLONIAL THEORY

The most vigorous debates on the dynamics of difference in contemporary culture have occurred within the field of post-colonial theory. Given the extremities of social and psychic upheaval generated by colonialism, it is no coincidence that the most radical critics of cultural transformation in modernity have come from places that have experienced these global changes most brutally.

In the context of rupture and violation, communication and identity are always problematical. For, as Stuart Hall argues, the emergence of 'other histories' in contemporary discourse is synchronous with the radicalisation of the notions of identity, history and language. If the experience of displacement has become the paradoxical starting point for understanding the parameters of belonging in the modern world, then this would entail a challenge to our conceptual framework for understanding identity and culture. On the one hand, there is still the Romantic claim that identity is grounded in the essential distinctiveness of a culture. On the other, the process of constructing identity through mixing and engaging with the Other has been given, as we have seen, a far more critical perspective. Recent writings within post-colonial theory routinely cite the work of Stuart Hall, Homi Bhabha and Gayatri Spivak as authorising hybrid identities. At the broadest level of conceptual debate there seems to be a consensus over the utility of hybridity as antidote to essentialist subjectivity. However, Spivak sharply dissents from both Bhabha's and Hall's suggestion that hybridity has purchase both in the Third World post-colonial arena and within the diasporic condition of minorities in the First World.

According to Stuart Hall, cultural identity is always hybrid, but he also insists that the precise form of this hybridity will be determined by specific historical formations and cultural repertoires of enunciation (Morley and Kuan-Hsing Chen 1996: 502). Homi Bhabha notes the rising influence of once-excluded voices now challenging the boundaries of what is seen as a Eurocentric project. The affinity between these interruptive voices, Bhabha suggests, offers the basis for rethinking the process of change and the subjects of modernity.

> For the demography of the new internationalism is the history of postcolonial migration, the narratives of cultural and political diaspora, the major social displacements of peasant and aboriginal communities, the poetics of exile and the grim prose of political and economic refugees. (Bhabha 1994: 5)

Hybridity may be a condition that is common to all those who have sharp memories of deprivation, but – as Bhabha also reminds us – it seems an insufficient basis on which to consolidate new forms of collectivity that can overcome the embeddedness of prior antagonisms. Nevertheless, Bhabha's work has focused on the psychic processes of identification and the cultural practices of performance to highlight the hybridisation that is intrinsic to all forms of radical transformation and traditional renewal. Gayatri Spivak is not so quick to embrace such a demography of post-colonials: she draws a sharp distinction between the diasporic communities in the First World and the subaltern in the Third. The subaltern and the diasporic are, in her view, incommensurable worlds, and projecting the concept of hybridity on to the former is not only misleading but akin to providing an alibi for global exploitation. By charting how hybridity is variously defined by Hall, Bhabha and Spivak we can break with the naive assumption that hybridity is itself a stable concept in post-colonial theory.

In Stuart Hall's writing the term 'hybridity' is integral to the Bakhtinian–Gramscian perspective that he brings to bear on his representations of social transformation. Nowhere in his work is there a theoretical model which could be transferred to particular sites of struggle and used to 'read off' examples of hybridity. Hall's understanding of the process of transformation is never constructed in terms of either an absolutist oppositionality – whereby one position demolishes its antagonist – or a neat succession, with each stage being a clean break from the one before. Transformation is seen as occurring in a more 'generative way': as ideas, world-views and material forces interact with each other, they undergo a process of being internally reworked until the old ones are displaced.

From this perspective, hybridity can be seen as operating on two levels: it refers to the constant process of differentiation and exchange between the centre and the periphery and between different peripheries, as well as serving as the metaphor for the form of identity that is being produced from these conjunctions. Hall's representation of hybrid identities as always incomplete does not imply that they aspire to a sense of wholeness and invariably fall short of becoming a finished product but, rather, that their energy for being is directed by the flows of an on-going process. This anti-essentialist perspective on identity has had significant impact on the debates over the 'politics of representation', and has been utilised by Hall like a spiralling coil to extract the concept of ethnicity out of its anti-racist paradigm, where it connotes the immutable difference of minority experience, and into a term which addresses the historical positions, cultural conditions and political conjunctures through which all identity is constructed. So ethnicity becomes a positive concept for the 'recognition that we all speak from a particular place, out of a particular history, out of a particular experience, a particular culture. ... We are all, in a sense, *ethnically* located and our ethnic identities are crucial to our subjective sense of who we are' (Hall 1988: 5). By initiating such a contestation over the boundaries of ethnicity, Hall opens up a mode for understanding identity which is paradoxically both inclusive and specific (see also discussions by Werbner, Yuval-Davis and Baumann, in Chapters 13, 11 and 12 above).

With the revelation of the multiple others in the self – or rather, the understanding that the history of the self 'as composed always across the silence of the other' (Hall 1991: 49) – and when language is framed by a broader politics of articulation – embedded, that is, within 'an infinite semiosis of meaning' (ibid.: 51) – the space is open for the process of reidentification and reterritorialisation of experiences previously deemed 'too marginal' to be worthy of representation. Hall describes this re-articulation of the symbolic order through the Gramscian theory of hegemony and counter-politics. The margin challenges the centre via a three-pronged strategy: first, through an opposition to the given order; second, via recovery of broken histories and the invention of appropriate narrative forms; third, through the definition of a position and a language from which speech will continue (ibid.: 35).

Hall's perspective presupposes that translation across cultural difference is always possible. But how do we map a culture whose own references do not correspond to ours? How do we represent a culture whose historical memory and conceptual apparatus have been so damaged by the colonial encounter that the very possibility of exchange or dialogue seems no longer to exist? These questions are central to Gayatri Spivak's essay 'Can the Subaltern Speak?' (1993). With characteristic bluntness, Spivak has answered her own question in the negative: she has stated that the subaltern cannot speak. Between posing the question and the negative response, however, lie profound implications for the languages of resistance, the structures of oppression and the role of the intellectual. Spivak argues that there are two sides to the meaning of representation, the political and rhetorical, which are articulated by Marx with separate

terms, proxy and portrayal; and against a tendency of Western intellectuals to conflate the two. Hence she suggests that there can be no representation of real subaltern consciousness, because any representation of
an authentic condition is always premised on 'contestatory replacement
as well as an appropriation (a supplement) of something that is artificial
to begin with – "economic conditions of existence that separate their
mode of life"' (Spivak 1993: 71).

Who knows how best to manage the Other? Spivak again casts a
suspicious glance towards the possibly benign identification with the subaltern, the well-meaning gesture of solidarity with a constituency that
First World intellectuals neither appreciate nor could find the language
to address. Against all those facile claims of unity, she reminds us that
subalternity is not a condition to be desired. Taking the rural and land-
less poor of India as her example, Spivak points out that the question of
understanding is not confined to the linguistic problem of translation,
for how would you translate a culture whose 'responsibility-based ethical
systems have been for centuries completely battered and compromised'[8]
into the other culture's notion of democratic rights and civil society?
The incommensurability between these two orders is such that the gaps
and silences would be more significant than any utterance. There is no
clear process by which the realities and experiences of the Indian subaltern can be translated into Western categories. Spivak insists that in this
instance there is no prior space that can facilitate a dialogue between the
West and its Other.

The moment the subaltern has stepped into the arena of representation and negotiation, this is the first mark of a movement away from his
or her former position. The ability to 'speak up' to the hegemonic forces
is a step towards becoming an organic intellectual. However, to become
such a representative is already a movement from the condition that is
being represented. The subaltern condition cannot even bear the privilege of its own 'organic intellectuals'. Spivak repeatedly warns against the
presumption that subaltern experiences are texts that are available for
translation. This prognosis is aimed particularly at radical historians:

> When we come to the concomitant question of the consciousness of the sub-
> altern, the notion of what the work *cannot* say becomes important. In the
> semiosis of the social text, elaborations of insurgency stand in the place of 'the
> utterance'. The sender – 'the peasant' – is marked only as a pointer to an
> irretrievable consciousness. (Spivak 1993: 82)

Spivak's reminder of the need for added reflexivity over the precise status
of who is speaking in place of the subaltern, and who would be able to
listen to the subaltern, is a precaution against both false delegation and

idle identifications. For as she reminds us, to be in the position to speak for the subaltern is both impossible and unenviable. The poverty and brutalised conditions of the subaltern imply that the very step towards representation involves, at first, a move *out* of its own context. Alienation is the price of every representation. This is the extreme edge of Benjamin's observation that no translation can find exact correspondences between different languages. Thus Spivak, unlike Hall, seems to limit the concept of hybridity as a metaphor for cultural identity.

In Homi Bhabha's writing, the concept of hybridity is initially used to expose the conflicts in colonial discourse, then extended to address both the heterogeneous array of signs in modern life and the various ways of living with difference. Hybridity becomes an interpretative mode for dealing with what Bhabha calls the juxtapositions of space, and the combination of 'time lag' out of which is constructed a sense of being that constantly oscillates between the axioms of foreign and familiar. Bhabha suggests that in order to apprehend the contemporary structures of agency we need to shift our attention away from the concrete production of discrete objects and consider, rather, the restless process of identification. He places great stress on the 'fact' that identity is never fixed once and for all, never coheres into an absolute form. For instance, he describes minority discourse as emerging from the 'in between of image and sign, the accumulative and the adjunct, presence and proxy' (Bhabha 1990: 307). However, the refusal to accept the primacy of an originary essence, or the inevitability of an ultimate destiny for identity, is not an invitation to celebrate the liberation from substantive strictures. The theoretical qualification on the processes of identity formation in no way implies that identity is constructed out of a political and cultural vacuum. To elaborate the elasticity in the trajectory of identity is not a vindication of the claims that the horizons are boundless, access is free and the past is without weight or shape. According to Bhabha, attention to the process of identification requires a finer recognition of the strategy of negotiation. Identity always presupposes a sense of location and a relationship with others. However, this attention to place does not presuppose closure, for the representation of identity most often occurs precisely at the point when there has been a displacement (Bhabha 1994: 185).

The stress Bhabha gives to belatedness in the representation of identity is also connected to a deeper problematic of the partiality of representation in general. The status of representation is defined more by its limitations and distortions than by its ability to capture an 'elusive' spirit or hold the totality of presence. Therefore any theory of agency must also include the process of 'bricolage'. Identity is always conceived in the 'twixt of displacement and re-invention'. Stepping between Benjamin and Bhabha, we could say that representations of identity are at best a 'rear view' of a part of the past that is pushing us forward into the future. For Bhabha, Jameson's attention to pastiche, Said's appreciation of the contrapuntal, Deleuze and Guattari's tracking of nomadology, are parallel metaphors for naming the forms of identity which emerge in a context of difference and displacement:

> The process of reinscription and negotiation – the insertion or intervention of something that takes on new meaning – happens in the temporal break in-between the sign, deprived of subjectivity, in the realm of the intersubjective. Through this time-lag – the temporal break in representation – emerges the process of agency both as a historical development and as the narrative agency of historical discourse. ... It is in the contingent tension that results, that sign and symbol overlap and are indeterminately articulated through the 'temporal break'. Where the sign deprived of the subject – intersubjectivity – returns as subjectivity directed towards the rediscovery of truth, then a (re)ordering of symbols becomes possible in the sphere of the social. When the sign ceases the synchronous flow of the symbol, it also seizes the power to elaborate – through the time-lag – new and hybrid agencies and articulations. (1994: 191)

The exilic drives that underline our understanding of language and identity in modernity are thus made available to highlight the complex structures of agency (see also Papastergiadis 1991). The misfit between the formal structures that confer identity in fixed terms like nation, class, gender, race, and more fluid practices by which identity moves across certain positions and manoeuvres around given borders is not taken as an index of modern freedom but, rather, highlighted in order to draw attention to the complex dynamics of agency.

Referring to the process of linguistic hybridisation in the renaming that the artist Guillermo Gomez-Peña stages in his performances and texts, Bhabha argues that their potency is not based on their capacity to hold all the earlier parts together, or fuse together all the divergent sources of identity, but found in the way they hold differences together. Like Bakhtin, he notes the sense of separateness and unity in a single semantic field. Hybrid identity is thus not formed in an acretic way whereby the essence of one identity is combined with another, and hybridity is simply a process of accumulation. 'Hybrid hyphenations emphasise the incommensurable elements – the stubborn chunks – as the basis of cultural identifications' (1994: 219). The hybrid is formed, he says, out of the dual process of displacement and correspondence in the act of translation. As every translator is painfully aware, meaning seldom moves across borders with pristine integrity. Every translation requires a degree of improvisation. The hybrid, therefore, is formed not out of an excavation and transferral of foreignness into the familiar, but out of this awareness of the untranslatable bits that linger on *in* translation. In this respect Bhabha would criticise critical work, such as that of Raphael, which stresses the possibility of simple appropriation.

In many ways Bhabha's strategy for understanding the formation of culture and identity by focusing on the interstitial and liminal moments of articulation and the proposal of terms like hybridity is both a timely and an effective counter to the essentialist and organic models that are still common within the social sciences. Certainly multiculturalist projects, for example, often posit a process of accretion and synthesis. Bhabha's strategy is not a redemptive one. His strongest work is not a chronicle of the strategies of political resistance; rather, it focuses on the more general processes through which the tactics of survival and continuity are articulated. Hence his theorising of hybridity is distinct from Freyre's theory of amalgamation, which attempts to re-evaluate the historical legacy and lend prestige to the contemporary status of cultural hybrids.

Bhabha's attention to hybridity must also be distinguished from Nandy's theory of co-optation. By grafting the Bakhtinian notion of the subversive and dialogical force of hybridity on to the ambivalence in the colonial encounter, Bhabha gives a new twist to the meaning of hybridity. Hybridity is the process by which the discourse of colonial authority attempts to translate the identity of the Other within a singular category, but then fails and produces something else. The interaction between the two cultures proceeds with the illusion of transferable forms and transparent knowledge, but leads increasingly into resistant, opaque and dissonant exchanges. It is in this tension that a 'third space' emerges which can effect forms of political change that go beyond antagonistic binarisms between rulers and ruled (for a critical comment on this point, see Werbner, Chapter 13 above). The case of hybridity is pressed because the process of translation is, in his view, one of the most compelling tasks for the cultural critic in the modern world. Yet – to paraphrase Spivak in her corrective notes to other prominent radical theorists – this evocation of hybridity is 'so macrological that it cannot account for the micrological texture of power' (Spivak 1993: 74). Indeed, if we are all hybridised subjects, but our encounters with otherness and our flexing of translation are not equal, then we may well need to return to a theory of ideology to demonstrate how the gaps and slants of representation have various effects on the subject.

NOTES

1. In *The Complicities of Culture: Hybridity and 'New Internationalism'* (Cornerhouse Communiqué 4, Manchester 1994) I explore the incorporation of the term 'hybridity' in art criticism and curatorial practice. As an indication of how similar inroads have been made in literary and cultural theory, see Iain Chambers' recent overview *Migrancy, Culture. Identity* (London: Routledge 1994). For a most comprehensive account of the concept of hybridity within nineteenth-century scientific racism and British colonialism and its legacies in contemporary theory, see Robert C. Young, *Colonial Desire: Hybridity in Theory* (London: Routledge 1995).

2. G.C. Spivak, 'The Narratives of Multiculturalism', ICCCR lecture, University of Manchester, February 1995.

3. Parenthetically, it can be noted that the origin of the word 'miscegenation', which is a transformation of the Greek word *elaleukatio*, referring to the passing from 'black to white', connotes both moral cleansing and self-correction. The word first appeared in an anonymous pamphlet in 1864 which set out to satirise Abraham Lincoln by suggesting that the salvation of the American people could be found only in the interbreeding between blacks and whites in order to produce a brown-skinned race (Aaron 1983: 169–90).

4. When he refers to the general development of such a culture, Freyre does not speak of a process of hybridity, preferring the term 'mestizo'; and when he addresses the specific formations of the Brazilian national identity, he proposes the term 'Luso–Tropical'.

5. In Brazil, Aryanisation alludes to the absorption of the 'inferior' races by 'superior' ones (i.e. the 'white' race) and the gradual shedding of 'hybrid' characteristics.

6. Raphael's account of the evolution of artistic practice draws ambiguously on Lévy-Bruhl's controversial distinction between the 'pre-logical' mentality of primitive peoples and Western rationality, in the conviction that the *rationality* of the latter can assimilate the *spirituality* of the former. While not commenting on the commensurability of these cultural and philosophical traditions, he does note that contradictory motivations can generate conflicting aesthetic forms and these seemingly endorse the privilege, albeit flawed, of Western rationality.

7. It was this transcendent androgyny that Gandhi revitalised when he founded the nationalist anti-colonial movement (see Nandy 1983: 51–3) – Ed.

8. Spivak, 'The Narratives of Multiculturalism'.

REFERENCES

Aaron, D. (1983) 'The "Inky" Curse: Miscegenation in the White American Literary Imagination'. *Social Science Information* 22, 2.

Bhabha, Homi (1994) *The Location of Culture*. London: Routledge.

Bhabha, Homi (ed.) (1990) *Nation and Narration*. London: Routledge.

Fisher, J. (1995) 'Introduction to Special Issue: Contamination'. *Third Text* 32, Autumn.

Freyre, Gilberto (1946) *The Masters and the Slaves*, trans. S. Putnam. New York: Knopf.

Freyre, Gilberto (1974) *The Gilberto Freyre Reader*, trans. B. Shelby. New York: Knopf.

Hall, Stuart (1988) 'New Ethnicities', in K. Mercer, (ed.) *Black Film, British Cinema*. London: Institute of Contemporary Arts.

Hall, Stuart (1991) 'Old and New Identities, Old and New Ethnicities', in A. King (ed.) *Culture, Globalization and the World-System*. London: Macmillan.

Lotman, J.M. (1991) *The Universe of the Mind*, trans. A. Shukman. London: I.B. Tauris.

Lotman, J. M. and B.A. Uspenskij, (1984) *The Semiotics of Russian Culture*, trans. A. Shukman. Ann Arbor, MI: Michigan Slavic Contribution no. 11.

Miller, D.F. (1992) *The Reason of Metaphor*. New Delhi: Sage.

Morley, D. and C. Kuan-Hsing (eds) (1996) *Stuart Hall: Critical Dialogues in Cultural Studies*. London: Routledge.

Nandy, Ashis (1983) *The Intimate Enemy*. New Delhi: Oxford University Press.

Nunes, Z. (1994) 'Anthropology and Race in Brazilian Modernism', in F. Barker *et al.* (eds) *Colonial Discourse/Postcolonial Theory*. Manchester: Manchester University Press.

Papastergiadis, Nikos (1991) 'Reading DissemiNation'. *Millennium, Journal of International Studies* 20, 3.

Paz, Octavio (1967) *The Labyrinth of Solitude*. London: Allen Lane.

Raphael, Max (1980) *Proudhon, Marx, Picasso*, trans. I. Marcuse. London: Lawrence & Wishart.

Rushdie, Salman (1988) *The Satanic Verses*. London: Viking.

Serres, Michel (1982) *Hermes*. Baltimore, MD: Johns Hopkins University Press.

Spivak, Gayatri Chakravorty (1993) 'Can the Subaltern Speak?', in P. Williams and L. Chrisman (eds) *Colonial Discourse and Post-Colonial Theory: A Reader*. Hemel Hempstead: Harvester Wheatsheaf.

Williamson, J. (1980) *New People: Miscegenation and Mulattoes in the U.S.* New York: The Free Press.

Young, Robert C. (1995) *Colonial Desire: Hybridity in Theory*. London: Routledge.

NOTES ON THE

CONTRIBUTORS

Zygmunt Bauman is Emeritus Professor of Sociology, Universities of Leeds and Warsaw. His most recent publications include *Modernity and Ambivalence* (Polity Press 1991); *Intimations of Postmodernity* (Routledge 1992); *Postmodern Ethics* (Blackwell 1993); and *Life in Fragments: Essays in Postmodern Morality* (Blackwell 1995).

Gerd Baumann is a Fellow of the Research Centre for Religion and Society, University of Amsterdam, and has also had fellowships at the Queens University Belfast, and at Wolfson College, Oxford. He received his PhD in Social Anthropology at Belfast, based on fieldwork conducted among the Islamic Nuba of the Sudan, and his research has also included a seven-year study of Southall, London's most densely populated multi-ethnic area. He is author of *Post-Migration Ethnicity: De-essentialising Cohesion, Commitments and Comparison* (Martinus Nijhoff for Spinhuis Press 1995); and *Contesting Culture: Discourse of Identity in Multi-Ethnic London* (Cambridge University Press 1996).

Alastair Bonnett is Lecturer in Human Geography at the University of Newcastle upon Tyne. His comparative research focuses on the development of ideologies of race equality, both within the United Kingdom and internationally. He is part of a Canadian Government-funded team at the University of Newcastle investigating the development of Canadian and British anti-racist initiatives in the public sector. He is the author of *Radicalism, Anti-Racism and Representation* (Routledge 1993), and the editor of a new urban cultural studies journal, *Transgressions: A Journal of Cultural Explorations*.

Jonathan Friedman is Professor of Social Anthropology at the University of Lund, Sweden. He has written on topics such as structuralism and Marxism, theories of social transformation, global systemic processes and the practice of cultural identity. He has done fieldwork in Hawaii studying the emergence of the sovereignty movement, as well as working in a fishing village, from 1979 to the present. He has also worked on the Congo and is currently working on multicultural Sweden. His books include *System, Structure and Contradiction in the Evolution of 'Asiatic' Social Formations* (National Museum of Denmark 1979); *Modernity and Identity*, co-edited with Scott Lash (Blackwell 1993); *Cultural Identity and Global Process* (Sage 1994); and *Consumption and Identity* (editor, Harwood 1994).

John Hutnyk lectures in the Department of Social Anthropology at the University of Manchester. He received his PhD from the University of Melbourne, and is author of *The Rumour of Calcutta: Tourism, Charity and the Poverty of Representation* (Zed Books 1996), and co-editor of *Dis-Orienting Rhythms: The Politics of the New Asian Dance Music* (Zed Books 1996). He is currently conducting research on popular music and South Asian youth culture in Britain.

Alberto Melucci is Professor of Clinical Psychology at the Postgraduate School of Clinical Psychology, University of Milan. He has taught extensively in Europe, the USA, Canada, Latin America and Asia, has published widely in international journals and readers, and is the author of fifteen books about social movements, cultural change and personal and collective identity. Of these, *Nomads of the Present: Social Movements and Individuals Needs in Contemporary Society* (Radius 1989); *The Playing Self* (1996); and *Challenging Codes* (Cambridge University Press 1996) have appeared in English. He received his PhD in Sociology and Clinical Psychology.

Tariq Modood is a Senior Fellow at the Policy Studies Institute, and has held fellowships at Nuffield College, Oxford and the University of Manchester, and lectureships in political theory at several universities. He has worked at the Commission for Racial Equality and served as Chair of the Oxford Council for Community Relations. He is a regular contributor to journals and newspapers; his publications include *Not Easy Being British: Colour, Culture and Citizenship* (Trentham Books for the Runnymede Trust 1992); *Racial Equality* (Institute for Public Policy Research 1994); *Changing Ethnic Identities* (co-authored, PSI 1994); *Ethnic Minorities and Higher Education: Why are there differential rates of entry?*

(co-authored, PSI 1994); *The Fourth National Survey of Ethnic Minorities* (Oxford University Press for the PSI 1997).

Nikos Papastergiadis is Lecturer in Sociology at the University of Manchester. Born in Australia, he received his PhD from the University of Cambridge. He has written extensively on issues of identity, stranger-hood, sociology, and art and visual anthropology, and is the author of *Modernity in Exile: The Stranger in John Berger's Writing* (Manchester University Press 1993); and *Conversations with Anthropological Film Makers* (with Anna Grimshaw; Prickly Pear Press 1995).

Peter van der Veer is Professor of Comparative Religion and Director of the Research Centre for Religion and Society at the University of Amsterdam. He is the author of *Gods of the Earth* (Athlone 1988); and *Religious Nationalism* (University of California Press 1994); and editor of *Orientalism and the Postcolonial Predicament* (with Carol Breckenridge, University of Pennsylvania Press 1993); *Nation and Migration: The Politics of Space in the South Asian Diaspora* (University of Pennsylvania Press 1995); and *Conversion to Modernities* (New York 1996).

Pnina Werbner is a Senior Lecturer in Social Anthropology at Keele University, and Research Administrator of the International Centre for Contemporary Cultural Research (ICCCR) at the universities of Manchester and Keele. Her publications include *The Migration Process: Capital, Gifts and Offerings among British Pakistanis* (Berg 1990); *Black and Ethnic Leaderships in Britain: The Cultural Dimensions of Political Action*, co-edited with Muhammad Anwar (Routledge 1991); and *Economy and Culture in Pakistan: Migrants and Cities in a Muslim Society*, co-edited with Hastings Donnan (Macmillan 1991). Her forthcoming book, *Diaspora and Millennium: Islamic Narrations, Identity Politics and the Aesthetics of the Religious Imagination*, is on the political imaginaries of British Pakistanis. She recently directed a two-year ESRC-funded research project on 'South Asian Popular Culture: Gender, Generation and Identity'.

Hans-Rudolf Wicker is Professor of Anthropology at the University of Berne, Switzerland, where he received his PhD in Social Anthropology. He is the author of numerous articles and books including a recent co-edited volume, *Das Fremde in der Gesellscaft: Migration, Ethnizität und Staat* (Seismo 1996). He has conducted fieldwork on St Lawrence Island, Alaska, in rural Paraguay and in Switzerland, and writes on issues of anthropological theory, applied anthropology, migration and medical anthropology.

Michel Wieviorka is Director of the Centre d'Analyse et d'Intervention Sociologique. He is Professor at the École des Hautes Études en Sciences Sociales, and Director (with Georges Balandier) of Les Cahiers Internationaux de Sociologie. His publications include books about social movements, democracy, political violence, race, and other issues. Translated into English are *The Making of Terrorism* (University of Chicago Press); *The Arena of Racism* (Sage 1995); and *The Working-Class Movement* (Cambridge University Press 1987). A forthcoming book in press is on 'Post-Communism in Russia'.

Nira Yuval-Davis is Professor and Postgraduate Course Leader in Gender and Ethnic Studies at the University of Greenwich, London. She has written extensively on theoretical and empirical aspects of nationalism, racism, fundamentalism and gender relations in Britain, in Israel and in settler societies. Among others, she has co-authored *Racialised Boundaries* (Routledge 1992) and co-edited *Women – Nation – State* (Macmillan 1989); *Refusing Holy Orders: Women and Fundamentalism in Britain* (Virago 1992); *Unsettling Settler Societies: Articulations of Gender, Ethnicity, Race and Class* (Sage 1995); and *Crossfires: Nationalism, Racism and Gender in Europe* (Pluto 1995). Her forthcoming book, *Gender and Nation*, will be published by Sage in 1997.

INDEX

Aaron, D., 280 n3
Abedi, Mehdi, 93, 239
Abel, E., 187, 188
Abu-Lughod, Lila, 23 n2
Actor Network Theory, 20
Adorno, Theodor, 19, 20, 107, 115–17,
126, 132–4
'The Culture Industry
Reconsidered', 106
Dialectic of Enlightenment
(with Max Horkheimer), 115
Negative Dialectics, 116
affirmative action, 150
Afrocentrism, 13, 127
Ahmad, Aijaz, 5, 21
Ahsan, 232
Airey, C., 166
Ali, Yasmin, 246
Allen, Theodore, 184
ambivalence, as term for hybridity,
16
Amin, Krutika, 162
Anderson, Benedict, 246
Anglomorphism, 198
Anthias, Floya, 33, 35, 168, 193, 196,
198, 243, 246, 247, 248, 250 n4,
250 n8
anthropology, 6, 32, 90–91, 93
anti-colonial struggles, 85
anti-essentialism, 183, 187, 188

anti-racism, 3, 8, 21
cultural racism and, 159
discourses of, 139–52, 242
politics of, 9, 10, 228
South Asians and, 158–60
Whiteness and, 174–190
anti-racists, activity of, 10, 11, 19,
122
anti-semitism, 139, 144–5, 147
Anwar, Muhammed, 247
Anzaldúa, Gloria, *Borderlands/
La Frontera: The New Mestiza,* 80
Appadurai, Arjun, 36, 91
Appiah, Anthony, 92, 187
Asad, Talal, 104
Ashton, E.B., 116
Asian culture, 125, 127, 129, 131
Asian Dub Foundation, 119, 128–32,
133
Facts and Fictions, 129, 130, 131
Asian, *see* South Asian
Asian Women's Refuge, 201
Asian Women's Shelter Group, 204
assimilation, 72
Atlas, Natasha, 108–9
Austen, Jane, *Mansfield Park,* 97
Australia, Office of Multicultural Affairs
in, 198
autonomy, of individual, 58, 59–60, 62,
63